THEATRE

WORLD

edited by

JOHN WILLIS

SEASON 1965-1966

Volume 22

CROWN PUBLISHERS, INC.

New York

ASSOCIATION OF THEATRICAL PRESS AGENTS and MANAGERS

To all press agents and managers, past and present, whose gracious cooperation and generous assistance have made THEATRE WORLD *possible, this volume is gratefully dedicated . . .*

Angela Lansbury
in
"MAME"

TABLE OF CONTENTS

Assistant Editor: Harold Stephens
Staff: Jane Monroe, Charlotte Rahaim, Lucy Williams, Stanley Reeves
Staff Photographers: Louis Mélançon, Friedman-Abeles, Alix Jeffry, Van Williams

REVIEWING THE NEW YORK SEASON

The theatre, as well as New York City in general, was plagued with misfortunes this season: two newspaper strikes, a public transportation strike, the Long Island Railroad strike, the airport bus strike, the air condition maintenance workers strike, the power and light failure (fortunately for only one night), and a manhole explosion on 44th Street that cancelled several matinees. Naturally, these catastrophes took their toll at the boxoffice. However, financially, according to VARIETY's annual statistical report, Broadway had a record-breaking season, topping the previous record set by the 1964-65 season. Twelve hits were recorded, and one out of three productions was profitable. Theatres were open for 64½% of the year. Consequently, the season can not be considered unsuccessful.

A return engagement of the musical "Oliver" opened the season, and of the subsequent 51 Broadway productions, 15 were musicals or revues. The best, "Mame," was the final opening of the season, and had "Tony" winning performances by its star Angela Lansbury, and by Beatrice Arthur, and Frankie Michaels, the most endearing child actor to appear in many seasons. "Man Of La Mancha" that was presented Off-Broadway at the ANTA Washington Square Theatre received every best musical award, as did its star Richard Kiley for his performance. Other musical performances worth noting were by Julie Harris in "Skyscraper," Gwen Verdon, John McMartin, Helen Gallagher, and Thelma Oliver in "Sweet Charity," Barbara Harris and John Cullum in "On A Clear Day You Can See Forever," Harry Secombe and Roy Castle in "Pickwick," Linda Lavin, Patricia Marand, Michael O'Sullivan, and Jack Cassidy in "It's A Bird . . . It's A Plane . . . It's Superman!", Lillian Gish in her first Musical "Anya," Lesley Ann Warren and Elliott Gould in "Drat! The Cat!", Menasha Skulnik and Louis Gossett in "The Zulu and The Zayda," and the entire cast of the imported revue "Wait A Minim." Bob Fosse received a well-deserved "Tony" for his choreography in "Sweet Charity."

Of the straight plays, the one receiving the most accolades was the limited-run, controversial import with the marquee-breaking title "The Persecution and Assassination of Marat as Performed by the Inmates of the Asylum of Charenton Under the Direction of the Marquis De Sade," more popularly known as "Marat/Sade." It received "Tonys" for best play, best director, best costume design, and best supporting actor Patrick Magee. Although very few awards were left for them, other impressive dramatic productions were "Philadelphia, Here I Come," "Inadmissible Evidence," "The Right Honourable Gentleman," "Royal Hunt Of The Sun," "The Devils," and "Hostile Witness," all by foreign playwrights, and several with imported actors. "Lion In Winter" and "Wait Until Dark" were the best dramas among the few by native writers, and they provided vehicles for a "Tony" award performance by Rosemary Harris, and a "Tony" nomination for Lee Remick, respectively. The season also had memorable dramatic performances by Nicol Williamson, Donal Donnelly and Patrick Bedford, Kate Reid, Eamon Kelly, Glenda Jackson, Mairin D. O'Sullivan, Christopher Plummer, David Carradine, Ruth White, Valerie French, Anne Bancroft, Ruth Gordon, Coral Browne, Charles D. Gray, and Geraldine Page.

Comedies of situation and character with noteworthy performances were "Cactus Flower" with Lauren Bacall, Barry Nelson, and Brenda Vaccaro provoking the many laughs, "Generation" with Henry Fonda, "Entertaining Mr. Sloane" with Sheila Hancock, Paul Ford and April Shawhan in "3 Bags Full," Alan King in "The Impossible Years," and Zoe Caldwell in "Slapstick Tragedy" for which she received a "Tony."

If "Mark Twain Tonight!," which won a "Tony" for Hal Holbrook, and which he had previously presented Off-Broadway in 1959, is counted as a revival, then Broadway was blessed with four this season. The others were "Oliver," "Ivanov" with a cast of stars and beautiful performances by John Gielgud, Vivien Leigh, and Roland Culver, and APA's "You Can't Take It With You" which was the only Pulitzer Prize play on the boards because the committee decided not to make an award this season. It ranked high among the best productions of any season, and gave the brilliant Rosemary Harris another chance to display her versatility, as well as the other talented members of the company who alternated in the various roles. It is gratifying to know that Ellis Rabb's Association of Producing Artists will return next season in repertory with Helen Hayes and Melvyn Douglas as additions to the company.

"Hello, Dolly," a hold-over from past seasons, was still a sell-out with Ginger Rogers in the title role. The eight other hold-overs were doing relatively good business with replacements for all the original stars.

The astute and discriminating Jean Dalrymple, director of the City Center, again revived 5 well-received musicals, at the usual bargain prices. The exciting Robert Joffrey Ballet Company, which had its first season at the City Center this year, has fortunately agreed to return annually, after building an enviable and well-deserved reputation outside New York, and abroad. The Comedie Francaise, Bavarian State Theater, Bunraku Puppets, and Marcel Marceau were welcomed additions to the season.

The Lincoln Center Repertory Company in its third season, and its first in the beautiful new Vivian Beaumont Theater, again failed to measure up to the anticipated quality. Of its four productions, only the last, "The Caucasian Chalk Circle", had a modicum of success, and its run was extended instead of bringing back the three earlier productions in repertory as had been announced originally. It is sincerely hoped that they will soon prove worthy of their environment.

Across the plaza at the New York State Theater, success was more evident. Three opulent, star-studded musicals were successfully revived, one with the incomparable Ethel Merman. After limited engagements, each made a profitable tour. The New York City Opera, and ballet programs rounded out the season.

Off-Broadway's record for 1965-66 was not very encouraging. Except for the previously mentioned "Man Of La Mancha," musicals and revues fared poorly. Only the American Savoyards, the phenomenally long-run "The Fantasticks," and "The Mad Show" made music at the boxoffice. Excluding the hold-over "A View From The Bridge," there were only 10 straight plays that reached 100 or more performances. Among these were the critically praised "Hogan's Goat" and "Serjeant Musgrave's Dance." Also cited were "Happy Ending" and "Day Of Absence," "Phedre," "An Evening's Frost," and "The White Devil." Individual performances worth listing were given by Faye Dunaway, Robert Hooks, Barbara Ann Teer, John Colicos, Eli Mintz, Estelle Parsons, Will Geer, Jeanne Hepple, Irene Dailey, James Earl Jones, Bramwell Fletcher, Madeleine Renaud, Ruth White, Richard Mulligan, Dody Goodman, Gloria Foster, Kevin O'Connor, Dustin Hoffman, Linda Lavin, Paul Sand, Robert Burr, and William Mooney.

Even though fewer companies were touring this season, record grosses were rung up by many of them. Cultural centers are appearing in most of the larger cities across the country, increasing the demand for live theatre and touring companies. Resident companies are educating audiences to good theatre, and creating a desire for something other than repertory revivals. The increasing importance of these professional resident companies, the acknowledged quality of many of their productions and performers, their active endeavors to encourage new audiences, and develop young talent to keep "The Fabulous Invalid" alive, has justifiably brought them recognition for the first time in this yearbook. "May their tribe increase!"

John Gielgud

Vivien Leigh

BROADWAY CALENDAR

June 1, 1965 through May 31, 1966

Lauren Bacall

Henry Fonda

Ray Milland

Rosemary Harris

Graphic House Photos

MARTIN BECK THEATRE

Opened Monday, August 2, 1965.°
David Merrick and Donald Albery present:

OLIVER!

Book, Music, and Lyrics by Lionel Bart;
Freely adapted from Charles Dickens' "Oliver
Twist"; Directed by Peter Coe; Designed by
Sean Kenny; Orchestrations, Eric Rogers; Mu-
sical Direction, Robert McNamee; Technical
Supervisor, Ian Albery; Lighting, John Wyck-
ham; Original Cast Album by Decca.

CAST

Oliver Twist	Victor Stiles
Mr. Bumble	Alan Crofoot
Mrs. Corney	Dawna Shove
Old Sally	Sherill Price
Mr. Sowerberry	John Miranda
Mrs. Sowerberry	Sherill Price
Charlotte	Lynda Sturner
Noah Claypole	Billy Brandon
Fagin	Robin Ramsay
The Artful Dodger	Joey Baio
Nancy	Maura K. Wedge
Bet	Donnie Smiley
Bill Sikes	Danny Sewell
Mr. Brownlow	Bram Nossen
Dr. Grimwig	Fred Miller
Mrs. Bedwin	Dodi Protero

WORKHOUSE BOYS AND FAGIN'S GANG:
Tommy Battreall, Ronnie K. Douglas, Paul
Dwyer, Anthony Endon, Eugene Endon, Harry
Gold, Lee Koenig, Bart Larsen, Christopher
Month, Jackie Perkuhn, Sonny Rocco, Ricky
Rosenthal, Brett Smiley

LONDONERS: Walter Blocher, Ted Bloecher,
Reese Burns, Dominic Chianese, Sally Cooke,
Marise Counsell, Georgia Dell, Walter Hook,
Lesley Hunt, Michael McCormick, Richard
Miller, Moose Peting, Terry Robinson, Virginia
Sandifur, Gretchen Van Aken, Richard Wulf

UNDERSTUDIES: Fagin, Richard Miller;
Nancy, Gretchen Van Aken; Bumble, Fred
Miller; Mrs. Corney, Georgia Dell; Brownlow,
Walter Hook; Grimwig, Walter Blocher; Bill,
Richard Wulf; Mrs. Sowerberry, Marise Coun-
sell; Sowerberry, Dominic Chianese; Oliver,
Brett Smiley, Ronnie K. Douglas; Dodger,
Harry Gold, Eugene Endon; Charlotte, Lesley
Hunt; Noah, Michael McCormick; Sally, Marise
Counsell; Bet, Lesley Hunt; Mrs. Bedwin,
Georgia Dell

MUSICAL NUMBERS: "Food, Glorious Food,"
"Oliver!," "I Shall Scream," "Boy For Sale,"
"That's Your Funeral," "Where Is Love?,"
"Consider Yourself," "You've Got To Pick A
Pocket Or Two," "It's A Fine Life," "I'd Do
Anything," "Be Back Soon," "Oom-Pah-Pah,"
"My Name," "As Long As He Needs Me,"
"Who Will Buy?," "Reviewing The Situation,"
Finale.

A Musical in two acts.

General Manager: Jack Schlissel
Manager: Irving L. Cone
Press: Lee Solters, Harvey B. Sabinson,
Jay Russell
Stage Managers: Ben D. Kranz,
Geoffrey Johnson, Moose Peting

° Closed September 25, 1965. (64 performances) This was the National Touring Company that played a limited engagement. The
original production opened Jan. 6, 1963 and
closed Nov. 14, 1964 after 774 performances.
See THEATRE WORLD, Vol. 19.

**Maura K. Wedge, Robin Ramsay, Victor Stiles
Top: Danny Sewell**

Arlene Francis

Sam Siegel Photos

JOHN GOLDEN THEATRE

Opened Wednesday, September 22, 1965.°
Martin Gabel presents:

MRS. DALLY

By William Hanley; Directed by Joseph Anthony, Setting and Lighting by David Hays; Costumes, Ann Roth.

PART I: "Mrs. Dally Has A Lover"

CAST

Evalyn _____ Arlene Francis
Frankie _____ Robert Forster

PART II: "Today Is Independence Day"

CAST

Evalyn _____ Arlene Francis
Sam _____ Ralph Meeker

Understudy for Frankie and Sam: Jim Oyster

Both plays take place at the present time in an apartment in New York City.

General Manager: Victor Samrock
Press: Harvey Sabinson, Lee Solters,
Bob Ullman
Stage Managers: Paul A. Foley, Jim Oyster

° Closed November 6, 1965. (52 performances)

Arlene Francis, Robert Forster (also at top)
Above: Arlene Francis, Ralph Meeker

Opened Thursday, September 30, 1965.°
Garson Kanin presents:

A VERY RICH WOMAN

By Ruth Gordon; Based on a Play by Philippe
Heriat; Directed by Garson Kanin; Settings,
Oliver Smith; Costumes, Audre; Lighting, John
Harvey; Fashions from Bergdorf-Goodman; As-
sociate Producer, Al Goldin; Associate Director,
David Pardoll.

CAST

Mrs. Lord	Ruth Gordon
Mrs. Minot	Madge Kennedy
Johnny	Larry Oliver
Mae	Ethel Griffies
Dennis	Jon Richards
Edith Shaw	Joan Wetmore
Ursula Bailey	Carrie Nye
Patrick	Raymond Walburn
Linus Bailey III	Peter Turgeon
Alex Rovenesco	Jack Ryland
Daphne Bailey	Heidi Murray
Oliver Sears	Ernest Truex
Pearl	Katharine Houghton
Miss Moran	Diana Muldaur
Supervisor	Stefan Schnabel

UNDERSTUDIES: Mrs. Lord, Sylvia Field;
Edith, Ursula, Eileen Letchworth; Dick Van
Patten, Jon Richards, Larry Oliver, Katharine
Houghton

A Comedy in three acts. The action takes
place at the present time in and around Boston, Massachusetts.

General Manager: Al Goldin
Press: Nat and Irvin Dorfman
Stage Manager: Dick Van Patten

° Closed October 23, 1965. (28 performances)

Ruth Gordon, Ernest Truex, Madge Kennedy,
Ethel Griffies

Friedman-Abeles Photos

Ruth Gordon, Ethel Griffies. Above:
Ruth Gordon, Joan Wetmore

Ruth Gordon

10

FORTY-SIXTH STREET THEATRE

Opened Monday, October 4, 1965.*
David Merrick in association with Bernard Delfont presents:

PICKWICK

Book by Wolf Mankowitz; Based on Charles Dickens' "Pickwick Papers"; Music, Cyril Ornadel; Lyrics, Leslie Bricusse; Directed by Peter Coe; Settings, Sean Kenny; Costumes, Roger Furse and Peter Rice; Lighting, Jules Fisher; Choreography, Gillian Lynne; Musical Direction and Vocal Arrangements, Ian Fraser; Orchestrations, Eric Rogers; Production Supervisor, Samuel Liff.

CAST

Hot Toddy Seller	Jim Connor
Cold Drinks Seller	Edmond Varrato
Bird Seller	Roger LePage
Hot Potato Man	Gerrit de Beer
Turnkey	Allan Lokos
Roker	Peter Costanza
Pickwick	Harry Secombe
Augustus Snodgrass	Julian Orchard
Tracy Tupman	John Call
Nathaniel Winkle	Oscar Quitak
Sam Weller	Roy Castle
Mr. Wardle	Michael Logan
Rachel	Helena Carroll
Isabella	Nancy Haywood
Emily	Sybil Scotford
Fat Boy	Joe Richards
Mrs. Bardell	Charlotte Rae
Bardell, Jr.	Brian Chapin
Mary	Nancy Barrett
Mr. Jingle	Anton Rodgers
Major Domo	Jim Connor
Dr. Slammer	Peter Costanza
First Officer	Richard Neilson
Second Officer	Haydon Smith
Landlord	Edmond Varrato
Mrs. Leo Hunter	Elizabeth Parrish
Mr. Leo Hunter	Gerrit de Beer
Dodson	Michael Darbyshire
Fogg	Tony Sympson
Wicks	Haydon Smith
Jackson	Keith Perry
Usher	Taylor Reed
Bailiff	Stanley Simmonds
Sgt. Buzfuz	Peter Bull
Judge	Richard Neilson
Sgt. Snubbins	Allan Lokos
Jury Foreman	Roger LePage

PASSERS-BY, DEBTORS, MAIDS, ETC.: Jill Alexander, Michael Amber, Bill Black, William Coppola, Ann Davies, Selma Marcus, Ann Tell, Bill Nuss, Edmond Varrato, Larry Whiteley, Gerrit de Beer, Clyde Laurents, Keith Perry, Taylor Reed, Bruce Becker, Susan Cartt, Jo Freilich, Mary Keller, Don Lawrence, Ginia Mason, Lani Michaels, Ross Miles, Nancy Stevens, Don Strong, Haydon Smith, Roger LePage

CHILDREN: Michael Easton, Richard Easton, Tracy Evans, Leslie Ann Mapes, Bonnie Turner

UNDERSTUDIES: Pickwick, Taylor Reed; Sam, Roger LePage; Snodgrass, Keith Perry; Winkle, Larry Whiteley; Tupman, Taylor Reed; Mrs. Bardell, Ann Tell; Wardle, William Coppola; Dodson, Keith Perry; Mary, Mary Keller; Fogg, Gerrit de Beer; Buzfuz, Peter Costanza; Jingle, Richard Neilson; Rachel, Elizabeth Parrish; Emily, Ann Davies; Isabella, Jill Alexander; Mrs. Hunter, Selma Marcus; Bardell, Jr., Michael Easton; Officer, Clyde Laurents; Roker, Stanley Simmonds

MUSICAL NUMBERS: "I Like The Company Of Men," "That's What I'd Like For Christmas," "The Pickwickians," "A Bit Of A Character," "There's Something About You," "A Gentleman's Gentleman," "You Never Met A Feller Like Me," "I'll Never Be Lonely Again," "Fizkin and Pickwick," "Very," "If I Ruled The World," "Talk," "That's The Law," "Damages," Finale.

A Musical Comedy in two acts and twelve scenes. The action takes place in and around London and Rochester, England in 1827.

General Manager: Jack Schlissel
Company Manager: Richard Highley
Press: Harvey B. Sabinson, Lee Solters, Lila King, David Powers
Stage Managers: William Dodds, Peter Stern, Stanley Simmonds

* Closed November 20, 1965. (56 performances)

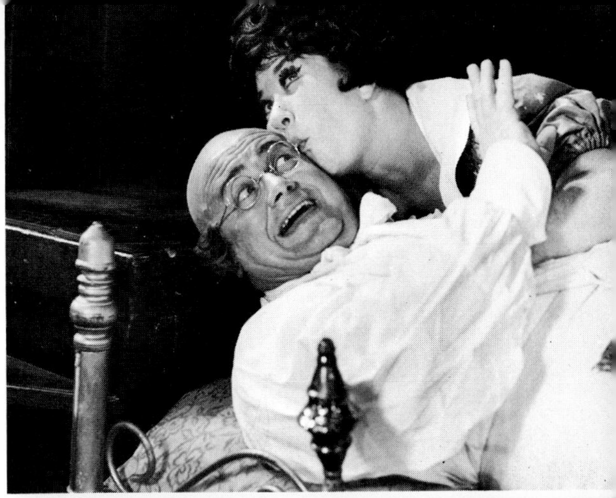

Sam Siegel Photos

John Call, Roy Castle, Oscar Quitak, Harry Secombe, Julian Orchard, Michael Logan. Above: Harry Secombe, and top with Charlotte Rae

MOROSCO THEATRE

Opened Wednesday, October 6, 1965.°
Frederick Brisson presents:

GENERATION

By William Goodhart; Directed by Gene Saks; Scenery and Lighting, George Jenkins; Costumes, Albert Wolsky; Incidental Music, Jerry Bock; Lyrics, William Goodhart; Production Manager, Fred Hebert; Associate Producer, Victor Samrock; Production Assistant, Roberta Robins.

CAST

Walter Owen	Richard Jordan†1
Jim Bolton	Henry Fonda
Doris Owen	Holly Turner
Stan Herman	A. Larry Haines
Winston Garand	Don Fellows
Ken Powell	Sandy Baron†2

UNDERSTUDIES: Lynn Morris, Joseph Bernard

A Comedy in three acts. The action takes place at the present time in the studio-loft apartment of Walter Owen in Lower Manhattan.

General Manager: Victor Samrock
Company Manager: Richard Seader
Press: Sol Jacobson, Lewis Harmon, Mary Ward
Stage Managers: Wayne Carson, Joseph Bernard

° Still playing May 31, 1966.

† Succeeded by: 1. Peter Lombard, 2. Michael Arquette, Paul Collins.

Graphic House Photos

Henry Fonda, Richard Jordan, Holly Turner
Top: Henry Fonda, Holly Turner

Don Fellows, A. Larry Haines, Henry Fonda
Above: Richard Jordan, Holly Turner

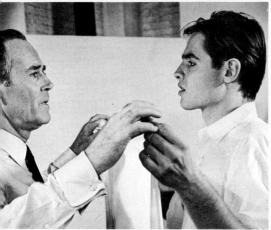

olly Turner, Richard Jordan, Henry Fonda, Sandy
Baron. Above: Henry Fonda, Richard Jordan

Richard Jordan, Henry Fonda, and top with
Holly Turner

13

HENRY MILLER'S THEATRE

Opened Thursday, October 7, 1965.°
Zev Bufman and Howard Erskine present:

MINOR MIRACLE

By Al Morgan; Adapted from his Novel;
Directed by Howard Erskine; Scenery, Robert
Randolph; Lighting, Tharon Musser; Costumes,
Theoni V. Aldredge; Production Assistant,
Marilyn H. Rubin.

CAST

Mrs. Doody	Pert Kelton
Father Maurice Britt	Lee Tracy
Herman Wekstein	Robert H. Harris
Mrs. Prosser	Julie Bovasso
Rickie Prosser	Glenn Scimonelli
Father Kincaid	Conard Fowkes
Bishop William O'Leary	Dennis King
Mrs. Fuller	Zamah Cunningham
Reporters	Douglas McLean,

Kate Tomlinson, Maurice Brenner, Roger
Johnson, Jr., Julia Curry, Joel Frederick,
Robert Horen

UNDERSTUDIES: Britt, O'Leary, Douglas Mc-
Lean; Doody, Prosser, Fuller, Kate Tomlinson;
Wekstein, Maurice Brenner; Kincaid, Roger
Johnson, Jr.; Rickie, Eugene Pressman

A Drama in three acts and five scenes. The
action takes place at the present time in the
parlor of the Parish House of St. Martin's Catholic Church in the Yorkville section of Manhattan.

General Manager: Edward H. Davis
Press: Harvey Sabinson, Lee Solters,
Bob Ullman
Stage Managers: Howard Whitfield,
Roger Johnson, Jr.

° Closed October 9, 1965. (4 performances)

Sam Siegel Photos

Dennis King, Pert Kelton, Lee Tracy

Lee Tracy, Conard Fowkes, Glenn Scimonelli,
Julie Bovasso, Pert Kelton. Above: Lee Tracy, and
top with Robert H. Harris

14

MARTIN BECK THEATRE

Opened Sunday, October 10, 1965.°
Jerry Adler and Norman Rosemont present:

DRAT! THE CAT!

Book and Lyrics, Ira Levin; Music, Milton
Schafer; Directed and Choreographed by Joe
Layton; Scenery and Lighting, David Hays;
Costumes, Fred Voelpel; Musical Direction and
Vocal Arrangements, Herbert Grossman; Orches-
trations, Hershy Kay and Clare Grundman;
Dance Music, Genevieve Pitot; Hair Styles,
Joseph Tubens; Production Assistant, Carole E.
Gister; Original Cast Album by Columbia.

CAST

The Mayor	Alfred Spindelman
Superintendent of Police Pincer	Charles Durning
Chief of Detectives Mallet	Gene Varrone
Former Chief of Detectives Roger "Bulldog" Purefoy	David Gold
Kate Purefoy	Lu Leonard
Patrolwoman Emma	Sandy Ellen
Bob Purefoy	Elliott Gould
Butler	Harry Naughton
Matilda Van Guilder	Jane Connell
Lucius Van Guilder	Jack Fletcher
Alice Van Guilder	Lesley Ann Warren
Maid	Jacque Dean
Minister	Al Lanti
Mayor's Wife	Marian Haraldson
Julietta Onderdonck	Mariana Doro
Judge	David Gold
Prosecutor	Leo Bloom

PATROLMEN: Leo Bloom, Ralph Farnworth,
Ian Garry, David Gold, Barney Johnston, Al
Lanti, William Lutz, George Marcy, Larry
Moss, Harry Naughton, Ronald Pare, James
Powers, Dan Siretta, Bill Starr.

ENSEMBLE: Jeri Barto, Nancy Lynch, Carmen
Morales, Mary Zahn, Lillian Bozinoff, Beth
Howland, Meg Walter, Margery Gray.

MUSICAL NUMBERS: "Drat! The Cat!," "My
Son, Uphold The Law," "Holmes and Watson,"
"She Touched Me," "Wild and Reckless,"
"She's Roses," "Ignoble Theft of The Idol's
Eyes," "Dancing With Alice," "Purefoy's La-
ment," "A Pox Upon The Traitor's Brow,"
"Deep In Your Heart," "Let's Go," "It's Your
Fault," "The Upside-Down Thief," "Today Is
A Day For A Band To Play," "I Like Him,"
"Justice Triumphant."

A Musical Spoof in two acts and sixteen
scenes. The action takes place in New York
City and environs during spring in the latter
part of the nineteenth century.

General Manager: Phil Adler
Company Manager: Sam M. Handelsman
Press: Mike Merrick, Barry Kobrin, Ruth Cage
Stage Managers: George Thorn, Tom Porter,
Bob Borod, Robert E. Maxwell, Jr.

° Closed October 16, 1965. (8 performances)

Elliott Gould, Lesley Ann Warren (also top and right)
Above: Elliott Gould

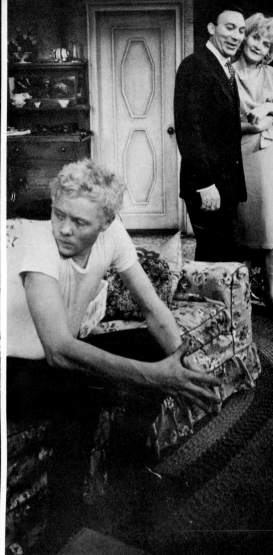

LYCEUM THEATRE

Opened Tuesday, October 12, 1965.°
Slade Brown, Tanya Chasman and E. A.
Gilbert in association with Michael Codron
and Donald Albery present:

ENTERTAINING MR. SLOANE

By Joe Orton; Directed by Alan Schneider;
Designed by William Ritman.

CAST

Kath	Sheila Hancock
Sloane	Dudley Sutton
The Dadda	George Turner
Ed	Lee Montague

UNDERSTUDIES: Kath, Michaele Myers;
Sloane, Geoff Garland; Ed, Dadda, Harry Bergman

A Comedy in three acts. The action takes
place at the present time in a house in London.

General and Company Manager: David Lawlor
Press: Dorothy Ross, Richard O'Brien,
Shirley Herz
Stage Managers: Duane Camp, Mark Wright
° Closed October 23, 1965. (13 performances)

George de Vincent Photos

Lee Montague, Sheila Hancock (above with
Dudley Sutton). Left: George Turner, Dudley Sutto

16

Janet Ward, Alan King, Jane Elliot
in
"THE IMPOSSIBLE YEARS"

Friedman-Abeles Photo

THE PLAYHOUSE

Opened Wednesday, October 13, 1965.✿
David Black and Walter A. Hyman present:

THE IMPOSSIBLE YEARS

By Bob Fisher and Arthur Marx; Directed by Arthur Storch; Scenery, William Pitkin; Lighting, Martin Aronstein; Costumes, Ann Roth; Hairstyles, The Kenneth Salon.

CAST

Dr. Jack Kingsley	Alan King†1
Linda Kingsley	Jane Elliot†2
Abbey Kingsley	Neva Small
Alice Kingsley	Janet Ward
Ricky Fleisher	Terrence Logan
Richard Merrick	Bert Convy
Miss Hammer	Sudie Bond
Francine	Donna Baccala
Wally	Kenneth Carr
Dennis	Jeff Siggins†3
Andy	Scott Glenn
Bartholomew Smuts	Michael Hadge
Dr. Harold Fleisher	Michael Vale
Arnold Brecher	Jack Hollander
Irwin Kniberg	Kenneth Kealey

UNDERSTUDIES: Kingsley, Fleisher, Brecher, Jack Sorian; Alice, Miss Hammer, Eulalie Noble; Linda, Francine, Pamela Murphy; Merrick, Robert Jundelin; Ricky, Dennis, Andy, Kenneth Carr; Smuts, Jeff Siggins; Abbey, Jan Rhodes

A Comedy in two acts and seven scenes. The action takes place at the present time in the den and living room of the Kingsley home in Old Westbury, Long Island.

General Manager: Eugene V. Wolsk
Company Manager: Emanuel Azenberg
Press: Frank Goodman, Martin Shwartz
Stage Managers: James Gelb, Doreen Richards, Robert Jundelin

✿ Still playing May 31, 1966.

† Succeeded by: 1. Ed McMahon for one week, 2. Pamela Murphy for one week, 3. Leland Mayforth.

Friedman-Abeles Photos

Jane Elliot, Alan King, Janet Ward. **Above:** Scott Glenn, Michael Hadge, Kenneth Carr, Donna Baccala, Jane Elliot, Jeff Siggins, Alan King, Bert Convy, Neva Small
Top: Janet Ward, Alan King, Sudie Bond
Left: Alan King

18

Charles Aznavour

AMBASSADOR THEATRE

Opened Thursday, October 14, 1965.°
Norman Twain and Sid Bernstein in association with Henri Goldgran present:

THE WORLD OF CHARLES AZNAVOUR

Scenery and Lighting by Ralph Alswang; Musical Director, Henry Byrs; All songs composed by Charles Aznavour.

A one-man show of Songs of Love and Other Sorrows sung by Charles Aznavour and presented in two parts.

PART I: "Le Temps," "Avec," "For Me Formidable," "Je Te Rechaufferais," "Who," "J'ai Perdu La Tete," "Never Again," "Parceque," "Isabelle," "The Boss Is Dead," "Reste," "Two Guitars," "Que C'est Triste Venice," "You've Let Yourself Go."

PART II: "I Dig You That Way," "C'est Fini," "The Time Is Now," "Quant Tu Viens Chez Moi," "L'amour C'est Comme Un Jour," "I'm Wrong," "Et Pourtant," "Les Comediens," "Love At Last You Have Found Me," "Paris Is At Her Best In May," "La Boheme," "You've Got To Learn," "La Mamma."

General Manager: Sherman Gross
Company Manager: Virginia Snow
Press: Max Eisen, Jeannie Gibson Merrick, Carl Samrock
Stage Manager: Martin Gold

° Closed November 6, 1965 after a limited engagement of 28 performances.

John Cullum, Barbara Harris
Above: Barbara Harris, Barbara Monte

MARK HELLINGER THEATRE

Opened Sunday, October 17, 1965.°
Alan Jay Lerner in association with Rogo
Productions presents:

ON A CLEAR DAY
YOU CAN SEE FOREVER

Book and Lyrics by Alan Jay Lerner; Music,
Burton Lane; Directed by Robert Lewis; Dances
and Musical Numbers Staged by Herbert
Ross; Scenery, Oliver Smith; Costumes, Freddy
Wittop; Lighting, Feder; Orchestrations, Robert
Russell Bennett; Music Continuity and Vocals,
Trude Rittman; Dance Music, Betty Walberg;
Musical Director, Theodore Saidenberg; Miss
Harris' modern clothes, Donald Brook; Pro-
duction Supervisor, Stone Widney; Production
Assistant, Greg Kayne; Hair Styles, Ronald De
Mann. Original Cast Album by RCA Victor.

CAST

Dr. Mark Bruckner	John Cullum
Mrs. Hatch	Rae Allen†1
Student	Gerald M. Teijelo, Jr.
Daisy Gamble	Barbara Harris
Muriel Bunson	Barbara Monte
James Preston	William Reilly
Samuel Welles	Gordon Dilworth
Mrs. Welles	Blanche Collins
Sir Hubert Insdale	Byron Webster
Dolly Wainwhistle	Hanne Marie Reiner
Blackamoor	Bernard Johnson
Bob Brody	Dan Resin
Jimmy Dern	Ken Richards
Millard Cross	Paul Reid Roman
Warren Smith	William Daniels
Prudence Cumming	Barbara Remington
Edward Moncrief	Clifford David
Flora	Carol Flemming
Dr. Paul Bruckner	Gerry Mathews
Dr. Conrad Bruckner	Michael Lewis
Evans Bolagard	Hamilton Camp†2
Themistocles Kriakos	Titos Vandis
T.A.A. Official	David Thomas
Melinda	Barbara Harris

SINGING ENSEMBLE: Rudy Challenger, Paul
Eichel, Eddie Erickson, Stokely Gray, Ben-
nett Hill, Art Matthews, Dan Resin, Ken
Richards, Rita Golden, Joy Holly, Zona Ken-
nedy, Pat Lysinger, Caroline Parks, Nancy
Reeves, Jeannette Seibert, Dixie Stewart

DANCING ENSEMBLE: Sterling Clark, Luigi
Gasparinetti, Bernard Johnson, Louis Kosman,
Kazimir Kokich, Marco Pogacar, Ronald B.
Stratton, Gerald M. Teijelo, Jr., William Reilly,
Rita Agnese, Carol Flemming, Marion Fels,
Leslie Franzos, Bettye Jenkins, Charlene Mehl,
Barbara Monte, Hanne Marie Reiner, Barbara
Remington

UNDERSTUDIES: Daisy, Mrs. Hatch, Pat
Lysinger; Mark, Paul, Warren, Dan Resin;
Kriakos, Gordon Dilworth; Edward, Conrad,
Art Matthews; Insdale, Welles, Michael Lewis;
Official, Ken Richards, David Thomas;
Mrs. Welles, Jeanette Siebert

MUSICAL NUMBERS: "Hurry! It's Lovely Up
Here," "Ring Out The Bells," "I'll Not Marry,"
"Tosy and Cosh," "On A Clear Day You Can
See Forever," "On The S.S. Bernard Cohn,"
"At The Hellrakers'," "Don't Tamper With My
Sister," "She Wasn't You," "Melinda," "When
I'm Being Born Again," "What Did I Have
That I Don't Have," "Wait 'Til We're Sixty-
five," "Come Back To Me."

A Musical in two acts and eleven scenes.
The action takes place at the present time, and
in the past.

General Manager: Irving Squires
Press: Mike Merrick Co., Barry Kobrin
Stage Managers: Ross Bowman, Pat Chandler,
Edward Preston, Bill Siegler,
Louis Kosman

° Still playing May 31, 1966.
† Succeeded by: 1. Evelyn Page, 2. Dan Resin.

Friedman-Abeles Photos

John Cullum, Barbara Harris
Top: Barbara Harris (center)

Barbara Harris. Above:
Barbara Harris, Clifford David

BILLY ROSE THEATRE

Opened Tuesday, October 19, 1965.°
Peter Cookson, Amy Lynn, and Walter
Schwimmer present:

THE RIGHT HONOURABLE
GENTLEMAN

By Michael Dyne; Directed by Frith Ban-
bury; Scenery and Costumes Designed by
Loudon Sainthill; Costume Supervisor, Ray Dif-
fen; Lighting, Lloyd Burlingame.

CAST

Mr. Bodley	Ed Zimmermann
Sir Charles Dilke	Charles D. Gray
Brookes	Frederick Young
Mrs. Ashton Dilke	Frances Sternhagen
Mrs. Emilia Pattison	M'El Dowd
Mr. Joseph Chamberlain	William Roerick
Mrs. Donald Crawford	Sarah Badel
Mr. Donald Crawford	Henderson Forsythe†
Sir James Russell	Staats Cotsworth
Mrs. Sarah Gray	Eve Collyer
Mrs. Lila Rossiter	Coral Browne
Mrs. Helen Garland	Marie Wallace
Mrs. Pelham	Louise Larabee
Captain Forster	Francis Bethencourt

UNDERSTUDIES: Dilke, Francis Bethencourt;
Lila, Eve Collyer; Nia, Maye, Helen, Nancy
Reardon; Emilia, Sarah, Mrs. Pelham, Brookes,
Sylvia O'Brien; Chamberlain, Henderson For-
sythe; Bodley, Crawford, Russell, Forster, Fred-
erick Young

A Drama in two acts and seven scenes. The
action takes place in London during the year
1885.

General Manager: Robert Rapport
Press: Sol Jacobson, Lewis Harmon,
Mary Ward
Stage Managers: John Maxtone-Graham,
William H. Batchelder

° Closed January 29, 1966. (118 performances)
† Succeeded by Philip Huston.

Sarah Badel, Charles D. Gray
Above: Coral Browne
Right: Charles D. Gray

Frances Sternhagen, Charles D. Gray
Above: Coral Browne, Charles D. Gray
Top: M'El Dowd, Charles D. Gray

Sarah Badel, Francis Bethencourt
Above: Charles D. Gray, Sarah Badel
Top: William Roerick, Charles D. Gray

23

George Rose, Gregory Rozakis, B. J. DeSimone
Above: Christopher Plummer, Gregory Rozakis

"The Massacre"
Above: David Carradine

ANTA THEATRE

Opened Tuesday, October 26, 1965.°
Theatre Guild Productions, Theodore Mann, Gerard Oestreicher in association with Hope Abelson present:

THE ROYAL HUNT OF THE SUN

By Peter Shaffer; Directed by John Dexter; Scenery and Costumes, Michael Annals; Lighting, Martin Aronstein; Mime, Madame Claude Chagrin; Music and Sound Effects, Marc Wilkinson; Musical Director, Herbert Harris; New York Production Supervised by George Jenkins and Ben Edwards; Associate Producer, Don Herbert; An ANTA presentation by arrangement with David Susskind and Daniel Melnick.

CAST

The Spaniards:

Martin Ruiz	George Rose
Martin Ruiz as a boy	Paul Collins†1
Francisco Pizarro	Christopher Plummer†2
Hernardo de Soto	John Vernon†3
Fray Vincente de Valverde, Chaplain	Ben Hammer
Diego de Trujillo	Michael Lamont
Salinas, blacksmith	Nelson Phillips†4
Rodas, tailor	Jake Dengel
Vasca	Tony Capodilupo
Domingo	George Sampson
Juan Chavez	Clyde Burton†5
Pedro Chavez	John Church
Felilillo, interpreter	Gregory Rozakis
Fray Marcos de Nizza, Franciscan Friar	Michael Levin†6
Pedro de Candia, Commander of Artillery	Cal Bellini†7
Miguel Estete, Royal Overseer	Thayer David

The Incas:

Atahuallpa, Sovereign Inca	David Carradine†8
Villac Umu, High Priest	Mylo Quam
Challcuchima, Inca General	Clayton Corbin
Manco, a messenger	Marc Maskin
Chieftain	Robert Berdeen†9
Headman	Judd Jones
Oello, a wife of Atahuallpa	Sandy Leeds
Inti Coussi, step-sister of Atahuallpa	Julie Sheppard

PERUVIAN INDIANS: Barry Burns, Paul Charles, Kurt Christian, Edilio Ferraro, Roy Lozano, Hector Mercado, Ken Novarro, B. J. Desimone, Don Silber

MUSICIANS: Herbert Harris, Norman Grossman, Charles Birch, Steve Silverman

A Drama in two acts: The Hunt, The Kill. Apart from two early scenes in Spain and Panama, the play is set in the Upper Province of the Inca Empire, what is now South Ecuador and North Western Peru. Act Two takes place in the town of Cajamarca. The time is from June 1529 to August 1533.

General Manager: Paul Libin
Press: Merle Debuskey, Violet Welles, Lawrence Belling
Stage Managers: Maxine S. Taylor, Robert Bishop

° Still playing May 31, 1966.

† Succeeded by: 1. Paul Charles, 2. Robert Burr, 3. Robert Burr, Don Filber, 4. Newt Sullivan, 5. B. J. DeSimone, 6. John Church, 7. Tony Lo Bianco, 8. Clayton Corbin, 9. Roy Lozano.

Friedman-Abeles Photos

Clayton Corbin, Robert Burr
Above: Christopher Plummer, David Carradine
Top: David Carradine. Left: Clayton Corbin

25

Edward Grover, Curt Lowens, John Karlen,
Alvin Epstein, John Heffernan, Hardy Kruger

Martha Swope Photos

BROOKS ATKINSON THEATRE

Opened Monday, November 1, 1965.°
Burton C. D'Lugoff, Robert Nemiroff and
Franklin Fried, in association with Triangle
Productions present:

POSTMARK ZERO

By Robert Nemiroff; Directed by Peter Kass;
Entire production Designed by Jack Blackman;
Production Associates, Howard Bennett, Joel
Dein; Special Film Sequences from Artkino
Productions; Film Technical Consultant, Abe
Weisburd; Sound, Sanford Rackow, Richard
Greenfield; Title Song by James Kpondes.

CAST

Hardy Kruger	Viveca Lindfors
John Heffernan	Alvin Epstein
Edward Grover	John Karlen
Curt Lowens	Jane Cronin

A Drama in two acts. The action takes
place in Germany and Russia, from the summer
of 1942 through January 31, 1943.

General Manager: Norman Maibaum
Company Manager: Clayton Coots
Press: Robert W. Larkin
Stage Managers: Norman Rothstein, Bud Coffey
° Closed November 6, 1965. (8 performances)

Viveca Lindfors

FIFTY-FOURTH STREET THEATRE
Opened Tuesday, November 2, 1965.°
The B. de Rothschild Foundation presents:

MARTHA GRAHAM
and Dance Company

Produced by Gertrude Macy; Conductor, Robert Irving; Assistant Conductor, Harry Fuchs; Lighting, Jean Rosenthal; Production Assistants, William H. Batchelder, Marion Kinsella; Costumes Supervised by Ursula Reed; Sets, Isamu Noguchi, Dani Karavan, Jean Rosenthal, Ming Cho Lee.

COMPANY: Bertram Ross, Helen McGehee, Robert Cohan, Yuriko, Mary Hinkson, Gene McDonald, Ethel Winter, Linda Hodes, David Wood, Matt Turney, Robert Powell, Clive Thompson, Takako Asakawa, Carol Fried, Peter Randazzo, Juliet Fisher, Noemi Lapzeson, William Louther, Dudley Williams, Phyllis Gutelius, Gus Solomons, Jr., Jeanne Nuchtern, Ross Parkes, Janet Aaron, Juanita Londono, Diane Gray, Toni Shimin, Marcia Lerner, Rozann Stephens

REPERTOIRE: Premieres of "The Witch of Endor" and "Part Real—Part Dream," "Acrobats of God," "Appalachian Spring," "Cave of The Heart," "Circe," "Clytemnestra," "Diversion of Angels," "Embattled Garden," "Legend of Judith," "Phaedra," "Primitive Mysteries," "Secular Games," "Seraphic Dialogue."

Manager: Gertrude Macy
Press: Isadora Bennett
Stage Manager: Anne Sullivan

° Closed November 20, 1965, after a limited engagement of 22 performances.

Clive Thompson, Yuriko, Martha Graham in "Legend Of Judith". Above: Matt Turney, Robert Cohan, Ethel Winter in "Appalachian Spring". Top: Martha Graham in "The Witch Of Endor". (R) "Part Real—Part Dream". Below: Bertram Ross, Martha Graham in "Clytemnestra"

EUGENE O'NEILL THEATRE

Opened Wednesday, November 3, 1965.°
Elliot Martin presents:

MATING DANCE

By Eleanor Harris Howard and Helen McAvity; Directed by Ronny Graham; Settings, Eldon Elder; Costumes, Florence Klotz; Lighting, John Harvey; Title Song, Albert A. Beach and Lawrence Grossman.

CAST

Kelly Lewis	Marian Hailey
Jeff	Rick Lenz
Mrs. Grindell	Ruth Newton
Oscar Davenport	J. D. Cannon
Deedee Dinehart	Judith Barcroft
Bruce Barrett	Van Johnson
Senator Lucia Barrett	Marian Winters
Lyn Hoyt	Esther Jane Coryell
Ramesh Ramru	Don Calfa
Junior	Robert H. Wiensko
Roger MacDougall	Richard Mulligan
Officer Lynch	Paul Sorvino

UNDERSTUDIES: Bruce, Robert H. Wiensko; Lucia, Ruth Newton; Kelly, Judith Barcroft; Roger, Rick Lenz; Lyn, Ruth Newton; Junior, Don Calfa

A Comedy in two acts and five scenes. The action takes place at the present time in Kelly's apartment.

General Manager: C. Edwin Knill
Company Manager: Helen Richards
Press: Mary Bryant, Fred Weterick, Robert Pasolli
Stage Managers: Wally Peterson, Nelle Nugent

° Closed Wednesday, November 3, 1965. (1 performance)

Van Williams Photos

Van Johnson, and top right with Marian Hailey

Marian Hailey, Marian Winters
Above: J. D. Cannon, Richard Mulligan

28

ETHEL BARRYMORE THEATRE

Opened Thursday, November 4, 1965.°
Fred Coe and David Karr present:

XMAS IN LAS VEGAS

By Jack Richardson; Directed by Fred Coe; Settings and Lighting, Robert Randolph; Costumes, Ruth Morley; Production Supervisor, Porter Van Zandt.

CAST

Edward T. Wellspot	Tom Ewell
Lionel Wellspot	Joe Ponazecki
Emily Wellspot	Judy Frank
Eleanor Wellspot	Shannon Bolin
Michel Wellspot	Heywood Hale Broun
Mrs. Edna Simon	Mabel Albertson
Willy	MacIntyre Dixon
Spiros Olympus	Robert H. Harris

UNDERSTUDIES: Edward, Olympus, Michel, John Cecil Holm; Eleanor, Edna, Sylvia Davis; Lionel, Willy, Ronald Roston; Emily, Anne Baker.

A Comedy in two acts and eight scenes. The action takes place at the present time, two days before Christmas, in Las Vegas, Nevada.

General Managers: Joseph Harris, Ira Bernstein
Press: Karl Bernstein, Michael Bruno
Stage Manager: Ellen Wittman

° Closed November 6, 1965. (4 performances)

Friedman-Abeles Photos

Judy Frank, Tom Ewell, and above with Shannon Bolin, Heywood Hale Broun. Top: Joe Ponazecki, Shannon Bolin. Left: Tom Ewell Below: Judy Frank, Joe Ponazecki

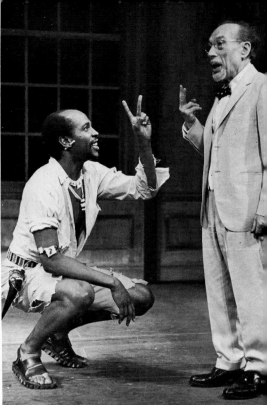

Ossie Davis, Louis Gossett. Above: Menasha
Skulnik, Joe Silver. Top: Philip Vandervort,
30 Sarah Cunningham, John Pleshette, Joe Silver
Right: Louis Gossett, Menasha Skulnik

CORT THEATRE

Opened Wednesday, November 10, 1965.°
Theodore Mann and Dore Schary present:

THE ZULU AND THE ZAYDA

By Howard Da Silva and Felix Leon; Music
and Lyrics by Harold Rome; Based on Story by
Dan Jacobson; Directed by Dore Schary; Set-
tings and Lighting, William and Jean Eckart;
Costumes, Frank Thompson; Musical Super-
vision and Orchestrations, Meyer Kupferman;
Conductor, Michael Spivakowsky; Language
Coach, Barbara Masekela; Production Assistant,
Phyllis Dukore; Original Cast Album by
Columbia.

CAST

Johannes	Ossie Davis
Koofer	James Higgins
Harry Grossman	Joe Silver
Helen Grossman	Sarah Cunningham
Arthur Grossman	Philip Vandervort
David Grossman	John Pleshette
Eric	John Randolph Jones
Zayda	Menasha Skulnik
Tommy Layton	Norman Barrs
Paulus	Louis Gossett
Woman with carriage	Sandra Kent
Policeman	David Mogck
Peter	Peter DeAnda
John	Yaphet Kotto
Joan	Christine Spencer
William	Ed Hall
Mr. Lamene	Charles Moore
Mrs. Lamene	Ella Thompson
Groenwald	Robert Hewitt
Dyckboom	Max Jacobs
Mourner	Sholom Ludvinsky
Nurse	Sandra Kent

UNDERSTUDIES: Sandra Kent, Charles Moore,
Ella Thompson

A Comedy with music in two acts. The
action takes place at the present time in
Johannesburg, Republic of South Africa.

General Manager: Paul Libin
Press: Merle Debuskey, Lawrence Belling,
Violet Welles, Reuben Rabinovitch
Stage Managers: Jeb Schary, Harry Young,
John Randolph Jones

° Closed April 16, 1966. (179 performances)

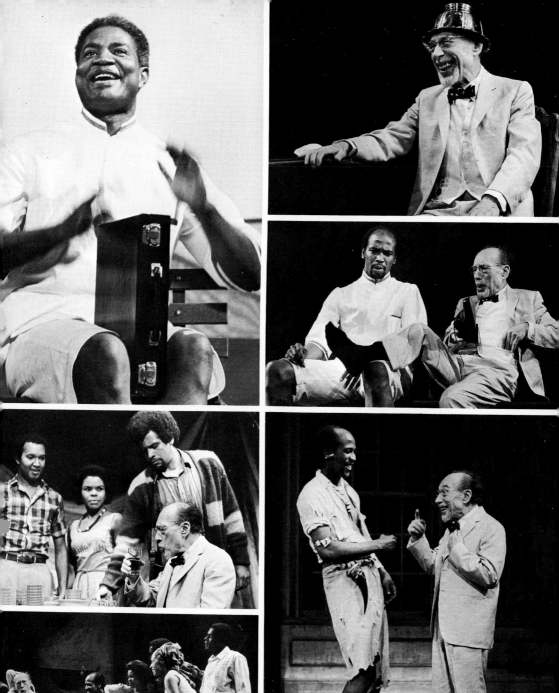

eter DeAnda, Menasha Skulnik, Louis Gossett,
istine Johnson, Ed Hall, Ella Thompson, Charles
ore. Above: Ed Hall, Christine Johnson, Peter
DeAnda, Menasha Skulnik. Top: Ossie Davis

Louis Gossett, Menasha Skulnik, and above
Top: Menasha Skulnik

31

LUNT-FONTANNE THEATRE

Opened Saturday, November 13, 1965.°
Feuer and Martin present:

SKYSCRAPER

Book by Peter Stone; Based on "Dream
Girl" by Elmer Rice; Music, James Van Heusen;
Lyrics, Sammy Cahn; Directed by Cy Feuer;
Dances and Musical Numbers Staged by Michael
Kidd; Scenery and Lighting, Robert Randolph;
Costumes, Theoni V. Aldredge; Musical Direc-
tor, John Lesko; Orchestrations, Fred Werner;
Dance Music, Arranged by Marvin Laird;
Associate Conductor, Fred Manzella; Hair Styles,
D. Rusty Bonaccorso. Original Cast Album by
Capital.

CAST

Georgina	Julie Harris
Mrs. Allerton	Nancy Cushman
Mr. Allerton	Donald Burr
Charlotte	Lesley Stewart
Mayor	Burt Bier
Doctor	Richard Korthaze
Herbert Bushman	Dick O'Neil
Stanley	Rex Everhart
Timothy Bushman	Peter L. Marshall
Roger Summerhill	Charles Nelson Reilly
Woman Customer	Georgia Creighton
Auctioneer	Burt Bier
Harry The Waiter	John Anania
Cab Driver	Ken Ayers
Jazz Musician	Walter P. Brown
Photographer	Christian Gray
In film sequence:	
Paola	Pola Chapelle
Francesco	Paul Sorvino

SINGERS: John Anania, Ken Ayers, Burt Bier,
Walter P. Brown, Christian Gray, Randy Phil-
lips, Casper Roos, Eleanor Bergquist, Georgia
Creighton, Ceil Delli, Maryann Kerrick

DANCERS: Ray Chabeau, Gene Gavin, Curtis
Hood, Gene Kelton, Ray Kirchner, Richard
Korthaze, Darrell Notara, Bill Starr, Ken
Thomas, Barbara Beck, Trudy Carson, Marilyn
Charles, Suzanne France, Ellen Graff, Laurel
Jones, Renata Powers

UNDERSTUDIES: Georgina, Lesley Stewart;
Roger, Christian Gray; Tim, Randy Phillips; Mrs.
Allerton, Georgia Creighton; Herbert, Burt Bier;
Mr. Allerton, Casper Roos; Stanley, John Ana-
nia; Charlotte, Maryann Merrick

MUSICAL NUMBERS: "Occasional Flight of
Fancy," "Run For Your Life," "Local 403,"
"Opposites," "Just The Crust," "Everybody Has
A Right To Be Wrong," "Wrong!," "The
Auction," "The Gaiety," "More Than One
Way," "Don't Worry," "I'll Only Miss Her
When I Think Of Her," "Spare That Building."

A Musical in two acts. The entire action
took place yesterday in New York City, in
and around a large skyscraper and a small
brownstone.

Company Manager: Milton M. Pollack
Press: Merle Debuskey, Lawrence Belling,
Violet Welles
Stage Managers: Phil Friedman,
Jack Leigh, Merritt Thompson, Gene Gavin
° Still playing May 31, 1966.

Peter L. Marshall, Julie Harris
Above: Julie Harris, Charles Nelson Reilly

ulie Harris, and above with Peter L. Marshall

"Construction Ballet". Above: Julie Harris,
Donald Burr, Nancy Cushman, Lesley Stewart
Top: Julie Harris and dream characters
Below: "Gaiety Delicatessen"

33

Shepperd Strudwick,
Jason Robards

Anne Bancroft,
John Colicos

Above: Anne Bnacroft (C), and top with Albert
Dekker, Patrick Hines, Michael Lombard
Below: Tom Klunis, Richard Lynch
Top Right: Lynda Day, Jason Robards

BROADWAY THEATRE

Opened Tuesday, November 16, 1965.°
Alexander H. Cohen presents:

THE DEVILS

By John Whiting; Based on "The Devils of
Loudun" by Aldous Huxley; Directed by Mi-
chael Cacoyannis; Designed by Rouben Ter-
Arutunian; Costumes, Motley; Lighting, Jules
Fisher; Production Associates, Hildy Parks, Mil-
ton Chwasky; Production Assistant, Davina
Crawford; Hair Styles, Phil Leto.

CAST

Mannoury, a surgeon	Bernard Kates
Adam, a chemist	Mark Gordon
Jean D'Armagnac, Governor of Loudun	Hugh Franklin
Guillame De Cerisay, Chief Magistrate	John Baragrey
Louis Trincant, Public Prosecutor	John Milligan
A Sewerman	James Coco
Urbain Grandier, Vicar of St. Peter's	Jason Robards
Ninon, a widow	Barbara Colby
De La Rochepozay, Bishop of Poitiers	Shepperd Strudwick
Father Rangier	Michael Lombard
Father Barre	Albert Dekker
Sister Jeanne of The Angels, Prioress of St. Ursula's Convent	Anne Bancroft
Richelieu	Tom Klunis
Louis XIII of France	Richard Lynch
De Laubardemont, the Cardinal's Special Emissary	John Colicos
Sister Claire	Karen Ludwig
Sister Louise	Erin Martin
Sister Gabrielle	Anna Shaler
Father Mignon	Patrick Hines
Prince Henri De Conde	Louis Turenne
Bontemps, a jailer	Alan Mixon
Father Ambrose	Edgar Stehli
Clerk	John Milligan
Old Man	Eugene R. Wood

TOWNSPEOPLE: Harry Clark, Linda Geiser,
Judy Granite, Patricia Hammack, George Morse,
Martha Neag, Frank Rowley, Lucretia Simmons,
Holland Taylor, Eugene R. Wood, Joseph Aulisi,
Richard Botham, Eleanor Bruno, Eric Bruno,
Susan Carr, Diane Deckard, Jonathan Fox, Ron
Frederic, Mary McKenzie Gordon, Adrienne
Hazzard, Betsy Langman, Terry Lomax, Robert
Nadder, P. L. Pfeiffer, Julie Prince, Robbie
Reed, Malcolm Taylor

UNDERSTUDIES: Sister Jeanne, Jenny Egan;
De Cerisay, De La Rochepozay, Richelieu,
Bontemps, Roy Shuman; Adam, Sewerman,
Rangier, Clerk, George Morse; Ninon, Anna
Shaler; Trincant, Ambrose, Eugene R. Wood;
Phillipe, Erin Martin; Mannoury, Sewerman,
Grandier, Alan Mixon; D'Armagnac, De Lau-
bardemont, De Conde, Tom Klunis; Barre,
Michael Lombard; Louis, Frank Rowley; Claire,
Lucretia Simmons; Louise, Holland Taylor;
Gabrielle, Linda Geiser; Mignon, John Milligan

A Drama in three acts. The action takes
place in and near the town of Loudun, and
briefly at Paris, between the years 1623 and
1634.

General Manager: Roy A. Somlyo
Company Manager: Seymour Herscher
Press: James D. Proctor, Louise Weiner,
Max Gendel
Stage Managers: Jean Barrere, Jake Hamilton,
Harry Clark, Frank Rowley

° Closed January 8, 1966. (31 performances)

Friedman-Abeles Photos

Seated: Donald Moffat, Paulette Waters, Rosemary Harris, Clayton Corzatte, Betty Miller
Standing: Dee Victor, Sydney Walker, Nat Simmons, Joseph Bird, Patricia Conolly,
Gordon Gould, Jennifer Harmon, Keene Curtis, Claribel Baird, Richard Woods in
"You Can't Take It With You"

LYCEUM THEATRE

Opened Tuesday, November 23, 1965.°
Phoenix Theatre (A Project of Theatre
Incorporated) T. Edward Hambleton,
Managing Director, presents The APA
Repertory Company in:

YOU CAN'T TAKE IT
WITH YOU

By Moss Hart and George S. Kaufman;
Directed by Ellis Rabb, Artistic Director of
APA; Scenery and Lighting, James Tilton;
New York Supervision by Norris Houghton;
Costumes, Nancy Potts.

CAST

Penelope Sycamore	Dee Victor
Essie	Jennifer Harmon
Rheba	Paulette Waters
Paul Sycamore	Sydney Walker
Mr. De Pinna	Joseph Bird
Ed	Gordon Gould
Donald	Nat Simmons
Martin Vanderhof	Donald Moffat
Alice	Rosemary Harris[1]
Henderson	James Greene
Tony Kirby	Clayton Corzatte
Boris Kolenkhov	Keene Curtis
Gay Wellington	Patricia Conolly
Mr. Kirby	Richard Woods
Mrs. Kirby	Betty Miller
Three Men	Chuck Daniel, Robert Moss, George Pentecost
Olga	Claribel Baird[2]

UNDERSTUDIES: Penny, Mrs. Kirby, Cavada
Humphrey; Essie, Olga, Alice, Patricia Conolly;
Rheba, Gay, Mira Waters; Paul, DePinna, James
Greene; Ed, Tony, Henderson, George Pente-
cost; Donald, Henderson, Chuck Daniel; Van-
derhof, Joseph Bird; Alice, Jennifer Harmon;
Kirby, Gordon Gould; Three Men, Sean Gil-
lespie

A Comedy in three acts. The action takes
place in the New York home of Martin Vander-
hof in 1936.

General Managers: Norman Kean,
Marilyn S. Miller
Press: Ben Kornzweig, Reginald Denenholz,
Anne Woll
Stage Managers: Robert Moss,
Bruce A. Hoover, Sean Gillespie

° Still playing May 31, 1966.

This Pulitzer Prize Play made its debut at
the Booth Theatre on Dec. 14, 1936 with
Josephine Hull, Paula Trueman, Henry Tra-
vers, Margot Stevenson, and Jess Barker.
It played 837 performances.

† Succeeded by: 1. Kathleen Widdoes, 2. Cavada Humphrey, Anne Francine. Company
alternates in parts.

36

Friedman-Abeles, Van Williams Photos

Kathleen Widdoes, Clayton Corzatte
Above: Jennifer Harmon, Gordon Gould,
Sydney Walker, Dee Victor. Top: (L) Rosemary
Harris, Donald Moffat (R) Joseph Bird,
Dee Victor (foreground). Below: Donald Moffat,
Richard Woods, Keene Curtis

ZIEGFELD THEATRE

Opened Monday, November 29, 1965.°
Fred R. Fehlhaber presents:

ANYA

Book by George Abbott and Guy Bolton; Based on "Anastasia" by Marcelle Maurette and Guy Bolton; Music and Lyrics, Robert Wright and George Forrest; Based on themes of Rachmaninoff; Directed by George Abbott; Choreography and Musical Numbers by Hanya Holm; Scenery, Robert Randolph; Costumes, Patricia Zipprodt; Lighting, Richard Casler; Musical Direction, Harold Hastings; Orchestrations, Don Walker; Hair Styles, D. Rusty Bonaccorso; Original Cast Album by United Artists Records.

CAST

Anya	Constance Towers
Nurse	Patricia Hoffman
Bounine	Michael Kermoyan
Josef	Boris Aplon
Count Drivinitz	Lawrence Brooks
Count Dorn	Adair McGowan
Sergei	Jack Dabdoub
Yegor	Walter Hook
Katrina	Irra Petina
Petrovin	Ed Steffe
Balalaika Player	Konstantin Pio-Ulsky
Genia, Countess Hohenstadt	Karen Shepard
Chernov	George S. Irving
Olga	Laurie Franks
Masha	Rita Metzger
Sleigh Driver	Lawrence Boyll
Anouchka	Elizabeth Howell
Tinka	Barbara Alexander
Mother	Maggie Task
Father	Michael Quinn
Dowager Empress	Lillian Gish
Prince Paul	John Michael King
Countess Drivinitz	Elizabeth Howell
First Policeman	Lawrence Boyll
Second Policeman	Bernard Frank
Police Sergeant	Howard Kahl
Baroness Livenbaum	Margaret Mullen

DANCERS: Barbara Alexander, Ciya Challis, Patricia Drylie, Juliette Durand, Kip Andrews, Steven Boockvor, Randy Doney, Joseph Nelson

SINGERS: Laurie Franks, Patricia Hoffman, Rita Metzger, Mia Powers, Lourette Raymon, Diane Tarleton, Maggie Task, Darrel Askey, Lawrence Boyll, Les Freed, Horace Guittard, Walter Hook, Howard Kahl, Adair McGowan, Richard Nieves, J. Vernon Oaks, Robert Sharp, John Taliaferro, Bernard Frank

UNDERSTUDIES: Anya, Karen Shepard; Bounine, Lawrence Brooks; Empress, Margaret Mullen; Katrina, Maggie Task; Chernov, Jack Dabdoub; Josef, Bernard Frank; Petrovin, Jack Dabdoub; Paul, Horace Guittard; Genia, Lourette Raymon; Baroness, Elizabeth Howell; Tinka, Ciya Challis

MUSICAL NUMBERS: "Anya," "A Song From Somewhere," "Vodka, Vodka!," "So Proud," "Homeward," "Snowflakes and Sweethearts," "On That Day," "Six Palaces," "Hand In Hand," "This Is My Kind of Love," "That Prelude!," "A Quiet Land," "Here Tonight, Tomorrow Where?," "Leben Sie Wohl," "If This Is Goodbye," "Little Hands," "All Hail The Empress," Finale.

A Musical in two acts and twelve scenes. The action takes place in 1925 in Berlin.

General Manager: Carl Fisher
Press: Mary Bryant, Robert Pasolli
Stage Managers: John Allen, Frank Gero, Bob Bernard

° Closed December 11, 1965. (16 performances)

Friedman-Abeles Photos

Constance Towers, Lillian Gish, also above with Michael Kermoyan, Irra Petina
Top: Constance Towers, Michael Kermoyan

BELASCO THEATRE

Opened Tuesday, November 30, 1965.°
(Moved February 8, 1966 to the Shubert
Theatre)
David Merrick Arts Foundation presents
the English Stage Company production of:

INADMISSIBLE EVIDENCE

By John Osborne; Directed by Anthony Page;
Sets and Costumes, Jocelyn Herbert; Lighting
and Design Supervision, Lloyd Burlingame;
Associate Producer, Samuel Liff.

CAST

Bill Maitland _____ Nicol Williamson
(James Patterson, matinees)†1
Hudson _____ Peter Sallis
Jones _____ Ted van Griethuysen
Shirley _____ Jeanne Hepple†2
Joy _____ Lois Daine
Mrs. Garnsey _____ Madeleine Sherwood
Jane Maitland _____ Jill Townsend
Liz _____ Valerie French

UNDERSTUDIES: Hudson, Jones, Mitchell
Erickson; Mrs. Garnsey, Liz, Barbara Lester;
Shirley, Joy, Jane, Susan Tabor

A Drama in two acts. The action takes place
at the present time in a solicitor's office in East
London.

General Manager: Jack Schlissel
Company Manager: Vince McKnight
Press: Max Eisen, Carl Samrock
Stage Managers: Ben Kranz, Mitchell Erickson

° Closed April 23, 1966. (167 performances)

† Succeeded by: 1. John Harkins, 2. Christine
Pickles.

Nicol Williamson (also at top), Lois Daine, Valerie French

Nicol Williamson, Jill Townsend
Top: Nicol Williamson, Jeanne Hepple

Nicol Williamson, Valerie French

39

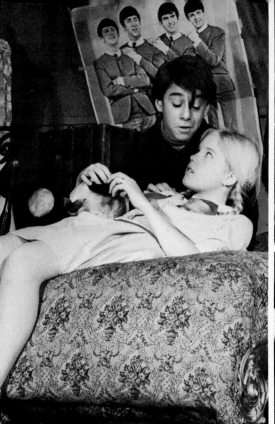

BROOKS ATKINSON THEATRE

Opened Sunday, December 5, 1965.°
Kermit Bloomgarden and Trude Heller in
association with Max Youngstein and David
Karr present:

THE PLAYROOM

By Mary Drayton; Directed by Joseph Anthony; Settings and Lighting, Jo Mielziner;
Costumes, Theoni V. Aldredge; Production Supervisor, Bill Ross; Songs, Linda Lauri, George
Goehring and Mary Drayton.

CAST

Christopher	Peter Kastner
Judy	Karen Black
Louise	Augusta Dabney
David	Tom Helmore
Eric	Richard Thomas
Pauline	Bonnie Bedelia
Charlot	Alan Howard
Ellen	Christopher Norris
Lt. McAfee	P. Jay Sidney
Detective Sullivan	Stan Watt
Patrolman Young	Jon DeHart

UNDERSTUDIES: David, Stan Watt; McAfee,
Sullivan, Don Doherty; Judy, Bonnie Bedelia;
Pauline, Ellen, Barbara Myers; Christopher,
Eric, Charlot, Don Scardino.

A Contemporary Thriller in two acts. The
action takes place in an apartment building in
New York City at the present time.

General Manager: Max Allentuck
Press: James D. Proctor, Louise Weiner
Stage Managers: Don Doherty, Jon DeHart

° Closed January 1, 1966. (33 performances)

Fred Fehl Photos

Tom Helmore, Karen Black. Above: Karen Black,
Richard Thomas, Bonnie Bedelia, Christopher Norris
Top: Alan Howard, Peter Kastner, Karen Black,
Richard Thomas. Left: Alan Howard,
Christopher Norris

Friedman-Abeles Photos

JOHN GOLDEN THEATRE

Opened Tuesday, December 7, 1965.°
Delancey Productions presents:

ME AND THEE

By Charles Horine; Directed by Perry Bruskin; Setting and Costumes, Charles Evans; Fashion Coordination, A. Christina Giannini; Lighting, V. C. Fuqua; Music, George Fischoff; Lyrics, Charles Horine, Hank Miles.

CAST

Alice Carter	Barbara Britton
Paul Carter	Durward Kirby
Roger Carter	Randy Kirby
Dr. Grant Reeves	Charles Braswell
Lela	Carolan Daniels

UNDERSTUDIES: Paul, Reeves, Earl Rowe; Lela, Alice, Lynn Bernay; Roger, David Eliscu.

A Comedy in two acts and five scenes. The action takes place in the living room of the Carters' New York City apartment at the present time.

Press: David Lipsky, Marian Graham
Stage Managers: Ben Janney, David Eliscu
° Closed December 7, 1965. (1 performance)

Randy Kirby, Durward Kirby, Barbara Britton. Top: Carolan Daniels, Randy Kirby

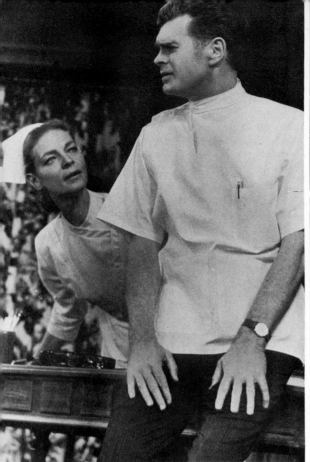

Lauren Bacall, and top with Barry Nelson
Right: Barry Nelson, Brenda Vaccaro, Burt
Brinckerhoff. Below: Barry Nelson, Brenda Vaccaro

42

ROYALE THEATRE

Opened Wednesday, December 8, 1965.°
David Merrick presents:

CACTUS FLOWER

By Abe Burrows; Based on Play by Pierre
Barillet and Jean Pierre Gredy; Directed by
Abe Burrows; Scenic Production, Oliver Smith;
Costumes, Theoni V. Aldredge; Lighting, Martin Aronstein; Associate Producer, Samuel Liff;
Music Consultant, Alfred Simon; Dance Advisor, Vernon Lusby; Miss Bacall's Clothes by
Norman Norell; Produced in Association with
Beresford Productions, Ltd.

CAST

Toni	Brenda Vaccaro
Igor	Burt Brinckerhoff
Stephanie	Lauren Bacall
Mrs. Durant	Eileen Letchworth
Julian	Barry Nelson
Harvey	Robert Moore
Senor Sanchez	Arny Freeman
Customer	Will Gregory
Waiter	Michael Fairman
Botticelli's Springtime	Marjorie Battles
Music Lover	Michael Fairman

UNDERSTUDIES: Stephanie, Eileen Letchworth; Julian, Will Gregory; Toni, Marjorie
Battles; Igor, Harvey, Michael Fairman.

A Comedy in two acts and fifteen scenes.
The action takes place at the present time in
uptown and downtown Manhattan.

General Manager: Jack Schlissel
Company Manager: Richard Highley
Press: Harvey B. Sabinson, Lee Solters,
Bob Ullman, Jane Friedman
Stage Managers: Charles Durand,
May Muth, Will Gregory

° Still playing May 31, 1966.

Lauren Bacall, Brenda Vaccaro
Above: Brenda Vaccaro, Burt Brinckerhoff
Top: Barry Nelson, Brenda Vaccaro
Lauren Bacall, Robert Moore

Brenda Vaccaro, Barry Nelson, and above with
Arny Freeman, Lauren Bacall

43

ALVIN THEATRE

Opened Friday, December 10, 1965.°
Lore Noto presents:

THE YEARLING

Book by Herbert Martin and Lore Noto;
Based on Novel by Marjorie Kinnan Rawlins;
Music, Michael Leonard; Lyrics, Herbert Martin; Directed by Lloyd Richards; Sets and
Costumes, Ed Wittstein; Lighting, Jules Fisher;
Music Direction and Vocal Arrangements, Julian
Stein; Orchestrations, Larry Wilcox; Dance
Music, David Baker; Choreography, Ralph Beaumont; Associate Producer, Michael Malistreri;
Original Cast Album by Mercury Records.

CAST

Jody Baxter	Steve Sanders
Ezra (Penny) Baxter	David Wayne
Ora Baxter	Dolores Wilson
Fodder-Wing	Peter Falzone
Ma Forrester	Fay Sappington
Buck Forrester	Allan Louw
Arch Forrester	Rodd Barry
Pack Forrester	Roy Barry
Gabby Forrester	Bob LaCrosse
Millwheel Forrester	Tom Fleetwood
Lem Forrester	Robert Goss
Mrs. Hutto	Carmen Mathews
Oliver Hutto	David Hartman
Eulalie	Janet Campano
Twink	Carmen Alvarez
Doc Wilson	Gordon B. Clarke
Preacher	Frank Bouley
Captain	David Sabin

TOWNSPEOPLE: Loyce Baker, Lynette Bennett, Lois Grandi, Bobbi Lange, Ruth Lawrence,
Barbara Miller, Bella Shalom, Myrna Strom,
Mimi Wallace, Trudy Wallace, Vito Durante,
Anthony Endon, Harrison Fisher, Scott Hunter,
Martin Ross, Herbert Sanders, Ted Sprague
UNDERSTUDIES: Ora, Lizabeth Pritchett;
Forrester Brothers, Oliver, Doc, David Sabin;
Jody, Fodder-Wing, Bryant Fraser; Twink, Mimi
Wallace; Eulalie, Lois Grandi; Pack, Arch,
Gabby, Vito Durante; Ma, Barbara Miller
MUSICAL NUMBERS: "Let Him Kick Up His
Heels," "Boy Talk," "Bear Hunt," "Some Day
I'm Gonna Fly," "Lonely Clearing," "Everything In The World I Love," "I'm All Smiles,"
"The Kind Of Man A Woman Needs," "What
A Happy Day," "Ain't He A Joy?," "Why Did
I Choose You?," "One Promise," "Nothing
More," "Everything Beautiful."

A Musical in two acts and sixteen scenes.
The action takes place in and around the Baxter
cabin, the Forrester cabin, the Hutto house, and
in the town of Volusia.

General Manager: Norman Maibaum
Company Manager: Morton Zolotow
Press: Harvey B. Sabinson, Lee Solters,
David Powers, Jane Friedman
Stage Managers: Mortimer Halpern,
Edward Julien, Frank Bouley

° Closed December 11, 1965. (3 performances)

Steve Sanders, Carmen Mathews. Above: Dolores
Wilson, Steve Sanders, David Wayne
Top: Robert Goss, David Wayne, David Hartman,
Allan Louw. Left: Gordon B. Clarke, Allan Louw,
Steve Sanders, Tom Fleetwood

Victor Spinetti (Center), Ronald Fraser
Top: Ronald Fraser, France Arnell
Right: France Arnell, John Maxim

Bob Colby, Friedman-Abeles Photos

FIFTY-FOURTH STREET THEATRE

Opened Tuesday, December 14, 1965.°
Joe Kipness and Arthur Lesser present:

LA GROSSE VALISE

Book by Robert Dhery; Music and Orchestrations, Gerard Calvi; Lyrics, Harold Rome; Directed by Robert Dhery; Choreography, Colette Brosset; Associate Choreographer, Tom Panko; Musical Director, Lehman Engel; Scenery and Costumes, Jacques Dupont; Scenery and Costumes Supervised by Frederick Fox; Lighting, John Gleason; Assistant Conductor, Karen L. Gustafson; Associate Producer, Arthur Cantor; Production Coordinator, Sammy Lambert; Hair Styles, Joseph Tubens; Original Cast Album by Mercury Records.

CAST

Traveler to Bordeaux	Jacques Ebner
Antoine, Customs inspector	Michel Modo
Spanish Tourists	Marcello Gamboa, Diane Coupe
Pepito, customs inspector	Guy Grosso
Jean-Loup Roussel, assistant chief of customs	Ronald Fraser
La Fouillette, and airport police officer	Tony Doonan
La Nana	France Arnell
Photographers	Max Vialle, Bernard Gauthron
Nicolas	Brigitte Valadin
Svatsou, the clown (M. Cheri)	Victor Spinetti
Vlaminsky	Guy Bertil
Raoul	Barry L. Martin
Chief of Customs	John Maxim
The Little Porter	Bert Michaels
DeWalleyne	Sybil Bartrop
Baby's Maid	Maureen Byrnes
Chef d'Etat, a diplomatic official	Max Vialle
Old Lady	Rita Charisse
Andre	Jean-Michel Mole
Baby	Joyce Jillson
Mireille	Mireille Chazal
Pedralini, head scout	John Maxim
First Scout	George Tregre
Bald Man	Bernard Gauthron
Berthozeau	Tony Doonan

AND: Diane Baffa, Maureen Byrnes, Diane Coupe, Ronn Forella, Marcello Gamboa, Pat Gosling, Carolyn Kirsch, Alex MacKay, Bert Michaels, Donna Sanders, George Tregre, Mary Zahn

MUSICAL NUMBERS: "La Grosse Valise," "A Big One," "C'est Defendu," "Hamburg Waltz," "Happy Song," "For You," "Sandwich For Two," "La Java," "Xanadu," "Slippy Sloppy Shoes," "Spanish Dance," "Delilah Done Me Wrong," "Hawaii."

A Musical in two acts. The action takes place at the present time at Customs, Orly Airport, Paris, France.

General Manager: Philip Adler
Company Manager: S. M. Handelsman
Press: Arthur Cantor, Arthur Solomon
Stage Managers: Bob Burland, Pierre Billon

° Closed December 18, 1965. (7 performances) **45**

Morris Newcombe Photos

Robert Lloyd, Clifford Rose, Brenda Kempner,
Ruth Baker. Above: Patrick Magee

MARTIN BECK THEATRE

Opened Monday, December 27, 1965.°
David Merrick Arts Foundation by arrangement with The Governors of the Royal Shakespeare Theatre, Stratford-upon-Avon, presents The Royal Shakespeare Company in:

THE PERSECUTION AND ASSASSINATION OF MARAT AS PERFORMED BY THE INMATES OF THE ASYLUM OF CHARENTON UNDER THE DIRECTION OF THE MARQUIS DE SADE

By Peter Weiss; English Version, Geoffrey Skelton; Verse Adaptation, Adrian Mitchell, Directed by Peter Brook; Setting and Properties Designed by Sally Jacobs; Costumes, Gunilla Palmstierna-Weiss; Choreographer, Malcolm Goddard; Original Lighting, David Read; Lighting and Design Supervision, Lloyd Burlingame; Music, Richard Peaslee; Production Supervisor, Samuel Liff.

CAST

M. Coulmier	Clifford Rose
Mme. Coulmier	Brenda Kempner
Mlle. Coulmier	Ruth Baker
Herald	Michael Williams
Cucurucu	Freddie Jones
Kokol	Hugh Sullivan
Polpoch	Jonathan Burn
Rossignol	Jeanette Landis
Jacques Roux	Robert Lloyd
Charlotte Corday	Glenda Jackson
Jean-Paul Marat	Ian Richardson
Simonne Evrard	Susan Williamson
Marquis de Sade	Patrick Magee
Duperret	John Steiner
Abbot	Mark Jones
A Mad Animal	Morgan Sheppard
Schoolmaster	James Mellor
The Military Representative	Ian Hogg
Mother	Mark Jones
Father	Henry Woolf
Newly-rich Lady	John Hussey
Voltaire	John Harwood
Lavoisier	Leon Lissek
Nuns	Heather Canning, Jennifer Tudor
Guards	Timothy Hardy, Stanford Trowell

PATIENTS: Mary Allen, Michael Farnsworth, Maroussia Frank, Tamara Fuerst, Guy Gordon, Sheila Grant, Michael Percival, Lyn Pinkney, Carol Raymont

MUSICIANS: Patrick Gowers, Richard Callinan, Michael Gould, Nicholas Moes, Rainer Schuelein

UNDERSTUDIES: Marat, Robert Lloyd; de Sade, Morgan Sheppard; Charlotte, Sheila Grant; Herald, John Steiner; Coulmier, John Hussey; Duperret, Mark Jones; Simonne, Maroussia Frank

A Drama in two parts. The action takes place in the Charenton Asylum in France sometime between 1803 and 1814.

General Manager: Jack Schlissel
Company Manager: Vince McKnight, Hal Rogers
Press: Harvey B. Sabinson, Lee Solters, David Powers, Jane Friedman
Stage Managers: Christine Staley, Diana Seaney, Lynne Holmes

° Closed April 30, 1966, after a limited engagement of 145 performances. Winner of Drama Critics Circle Award.

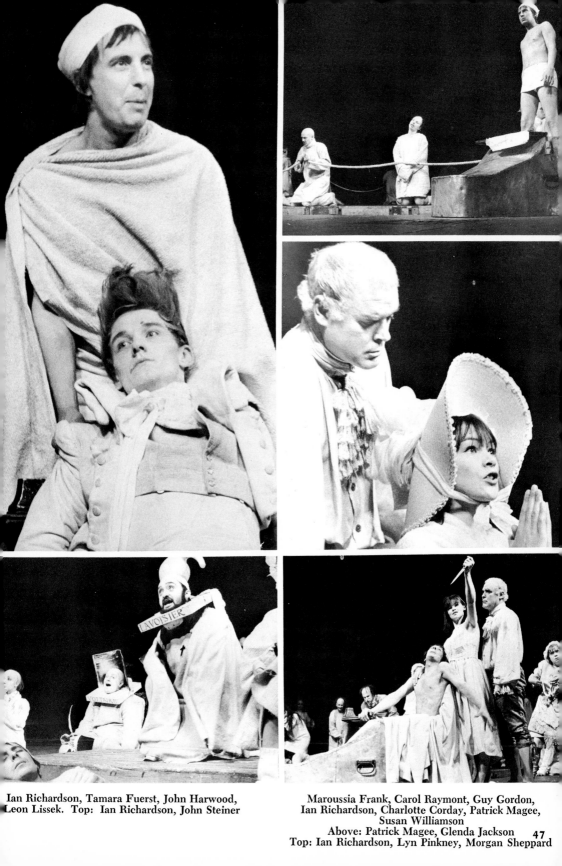

Ian Richardson, Tamara Fuerst, John Harwood,
Leon Lissek. Top: Ian Richardson, John Steiner

Maroussia Frank, Carol Raymont, Guy Gordon,
Ian Richardson, Charlotte Corday, Patrick Magee,
Susan Williamson
Above: Patrick Magee, Glenda Jackson
Top: Ian Richardson, Lyn Pinkney, Morgan Sheppard

HELEN HAYES THEATRE

Opened Tuesday, January 4, 1966.°
Lyn Austin presents:

UTBU
(Unhealthy To Be Unpleasant)

By James Kirkwood; Directed by Nancy
Walker; Setting and Lighting, David Hays;
Costumes, Theoni V. Aldredge; Associate Pro-
ducer, Bruce W. Stark; Production Associate,
Ronald Bernstein.

CAST

Connie Tufford	Margaret Hamilton
Anastasia Amber	Cathryn Damon
William Uggims	Alan Webb
Madge Kempton	Doris Rich
Shirley Amber	Thelma Ritter
J. Francis Amber	Tony Randall
Eugene Boyer	Tom Aldredge
Valerie Rogers	Constance Ford
Miss-----Rogers	Susan Priolo
Jimmy Newton	Clyde Williams

UNDERSTUDIES: Uggims, J. Francis, Tom
Aldredge; Connie, Madge, Shirley, Mary Far-
rell; Anastasia, Valerie, Laurinda Barrett; Boyer,
Charles Gray; Miss Rogers, Trudy Bordoff;
Jimmy, Valdo Williams

A Comedy in two acts and three scenes. The
action takes place at the present time in the
Manhattan apartment of J. Francis Amber overlooking the East River.

General Manager: Oscar Olesen
Press: Samuel Lurie, Stanley F. Kaminsky
Stage Managers: Frederic de Wilde,
Charles Gray

° Closed January 8, 1966. (7 performances)

Friedman-Abeles Photos

Alan Webb, Tony Randall, Thelma Ritter
Above: Tony Randall, Margaret Hamilton

Alan Webb, Tony Randall
Above: Thelma Ritter, Tony Randall

48

Jennifer West, Matthew Cowles, Alan Yorke
Right: Alice Drummond, Matthew Cowles,
Donald Hotton. Top: Matthew Cowles,
Estelle Parsons, Alan Yorke, Henderson Forsythe

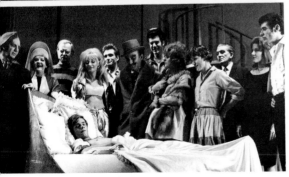

Henderson Forsythe, John Heffernan, Ruth White,
Donald Hotton, Jennifer West, Robert Viharo,
Wyman Pendleton, Alan Yorke, Estelle Parsons,
Alice Drummond, William Callan, Vicki
Blankenship, Victor Arnold, Matthew Cowles (in bed)
Above: Matthew Cowles, Ruth White,
Wyman Pendleton

Alix Jeffry Photos

SAM S. SHUBERT THEATRE

Opened Tuesday, January 11, 1966.°
Theatre 1966 (Richard Barr, Clinton
Wilder) presents:

MALCOLM

By Edward Albee; From the Novel by James
Purdy; Directed by Alan Schneider; Designed
by William Ritman; Costumes, Willa Kim;
Lighting, Tharon Musser; Music, William Flan-
agan; Administrative Director, Barry Plaxen;
Produced by A.B.W. Productions, Inc. and
Pisces Productions Inc.; Song, William Flan-
agan, Edward Albee; Painting, Paul Jasmin.

CAST

Malcolm	Matthew Cowles
Cox	Henderson Forsythe
Laureen	Estelle Parsons
Kermit	John Heffernan
A Young Man	Victor Arnold
Madame Girard	Ruth White
Girard Girard	Wyman Pendleton
A Street Walker	Estelle Parsons
Eloisa Brace	Alice Drummond
Jerome Brace	Donald Hotton
Gus	Alan Yorke
Jocko	Robert Viharo
Melba	Jennifer West
Miles	Henderson Forsythe
Madame Rosita	Estelle Parsons
Heliodoro	Victor Arnold
A Man	William Callan
Washroom Attendant	Henderson Forsythe
Doctor	Henderson Forsythe
Various People	Vicki Blankenship, Joseph Cali, William Callan, Robert Viharo

UNDERSTUDIES: Malcolm, Douglas Henderson; Laureen, Melba, Vicki Blankenship; Kermit, Girard, Cox, William Callan; Jerome,
Victor Arnold; Gus, Heliodoro, Robert Viharo;
Madame Girard, Eloisa, Doris Roberts

A Drama in two acts.
General Manager: Michael Goldreyer
Press: Howard Atlee, David Roggensack
Stage Managers: Mark Wright,
Arthur Pepine, Joseph Cali

° Closed January 15, 1966. (7 performances)

49

Opened Wednesday, January 19, 1966.°
Garrick Productions and Martin Lee present:

THE WAYWARD STORK

By Harry Tugend; Directed by Dan Levin; Settings, Will Steven Armstrong; Costumes, Ann Roth; Lighting, Peter Hunt; Production Assistant, Gail MacAndrew.

CAST

Robert Stevens	Bob Cummings
Mrs. Julia Stevens	Lois Nettleton
Mrs. Maggie Stevens	Arlene Golonka
Mrs. Peters	Arlene Walker
Mrs. Hoyt	Rosalind Cash
Mrs. Galbraith	Molly Ardrey
Nurse	Linn Mason
Dr. Justin Kempp	Bernie West
Dr. Stanley Carter	Gary Pillar
Roy Bailey	Art Lund

UNDERSTUDIES: Stevens, Bernie West; Julia, Maggie, Nurse, Mrs. Peters, Mrs. Hoyt, Molly Ardrey; Kempp, Art Lund; Roy, Carter, Chet Leaming

A Comedy in two acts and seven scenes. The action takes place at the present time in the Stevens' home and Dr. Kempp's offices in Los Angeles, California.

General Manager: Victor Samrock
Company Manager: David Wyler
Press: Nat and Irvin Dorfman,
Marcia Katz
Stage Managers: Kenneth Mays, Chet Leaming

° Closed January 22, 1966. (5 performances)

Friedman-Abeles Photos

Gary Pillar, Arlene Golonka, Art Lund
Above: Arlene Golonka, Bob Cummings,
Lois Nettleton

Bob Cummings, Lois Nettleton. Above: Gary Pillar
Bob Cummings, Bernie West

Gwen Verdon
as
"SWEET CHARITY"

Friedman-Abeles Photos

John McMartin, Gwen Verdon
Above: "Big Spender" Number
Top: Gwen Verdon, Helen Gallagher, Thelma Oliver

PALACE THEATRE

Opened Saturday, January 29, 1966.°
Fryer, Carr and Harris present:

SWEET CHARITY

Book by Neil Simon; Music, Cy Coleman;
Lyrics, Dorothy Fields; Based on film "Nights
Of Cabiria" by Federico Fellini, Tullio Pinelli,
Ennio Flaino; Staged and Choreographed by
Bob Fosse; Scenery and Lighting, Robert Ran-
dolph; Costumes, Irene Sharaff; Musical Direc-
tion and Dance Music Arranged by Fred Wer-
ner; Orchestrations, Ralph Burns; Production
Manager; Robert Linden; Associate Producer,
John Bowab; Hair Styles, Ronald De Mann; Miss
Verdon's Hair Styles, Romaine Green; Assistant
Conductor, Oscar Kosarin. Original Cast Al-
bum by Columbia.

CAST

Charity	Gwen Verdon
Dark Glasses	Michael Davis
Bystander	John Stratton
Married Couple	Bud Vest, Elaine Cancilla
Woman with hat	Ruth Buzzi
Football Player	John Sharpe
Ice Cream Vendor	Gene Foote
Ballplayers	Harold Pierson, Eddie Gasper
Career Carl	Barbara Sharma
Young Spanish Man	Lee Roy Reams
First Cop	John Wheeler
Second Cop	David Gold
Helene	Thelma Oliver
Carmen	Carmen Morales
Nickie	Helen Gallagher
Herman	John Wheeler
Doorman	I. W. Klein
Ursula	Sharon Ritchie†
Vittorio Vidal	James Luisi
Waiter	John Stratton
Manfred	Bud Vest
Receptionist	Ruth Buzzi
Old Maid	Elaine Cancilla
Oscar	John McMartin
Daddy Johann Sebastian Brubeck	Arnold Soboloff
Brother Harold	Harold Pierson
Brother Eddie	Eddie Gasper
Policeman	Harold Pierson
Rosie	Barbara Sharma
Barney	David Gold
Mike	Michael Davis
Good Fairy	Ruth Buzzi

SINGERS AND DANCERS OF TIMES
SQUARE: I. W. Klein, Mary Louise, Alice
Evans, Betsy Dickerson, Kathryn Doby, Su-
zanne Charny, Elaine Cancilla, Carmen Mo-
rales, Christine Stewart, Charlene Ryan, David
Gold, Gene Foote, Harold Pierson, Bud Vest,
Lee Roy Reams, John Sharpe, Eddie Gasper,
Michael Davis

UNDERSTUDIES: Charity, Helen Gallagher;
Oscar, John Stratton; Vidal, Michael Davis;
Nickie, Elaine Cancilla; Helene, Barbara Shar-
ma; Ursula, Charlene Ryan; Rosie, Suzanne
Charney

MUSICAL NUMBERS: "You Should See
Yourself," "The Rescue," "Big Spender,"
"Charity's Soliloquy," "Rich Man's Frug," "If
My Friends Could See Me Now," "Too Many
Tomorrows," "There's Gotta Be Something Bet-
ter Than This," "I'm The Bravest Individual,"
"Rhythm Of Life," "Baby Dream Your Dream,"
"Sweet Charity," "Where Am I Going?," "I'm
A Brass Band," "I Love To Cry At Weddings."

A Musical in two acts and eighteen scenes
with a prologue. The action takes place in
and around New York City at the present
time.

General Manager: Joseph P. Harris
Company Manager: Sam Pagliaro
Press: Betty Lee Hunt, Fred Weterick
Stage Managers: Paul Phillips,
Michael Sinclair, Nick Malekos

° Still playing May 31, 1966.
† Succeeded by Marie Wallace.

Friedman-Abeles Photos

Geraldine Page
Above with Margaret Ladd, Clarence Williams III
Top: Clarence Williams III, Curt Jurgens, Hans
Gudegast, Logan Ramsey
Right: Geraldine Page, Curt Jurgens

EUGENE O'NEILL THEATRE

Opened Tuesday, February 1, 1966.°
George W. George and Frank Granat present:

THE GREAT INDOORS

By Irene Kamp; Directed by George Schaefer; Setting, Peter Larkin; Lighting, Tharon Musser; Costumes, Noel Taylor; "Cold" Music, Jacques Urbont, Lyrics, Irene Kamp; Hair Styles, Francesca Ruta of Orcel; Recorded song performed by Ruth Kobart; Technical Supervisor, Ralph O. Willis.

CAST

Hattie Gaines	Rosetta LeNoire
Oriane Brice	Geraldine Page
Arnolt Zend	Curt Jurgens
Hector Case	Clarence Williams III
Billie Mae McCune	Margaret Ladd
Willy Kane	Logan Ramsey
Bonnie Doon	Dolph Sweet
Kurt Schonforn	Hans Gudegast
Francis X. Daugherty	House Jameson
Lila Sparrow	Joan Wetmore

UNDERSTUDIES: Oriane, Lila, Eunice Anderson; Zend, House Jameson; Hector, Gene Boland; Billie Mae, Carol Guilford; Willy, Bonnie, Daugherty, Wallace Englehardt; Kurt, Reinhard Jahn

A Drama in three acts. The action takes place in the Belvedere, a summerhouse on a former plantation in the Delta region of the American South, late in the summer of 1964.

General Manager: Edward H. Davis
Press: Harvey B. Sabinson, Lee Solters, Lila King, David Powers
Stage Managers: Robert Downing, Nelle Nugent
° Closed February 5, 1966. (7 performances)

Friedman-Abeles Photos

ETHEL BARRYMORE THEATRE

Opened Wednesday, February 2, 1966.°
Fred Coe presents:

WAIT UNTIL DARK

By Frederick Knott; Directed by Arthur
Penn; Scenery Designed and Lighted by
George Jenkins; Costumes, Ruth Morley; Pro-
duction Supervisor, Porter Van Zandt; Wigs and
Makeup, Dick Smith; Produced in association
with Hiller Productions, Ltd.

CAST

Mike Talman	Mitchell Ryan
Sgt. Carlino	Val Bisoglio
Harry Roat, Jr.	Robert Duvall
Susy Hendrix	Lee Remick
Sam Hendrix	James Congdon
Gloria	Julie Herrod
Policemen	William Jordan, Richard Kuss

UNDERSTUDIES: Susy, Dixie Marquis; Roat,
James Tolkan; Talman, Sam, William Jordan;
Carlino, Richard Kuss; Gloria, Susan Dunfee

A Suspense Drama in three acts and seven
scenes. The action takes place at the present
time in a basement apartment in Greenwich
Village.

General Managers: Joseph Harris,
Ira Bernstein
Assistant: Nancy Simmons
Press: Karl Bernstein, Michael Bruno
Stage Manager: Ellen Wittman

° Still playing May 31, 1966.

Lee Remick, James Congdon
Top: Mitchell Ryan, Val Bisoglio

Julie Herrod, Lee Remick

Val Bisoglio, Robert Duvall
Top: Val Bisoglio, Lee Remick

Lee Remick, Mitchell Ryan
Top: Robert Duvall, Lee Remick

Donal Donnelly, Patrick Bedford, Mavis Villiers, Joseph Warren, John Cecil Holm
Above: Donal Donnelly, Patrick Bedford, Mairin D. O'Sullivan

HELEN HAYES THEATRE

Opened Wednesday, February 16, 1966.°
David Merrick Arts Foundation by arrangement with Oscar Lewenstein and Michael White presents:

PHILADELPHIA, HERE I COME!

By Brian Friel; Directed by Hilton Edwards; Designed by Lloyd Burlingame; Associate Producer, Samuel Liff.

CAST

Madge	Mairin D. O'Sullivan
Gareth O'Donnell:	
In Public	Patrick Bedford
In Private	Donal Donnelly
S. B. O'Donnell, County Councillor	Eamon Kelly
Kate Doogan	Lanna Saunders
Senator Doogan	William Griffis
Master Boyle	Joseph Boland
Lizzy Sweeney	Mavis Villiers
Con Sweeney	Joseph Warren
Ben Burton	John Cecil Holm
Ned	Thomas Connolly
Tom	Dermot McNamara
Joe	Eamon Morrissey
Canon Mick O'Byrne	Donald Marye

UNDERSTUDIES: Gar (Private), Dermot McNamara; Gar (Public), Ned, Tom, Joe, David Haviland; S. B., Joseph Boland; Boyle, Canon, John Cecil Holm; Con, Ben, Senator, Joseph Hill; Lizzy, Madge, Grace Carney; Kate, Lesley Hunt

A Comedy in three acts. The action takes place at the present time in the living quarters behind the general store of County Councillor O'Donnell in the small village of Ballybeg in Ireland on the night before Gar's departure for Philadelphia.

General Manager: Jack Schlissel
Company Manager: Richard Highley
Press: Harvey B. Sabinson, Lee Solters, Jay Russell, Jane Friedman
Stage Managers: Mitchell Erickson, Joseph Hill

° Still playing May 31, 1966.

Sam Siegel Photos

Donald Marye, Donal Donnelly, Eamon Kelly
Top: Donal Donnelly, Patrick Bedford
Left: Patrick Bedford, Lanna Saunders, William Griffis 57

Angela Thornton, Norman Barrs, Ray Milland, Michael Allinson
Top: (L) Melville Cooper, Ray Milland. (R) Michael Allinson, Ray Milland

THE MUSIC BOX

Opened Thursday, February 17, 1966.°
Jay Julien and Andre Goulston by arrangement with Peter Saunders present:

HOSTILE WITNESS

By Jack Roffey; Directed by Reginald Den-
ham; Scenery and Lighting, Ralph Alswang;
Associate Producer, Anthony Parella; Assistant
to the Producers, Janet Stewart.

CAST

Charles Milburn .... Norman Barrs
Percy .... Harvey Jason
Sheila Larkin .... Angela Thornton
Simon Crawford .... Ray Milland
Sir Peter Crossman .... Michael Allinson
Hamish Gillespie .... Edgar Daniels
Major Hugh Maitland .... Geoffrey Lumsden
Court Usher .... Stafford Dickens
Mr. Naylor .... Anthony Kemble Cooper
Clerk of the Court .... Walter Thomson
Policeman .... Arthur Marlowe
Superintendent Eley .... Gerald Peters
Dr. Wimborne .... Peter Pagan
Mr. Justice Osborne .... Melville Cooper
Prison Officer .... John Clark
Lady Gregory .... Margot Stevenson

SPECTATORS AND COURT PERSONNEL:
Katherine Hynes, Dorothy James, Robert Murch,
Alex Reed, Tom McDermott, Jim Oyster

UNDERSTUDIES: Milburn, Eley, Alex Reed;
Crossman, Naylor, Tom McDermott; Maitland,
Peter Pagan; Sheila, Dorothy James; Gillespie,
Walter Thomson; Osborne, Stafford Dickens;
Usher, Clerk, Arthur Marlowe; Wimborne, Of-
ficer, Policeman, Jim Oyster; Lady Gregory,
Katherine Hynes; Percy, John Clark

A Courtroom Melodrama in two acts and
four scenes. The action takes place at the
present time in the chambers of Simon Crawford in London, in the Central Criminal Court
of Old Bailey, and in a consultation cell of
Old Bailey.

General Manager: Norman Maibaum
Company Manager: Paul Groll
Press: Harvey B. Sabinson,
Lee Solters, Leo Stern
Stage Managers: Paul A. Foley,
Arthur Marlowe, Jim Oyster

° Still playing May 31, 1966.

Henry Grossman Photos

Melville Cooper, Ray Milland,
Angela Thornton, Edgar Daniels
Top: Edgar Daniels, Angela Thornton, Ray Milland **59**

LONGACRE THEATRE

Opened Tuesday, February 22, 1966.°
Charles Bowden and Lester Persky in association with Sidney Lanier present:

SLAPSTICK TRAGEDY

By Tennessee Williams; Directed by Alan Schneider; Sets, Ming Cho Lee; Costumes, Noel Taylor; Music, Lee Hoiby; Lyrics, Tennessee Williams; Lighting, Martin Aronstein; Produced in association with Frenman Productions Ltd.; Choral Director, Zev Babbitt.

CAST

"The Mutilated"

Celeste	Kate Reid
Henry	Ralph Waite
Trinket	Margaret Leighton
Slim	James Olson
Bruno	Ralph Waite
Maxie	David Sabin
Bird Girl	Renee Orin
Cop	Jordan Charney
Bernie	Tom Aldredge
Woman at Bar	Adelle Rasey
Pious Queen	Dan Bly
Tiger	Henry Oliver
Shore Police	Hank Brunjes

SINGERS: Hank Brunjes, Jordan Charney, Alan Crofoot, Larry Ellis, Ronn Hansen, Henry Oliver, Renee Orin, Art Ostrin, Adelle Rasey, David Sabin.

The action takes place during the 1930's in the Old French Quarter of New Orleans.

"The Gnadiges Fraulein"

Polly	Zoe Caldwell
Molly	Kate Reid
Permanent Transient	Dan Bly
The Gnadiges Fraulein	Margaret Leighton
Cocaloony	Art Ostrin
Indian Joe	James Olson

UNDERSTUDIES: Trinket, Fraulein, Adelle Rasey; Polly, Molly, Renee Orin; Slim, Indian, Hank Brunjes; Bruno, Jordan Charney; Bernie, Henry, Dan Bly.

The action takes place at the present time on Cocaloony Key, Florida, in and around Molly's boarding house.

Managers: Michael Wilding, Arthur Waxman
Press: David Rothenberg, Lawrence Schneider
Stage Managers: Mark Wright,
Patrick Horrigan, Elizabeth Roberts

° Closed February 26, 1966. (7 performances)

Friedman-Abeles Photos

James Olson, Ralph Waite, Margaret Leighton
Above: Zoe Caldwell, Kate Reid, Margaret Leighton
Top: Margaret Leighton, Kate Reid
Left: James Olson, Zoe Caldwell, Kate Reid

Friedman-Abeles Photos

BROOKS ATKINSON THEATRE

Opened Friday, February 25, 1966.°
Philip Rose, Jeanne Otto and Herschel
Bernardi present:

NATHAN WEINSTEIN, MYSTIC, CONNECTICUT

By David Rayfiel; Directed by Peter Kass;
Setting and Lighting, Ben Edwards; Costumes,
Jane Greenwood; Music Composed and Ar-
ranged by Joseph Garvey.

CAST

Rachel Weinstein	Zohra Lampert
Arnold Rose	Anthony Holland
Nathan Weinstein	Sam Levene
Dr. Lance Augenblick	Gerry Matthews
Goldfish Girl	Alixandria Walsh
Lady Visitor	Sylvia Davis
Hospital Attendant	David Miller
Man Patient	Michael Becket
Ticket Seller	David Miller
Mrs. Snow	Estelle Winwood
Harry Wang	Robert Barend
Deborah Wang	Doris Belack
Lem Fowler	John Wardwell
Chief Kim Bong Choy	Saeed Jaffrey

UNDERSTUDIES: Nathan, Robert Barend;
Rachel, Deborah, Anna Shaler; Harry, Norman
Shelly; Mrs. Snow, Sylvia Davis; Chief, Lem,
David Miller; Arnold, Doctor, Michael Becket

A Comedy in three acts and ten scenes.
The action takes place at the present time.

General Manager: Walter Fried
Company Manager: Helen Richards
Press: Merle Debuskey, Violet Welles,
Mae S. Hong, Lawrence Belling
Stage Managers: Leonard Auerbach,
Norman Shelly

° Closed February 26, 1966. (3 performances)

Gerry Matthews, Zohra Lampert
Above: Saeed Jaffrey, Sam Levene, Zohra Lampert
Top: Estelle Winwood, Sam Levene
Right: Sam Levene

Friedman-Abeles Photos

BELASCO THEATRE

Opened Saturday, February 26, 1966.°
Edgar and Bruce Lansbury present:

FIRST ONE ASLEEP, WHISTLE

By Oliver Hailey; Directed by John Berry;
Setting and Lighting, Lloyd Burlingame; Costumes, Theoni V. Aldredge.

CAST

Elaine	Salome Jens
Susan	Marya Zimmet
	(matinees: Elissa Leeds)
David	Frank Converse
Esther	Louise Shaffer

UNDERSTUDIES: Elaine, Nina Wilcox;
David, Sam Waterston.

A Comedy in two acts and six scenes. The action takes place at the present time in Elaine's apartment in New York City.

General Manager: Joseph Beruh
Company Manager: M. Weinberg
Press: Max Eisen, Robert Larkin, Carl Samrock, Jeannie Gibson Merrick
Stage Managers: Gigi Cascio, Sam Waterston

° Closed February 26, 1966. (1 performance)

Louise Shaffer, Salome Jens
Top: Salome Jens, Marya Zimmet, Frank Converse
Right: Frank Converse, Salome Jens

62

BILLY ROSE THEATRE

Opened Wednesday, March 2, 1966.°
Michael Wager (by arrangement with Robert Whitehead) presents:

WHERE'S DADDY?

Directed by Harold Clurman; Setting and Lighting, Ben Edwards; Clothes, Jane Greenwood.

CAST

Teena	Barbara Dana
Tom	Beau Bridges
Mrs. Bigelow	Betty Field
Helen	Barbara Ann Teer
Razz	Robert Hooks
Pinky	Hiram Sherman

UNDERSTUDIES: Teena, Katharine Houghton; Tom, John Crowther; Mrs. Bigelow, Dortha Duckworth; Helen, Abigail Rosen; Razz, Booker T. Bradshaw, Jr.; Pinky, Howard Fischer.

A Comedy in two acts. The action takes place at the present time in Midtown Manhattan.

General Manager: Oscar Olesen
Company Manager: Thomas Bodkin
Press: Samuel Lurie, Stanley F. Kaminsky
Stage Managers: Frederic de Wilde, Howard Fischer

° Closed March 19, 1966. (21 performances)

Beau Bridges, Hiram Sherman, Barbara Dana (also top with Robert Hooks)
Above: Betty Field, Barbara Dana
Left: Barbara Ann Teer, Robert Hooks, Barbara Dana

63

Robert Preston, Rosemary Harris

Robert Preston, Bruce Scott, Rosemary Harris,
Christopher Walken. Top: Dennis Cooney,
Bruce Scott, Christopher Walken, Robert Preston,
Rosemary Harris, James Rado, Suzanne Grossmann

AMBASSADOR THEATRE

Opened Thursday, March 3, 1966.°
Eugene V. Wolsk, Walter A. Hyman and
Alan King with Emanuel Azenberg
present:

THE LION IN WINTER

By James Goldman; Directed by Noel Will-
man; Scenery and Costumes, Will Steven Armstrong; Lighting, Tharon Musser; Incidental
Music, Thomas Wagner; Production Manager,
Jose Vega.

CAST

Henry II, King of England _____ Robert Preston
Alais, a French Princess ____ Suzanne Grossmann
John, the youngest son _____ Bruce Scott
Geoffrey, the middle son _____ Dennis Cooney
Richard, the oldest son, sometimes
   called the Lionheart _____ James Rado
Eleanor, Henry's Wife _____ Rosemary Harris
Philip, King of France _____ Christopher Walken
UNDERSTUDIES: Eleanor, Ludi Claire;
Henry, Bruce Glover; Geoffrey, John, Philip,
Ty McConnell; Alais, Leslie Vega; Richard,
Bruce Glover

An Historical Drama in two acts and nine
scenes. The action takes place in Henry's
castle at Chinon, France on Christmas in 1183.

General Manager: Emanuel Azenberg
Press: Frank Goodman, Martin Shwartz,
   Ruth Cage, Arlene Gordon
Stage Managers: Roger Johnson, Jr.,
   Ty McConnell

° Closed May 21, 1966. (92 performances)

Friedman-Abeles Photos

Suzanne Grossmann, Dennis Cooney, Bruce Scott, Rosemary Harris, James Rado, Robert Preston
Top Right: Rosemary Harris, Robert Preston

HENRY MILLER'S THEATRE

Opened Sunday, March 6, 1966.°
Leonard S. Field presents:

THREE BAGS FULL

By Jerome Chodorov; Based on Play by Claude Magnier; Directed by Gower Champion; Setting and lighting, Will Steven Armstrong; Costumes, Freddy Wittop; Produced by the Astounding Company (Leonard Field, Jerome Chodorov, Grandandy Productions, and Gower Champion).

CAST

Jenkins	Jon Richards
Kathleen	Sharon Gans
Bascom Barlow	Paul Ford
Richard Foyle	Joe Ponazecki
Angela	April Shawhan
Genevieve	Nancy Marchand
Jeanette	Leigh Taylor-Young
Boris	Dick Sabol
Mr. Cottingham	Rufus Smith
Charlotte	Iris Whitney
Preston Cottingham	Philip Cusack

UNDERSTUDIES: Barlow, Gordon B. Clarke; Genevieve, Charlotte, Parker McCormick; Richard, Philip Cusack; Boris, Cottingham, Jenkins, Preston, John Hallow.

A Comedy in two acts. The action takes place in a private residence on Madison Avenue in New York City during a summer in the early 1900's.

Business Manager: Ben Rosenberg
Company Manager: Richard Osorio
Press: Abner D. Klipstein
Stage Managers: John Drew Devereaux,
John Hallow

° Closed April 2, 1966. (33 performances)
Pre-Broadway tour and previews played under the title "Bascom Barlow."

Friedman-Abeles Photos

Jon Richards, Paul Ford, Dick Sabol, Joe Ponazeck
Above: Dick Sabol, April Shawhan, Nancy Marchan
Top: Iris Whitney, Leigh Taylor-Young,
Joe Ponazecki, Paul Ford, Rufus Smith
Left: Paul Ford, Sharon Gans

JOHN GOLDEN THEATRE
Opened Monday, March 7, 1966.°
Frank Productions, Inc. presents:

WAIT A MINIM!

Devised and Directed by Leon Gluckman; Musical Arrangements and Direction, Andrew Tracey; Decor and Lighting, Frank Rembach, Leon Gluckman; Decor Executed by Frank Rembach; Costumes, Heather Macdonald-Rouse; Choreography, Frank Staff, Kendrew Lascelles; Lighting and Design Supervision, Klaus Holm; Costume Supervision, Patton Campbell; Production Supervisor, Lanier Davis; Original Cast Album by London Records.

CAST

Andrew Tracey	Nigel Pegram
Paul Tracey	April Olrich
Kendrew Lascelles	Dana Valery
Michel Martel	Sarah Atkinson

PROGRAM

PART I: "This Is The Land," "Ndinosara Nani?," "Hoe Ry Die Boere," "This Is Worth Fighting For," "Subuhi Sana," "Jikel' Emaweni," "Ajade Papa," "Dingere Dingale," "Over The Hills," "I Know Where I'm Going," "I Gave My Love A Cherry," "Black-White Calypso," "Die Meistertrinker," "Butter Milk Hill," "Aria," "Out Of Focus," "Dirty Old Town," "Last Summer," "Vive La Difference," "Lalirette, Le Roi A Fait Battre Tambour," "Tour De France," "A Piece of Ground," "Ayama," "North Of The Popo," "Kupura Kupika," "Izicatulo Gumboot Dance."

PART II: "Tunes of Glory," "The Wee Cooper o' Fife," "Red Red Rose," "Hammer Song," "London Talking Blues," "The Love Life Of A Gondolier," "Foyo," "Cool," "On Guard," "Sir Oswald Sodde," "Opening Knight," "Table Bay," "This Is South Africa," "Marabi Dance Song," "Celeste Aida," "Cingoma Chakabaruka," "Skalo-Zwi," "Samandoza-we!," "Amasalela."

A Musical Entertainment in two parts.

General Manager: Ira Bernstein
Press: Reuben Rabinovitch,
John Springer Associates
Stage Manager: Frank Rembach

° Still playing May 31, 1966.

Friedman-Abeles Photos

April Olrich, Kendrew Lascelles, Andrew Tracey, Paul Tracey, Michel Martel, Nigel Pegram, Sarah Atkinson, Dana Valery. Above: April Olrich, Kendrew Lascelles. Top: Paul Tracey, Sarah Atkinson, Andrew Tracey, Nigel Pegram

Kendrew Lascelles, Michel Martel, April Olrich

EUGENE O'NEILL THEATRE

Opened Thursday, March 10, 1966.°
George W. George and Frank Granat
present:

HAPPILY NEVER AFTER

By J. A. Ross; Directed by Joseph Anthony;
Scenery, Peter Larkin; Costumes, Theoni V.
Aldredge; Lighting, Jean Rosenthal; Hair
Styles, Enrico Caruso; Production Assistant,
Gloria Banta; Technical Supervisor, Ralph O.
Willis; Set Accessories, David Barrett.

CAST

Harry Mills	----------------------	Gerald S. O'Loughlin
Joan Mills	-------------------------	Barbara Barrie
Mary Kingsley	----------------------	Rochelle Oliver
Peter Kingsley	-----------------------	Ken Kercheval
Sarah Mills	--------------------------	Karen Black†

UNDERSTUDIES: Harry, Robert Baines;
Mary, Sarah, Nancy Tribush; Peter, Don
Travanty; Joan, Nancy Franklin

A Comedy in three acts and four scenes.
The action takes place on a weekend in
June of the present time in a beach house on
the North Shore of Long Island.

General Manager: Edward H. Davis
Press: Harvey B. Sabinson, Lee Solters,
David Powers
Stage Managers: William Dodds,
Robert Baines

° Closed March 12, 1966. (4 performances)
† Played by Bonnie Bedelia in pre-Bdwy tour.

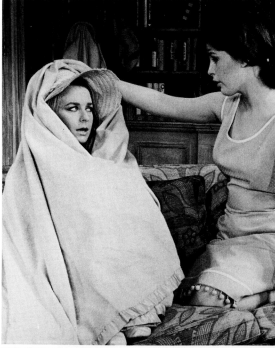

Gerald S. O'Loughlin, Ken Kercheval, Rochelle Oliver
Above: Barbara Barrie, Gerald S. O'Loughlin

Gerald S. O'Loughlin, Barbara Barrie
Above: Rochelle Oliver, Bonnie Bedelia
Top: Ken Kercheval, Barbara Barrie, Rochelle Oliv
Bonnie Bedelia, Gerald S. O'Loughlin

FORTY-SIXTH STREET THEATRE

Opened Friday, March 18, 1966.°
Guy De La Passardiere presents:

POUSSE-CAFÉ

Book, Jerome Weidman; Music, Duke Ellington; Lyrics, Marshall Barer, Fred Tobias; Director, José Quintero; Scenery, Will Steven Armstrong; Costumes, Patricia Zipprodt, Albert Wolsky; Lighting, V. C. Fuqua; Musical Direction, Sherman Frank; Production Consultant, Charles Conaway; Orchestrations, Larry Wilcox; Associate Producer, Monty Shaff; Choreography, Valerie Bettis; Musical Numbers and Dances Staged by Marvin Gordon; Hair Styles, D. Rusty Bonaccorso.

CAST

Ellis	Ellis Larkins
Havana	Travis Hudson
Duchess	Madge Cameron
Monty	Al Nesor
Harry	Tommy Karaty
Sourball	Robert Rovin
Bill	Ben Bryant
Arthur Owen, Jr.	Jeff Siggins
John Harmon	Gary Krawford
Prof. George Ritter	Theodore Bikel
Solange	Lilo
Sailor	Dom Angelo
Policeman	Hal Norman
Paul	Don Crabtree
Maurice	Charles Durning
Artie	Coley Worth
Tourist Lady	Fran Stevens
Louise	Marlene Lustik
Dean Stewart	Charles Durning
Danny	Richard Tone

ENSEMBLE: Dom Angelo, Kay Cole, Joel Conrad, Mervin Crook, Elaine Giftos, Altovise Gore, Peter Hamparian, Jo Ann Lehmann, Marlene Lustik, Iva March, Simon McQueen, Rita O'Connor, Martin Ross, Barbara Saatan, Scotty Salmon

UNDERSTUDIES: Solange, Simon McQueen; Ritter, Peter Johl; Havana, Madge Cameron; Danny, Dom Angelo; Harmon, Tommy Karaty; Sourball, Bill, Monty, Marty Ross; Harry, Joel Conrad; Owen, Scotty Salmon; Artie, Charles Durning; Dean, Paul, Maurice, Hal Norman; Duchess, Fran Stevens.

MUSICAL NUMBERS: "The Spider and The Fly," "Rules and Regulations," "Follow Me Up The Stairs," "Goodbye Charlie," "C'est Comme Ca," "Thank You, Ma'am," "The Eleventh Commandment," "Someone To Care For," "The Wedding," "Entre Acte," "Let's," "The Good Old Days," "Easy To Take," "Old World Charm."

A Musical in two acts and seventeen scenes with prologue. The entire action takes place in New Orleans during the early 'twenties.

General Manager: Monty Shaff
Business Manager: Martin Cohen
Press: Bill Doll & Co., Midori Tsuji, Robert Ganshaw, Dick Spittel
Stage Managers: Herman Magidson, Hal Norman

° Closed March 19, 1966.   (3 performances)

Doris Spremo Photos

Gary Krawford, Lilo (above with Theodore Bikel) Top: Al Nesor, Coley Worth, Barbara Saatan, Iva March. Left: Barbara Saatan, Rita O'Connor

69

LONGACRE THEATRE

Opened Wednesday, March 23, 1966.°
Emanuel Azenberg, Eugene Wolsk and
Leonard Soloway in association with John
Lotas present:

Hal Holbrook
in
MARK TWAIN TONIGHT!

A one-man reading of selections from the
books, notes, and letters of Mark Twain, presented in three parts. The program was recorded by Columbia Records.

Production Supervisor: Jerry Adler
General Manager: Max Allentuck
Press: Harvey B. Sabinson, David Powers

° Still playing May 31, 1966.

Friedman-Abeles Photos

BROOKS ATKINSON THEATRE

Opened Friday, March 25, 1966.°
Hillard Elkins in association with Donald
J. Mitchell presents:

THE BEST LAID PLANS

By Gwen Davis; Directed by Jack Percival;
Scenic Production, Oliver Smith; Costumes,
Florence Klotz; Lighting, Peggy Clark; Associate Producer, George Platt; Production
Supervisor, Michael Thoma; Men's Wardrobe,
Oleg Cassini.

CAST

Alicia Hopper _____ Marian Hailey
Jason Beckman _____ Edward Woodward
Lorna _____ Cynthia Harris
Dr. Ralph Brodie _____ Kenneth Mars
Evelyn Hopper _____ Polly Rowles

UNDERSTUDIES: Jason, Ralph, Lawrence
Keith; Alicia, Lorna, Rue McClanahan; Evelyn,
Ethel Britton.

A Comedy in three acts and nine scenes.
The action takes place at the present time
in the apartments of Alicia Hopper and Jason Bleckman, and in Dr. Brodie's office.

General Manager: Bill Levine
Press: Lee Solters, Harvey B. Sabinson,
Harry Nigro
Stage Managers: Vincent Lynne,
Lawrence Keith

° Closed March 26, 1966. (3 performances)

Kenneth Mars, Edward Woodward
Above: Polly Rowles, Marian Hailey
Top: Edward Woodward

Marian Hailey, Edward Woodward, also above

71

ALVIN THEATRE

Opened Tuesday, March 29, 1966.°
Harold Prince in association with Ruth Mitchell presents:

"IT'S A BIRD . . .
IT'S A PLANE . . .
IT'S SUPERMAN"

Book by David Newman and Robert Benton; Based on comic strip "Superman;" Music, Charles Strouse; Lyrics, Lee Adams; Directed by Harold Prince; Dances and Musical Numbers Staged by Ernest Flatt; Scenery and Lighting, Robert Randolph; Costumes, Florence Klotz; Musical Direction, Harold Hastings; Orchestrations, Eddie Sauter; Dance Arrangements, Betty Walberg; Hair Styles, D. Rusty Bonaccorso; Filmed sequences by MPO Pictures, Inc.; Original Cast Album by Columbia.

CAST

Superman/Clark Kent	Bob Holiday
Max Mencken	Jack Cassidy
Lois Lane	Patricia Marand
Perry White	Eric Mason
Sydney	Linda Lavin
Dr. Abner Sedgwick	Michael O'Sullivan
Jim Morgan	Don Chastain
Father Ling	Jerry Fujikawa
Dong Ling	Bill Starr
Tai Ling	Murphy James
Fan Po Ling	Juleste Salve
Ming Foo Ling	Michael Gentry
Joe Ling	Joseph Gentry

Suspects:

One	Les Freed
Two	Dick Miller
Three	Dal Richards
Four	John Grigas
Five	John Smolko
Byron, the Bank Guard	Eugene Edwards
Harvey, the Tour Guide	Bob Scherkenbach
Bonnie, the Moll	April Nevins
Sue-Ellen, the Teenager	Tina Faye
Marnie, the Model	Judy Newman
Gordon, the Student	Bick Goss
Annette, the Secretary	Michelle Barry
Wanda, the Waitress	Gay Edmond
Rosalie, the High School Girl	Marilyne Mason
Leslie, the Shopper	Jayme Mylroie
Cathy, the Child	Lori Browne
Barbie, the Receptionist	Mara Landi
Al, the Bank Robber	George Bunt
Milton, the Hood	Dallas Edmunds
Kevin, the College Boy	Roy Smith
William, the Exchange Student	Haruki Fujimoto

UNDERSTUDIES: Max, Dick Miller; Sedgwick, Dal Richards; Superman, John Smolko; Lois, Marilyne Mason; Morgan, Eric Mason; Sydney, Jayme Mylroie; The Flying Lings, Haruki Fujimoto; Father Ling, Juleste Salve

MUSICAL NUMBERS: "Doing Good," "We Need Him," "It's Superman," "We Don't Matter At All," "Revenge," "The Woman For The Man," "You've Got Possibilities," "What I've Always Wanted," "Everything's Easy When You Know How," "It's Super Nice," "So Long, Big Guy," "The Strongest Man In The World," "Ooh, Do You Love You!," "You've Got What I Need," "I'm Not Finished Yet," "Pow! Bam! Zonk!"

A Musical in two acts and eighteen scenes. The action takes place at the present time in and around the city of Metropolis, U.S.A.

General Manager: Carl Fisher
Press: Mary Bryant, Robert Pasoli
Stage Managers: Ruth Mitchell, Ben Strobach, Nicholas G. Rinaldi

° Still playing May 31, 1966.

Bob Holiday, and top with Michael O'Sullivan (L), Patricia Marand (C), Don Chastain

Linda Lavin, Jack Cassidy
Above: Jack Cassidy, Michael O'Sullivan
Top: Bob Holiday, Patricia Marand

Patricia Marand (Center). Above: Bob Holiday,
Linda Lavin. Top: The Company

METROPOLITAN OPERA HOUSE

Opened Tuesday, April 19, 1966.°
S. Hurok presents:

BOLSHOI BALLET

Director General, Mikhail Chulaki; Principal Choreographer, Yuri Grigorovich; Conductors, Gennady Rozhdestvensky, Alexander Kopylov, Kiril Tikhonov; Guest Conductor, Arthur Lief; Assistant Director, Mikhail Anastasiev; Ballet Coordinator, Alexander Tomsky; Manager, Mikhail Lakhman; Interpreter, Helen Gillespie.

SOLOISTS

Maya Plisetskaya, Ekaterina Maximova, Natalia Bessmertnova, Rimma Karelskaya, Nina Sorokina, Maya Samokhvalova, Nicolai Fadeyechev, Vladimir Vasiliev, Vladimir Tikhonov, Mikhail Lavrovsky, Vladimir Levashev, Yuri Vladimirov, Alla Boguslavskaya, Ida Vasilieva, Larisa Dmitrieva, Natalia Kasatkina, Faina Kuznetsova, Natalia Pozniakova, Natalia Ryzhenko, Natalia Taborko, Elena Kholina, Elmira Kosterina, Dmitri Begak, Stanislav Vlasov, Esfandiar Kashani, Alexander Lavreniuk, Vladimir Koshelev, Valery Lagunov, Nicolai Simachev, Anatoli Simachev, German Sitnikov.

REPERTOIRE

Swan Lake, The Nutcracker, Don Quixote, Giselle, The Rite Of Spring, Chopiniana, Raymonda, Divertissements, Highlights Program.

Company Manager: Edward A. Perper
Press: Martin Feinstein, Michael Sweeley, Edward Parkinson, Myra Armstrong
Stage Managers: Alexander Tsarman, Anatoly Pavlinov, John L. Moorehead, Jay Kingwill

° Closed Sunday, May 8, 1966 (24 performances) with a Gala Program for the final performance to be presented on the stage of the Met before its move to Lincoln Center. Bolshoi Company returned to Madison Square Garden Tuesday, May 17, 1966 for 7 additional performances, closing Sunday, May 22, 1966.

Nina Sorokina, Yuri Vladimirov in "The Rite Of Spring"

Maya Plisetskaya, Vladimir Tikhonov in "Don Quixote"
Above: Vladimir Vasiliev in "The Nutcracker"

74

John Gielgud, Vivien Leigh
in
"IVANOV"

SHUBERT THEATRE

Opened Tuesday, May 3, 1966.°
Alexander H. Cohen presents the Tennent
Production of:

IVANOV

By Anton Chekhov; Adapted by John Giel-
gud; Based on original translation by Ariadne
Nicolaeff; Directed by John Gielgud; Scenery
and Costumes, Rouben Ter-Arutunian; Lighting,
Jean Rosenthal; Production Associate, Hildy
Parks; Production Manager, Jean Barrere; Pro-
duction Associate, Milton Chwasky; Production
Assistant, Davina Crawford; Staff Assistant,
Sean Brancato; Hair Stylist, Phil Leto; Origin-
al Cast Album by RCA Victor.

CAST

Nikolai Alekseyevitch Ivanov, full time member of Department of Peasant Affairs	John Gielgud
Mikhail Mikhailovitch Borkin (Misha Mishelitch), distant relative of Ivanov and his estate manager	Ronald Radd
Anna Petrovna, nee Sarah Abramson, wife of Ivanov	Vivien Leigh
Count Matvei Semyonovitch Shabelsky, his maternal uncle	Edward Atienza
Yevgeny Konstantinovitch Lvov, young country doctor	John Merivale
Zinaida Savishna (Zyuzyushka), wife of Lebedev	Paula Laurence
Marfa Yegorovna Babakina, young widow, landowner, daughter of rich merchant	Helen Christie
Kossykh, a card addict	Dillon Evans
Avdotya Nazarovna, a marriage broker	Ethel Griffies
Pavel Kirilytch Lebedev (Pashenka), Chairman of the Rural Council	Roland Culver
Sasha (Shura), his daughter	Jennifer Hilary
Young Men	Brooks Morton, Miller Lide, Tom Klunis
Young Girls	Esther Benson, Linda Geiser
Old Lady	Betty Sinclair
Gavrila (Butler)	Guy Spaull
Maid	Anna Minot
Pyotr, Ivanov's servant	Michael Miller

UNDERSTUDIES: Ivanov, Tom Klunis; Anna,
Marfa, Esther Benson; Lebedev, Count, Guy
Spaull; Sasha, Linda Geiser; Zinaida, Betty
Sinclair; Borkin, Michael Miller, Brooks Mor-
ton; Nazarovna, Betty Sinclair; Young Girls,
Anna Minot; Young Man, Michael Miller.

A Drama presented in two acts and four
scenes. The action takes place in a district
in Central Russia at the end of the last century.

General Manager: Roy A. Somlyo
Company Manager: Seymour Herscher
Press: James D. Proctor, Robert W. Larkin,
Sally Zeitlin
Stage Managers: Harry Young, Anna Minot
° Still playing May 31, 1966.

Friedman-Abeles Photos

Jennifer Hilary, John Gielgud
Above: Paula Laurence, John Gielgud
Top: Ronald Radd, Edward Atienza, Roland Culver
Ethel Griffies. Left: John Merivale, Vivien Leigh

Laurence Naismith, Shani Wallis, Ivor Emmanuel, Tessie O'Shea
in
"A TIME FOR SINGING"

George Mathews, John Call, Frank Griso,
Laurence Naismith
Above: Ivor Emmanuel, Shani Wallis

BROADWAY THEATRE

Opened Saturday, May 21, 1966.°
Alexander H. Cohen presents:

A TIME FOR SINGING

Book and Lyrics, Gerald Freedman and John Morris; Based on Novel "How Green Was My Valley" by Richard Llewellyn; Music, John Morris; Director, Gerald Freedman; Choreography, Donald McKayle; Designed by Ming Cho Lee; Costumes, Theoni V. Aldredge; Lighting, Jean Rosenthal; Musical Direction, Jay Blackton; Orchestrations, Don Walker; Production Associate, Hildy Parks; Production Supervisor, Jerry Adler; Produced in Association with Joseph Wishy; Production Associate, Milton Chwasky; Hair Stylists, Phil Leto, Barry Brown; Original Cast Album by Warner Bros. Records.

CAST

David Griffith	Ivor Emmanuel
Paymaster	Jay Gregory
Dai Bando	John Call
Cyfartha Lewis	George Mathews
Gwillym Morgan (Dada)	Laurence Naismith
Davey Morgan	Gene Rupert
Ivor Morgan	Brian Avery
Ianto Morgan	George Hearn
Owen Morgan	Harry Theyard
Evan Morgan	Philip Proctor
Huw Morgan	Frank Griso
Beth Morgan	Tessie O'Shea
Angharad Morgan	Shani Wallis
Bronwen Jenkins	Elizabeth Hubbard
Mr. Evans	John Malcolm
Iestyn Evans	David O'Brien
School Teacher	David Thomas

CHILDREN: Paul Dwyer, Peter Falzone, Dewey Golkin, Laura Michaels, Janice Notaro.

SINGERS: Robert Carle, Ed Ericksen, Jay Gregory, Marian Haraldson, Zona Kennedy, Reid Klein, Henry LeClair, Constance Moffit, Jack Murray, Mari Nettum, Joyce O'Neil, Michael Quinn, Maggie Task, Ann Tell, David Thomas, Maggie Worth.

DANCERS: Bruce Becker, Steven Boockvor, Sandra Brewer, Roger Briant, Sterling Clark, Carolyn Dyer, Mary Ehara, Rodney Griffin, Sue Babel, Mimi Wallace.

UNDERSTUDIES: Beth, Travis Hudson; Angharad, Bronwen, Mari Nettum; Griffith, George Hearn; Dada, George Mathews; Ivor, Davey, Harry Theyard; Owen, Reid Klein; Evan, Sterling Clark; Huw, Peter Falzone and Dewey Golkin; Evans, Lewis, Mike Quinn; Iestyn, Jay Gregory; Dai, David Thomas.

MUSICAL NUMBERS: "Come You Men," "How Green Was My Valley," "Old Long John," "Here Come Your Men," "What A Good Day Is Saturday," "Peace Come To Every Heart," "Someone Must Try," "Oh, How I Adore Your Name," "That's What Young Ladies Do," "When He Looks At Me," "Far From Home," "I Wonder If," "What A Party," "Let Me Love You," "Why Would Anyone Want To Get Married," "A Time For Singing," "When The Baby Comes," "I'm Always Wrong," "There Is Beautiful You Are," "Three Ships," "Tell Her," "And The Mountains Sing Back," "Gone In Sorrow."

A Musical in two acts. The action takes place about 1900 in the memory of David Griffith and flows freely in time in the environment of The Valley, The Town, and The Morgan Home, in South Wales.

General Manager: Roy A. Somlyo
Press: James D. Proctor, Robert W. Larkin, Sally Zeitlin
Stage Managers: Jake Hamilton, George Thorn, Tom Porter

° Still playing May 31, 1966.

Top Left: **Bruce Becker, Steve Boockvor, Shani Wallis, Sterling Clark, Roger Briant, Ivor Emmanuel**

David O'Brien, Shani Wallis, Laurence Naismith, Frank Griso, Tessie O'Shea,
Elizabeth Hubbard, Brian Avery. Above: (L) Shani Wallis, David O'Brien
(R) Frank Griso, Laurence Naismith, Tessie O'Shea

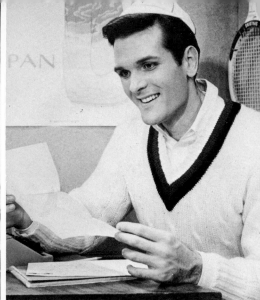

Jane Connell, Beatrice Arthur, Angela Lansbury
Above: (L) Frankie Michaels. (R) Jerry Lanning

WINTER GARDEN THEATRE

Opened Tuesday, May 24, 1966.*
Fryer, Carr and Harris present:

MAME

Book, Jerome Lawrence, Robert E. Lee;
Based on Novel "Auntie Mame" by Patrick
Dennis, and Play by Lawrence and Lee; Music
and Lyrics, Jerry Herman; Director, Gene Saks;
Dances and Musical Numbers Staged by Onna
White; Settings, William and Jean Eckart;
Costumes, Robert Mackintosh; Lighting, Tharon
Musser; Musical Direction and Vocal Arrange-
ments, Donald Pippin; Orchestrations, Philip
J. Lang; Dance Music Arranged by Roger
Adams; Hair Styles, Ronald DeMann; Asso-
ciate Producer, John Bowab; Production As-
sistants, Maxine Fox, Danny Banks; Original
Cast Album by Columbia Records.

CAST

Patrick Dennis, age 10	Frankie Michaels
Agnes Gooch	Jane Connell
Vera Charles	Beatrice Arthur
Mame Dennis	Angela Lansbury
Ralph Devine	Ron Young
Bishop	Jack Davison
M. Lindsay Woolsey	George Coe
Ito	Sab Shimono
Doorman	Art Matthews
Elevator Boy	Stan Page
Messenger	Bill Stanton
Dwight Babcock	Willard Waterman
Art Model	Jo Tract
Dance Teacher	Johanna Douglas
Leading Man	Jack Davison
Stage Manager	Art Matthews
Madame Branislowski	Charlotte Jones
Gregor	John Taliaferro
Beauregard Jackson Pickett Burnside	Charles Braswell
Uncle Jeff	Clifford Fearl
Cousin Fan	Ruth Ramsey
Sally Cato	Margaret Hall
Mother Burnside	Charlotte Jones
Patrick Dennis, age 19-29	Jerry Lanning
Junior Babcock	Tommy Karaty
Mrs. Upson	Johanna Douglas
Mr. Upson	John C. Becher
Gloria Upson	Diana Walker
Pegeen Ryan	Diane Coupe
Peter Dennis	Michael Maitland

MAME'S FRIENDS: Diana Baffa, Jack Blackton, David Chaney, Pat Cummings, Jack Davison, Hilda Harris, Tommy Karaty, Nicole Karol,
Gene Kelton, Nancy Lynch, Art Matthews, Ross
Miles, Stan Page, Ruth Ramsey, Betty Rosebrock, Scotty Salmon, Bella Shalom, Bill Stanton, John Taliaferro, Jo Tract, Jodi Williams,
Kathy Wilson

UNDERSTUDIES: Mame, Charlotte Fairchild;
Jodi Williams for Agnes, Fan, Mrs. Upson;
Clifford Fearl for Babcock, Upson; Art Matthews
for Beauregard; Jack Blackton for older Patrick;
Michael Maitland for young Patrick; Jo Tract
for Sally Cato, Mme. Branislowski; Jack Davi-
son for Lindsay; Hilda Harris for Ito; Betty
Rosebrock for Pegeen; Laurie Franks for Gloria;
David Chaney for Gregor; Stan Page for Uncle
Jeff

MUSICAL NUMBERS: "St. Bridget," "It's
Today," "Open A New Window," "The Man
In The Moon," "My Best Girl," "We Need
A Little Christmas," "The Fox Hunt,"
"Mame," "Bosom Buddies," "Gooch's Song,"
"That's How Young I Feel," "If He Walked
Into My Life," Finale.

A Musical in two acts and sixteen scenes.
The action takes place between 1928 and 1946.

General Manager: Joseph P. Harris
Company Manager: Richard Grayson
Press: David Lipsky, Lisa Lipsky
Stage Managers: Terence Little,
Ralph Linn, Delmar Hendricks

* Still playing May 31, 1966.

Friedman-Abeles Photos

Angela Lansbury (C) and above with
Michael Maitland and top with Frankie Michaels

BILTMORE THEATRE

Opened Wednesday, October 23, 1963.°
Saint Subber presents:

BAREFOOT IN THE PARK

By Neil Simon; Director, Mike Nichols;
Setting, Oliver Smith; Costumes, Donald Brooks;
Lighting, Jean Rosenthal.

CAST

Corie Bratter	Penny Fuller†1
Telephone Man	Stephen Pearlman†2
Delivery Man	Joseph Keating
Paul Bratter	Anthony Roberts
Mrs. Banks	Mildred Natwick†3
Victor Velasco	Kurt Kasznar†4

UNDERSTUDIES: Corie, Beverlee McKinsey;
Paul, Jed Allan; Mrs. Banks, Ruth Matteson;
Victor, Joseph Keating

A Comedy in three acts and four scenes.
The action takes place at the present time
in the Bratter apartment on East 48th Street
in Manhattan.

General Manager: C. Edwin Knill
Company Manager: William Craver
Press: Harvey B. Sabinson, Harry Nigro,
David Powers
Stage Managers: Harvey Medlinsky,
Robert Merriman, Joseph Keating

° Still playing May 31, 1966. For original
production, see THEATRE WORLD, Vol. 20.

† Succeeded by: 1. Joan Van Ark, 2. Judd
Hirsch, 3. Eileen Heckart, Ilka Chase, 4.
Erik Rhodes for vacation, then Charles Kor-
vin, Jules Munshin.

Friedman-Abeles Photos

Jules Munshin, Ilka Chase
Above: Jules Munshin, Eileen Heckart
Top Left: Penny Fuller, Charles Korvin,
Anthony Roberts
Below: Joan Van Ark, Anthony Roberts

ST. JAMES THEATRE

Opened Thursday, January 16, 1964.°
David Merrick presents:

HELLO, DOLLY!

Book, Michael Stewart; Based on Play
"The Matchmaker" by Thornton Wilder; Music and Lyrics, Jerry Herman; Directed and
Choreographed by Gower Champion; Settings,
Oliver Smith; Costumes, Freddy Wittop; Lighting, Jean Rosenthal; Musical Direction and
Dance and Incidental Music Arrangements,
Peter Howard; Orchestrations, Philip J. Lang;
Vocal Arrangements, Shepard Coleman; Assistant to Director, Lucia Victor; Production Supervisor, Neil Hartley; A David Merrick and
Champion-Five, Inc. Production; Original Cast
Album by RCA Victor.

CAST

Mrs. Dolly Gallagher Levi	Carol Channing[1]
Ernestina	Mary Jo Catlett
Ambrose Kemper	Charles Karel[2]
Horse	Jan LaPrade[3], Bonnie Mathis[4]
Horace Vandergelder	David Burns
Ermengarde	Alice Playten
Cornelius Hackl	Charles Nelson Reilly[5]
Barnaby Tucker	Jerry Dodge
Irene Molloy	Eileen Brennan[6]
Minnie Fay	Sondra Lee
Mrs. Rose	Amelia Haas
Rudolph	David Hartman[7]
Judge	Gordon Connell
Court Clerk	Ken Ayers[8]

TOWNSPEOPLE, WAITERS, ETC.: Nicole
Barth, Monica Carter, Joyce Dahl, Elisa De
Marko, Diane Findlay, Lee Hopper, Katherine
Hull, Joan Buttons Leonard, Anne Nathan,
Patti Pappathatos, Yolanda Poropat, Jane Quinn,
Bonnie Schon, Mary Ann Snow, Pat Trott,
Paul Berne, George Blackwell, Joel Craig, Dick
Crowley, David Evans, Tony Falco, Ian
Garry, Gene Gebauer, Joe Helms, Eddie James,
Neil Jones, Keith Kaldenberg, J. David Kirby,
Jim Maher, Ed Mastin, John Mineo, Dan Siretta, Paul Solen, Lou Zeldis

UNDERSTUDIES: Dolly, Bibi Osterwald;
Vandergelder, Gordon Connell; Cornelius,
Charles Karel; Irene, Mary Ann Snow; Minnie Fay, Bonnie Schon; Barnaby, John Mineo;
Ambrose, David Evans; Ernestina, Amelia
Haas; Mrs. Rose, Yolanda Poropat; Ermengarde, Patti Pappathatos; Rudolph, Ed Mastin;
Judge, Richard Hermany. Alternates: Vandergelder, George Blackwell; Cornelius, Gene Gebauer; Irene, Joyce Dahl; Barnaby, Neil Jones;
Judge, Keith Kaldenberg

MUSICAL NUMBERS: "I Put My Hand
In," "It Takes A Woman," "Put On Your
Sunday Clothes," "Ribbons Down My Back,"
"Motherhood," "Dancing," "Before The Parade
Passes By," "Elegance," "The Waiters' Gallop," "Hello, Dolly!," "It Only Takes A Moment," "So Long Dearie," Finale.

A Musical in two acts and fifteen scenes.
The action takes place in Yonkers and Manhattan, in the past.

General Manager: Jack Schlissel
Press: Lee Solters, Harvey B. Sabinson,
Lila King, David Powers
Stage Managers: Frank Dudley, Tony Manzi

° Still playing May 31, 1966. For original
production, see THEATRE WORLD, Vol. 20.
† Succeeded by: 1. Ginger Rogers, 2. Richard
Hermany, 3. Patti Pappathatos, 4. Elisa De
Marko, 5. Lawrence Holofcener, Carlton
Carpenter, Will Mackenzie, 6. Patte Finley,
7. Dan Merriman, 8. Keith Kaldenberg.

Friedman-Abeles Photos

David Burns, Ginger Rogers (also above)
Top: Ginger Rogers (C) and entire company

THE MUSIC BOX

Opened Tuesday, February 18, 1964.°
(Moved February 14, 1966 to George
Abbott Theatre)
George W. George, Frank Granat, Howard
Erskine, Edward Specter Productions,
Peter S. Katz present:

ANY WEDNESDAY

By Muriel Resnik; Director, Henry Kaplan;
Scenery, Robert Randolph; Costumes, Theoni
V. Aldredge; Lighting, Tharon Musser; Hair
Styles, Mr. Kenneth; Production Assistant,
Nelle Nugent; Technical Supervisor, Ralph O.
Willis.

CAST

John Cleves .... George Gaynes†1
Ellen Gordon .... Barbara Cook†2
Cass Henderson .... Kenneth Mars†3
Dorothy Cleves .... Rosemary Murphy†4
UNDERSTUDIES: John, Cass, Franklin Cover;
Ellen, Loretta Swit; Dorothy, Mary K. Wells

A Comedy in two acts and four scenes.
The action takes place at the present time in
a garden apartment in the East Sixties in
Manhattan.

General Manager: Edward H. Davis
Press: Lee Solters, Harvey B. Sabinson,
Lila King, David Powers
Stege Managers: John K. Maxtone-Graham,
William H. Batchelder

° Still playing May 31, 1966. For original
production, see THEATRE WORLD, Vol.
20.

† Succeeded by: 1. Jeffrey Lynn during
month's vacation, 2. Sandra Smith, 3.
Maurice Ottinger, 4. Patricia Cutts.

Left: Sandra Smith, Maurice Ottinger
Top: George Gaynes, Sandra Smith

ROYALE THEATRE

Opened Monday, May 25, 1964.°
(Moved to Winthrop Ames Theatre, to
Helen Hayes Theatre, to Henry Miller's
Theatre, to the Belasco Theatre)
Edgar Lansbury presents:

THE SUBJECT WAS ROSES

By Frank D. Gilroy; Directed by Ulu Gros-
bard; Scenery, Edgar Lansbury; Lighting, Jules
Fisher; Costumes, Donald Foote; Production
Assistants, Linda Gaydos, Al Isaac.

CAST

John Cleary .... Jack Albertson†1
Nettie Cleary .... Irene Dailey†2
Timmy Cleary .... Martin Sheen†3
UNDERSTUDIES: John, Joseph Sullivan;
Nettie, Peg Murray; Timmy, Matt Clark

A Drama in two acts and seven scenes.
The action takes place in May 1946 in a
middle class New York apartment.

General Manager: Joseph Beruh
Press: Max Eisen, Jeannie Gibson Merrick,
Carl Samrock, Dan Rosen, Paul Solomon
Stage Managers: Paul Leaf,
Dustin Hoffman

° Closed May 21, 1966. (834 performances)
Winner of Pulitzer Prize, Antoinette Perry,
and Drama Critics Circle Awards. For original production, see THEATRE WORLD,
Vol. 20.

† Succeeded by: 1. Chester Morris, 2. Martha
Scott, then Maureen O'Sullivan, 3. Walter
McGinn.

Maureen O'Sullivan, Walter McGinn, Chester Mor

Opened Thursday, March 26, 1964.°
(Moved March 14, 1966 to Majestic
Theatre)
Ray Stark presents:

FUNNY GIRL

Book and Story, Isobel Lennart; Music,
Jule Styne; Lyrics, Bob Merrill; Director,
Garson Kanin; Musical Numbers Staged by
Carol Haney; Scenery and Lighting, Robert
Randolph; Costumes, Irene Sharaff; Musical
Direction, Paul Cianci; Orchestrations, Ralph
Burns; Vocal Arrangements, Buster Davis; Dance
Orchestrations, Luther Henderson; Associate
Producer, Al Goldin; Associate Director, Law-
rence Kasha; Presented in association with
Seven Arts Productions; Hairstyles, Ronald De-
Mann; Original Cast Album, Capitol Records.

CAST

Fanny Brice	Barbra Streisand†1
John	Robert Howard
Emma	Royce Wallace
Mrs. Brice	Kay Medford†2
Mrs. Strakosh	Fritzi Burr†3
Mrs. Meeker	Lydia S. Fredericks†4
Mrs. O'Malley	Joyce O'Neil†5
Tom Keeney	Joseph Macaulay
Eddie Ryan	Lee Allan†6
Heckie	Richard Ianni†7
Workmen	Robert Howard, Robert Henson†8
Snub Taylor	Buzz Miller
Trombone Smitty	Blair Hammond†9
Five Finger Finney	Alan E. Weeks
Trumpet Soloist	Dick Perry
Bubbles	Shellie Farrell
Polly	Joan Lowe
Maude	Ellen Halpint†10
Nick Arnstein	Sydney Chaplin†11
Showgirls	Sharon Vaughn†12, Diana Lee Nielsen†13
Stage Director	Marc Jordan
Florenz Ziegfeld, Jr.	Alan Manson
Mimsey	Sharon Vaughn†12
Ziegfeld Tenor	John Lankston†17
Ziegfeld Lead Dancer	George Reeder
Adolph	John Lankston†17
Mrs. Nadler	Rose Randolf
Paul	Larry Fuller†14
Cathy	Joan Cory
Vera	Lainie Kazan†15
Jenny	Diane Coupe†16
Ben	Buzz Miller
Mr. Renaldi	Marc Jordan
Mike Halsey	Robert Howard

Friedman-Abeles Photos

SHOWGIRLS: Lynette Bennett, Joan Cory,
Linda Jorgens, Virginia Kerr, Donna Monroe,
Barbara Rhoades

SINGERS: Barbara Ann Walters, Jeanne Mc-
Laren, Janet Moody-Morris, Rose Randolf,
Stephanie Reynolds, Larry Brucker, Victor Helou, Robert Howard, Marc Jordan, Albert Zimmerman

DANCERS: Rosemarie Barre, Edie Cowan,
Pat Dalsey, Shellie Farrell, Karen Kristin, Joan
Lowe, Billy Brandon, Bud Fleming, John Nola,
Bud Spencer, Ted Sprague, Terry Violino, Alan
E. Weeks

UNDERSTUDIES: Fanny, Linda Gerard; Nick,
George Reeder; Eddie, Bud Fleming; Mrs.
Strakosh, Barbara Ann Walters; Ziegfeld, Marc
Jordan; Tom, Robert Howard; Emma, Janet
Moody-Morris; Snub, Bud Spencer; Lead
Dancer, Ted Sprague

MUSICAL NUMBERS: "If A Girl Isn't Pretty,"
"I'm The Greatest Star," "Cornet Man," "Who
Taught Her Everything?," "His Love Makes
Me Beautiful," "I Want To Be Seen With
You Tonight," "Henry Street," "People," "You
Are Woman," "Don't Rain On My Parade,"
"Sadie, Sadie," "Find Yourself A Man," "Rat-
Tat-Tat-Tat," "Who Are You Now?," "The
Music That Makes Me Dance," Finale.

A Musical in two acts and twenty-four
scenes. Based on incidents in the life of
Fanny Brice shortly before and after World
War I, the action takes place in various
theatres, onstage and backstage, on New York's
lower East Side, in Baltimore, and on Long
Island.

General Manager: Al Goldin
Company Manager: John Larson
Press: Frank Goodman, Martin Shwartz,
Arlene Gordon
Stage Managers: William O'Brien,
Daniel Broun, Joseph Dooley, Robert Howard

° Still playing May 31, 1966. For original
production, see THEATRE WORLD, Vol. 20.

† Succeeded by: 1. Mimi Hines, 2. Fritzi
Burr, 3. Beulah Garrick, 4. Barbara Ann
Walters, 5. Jeanne McLaren, 6. Phil Ford,
7. Victor Helou, 8. Albert Zimmerman, 9.
Ted Sprague, 10. Edie Cowan, 11. Johnny
Desmond, 12. Joan Cory, 13. Lynette Ben-
nett, 14. John Nola, 15. Donna Monroe,
16. Linda Jorgens, 17. Larry Brucker.

Mimi Hines (Center)

Mimi Hines, Johnny Desmond

Friedman-Abeles Photos

Herschel Bernardi, Paul Lipson
Above: Maria Karnilova, Herschel Bernardi

IMPERIAL THEATRE

Opened Tuesday, September 22, 1964.°
Harold Prince presents:

FIDDLER ON THE ROOF

Book, Joseph Stein; Based on Sholom Aleicheim's stories; Music, Jerry Bock; Lyrics, Sheldon Harnick; Direction and Choreography, Jerome Robbins; Settings, Boris Aronson; Costumes, Patricia Zipprodt; Lighting, Jean Rosenthal; Orchestrations, Don Walker; Musical Direction and Vocal Arrangements, Milton Greene; Dance Music Arranged by Betty Walberg; Hair Stylist, D. Rusty Bonaccorso; Original Cast Album by RCA Victor.

CAST

Tevye	Zero Mostel†1
Golde	Maria Karnilova
Tzeitel	Ann Marisse
Hodel	Julia Migenes
Chava	Tanya Everett
Shprintze	Marilyn Rogers
Bielke	Pia Zadora
Yente	Beatrice Arthur†2
Motel	Austin Pendleton†3
Perchik	Leonard Frey†4
Lazar Wolf	Michael Granger†5
Mordcha	Zvee Scooler
Rabbi	Gluck Sandor
Mendel	Dan Jasin†6
Avram	Paul Lipson†7
Nachum	Maurice Edwards
Grandma Tzeitel	Sue Babel†8
Fruma-Sarah	Carol Sawyer
Constable	Joseph Sullivan
Fyedka	Joe Ponazecki†9
Shandel	Helen Verbit
The Fiddler	Ken LeRoy†10

THE VILLAGERS: Shloime the Bagel Man, John C. Attle; Itsuk, the Streetsweeper, Larry Ross; Chaim the Fishmonger, Lorenzo Bianco; Duvidel the Seltzer Man, Duane Bodin; Surcha, Sarah Felcher; Label the Woodsman, Tony Gardell; Hershel the Potseller, Louis Genevrino; Yankel the Grocer, Ross Gifford; Schmeril the Baker, Dan Jasin; Fredel, Victoria Wyndham; Yakov the Knifeseller, Thom Koutsoukos; Bluma, Jane Bergere; Berille, Jennie Lou Blackton; Mirala, Naomi Riseman; Sima, Peff Modelski; Rivka, Irene Paris; Moishe the Cobbler, Charles Rule; Anya, Phyllis Wallach; Yussel the Hatmaker, Mitch Thomas; Vladimir, Kip Andrews; Sasha, Robert Berdeen

UNDERSTUDIES: Tevye, Paul Lipson; Golde, Yente, Helen Verbit; Tzeitel, Irene Paris; Hodel, Victoria Wyndham; Chava, Jennie Lou Blackton; Perchik, Thom Klousoukos; Shprintze, Bielke, Phyllis Wallach; Rabbi, Maurice Edwards; Motel, John C. Attle; Lazar, Harry Goz; Nachum, John C. Attle; Avram, Maurice Edwards; Constable, Ross Gifford; Mendel, Dan Jasin; Mordcha, Thom Koutsoukos; Fruma, Irene Paris; Fiddler, Larry Ross; Fyedka, Robert Berdeen

MUSICAL NUMBERS: "Tradition," "Matchmaker," "If I Were A Rich Man," "Sabbath Prayer," "To Life," "Miracle of Miracles," "The Tailor, Motel Kamzoil," "Sunrise, Sunset," "Bottle Dance," "Wedding Dance," "Now I Have Everything," "Do You Love Me?," "I Just Heard," "Far From The Home I Love," "Anatevka," Epilogue.

General Manager: Carl Fisher
Company Manager: Clarence Jacobson
Press: Sol Jacobson, Lewis Harmon, Faith Geer
Stage Managers: Ruth Mitchell, James Bronson, Edmund Baylies

° Still playing May 31, 1966. For original production, see THEATRE WORLD, Vol. 21.

† Succeeded by: 1. Luther Adler, Herschel Bernardi, 2. Florence Stanley, 3. Leonard Frey, 4. Gordon Gray, 5. Paul Lipson, 6. Ken LeRoy, 7. Harry Goz, 8. Duane Bodin, 9. Don Atkinson, 10. Sammy Bayes.

Top Left: Leonard Frey, Herschel Bernardi, Gordon Gray, Maria Karnilova, Ann Marisse, Julia Migenes, Tanya Everett, Marilyn Rogers, Pia Zadora

Eddie Bracken, Nathaniel Frey, John Fiedler,
Alfred Sandor, Pat Hingle, Sidney Armus

Nathaniel Frey, Alfred Sandor, John Fiedler,
Eddie Bracken, Sidney Armus, Jack Klugman

Friedman-Abeles Photos

PLYMOUTH THEATRE

Opened Wednesday, March 10, 1965.°
Saint Subber presents:

THE ODD COUPLE

By Neil Simon; Director, Mike Nichols; Set,
Oliver Smith; Costumes, Ann Roth; Lighting,
Jean Rosenthal; Production Assistant, James
Turner.

CAST

Speed	Paul Dooley[†1]
Murray	Nathaniel Frey
Roy	Sidney Armus
Vinnie	John Fiedler
Oscar Madison	Walter Matthau[†2]
Felix Ungar	Art Carney[†3]
Gwendolyn Pigeon	Carole Shelley
Cecily Pigeon	Monica Evans

UNDERSTUDIES: Oscar, Alfred Sandor;
Gwendolyn, Cecily, Carol Gustafson

A Comedy in three acts and four scenes.
The action takes place at the present time
on a hot summer night in an apartment on
Riverside Drive in New York City.

General Manager: C. Edwin Knill
Company Manager: William Craver
Press: Harvey B. Sabinson, Lee Solters,
Harry Nigro, David Powers
Stage Managers: Bernard Pollock,
Roger Johnson, Jr.

° Still playing May 31, 1966. For original
production, see THEATRE WORLD, Vol. 21.

† Succeeded by: 1. Alfred Sandor, 2. Jack
Klugman, Pat Hingle, 3. Paul Dooley, Eddie
Bracken.

Eddie Bracken, Jack Klugman
Above: Pat Hingle, Eddie Bracken,
also right with Monica Evans, Carole Shelley

Rosanna Huffman, Tony Tanner
Above: Tony Tanner, also top center

BROADHURST THEATRE

Opened Sunday, April 25, 1965.°
Allen-Hodgdon, Stevens Productions, and
Harold Fielding present:

HALF A SIXPENCE

Book, Beverley Cross; Music and Lyrics,
David Heneker; Based on H. G. Wells' "Kipps;"
Director, Gene Saks; Dances and Musical Num-
bers Staged by Onna White; Scenery and
Costumes, Loudon Sainthill; Musical Direction,
Stanley Lebowsky; Lighting, Jules Fisher; Cos-
tume Supervision, Jane Greenwood; Opening
Ballet Music, Robert Prince; Vocal Arrange-
ments, Buster Davis; Orchestrations, Jim Ty-
ler; Dance Arrangements and Orchestrations,
Robert Prince; Associate Producer, Jane C.
Nusbaum; Production Assistant, Joyce Meyer-
son; Hair Dresser, Bari Braoun; Original Cast
Album by RCA Victor.

CAST

Arthur Kipps	Tommy Steele†1
Sid Pornick	Will Mackenzie†2
Buggins	Norman Allen
Pearce	Grover Dale†3
Carshot	William Larsen†4
Flo	Michele Hardy
Emma	Reby Howells
Kate	Louise Quick
Victoria	Sally Lee
Mr. Shalford	Mercer McLeod
Mrs. Walsingham	Ann Shoemaker†5
Mrs. Botting	Trescott Ripley
Ann Pornick	Polly James†6
Young Walsingham	John Cleese†7
Helen Walsingham	Carrie Nye†8
Chitterlow	James Grout†9
Laura	Eleonore Treiber
Girl Student	Rosanna Huffman†10
Boy Student	Sterling Clark†11
Photographer	Sean Allan
Photographer's Assistant	Robert Gorman
First Reporter	Reid Klein†12
Second Reporter	Fred Cline†13
Gwendolin	Ann Rachel†14

DANCERS: Diane Blair, Kathy Doherty, Alex
Mackay, Loren Hightower, Bert Michaels, Sally
Ransone, Ron Schwinn, Fabian Stuart, Vernon
Wendorf, Denise Winston

SINGERS: Sean Allan, Rosalind Ammons,
Fred Cline, Robert Gorman, Glenn Kezer, Dar-
rell Askey, Jack Knapp, Max Norman, Carol
Joplin, Jeanne Shea, Henrietta Valor

UNDERSTUDIES: Arthur, Kenneth Nelson;
Sid, Ron Schwinn; Flo, Reby Howells; Victoria,
Sally Ransone; Emma, Kate, Diane Blair; Shal-
ford, Stanley Simmonds; Mrs. Botting, Hen-
rietta Valor; Mrs. Walsingham, Trescott Ripley;
Ann, Jeanne Shea; Chitterlow, Remak Ramsay;
Laura, Sally Ransone; Helen, Eleonore Treiber;
Students, Carol Joplin, Bert Michaels; Pearce,
Sean Allan; Buggins, Bert Michaels; Walsing-
ham, Carshot, Jack Knapp

MUSICAL NUMBERS: "All In The Cause Of
Economy," "Half A Sixpence," "Money To
Burn," "A Proper Gentleman," "She's Too Far
Above Me," "The Rain's Got To Fall," "The
Old Military Canal," "Long Ago," "Flash
Bang Wallop," "I Know What I Am," "The
Party's On The House," Finale.

A Musical Comedy in two acts.

General Manager: Victor Samrock
Company Manager: Ben Rosenberg
Press: Bill Doll & Co., Midori Tsuji,
Robert Ganshaw, Richard Spittel
Stage Managers: Joe Calvan, Ernest Austin,
Stanley Simmonds

° Still playing May 31, 1966. For original
production, see THEATRE WORLD, Vol. 21

† Succeeded by: 1. Tony Tanner, and Joel
Grey during vacation, 2. Carl Esser, 3. Larry
Roquemore, 4. Stanley Simmonds, 5. Jean
Cameron, 6. Rosanna Huffman, 7. Remak
Ramsay, 8. Gwyda Donhowe, 9. Robert
Urquhart, William Larsen, 10. Jeanne Shea,
11. Patrick Cummings, Robert Gorman, 12.
Fred Cline, 13. Jack Knapp, 14. Henrietta
Valor.

Gabriel Dell, Barbara Bel Geddes,
Larry Blyden (also below)

BOOTH THEATRE

Opened Wednesday, November 11, 1964.°
Claire Nichtern presents:

LUV

By Murray Schisgal; Director, Mike Nichols;
Designed by Oliver Smith; Lighting, Jean
Rosenthal; Costumes, Theoni V. Aldredge;
Song, Irving Joseph; Production Assistant,
Jacqueline Awad; Acrobatic stunt staged by
Wayne Storm; Original Cast Album by Columbia.

CAST

Harry Berlin	Alan Arkin†1
Milt Manville	Eli Wallach†2
Ellen Manville	Anne Jackson†3

Understudies: Renee Taylor, Gene Wilder

A Comedy in two acts. The action takes
place at the present time on a bridge.

General Manager: Robert Kamlot
Assistant: Maurice Schaded
Press: Ben Kornzweig, Reginald Denenholz
Stage Managers: Ian Cadenhead,
Robert Darnell

° Still playing May 31, 1966. For original
production, see THEATRE WORLD, Vol. 21.

† Succeeded by: 1. Gabriel Dell, 2. Larry
Blyden, 3. Barbara Bel Geddes.

PLAYS FROM OTHER SEASONS THAT CLOSED
DURING THIS SEASON

Play	Opened	Closed	Performances
The Subject Was Roses	May 25, 1964	May 21, 1966	832
Golden Boy	Oct. 20, 1964	March 5, 1966	569
What Makes Sammy Run?	Feb. 27, 1964	June 12, 1965	540
The Owl and The Pussycat	Nov. 18, 1964	Nov. 27, 1965	428
Baker Street	Feb. 16, 1965	Nov. 14, 1965	313
Bajour	Nov. 23, 1964	June 12, 1965	232
The Roar Of The Greasepaint—The Smell Of The Crowd	May 16, 1965	Dec. 4, 1965	232
Do I Hear A Waltz?	March 18, 1965	Sept. 25, 1965	220
I Had A Ball	Dec. 15, 1964	June 12, 1965	199
The Glass Menagerie	May 4, 1965	Oct. 2, 1965	176
Catch Me If You Can	March 9, 1965	June 5, 1965	103
This Was Burlesque	March 16, 1965	June 6, 1965	96
Flora, The Red Menace	May 11, 1965	July 24, 1965	87
The Amen Corner	April 15, 1965	June 26, 1965	84

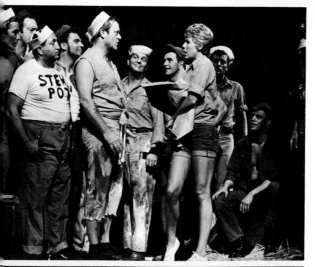

Alix Jeffry Photos

NEW YORK CITY CENTER

Opened Wednesday, June 2, 1965.°
The New York City Center Light Opera
Company presents:

SOUTH PACIFIC

Music, Richard Rodgers; Lyrics, Oscar Hammerstein 2nd; Book, Oscar Hammerstein 2nd and Joshua Logan; Adapted from James M. Michener's "Tales Of The South Pacific"; Director, James Hammerstein; Musical Director, Anton Coppola; Dances by Albert Popwell; Scenery, Jo Mielziner; Costumes, Stanley Simmons; Lighting, Peggy Clark; Orchestrations, Robert Russell Bennett; Hair Styles, Ernest Adler; Production Assistant, Ernest Dobbs.

CAST

Ngana	Dana Shimizu
Jerome	Keenan Shimizu
Henry	Sab Shimono
Ensign Nellie Forbush	Betsy Palmer
Emile de Becque	Ray Middleton
Bloody Mary	Honey Sanders
Bloody Mary's Assistant	Maureen Tionco
Abner	Victor Duntiere
Stewpot	Tom Pedi
Luther Billis	Alan North
Professor	Mickey Karm
Lt. Joseph Cable	Richard Armbruster
Capt. George Brackett	Murvyn Vye
Cmdr. William Harbison	Sam Kirkham
Yeoman Herbert Quayle	Walter P. Brown
Marine Sgt. Kenneth Johnson	William C. Wendt
Seaman Richard West	Ken Ayers
Seabee Morton Wise	Scott Blanchard
Seaman Tom O'Brien	Mel Gordan
Radio Operator	
Bob McCaffrey	Gregg Nickerson
Staff Sgt. Thomas Hassinger	Philip Lucas
Lt. Genevieve Marshall	Carol Joplin
Ensign Dinah Murphy	Terri Baker
Ensign Janet MacGregor	Nancy McGeorge
Ensign Cora MacRae	Renee Gorsey
Ensign Bessie Noonan	Patricia O'Riordan
Ensign Connie Walewska	Marlene Kay
Ensign Pamela Whitmore	Dorothy Hanning
Ensign Sue Yaeger	Jody Lane
Ensign Teya Ryan	Mary E. Small
Ensign Lisa Minelli	Maria Hero
Seaman James Hayes	Philip Rash
Marine Cpl. Hamilton Steeves	Michael Quinn
Seaman John Clark	Don Yule
Liat	Eleanor A. Calbes
Lt. Buzz Adams	Stan Page
Shore Patrol Officer	Joe Bellomo

UNDERSTUDIES: Bloody Mary, Doris Galiber; Billis, Mickey Karm; Cable, Stan Page; Brackett, Phil Lucas; Harbison, Scott Blanchard; Stewpot, Mike Quinn; Buzz, Joe Bellomo; Professor, Phil Rash; Liat, Maureen Tionco

MUSICAL NUMBERS: "Dites-Moi Pourquoi," "A Cockeyed Optimist," "Twin Soliloquies," "Some Enchanted Evening," "Bloody Mary Is The Girl I Love," "There's Nothing Like A Dame," "Bali Ha'i," "I'm Gonna Wash That Man Right Out Of My Hair," "I'm In Love With A Wonderful Guy," "Younger Than Springtime," "Soft Shoe Dance," "Happy Talk," "Honey Bun," "You've Got To Be Taught," "This Nearly Was Mine," Finale.

A Musical Play in two acts. The action takes place on two islands in the South Pacific during World War II.

General Manager: Homer Poupart
Company Manager: Catherine Parsons
Press: Tom Trenkle
Stage Managers: Herman Shapiro,
Chris Ryan, Beau Tilden

° Closed Sunday, June 13, 1965 after a limited engagement of 15 performances. Original production opened April 7, 1949 with Mary Martin and Ezio Pinza and ran for 1,925 performances. See THEATRE WORLD, Vol. 5.

Richard Armbruster, Eleanor A. Calbes
Above: Ray Middleton, Betsy Palmer
Top: Betsy Palmer (C)

Opened Wednesday, June 16, 1965.°
The New York City Center Light Opera
Company presents:

THE MUSIC MAN

Book, Music, and Lyrics by Meredith Willson; Story by Meredith Willson and Franklin Lacey; Directed by Gus Schirmer, Jr.; Musical Director, Liza Redfield; Choreography by Vernon Lusby based on original by Onna White; Associate Choreographer, Betty Hyatt Linton; Settings and Lighting, Howard Bay; Costumes, Raoul Pene Du Bois; Vocal Arrangements, Herbert Greene; Orchestrations, Don Walker; Dance Arrangements, Lawrence Rosenthal; Hair Styles, Ernest Adler; Production Assistant, Ernest Dobbs.

CAST

Travelling Salesmen	Russell Goodwin, John Herbert, Jack Davison, Ronald Stratton, Howard Kahl, Joseph Carow, Ronn Forello
Charlie Cowell	Alan Dexter
Conductor	Van Stevens
Harold Hill	Bert Parks
Mayor Shinn	Milo Boulton
Ewart Dunlop	Al Shea
Oliver Hix	Wayne Ward
Jacey Squires	Vern Reed
Olin Britt	Dale Jones
Marcellus Washburn	Art Wallace
Tommy Djilas	William Glassman
Marian Paroo	Gaylea Byrne
Mrs. Paroo	Sibyl Bowan
Amaryllis	Garda Hermany
Winthrop Paroo	Dennis Scott
Eulalie Mackecknie Shinn	Doro Merande
Zaneeta Shinn	Sandy Duncan
Gracie Shinn	Roma Hermany
Alma Hix	Adnia Rice
Maud Dunlop	Jeanne Schlegel
Ethel Toffelmier	Amelia Varney
Mrs. Squires	Paula Trueman
Constable Locke	Van Stevens

RIVER CITY TOWNSPEOPLE: Robin Adair, Rita Agnese, Barbara Beck, Carol B. Bostick, Bonnie Gene Card, Joanne Crosson, Suzanne Crumpler, Joan Lindsay, Sandra Ray, Alice Mary Riley, Joy Serio, Betty Chretien, Peggy Cooper, Laurie Franks, Jodell Ann Kenting, Ora McBride, Addi Negri, Jeannette Seibert, Peggy Wathen, Lynn Wendell, Joseph Carow, Ronn Forella, Carlos Macri, David Moffat, Eric Paynter, Michael Scotlin, Ronald Stratton, George Tregre, Gary Wales, Arthur Whitfield, Austin Colyer, Jack Davison, Russell Goodwin, John Herbert, Howard Kahl, Ben Laney, Ripple Lewis, Dan Resin, Van Stevens

UNDERSTUDIES: Marian, Laurie Franks; Mayor, Russell Goodwin; Mrs. Paroo, Adnia Rice; Marcellus, Ripple Lewis; Tommy, Arthur Whitfield; Zaneeta, Bonnie Gene Card; Winthrop, Michael Maitland; Alma, Betty Chretien; Ethel, Addi Negri; Amaryllis, Roma Hermany; Jacey, Ben Laney; Ewart, Austin Colyer; Oliver, Dan Resin; Olin, Russell Goodwin; Maud and Mrs. Squires, Lynn Wendell

MUSICAL NUMBERS: "Rock Island," "Trouble," "Piano Lesson," "Goodnight, My Someone," "Seventy-six Trombones," "Sincere," "The Sadder-But-Wiser Girl," "Pickalittle," "Goodnight, Ladies," "Marian The Librarian," "My White Knight," "Wells Fargo Wagon," "It's You," "Shipoopi," "Lida Rose," "Will I Ever Tell You," "Gary, Indiana," "Till There Was You," Finale.

A Musical Comedy in two acts and sixteen scenes. The action takes place in 1912 in River City, Iowa.

General Manager: Homer Poupart
Company Manager: Catherine Parsons
Press: Tom Trenkle
Stage Managers: Chester O'Brien, Bert Wood, Maxine Taylor

° Closed Sunday, June 27, 1965 after a limited engagement of 15 performances. Original production opened December 19, 1957 with Robert Preston and Barbara Cook, and ran for 1,375 performances. See THEATRE WORLD, Vol. 14.

Alix Jeffry Photos

Bert Parks (C). Above: Doro Merande (C)
Top: Gaylea Byrne, Dennis Scott, Bert Parks

NEW YORK CITY CENTER

Opened Wednesday, November 17, 1965.°
New York City Center Drama Company
(Jean Dalrymple, Director) in association
with Ronald A. Wilford Associates, Inc.,
presents:

MARCEL MARCEAU
and his partner Pierre Verry

in a program of pantomimes

PART I: The Kite, The Man and His Boat,
The Magician, The Bureaucrats, The Cage,
Circus Performer, The Seven Deadly Sins,
Walking, Walking Against the Wind, The
Staircase, The Sculptor, The Public Garden,
The Mask Maker, Youth, Maturity, Old Age
and Death

PART II: BIP—goes to an Audition, as a
Matador, dreams he is Don Juan, as a Soldier,
goes traveling, in the Subway, as a Baby
Sitter, at a Society Party, as a Lion Tamer,
takes an Ocean Voyage, hunts Butterflies,
plays David and Goliath, the Street Musician,
looks for a job on New Year's Eve

General Manager: Homer Poupart
Company Manager: John Trelfall
Administrative Director: Alain Mangel
Press: Herbert Breslin
Stage Managers: Louis Thomas,
Tennent McDaniel

° Closed Sunday, December 12, 1965. (24
performances) Tenth United States anniversary tour.

92

NEW YORK CITY CENTER

Opened Wednesday, December 15, 1965.°
The New York City Center Light Opera
Company (Jean Dalrymple, Director), by
arrangement with Rodgers and Hammerstein presents:

OKLAHOMA!

Book and Lyrics, Oscar Hammerstein II;
Based on Play "Green Grow The Lilacs"
by Lynn Riggs; Music, Richard Rodgers; Original Dances by Agnes de Mille; Restaged by
Gemze de Lappe; Entire Production Directed
by John Fearnley; Music Director, Pembroke
Davenport; Settings, Lemuel Ayers; Lighting,
Peggy Clark; Costumes, Stanley Simmons; Assistant Conductor, Abba Bogin; Production Assistant, Ernest Dobbs.

CAST

Aunt Eller	Ruth Kobart
Curly	John Davidson
Laurey	Susan Watson
Will Parker	Richard France
Jud Fry	Daniel P. Hannafin
Ado Annie Carnes	Karen Morrow
Ali Hakim	Jules Munshin
Gertie Cummings	Loi Leabo
Andrew Carnes	Sammy Smith
Cord Elam	Herbert Surface

DANCERS: Cathy Conklin, Joanna Crosson,
Carolyn Dyer, Carol Estey, Sharon Herr, Loi
Leabo, Jane Levin, Marie Patrice, Betty Ann
Rapine, Rande Rayburn, Julie Theobald, Too-
die Wittmer, Don Angelo, Dean Crane, Gerry
Dalton, Jeremy Ives, Brynnar Mehl, Phillip
Rice, Bud Spencer, Fabian Suart

SINGERS: Vicki Belmonte, Maria Bradley,
Judie Elkins, Jeanne Frey, Marie Hero, Joyce
Olson, Susan Sidney, Maggie Worth, Kenny
Adams, Brown Bradley, Roger Alan Brown,
Joseph Corby, Peter Clark, Lance Des Jardins,
Konstantin Moskalenko, Stephen John Rydell,
Herbert Surface, Victor Helou

UNDERSTUDIES: Curly, Joseph Corby; Laurey,
Laurie Franks; Ali, Andrew, Victor Helou; Ado
Annie, Maria Hero; Will, Kenny Adams;
Aunt Eller, Maggie Worth; Jud, Roger Alan
Brown; Gertie, Carolyn Dyer; Dancers, Dean
Crane, Sharon Herr; Swing Girl, Carolyn
Dyer

MUSICAL NUMBERS: "Oh, What A Beauti-
ful Mornin'," "The Surrey With The Fringe
On The Top," "Kansas City," "I Cain't Say
No," "Many A New Day," "It's A Scandal!
It's An Outrage!," "People Will Say," "Pore
Jud," "Lonely Room," "Out Of My Dreams,"
"The Farmer and The Cowman," "All er
Nothin'," "Oklahoma!," Finale.

A Musical in two acts and six scenes. The
action takes place just after the turn of the
century in Indian Territory, now Oklahoma.

General Manager: Homer Poupart
Company Manager: Cathy Parsons
Stage Managers: Herman Shapiro,
Chet O'Brien, Sean Cunningham

° Closed Sunday, January 2, 1966.
(24 performances)

For original production, see THEATRE
WORLD, Vol. 1. Last revival May 15,
1963 at City Center with Peter Palmer,
Louise O'Brien, Fay DeWitt, and Gabriel
Dell.

Alix Jeffry Photos

**Ruth Kobart, Jules Munshin, Karen Morrow,
Susan Watson. Above: Susan Watson, John Davidson
Top: Richard France, Karen Morrow** 93

NEW YORK CITY CENTER

Opened Tuesday, January 4, 1966.*
S. Hurok presents:

ANTONIO
and
THE BALLETS DE MADRID

GUEST ARTIST, ROSARIO

Direction, Choreography, and Lighting by Antonio; Assistant Director, Juan Ayala; Musical Director, Silvio Masciarelli; Balletmaster, Dino Lucchetta.

DANCERS: Alicia Diaz, Paco Romero, Mariana, Angela Del Moral, Carmen Roche, Pastora Ruiz, Jose Antonio, Enrique Gutierrez, Angel Garcia, Luis Ardiz, Teo Santelmo, Dino Lucchetta, Fabian Alonzo, Paco Alonzo, Paloma Andia, Emilia Baylo, Carlos Fernandez, Luis Flores, Elena Gandia, Mary Nieves, Ricardo Monte, Lina Montes, Salvador Napolitano, Flora Navarrete, Julia Perez, Jesus Ramos, Conchita Vidal

SINGERS: Clara Maria Alcala, Chaleco, Chano Lobato, Sernita de Jerez

GUITARISTS: Ricardo Modrego, Rafael Nogales, Carlos Sanchez, Currito de Jerez

PROGRAM: "Eritana," "Cana," "Baile Por Mirabra," "Viva Navarra," "El Amor Brujo," "Estampa Flamenca."

Company Manager: Kurt Neumann
Press: Martin Feinstein, Michael Sweeley, Edward Parkinson
Stage Manager: Roger Johnson

* Closed Sunday, January 16, 1966.
(16 performances)

John Blomfield Photos

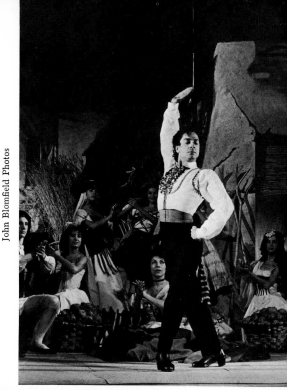

Antonio and Rosario

Antonio, Rosita Segovia. Above: Antonio

94

NEW YORK CITY CENTER

Opened Wednesday, January 19, 1966.°
Columbia Artists Management in association with The New York City Center presents:

THE HUNGARIAN NATIONAL BALLET And Folk Ensemble

General Manager, Istvan Feher; Artistic Director, Miklos Rabai; Director of Chorus, Miklos Paszti; Director of Dancers, Zoltan Matyus; Conductor, Rezso Lantos; Leader of Gypsy Orchestra (Primas), Istvan Albert; Technical Director, Vince Horvath; Choreography, Miklos Rabai, Dezso Letai.

SOLOISTS

Edith Varnai	Tibor Erdelyi
Imre Farkas	Sandor Sajti
Erzsebet Varga	Irdiko Erczhegyi
Anna Czako	Laszlo Tarczi
Geza Leka	

PROGRAM: "Kallai Kettos," "Two Songs," "Dance of The Hussars," "The Bottle Dance," "The Gypsy Orchestra," "An Evening In The Spinning Room," "Hungarian Gypsy Dance," "Gypsy Music," "Dance of The Shepherds," "Three Leaps," "Songs For Chorus and Orchestra," "Wedding In Ecser."

° Closed Sunday, January 30, 1966. (15 performances) Returned for 15 additional performances Wednesday, March 2 through Sunday, March 13, 1966.

"Double Dance". Above: "Shepherd's Dance"

"Gypsy Dance". Above: "Three Leaps"

NEW YORK CITY CENTER

Opened Tuesday, February 1, 1966.°
S. Hurok presents:

THE RUMANIAN
FOLK BALLET
(Ciocirlia)
with
FOLK ORCHESTRA

Petre Nastovici, Director; Victor Predescu,
Conductor; Ballet Master, Gheorghe Popescu-
Judet; Artistic Director, Hero Lupescu;
Choreography, Tamara Cap, Ion Ilie, Ghe-
orghe Popescu-Judet, Iacob Lascu, Gheorghe
Ilie.

SOLOISTS

DANCERS: Magda Popescu, Elena Tircolea,
Ion Ilie, Marin Alecu, Gheorghe Ilie, Vasile
Paraschivescu

VOCALISTS: Maria Stoica, Simion Pop

INSTRUMENTALISTS: Tudor Pana, Violinist;
Damian Luca, Pan Pipes; Tony Iordache, Ilie
Alecu, Cymbalom; Remus Bistrita, Clarinet;
Ion Serbon, Kobsa; Dumitru Zamfira, Shep-
herd's Flute and Long Pipe

PROGRAM

PART I: Dance From The Oltenia Region,
Hora Staccato, Come Out Moon And Look
On Dance From The Almajului Valley, My
Lad From Grui, The Flower Of The Slopes,
Geamparalele, Suite of Dances From The Codru
Mountains, Song From The Neadow Hora
From Gorj, Dialogue On Two Cymbaloms,
Bruil, Doina, The River Olt, Sirba, The Girls
of Capilna, The Calushari Dance

PART II: Suite of Walachian Dances, Dianca,
Who Has Made The Song, Dear To Me Is
The Somesh Dance, Moldavian Dance, Sirba In
The Cart, This Is My Love, Ciocirlia (The
Skylark), The Somesh Wedding

Company Manager: Oscar J. Berlin
Press: Martin Feinstein, Michael Sweeley,
Edward Parkinson, Myra Armstrong
Stage Manager: Jay Kingwell

° Closed Sunday, February 6, 1966 after a
limited engagement of 8 performances. Returned to Carnegie Hall for 2 performances
on Saturday, April 9, 1966.

The Folk Orchestra
Above: The Folk Ballet

Christine Fersen, Paul-Emile Deiber
in "La Reine Morte"
Above: Genevieve Casile, Michel Aumont,
Jean-Louis Jemma in "L'Avare". Right: "Le Cid"

NEW YORK CITY CENTER

Opened Tuesday, February 8, 1966.°
S. Hurok by arrangement with the French
Government presents The Comedie Fran-
caise in:

L'AVARE
(The Miser)

A Comedy in five acts by Moliere; Directed
by Jacques Mauclair; Decor and Costumes by
Jacques Noel; Music, Georges Delerue.

CAST

Anselme, father of Valere
  and Mariane .... Francois Chaumette
Valere, son of Anselme,
  in love with Elise .... Jacques Toja
Harpagon, Father of Cleante
  and Elise, Mariane's suitor .. Michel Aumont
Cleante, Harpagon's son, in love
  with Mariane .... Jean-Louis Jemma
Maitre Jacques, cook
  and coachman .... Jean-Claude Arnaud
La Merluche, Harpagon's lackey..Alain Feydeau
Le Commissaire .... Max Fournel
Maitre Simon,
  an intermediary .... Michel Duchaussoy
La Fleche, Cleante's valet .... Alain Pralon
Brindavoine,
  Harpagon's lackey .... Jacques Destoop
Frosine, une femme d'intrigue .. Lise Delamare
Elise, Harpagon's daughter,
  in love with Valere .... Genevieve Casile
Dame Claude,
  Harpagon's servant .... Francoise Kanel
Mariane, Cleante's sweetheart,
  courted by Harpagon .... Catherine Hubeau
A Baker .... Michel Martin

NEW YORK CITY CENTER

Opened Friday, February 11, 1966.°
S. Hurok by arrangement with the French
Government presents The Comedie Fran-
caise in:

LE CID

A Tragedy in five acts by Pierre Corneille;
Directed by Paul-Emile Deiber; Decor and
Costumes, Andre Delfau; Music, Marcel Lan-
dowski.

CAST

Don Diegue, father of
  Don Rodrigue .... Paul-Emile Deiber
Don Gomes, father of
  Chimene .... Francois Chaumette
Don Fernand, King of
  Castile .... Maurice Escande
Don Sanche, in love with
  Chimene .... Jean-Louis Jemma
Don Alonse .... Max Fournel
Don Arias .... Michael Duchaussoy
Don Rodrigue, Le Cid,
  in love with Chimene .... Jacques Destoop
Leonor, the Infanta's governess .. Lise Delamare
The Infanta,
  the King's daughter .... Genevieve Casile
Dona Elvire,
  Chimene's governess .... Francoise Kanel
Chimene, daughter of
  Don Gomes .... Christine Fersen
A Page .... Michel Martin

Opened Tuesday, February 15, 1966.°
S. Hurok by arrangement with the French
Government presents The Comedie Fran-
caise in:

LA REINE MORTE
("The Dead Queen")

A Drama in three acts and five scenes by
Henri de Montherlant; Directed by Pierre
Franck; Designed by Pierre Simonini.

CAST

Ferrante	Paul-Emile Deiber
Egas Coelho	Francois Chaumette
Prince Don Pedro	Jacques Toja
Don Christoval	Jean-Louis Jemma
Don Eduardo, Captain Bathala	Jean-Claude Arnaud
Don Manuel Goncalves	Max Fournel
Alvar Goncalves	Michel Duchaussoy
A Servant	Alain Pralon
Lieutenant Martins	Jacques Destoop
Ines de Castro	Genevieve Casile
The Infanta of Navarre	Christine Fersen
Dino del Moro	Michel Martin

Opened Friday, February 18, 1966.°
S. Hurok by arrangement with the French
Government presents The Comedie Fran-
caise in:

UN FIL A LA PATTE
("How To Cut The Thread That Ties You To Your Mistress")

A Farce in three acts by Georges Feydeau;
Directed by Jacques Charon; Designed by
Andre Levasseur.

CAST

Bois-d'Enghien	Jacques Charon
The General	Paul-Emile Deiber
Antonio	Jacques Toja
Bouzin	Michel Aumont
Lantery	Jean-Louis Jemma
Firmin	Jean-Claude Arnaud
Fontanet	Alain Feydeau
Emile	Max Fournel
Chennevitte	Michel Duchaussoy
Jean	Alain Pralon
A Gentleman	Jacques Destoop
Marceline	Lise Delamare
Lucette	Catherine Samie
Nini	Genevieve Casile
Miss Betting	Francoise Kanel
The Baroness	Martha Alycia
Viviane	Catherine Hubeau
A Lady	Christine Fersen
A Florist	Michel Martin

Company Manager: Edward A. Perper
Press: Martin Feinstein, Michael Sweeley,
Myra Armstrong
Stage Managers: Max de Guy, Irving Sudrow
° Closed Sunday, February 27, 1966 after a
limited engagement of 24 performances.

Left: Catherine Samie (in chair),
Jacques Charon (center), Marthe Alycia (right)
in "Un Fil A La Patte"

Opened Tuesday, March 15, 1966.°
Paul Szilard in association with the New
York City Center of Music and Drama,
Inc., under the distinguished patronage of
His Excellency Ryuji Takeuchi, His Excel-
lency Akira Matsui, and the Honorable
Fumihiko Togo presents:

BUNRAKU
(Classic Puppet Theatre of Japan)

Director Advisory Board, Hiroshi Kawazoe;
General Manager, Masahiko Imai; Set Director,
Kazuo Sugimoto; Lighting and Set Supervision, Ronald Bates; Simultaneous Translation
by Miss Kazu Obayashi; Stage Manager, Ei-
suke Kamada.

PROGRAM A: "Musume Kagekiyo Yashima
Nikki" (The General's Daughter), "Tsuri Onna"
(Fishing For Wives), "Date Musume Koi No
Higanoko" (The Greengrocer's Daughter)

PROGRAM B: Opened Thursday, March 17,
1966: "Kanadehon Chushingura" (The Revenge of The Forty-seven Ronin), "Sho-Utsushi
Asagao Banashi" (The Tale of The Morning
Glory)

Company Manager: David Lawlor
Press: Shirley E. Herz
Stage Manager: Ronald Bates
° Closed Sunday, March 27, 1966, after a
limited engagement of 16 performances.

Bunraku Puppets

Jack Mitchell, Arnold Eagle Photos

NEW YORK CITY CENTER

Opened Wednesday, March 30, 1966.°
The Foundation For American Dance in association with New York City Center presents:

ROBERT JOFFREY BALLET

Director, Robert Joffrey; Assistant Director and Choreographer, Gerald Arpino; Executive Director, Alexander Ewing; Musical Director, Maurice Peress; Guest Conductors, David Epstein, Teo Macero; Lighting, Thomas Skelton; Ballet Mistress, Rochelle Zide; Production Supervisor, Jack Harpman; Production Assistant, Larry Metzler; Costume Supervisor, Regina Quintana; Choreographers, Gerald Arpino, Fernand Nault, Norman Walker, Anna Sokolow; Music, Peter Ludwig Hertel, Paul Fetler, Charles Ives, Anton Webern, Antonio Vivaldi, Teo Macero; Sets and Costumes, William Pitkin, Ming Cho Lee, Lewis Brown.

COMPANY: Charthel Arthur, Lisa Bradley, Zelma Bustillo, Diana Cartier, Ivy Clear, Edwina Dingman, Christine Hennessy, Susan Magno, Noel Mason, Marjorie Mussman, Margo Sappington, Donna Silva, Trinette Singleton, Frank Bays, Rex Bickmore, Robert Blankshine, Dermot Burke, Jon Cristofori, Luis Fuente, Richard Gain, Ian Horvath, James Howell, John Jones, Nels Jorgensen, Dennis Nahat, George Ramos, Don Richard, Michael Uthoff.

REPERTOIRE: "Viva Vivaldi," "Sea Shadow," "Incubus," "Opus '65," "La Fille Mal Gardee," "Contrasts," "Ropes."

Manager: Wayne Richardson
Press: Isadora Bennett
Stage Manager: John Fenn

° Closed Sunday, April 3, 1966 after a limited engagement of 7 performances.

Susan Magno, George Ramos, Luis Fuente,
Zelma Bustillo, Ian Horvath in "Viva Vivaldi!"
Top: "Olympics"

NEW YORK CITY CENTER

Opened Tuesday, April 5, 1966.°
Gert Von Gontard and Felix G. Gerstman and Deutsches Theater, Inc., in association with The New York City Center under the patronage of the German Federal Republic and the Bavarian Government present The Bavarian State Theater of Munich, (Helmut Henrichs, General Manager) in:

DIE MITSCHULDIGEN
(The Accomplices)

By Johann Wolfgang von Goethe; Director, Hans Lietzau; Settings and Costumes, Jurgen Rose; Music, Mark Lothar; Lighting, Frithjof Elbertshagen.

CAST

The Innkeeper _____ Max Mairich
Soller, his son-in-law _____ Herbert Mensching
Sophie, his daughter _____ Elisabeth Orth
Alcest _____ Martin Benrath
A Waiter _____ Horst Sachtleben

Presented in three scenes.

and
WOYZECK

By Georg Buchner; Director, Hans Lietzau; Settings and Costumes, Jurgen Rose; Music, Peter Zwetkoff; Choreographer, Heino Hallhuber; Technical Director, Dieter Ganzenmuller; Lighting, Frithjof Elbertshagen; Assistant to Director, Ursula Heilmann; Translations, Iris Merlis, Liza Smart.

CAST

Woyzeck _____ Heinrich Schweiger
Andres _____ Peter Fricke
Marie _____ Elisabeth Orth
Marie's Child _____ A. Moosholzer
Margret _____ Carin Braun
Drum-Major _____ Helmut Schmid
Old Man _____ Erwin Faber
Barker _____ Friedrich Maurer
Sergeant _____ Edmund Saussen
Captain _____ Max Mairich
Doctor _____ Klaus Schwarzkopf
First Apprentice _____ Herbert Mensching
Second Apprentice _____ Horst Sachtleben
A Jew _____ Walter Kohutek
Karl, a fool _____ Jurgen Arndt
A Girl _____ Ilse Ritter
Grandmother _____ Edith Schultze-Westrum
First Man _____ Harry Hertzsch
Second Man _____ Hannes Kaetner
Kathe _____ Annemarie Wernicke
Innkeeper _____ Karl Hanft
Policeman _____ Sigfrit Steiner
Monkey _____ Darel Glaser
Children _____ Silvia Lemberger,
Robert Puleo, Lisa Puleo
SOLDIERS, STUDENTS, CITIZENS: Patricia Aldrich, Lee Callahan, Lynne Garmston, Zola Long, Nikki Nardone, Erna Rossmann, Patricia Sinnott, Ludmilla Tchor, Chris Yule, Robert Coldiron, James G. Demas, Lee H. Doyle, Cornelius T. Frizell, Werner T. Graber, John Keeler, Fred H. Kolouch, Alec Murphy, Mell Reynolds, Walter Rivera, Frederick S. Roffman, Ivan Smith, Carl W. Stewart.

A Drama in twenty-four scenes.

Rudolf Betz Photos

Opened Tuesday, April 12, 1966.°

DIE RATTEN
(The Rats)

By Gerhart Hauptmann; Directed by Helmut Henrichs; Settings and Costumes, Jurgen Rose; Technical Director, Dieter Ganzenmuller; Lighting, Frithjof Elbertshagen; Assistant to Director, Ursula Laerum.

CAST

Mrs. John _____ Maria Wimmer
Pauline Piperkarcka,
a servant _____ Christine Ostermayer
Bruno Mechelke,
Mrs. John's brother _____ Martin Benrath
Walburga Hassenreuter _____ Carin Braun
Harro Hassenreuter,
her father _____ Karl Maria Schley
Nathaniel Jettel, actor _____ Walter Kohutek
Alice Rutterbusch, actress _____ Elisabeth Orth
Erich Spitta, a student _____ Peter Fricke
John, foreman-mason _____ Gerd Brudern
Selma Knobbe _____ Gustl Halenke
Mrs. Hassenreuter _____ Edith Schultze-Westrum
Kaferstein, a student _____ Jorg Holm
Dr. Kegel, student _____ Jurgen Arndt
Quaquaro, superintendent _____ Max Mairich
Pastor Spitta _____ Friedrich Maurer
Mrs. Kielbacke _____ Annemarie Wernicke
Policeman Schierke _____ Harry Hertzsch
Mrs. Sidonie Knobbe _____ Elfriede Kuzmany

A Tragicomedy in five acts, presented in two parts. The action takes place in Berlin about 1910 in the attic of a former barracks, now an apartment house.

General Managers: Bill Levine, Joseph Beruh
Company Manager: Sidney Bernstein
Press: Jean Dalrymple, Homer Poupart, Paul Bosten
Production Coordinator: Hans Sondheimer

° Closed Sunday, April 17, 1966 after a limited engagement of 16 performances: 8 for the double bill and 8 for "Die Ratten."

Top Right: (center) Herbert Mensching in "Woyzeck"
Below: Edithe Schultze-Westrum, Gerd Brudern, Karl Maria Schley in "Die Ratten"

NEW YORK CITY CENTER

Opened Wednesday, April 20, 1966.°
The New York City Center Light Opera Company (Jean Dalrymple, Director) presents:

HOW TO SUCCEED IN BUSINESS WITHOUT REALLY TRYING

Book, Abe Burrows, Jack Weinstock, and Willie Gilbert; Based on Book by Shepherd Mead; Music and Lyrics, Frank Loesser; Director, Gus Schirmer; Scenery, Robert Randolph; Costumes, Stanley Simmons; Lighting, Peggy Clark; Musical Direction, Anton Coppola; Hair Styles, Ernest Adler; Production Assistant, Paul Bosten.

CAST

Finch	Len Gochman
Gatch	Lang Des Jardins
Jenkins	Austin Colyer
Peterson	Reese Burns
Tackaberry	Henry Lawrence
J. B. Biggley	Billy De Wolfe
Rosemary	Sheila Sullivan
Bratt	Art Barnett
Smitty	Pat McEnnis
Frump	Lee Goodman
Miss Jones	Justine Johnston
Mr. Twimble	Lou Cutell
Hedy	Betty Linton
Scrubwomen	Natasha Grishin, Renee Gorsey
Miss Krumholtz	Del Green
Ovington	Richard Marr
Policeman	Paul Adams
Womper	Lou Cutell

SINGERS: Paul Adams, Reese Burns, Austin Colyer, Lang Des Jardins, Walter E. Hook, Mickey Karm, Henry Lawrence, Richard Marr, Marie Bradley, Jane Coleman, Jacque Dean, Renee Gorsey, Del Green, Maria Hero, Judy McMurdo

DANCERS: Doria Avila, Richard Denny, Garold Gardner, Jerry Kent, Stan Mazin, Leo J. Muller, Terry Nicholson, Roger Allan Raby, Nephele Buecher, Patricia Cope, Mickey Gunnersen, Natasha Grishin, Rosie Holotik, Beth Howland, Joan Lindsay, Sharron Miller

UNDERSTUDIES: Finch, Mickey Karm; Biggley, Art Barnett; Rosemary, Maria Hero; Frump, Paul Adams; Bratt, Richard Marr; Hedy, Judy McMurdo

MUSICAL NUMBERS: "How To," "Happy To Keep His Dinner Warm," "Coffee Break," "The Company Way," "A Secretary Is Not A Toy," "Been A Long Day," "Grand Old Ivy," "Paris Original," "Rosemary," "Finaletto," "Cinderella," "Love From A Heart Of Gold," "I Believe In You," "The Yo Ho Ho," "Brotherhood Of Man," Finale.

General Manager: Homer Poupart
Company Manager: Catherine Parsons
Press: Jean Dalrymple, John Clugstone, Paul Bosten
Stage Managers: Herman Shapiro, Herman Magidson

° Closed Sunday, May 8, 1966 after a limited engagement of 23 performances. The original production (see THEATRE WORLD, Vol. 18) opened Oct. 14, 1961 and ran for 1,415 performances. The cast included Robert Morse, Rudy Vallee, Bonnie Scott, and Virginia Martin.

Alix Jeffry Photos

Betty Linton, Billy De Wolfe (also top left)
Above: (C) Lee Goodman, Pat McEnnis
Top: Pat McEnnis, Len Gochman, Sheila Sullivan

Norman Atkins, Barbara Meister

NEW YORK CITY CENTER

Opened Wednesday, May 11, 1966.°
The New York City Center Light Opera
Co. (Jean Dalrymple, Director) presents:

THE MOST HAPPY FELLA

Book, Music, and Lyrics by Frank Loesser;
Based on Sidney Howard's "They Knew What
They Wanted;" Direction and Choreography,
Ralph Beaumont; Musical Direction, Abba Bo-
gin; Settings, Jo Mielziner; Costumes, Frank
Thompson; Lighting, Peggy Clark; Production
Assistant, Paul Bosten; Hair Styles, Ernest
Adler.

CAST

The Cashier	Lee Cass
Cleo	Karen Morrow
Rosabella	Barbara Meister
Waitresses	Joanna Crosson, Rita O'Connor, Joy Serio, Susan Sigrist
Postman	Lee Cass
Tony	Norman Atkins
Marie	Fran Stevens
Max	Joe McGrath
Herman	Jack DeLon
Clem	James Hobson
Jake	Robert E. Maxwell, Jr.
Al	John A. Boni
Joe	Art Lund
Giuseppe	Montes de Oca
Pasquale	Will Roy
Ciccio	Edward Becker
Doctor	Carl Nicholas
Priest	Dick Ensslen
Tessie	Karen Grant
Gussie	Jody LaRocco
Sissy	Marci Phillips
Neighbors	Joyce Olson, Rosemary McNamara, Rita Metzger
Brakeman	Dale Westerman
Bus Driver	Doug Hunt

NEIGHBORS: Lillian Bozinoff, Susan Cogan,
Jeanne Frey, Marlene Kay, Evelyn Kingsley,
Rosemary McNamara, Rita Metzger, Barbara
Miller, LaVergne Monette, Joyce Olson, Patti
Winston, Gene Albano, John A. Boni, Marvin
Goodis, James Hobson, Doug Hunt, Philip
Lucas, Stuart Mann, Robert E. Maxwell, Jr.,
Joe McGrath, George T. McWhorter, Dale
Westerman, Wilson Robey, Diane Arnold, Linda
Bonem, Connie Burnett, Kay Cole, Joanna
Crosson, Judith Dunford, Ina Kurland, Rita
O'Connor, Joy Serio, Susan Sigrist, Myrna
Strom, Dom Angelo, Frank Coppola, Vito
Durante, Jerry Fries, Bob LaCrosse, Teak Lewis,
Carlos Macri, Donald Mark, Victor Pieran,
Dom Salinaro, Marc Scott

UNDERSTUDIES: Tony, Dick Ensslen; Rosa-
bella, Jeanne Frey; Joe, John A. Boni; Marie,
Rita Metzger; Herman, Wilson Robey; Cleo,
Rosemary McNamara; Doctor, Dale Wester-
man; Postman, Cashier, Dick Ensslen; Giuseppe,
Joe McGrath; Pasquale, Marvin Goodis; Ciccio,
Stuart Mann; Clem, Phil Lucas; Jake, Doug
Hunt; Al, George McWhorter

A Musical in three acts and eleven scenes.
The action takes place in California in 1927.

General Manager: Homer Poupart
Company Manager: Catherine Parsons
Press: Jean Dalrymple
Stage Managers: Chet O'Brien,
Phil King, Sean Cunningham

° Closed Sunday, May 22, 1966 after a limited
engagement of 15 performances. For original Broadway production, see THEATRE
WORLD, Vol. 12, which cast included Robert Weede, Jo Sullivan, Art Lund and
Susan Johnson.

Top Left: Norman Atkins (C)
Left Center: Karen Morrow, Jack DeLon,
Art Lund, Norman Atkins, Barbara Meister

NEW YORK CITY CENTER

Opened Wednesday, May 25, 1966.°
The New York City Center Light Opera
Company (Jean Dalrymple, Director) presents:

WHERE'S CHARLEY?

Book, George Abbott; Based on Brandon
Thomas' Play "Charley's Aunt;" Music and
Lyrics, Frank Loesser; Director, Christopher
Hewett; Choreography, John Sharpe; Costumes,
Frank Thompson; Ballet Music Adapted by
Marvin Laird; Musical Direction, Pembroke
Davenport; Lighting and Additional Settings
Designed by Peggy Clark; Production Assistant,
Paul Bosten; Hair Styles, Roberto Donzi.

CAST

Brassett	Tom Bate
Professor Fortesque	Donald Barton
Jack Chesney	David Smith
Charley Wykeham	Darryl Hickman
Kitty Verdun	Karen Shepard
Amy Spettigue	Susan Watson
Wilkinson	Emory Bass
Sir Francis Chesney	Ferdinand Hilt
Mr. Spettigue	Mort Marshall
Donna Lucia D'Alvadorez	Eleanor Steber
Photographer	Stan Mazin
Patricia	Maria Hero
Reggie	Austin Colyer
Photographer's Assistants	Violetta Landek, Zebra Nevins

BAND MEMBERS: Rodd Barry, Dennis Cole,
Gordon Cook, Jack Fletcher, Mario Maroze,
Doug Spingler

DANCERS: Rodd Barry, Dennis Cole, Myron
Curtis, Richard Denny, Jerry Kent, Don Lawrence, Mario Maroze, Richard Maxon, Stan
Mazin, Doug Spingler, Clive Thompson, Cathy
Conklin, Mickey Gunnersen, Beth Howland,
Violetta Landek, Sara Letton, Sharron Miller,
Zebra Nevins, Rande Rayburn, Alice Mary Riley,
Skiles Ricketts, Toodie Wittmer

SINGERS: Paul Adams, Austin Colyer, Gordon
Cook, Stephen Everett, Jack Fletcher, William
James, Konstantin Moskalenko, Hal Norman,
Fred Osin, David Wilder, Laverne Burden,
Jane Coleman, Renee Gorsey, Maria Hero, Nina
Hirschfeld, Miriam Lawrence, Joyce McDonald,
Betsy Norden, Mary Ann Rydzeski, Susan Stockwell, Elise Warner

UNDERSTUDIES: Charley, Lee Goodman;
Amy, Cathy Conklin; Jack, William James;
Kitty, Maria Hero; Sir Francis, Austin Colyer;
Spettigue, Emory Bass; Donna Lucia, Laverne
Burden; Brasset, Jack Fletcher; Fortesque, Wilkinson, Stephen Everett

MUSICAL NUMBERS: "The Years Before
Us," "Better Get Out Of Here," "The New
Ashmolean Marching Society and Students' Conservatory Band," "My Darling, My Darling,"
"Make A Miracle," "Serenade With Asides,"
"Lovelier Than Ever," "The Woman In His
Room," "Pernambuco," "Where's Charley?,"
"Once In Love With Amy," "The Gossips,"
"At The Red Rose Cotillion," Finale.

A Musical Comedy in two acts and nine
scenes. The action takes place in 1892 at St.
Olde's College, Oxford University.

General Manager: Homer Poupart
Company Manager: Catherine Parsons
Press: Jean Dalrymple, Homer Poupart,
Paul Bosten
Stage Managers: William Batchelder,
George Rondo, Elisa Ronstadt

° Still playing May 31, 1966. For original
Broadway production, see THEATRE
WORLD, Vol. 5. Ray Bolger, Allyn McLerie
were in company which opened Oct. 11, 1948
and played 792 performances.

Alix Jeffry Photos

Top Right: Susan Watson, Darryl Hickman
Right Center: Eleanor Steber, Darryl Hickman

Ferdinand Hilt, Eleanor Steber, Mort Marshall,
Darryl Hickman, Karen Shepard, David Smith

NEW YORK STATE THEATER
Opened Tuesday, June 1, 1965.°
The City Center of Music and Drama, Inc.
(Jean Dalrymple, Director) presents:

NEW YORK CITY BALLET

General Director, Lincoln Kirstein; Ballet Masters, George Balanchine, John Taras; Associate Ballet Mistress, Una Kai; Assistant Ballet Mistress, Francia Russell; Costumes, Karinska; NYC Ballet Orchestra Principal Conductor, Robert Irving; Associate Conductor, Hugo Fiorato.

PRINCIPAL DANCERS
Jacques D'Amboise, Melissa Hayden, Jillana, Allegra Kent, Conrad Ludlow, Nicholas Magallanes, Patricia McBride, Arthur Mitchell, Francisco Moncion, Andre Prokovsky, Maria Tallchief, Violette Verdy, Edward Villella, Patricia Wilde, Anthony Blum, Suzanne Farrell, Gloria Govrin, Deni Lamont, Sara Leland, Patricia Neary, Mimi Paul, Richard Rapp, Robert Rodham, Suki Schorer, Earle Sieveling, Victoria Simon, Kent Stowell, Carol Sumner, Roland Vazquez, William Weslow, Karin von Aroldingen, Karen Barizi, Diane Bradshaw, Marjorie Bresler, Elaine Comsudi, Gail Crisa, James DeBolt, Rosemary Dunleavy, Suzanne Erlon, Truman Finney, Penelope Gates, Ericca Goodman, Janet Greschler, Susan Hendl, Gail Kachadurian, Lise Kenniff, Ruth Ann King, Robert Maiorano, Kay Mazzo, Teena McConnell, Karen Morell, Marnee Morris, Larry O'Brien, Shaun O'Brien, Frank Ohman, Delia Peters, Roger Peterson, Roger Pietrucha, Susan Pillersdorf, John Prinz, David Richardson, Leslie Ruchala, Ellen Shire, Bettijane Sills, Michael Steele, Lynne Stetson, Virginia Stuart, Margaret Wood

REPERTOIRE
Don Quixote, Raymonda Variations, Tarantella, Stars and Stripes, Agon, Irish Fantasy, Liebeslieder Walzer, Harlequinade, La Valse, Swan Lake, Allegro Brillante, Meditation, Symphony In C, Firebird, Concerto Barocco, Prodigal Son, Pas De Deux and Divertissement, Scotch Symphony, Four Temperaments, Con Amore, Piege De Lumiere, Ballet Imperial, Episodes, La Sonnambula, Interplay, Bugaku, Monumentum Pro Gesualdo, Donizetti Variations, Movements For Piano and Orchestra, The Nutcracker, The Cage, Serenade, Ebony Concerto, Apollo, Meditation, Afternoon Of A Faun, Divertimento No. 15, Piege De Lumiere, Dim Lustre, A Midsummer Night's Dream.
PREMIERES: Variations, Summerspace, Brahms-Schoenberg Quartet, Jeux, La Guirlande De Campra.

General Manager: Betty Cage
Assistant Manager: Edward Bigelow
Company Manager: Zelda Dorfman
Press: Virginia Donaldson, Doris Luhrs
Stage Managers: Ronald Bates, Kevin Tyler

° Closed Sunday, June 13, 1965 after 16 performances of "Don Quixote." Returned Thursday, Sept. 23, 1965 for 48 performances in repertory which closed Oct. 31, 1965. Returned to give 32 performances of "The Nutcracker" from Friday, Dec. 24, 1965 through Sunday, Jan. 16, 1966. Spring season in repertory opened Tuesday, March 29, and closed Sunday, May 22, 1966 after 62 performances in repertory.

Top Right: George Balanchine in "Don Quixote"
Below: "The Nutcracker"

Martha Swope Photos

"Ballet Imperial." Above: Arthur Mitchell, Edward Villella, Melissa Hayden in "A Midsummer Night's Dream"

NEW YORK STATE THEATER

Opened Tuesday, June 22, 1965.°
Music Theater of Lincoln Center, Richard
Rodgers President and Producing Director,
presents:

KISMET

Book, Charles Lederer and Luther Davis;
Based on Play by Edward Knoblock; Music
and Lyrics, Robert Wright and George Forrest; Based on themes by Alexander Borodin; Directed by Edward Greenberg; Choreography and
Musical Staging, Jack Cole; Designed by Lemuel Ayers; Costumes, Frank Thompson;
Lighting, Peter Hunt; Orchestrations and Choral
Arrangements, Arthur Kay; Musical Director,
Franz Allers; Hair Styles, Ronald DeMann; Administrative Assistant, Cynthia Chisholm; General Assistant, Stephen Stoneburn.

CAST

Iman	Rudy Vejar
Muezzins	Grant Spradling, Paul Veglia, Vincent Henry, Martin Jewell
Mullah	Julius Fields
Beggars	Earle MacVeigh, Robert Lamont, Andre St. Jean
Dervishes	Buddy Bryan, Eddie James
Omar	Don Beddoe
The Poet Hajj	Alfred Drake
Marsinah	Lee Venora†1
Merchant	Neil McNelis
Hassan-Ben	Frank Coleman
Jawan	Truman Gaige
Bangle Man	Rudy Vejar
Street Dancer	Sally Neal
Akbar	Buddy Bryan
Assiz	Eddie James
Chief Policeman	Alfred Toigo
Second Policeman	Allen Peck
The Wazir of Police	Henry Calvin
Wazir's Guards	Nick Littlefield, Jerry Meyers
Lalume	Anne Jeffreys†2
Attendants	Henry Baker, James Wamen
Princesses of Ababu	Reiko Sato, Diana Banks, Nancy Roth
The Caliph	Richard Banke
Slave Girls	Michele Evans, Carol Hallock, Eleanore Kingsley, Ingeborg Kjeldsen
Servant	Paul Veglia
Princess Zubbediya of Damascus	Sally Neal
Ayah to Zubbediya	Anita Alpert
Princess Samaris of Bangalore	Beatrice Kraft
Prosecutor	Earle MacVeigh
Widow Yussef	Anita Alpert

SINGERS: Bonnie Glasgow, Bobbi Lange,
Joyce McDonald, Lucille Perret, Susan San-
ders, Wanda Saxon, Bonnie Ellen Spark, Hen-
ry Baker, Frank Coleman, Vincent Henry,
Martin Jewell, Richard Khan, Nick Littlefield,
Neil McNelis, Bob Neukum, Allen Peck, Grant
Spradling, Paul Veglia

Dancers: Joanne DiVito, Marti Hespen, Shai
Holsaert, Indra-nila, Bette Scott, Susan Sigrist,
Jenny Workman, Julius Fields, Andre St. Jean

UNDERSTUDIES: Hajj, Earle MacVeigh; La-
lume, Ingeborg Kjeldsen; Marsinah, Joyce Mc-
Donald; Wazir, Alfred Toigo; Caliph, Rudy
Vejar; Omar, Truman Gaige; Jawan, Robert
Lamont; Chief of Police, Allen Peck; Ayah,
Susan Sanders; Policeman, Nick Littlefield;
Beggars, Richard Khan, Andre St. Jean; Hassan-
Ben, Neil McNelis; Princesses of Ababu, Joanne
DiVito; Akbar and Assiz, Julius Field; Zubbe-
diya, Jenny Workman; Samaris, Bette Scott;
Slavegirls, Bobbi Lange; Widow, Bonnie Ellen
Spark

MUSICAL NUMBERS: "Sands Of Time,"
"Rhymes Have I," "Fate," "Bazaar of The
Caravans," "Not Since Nineveh," "Baubles,
Bangles and Beads," "Stranger In Paradise,"
"He's In Love," "Gesticulate," "Bored." "Night
Of My Nights," "Was I A Wazir?," "Rahadla-
kum," "And This Is My Beloved." "The Olive
Tree," "Presentation of Princesses," Finale.

Top Right: Lee Venora, Richard Banke
Below: Alfred Drake, Patricia Welting

A Musical Play in two acts and thirteen
scenes with prologue and epilogue. The action
takes place during one day in Baghdad.

General Manager: Henry Guettel
Company Manager: Charles Mooney
Press: Richard Maney
Stage Managers: Bill Ross, Ben Strobach,
Henry Velez

° Closed July 31, 1965 after limited engagement of 39 performances. Began national
tour Monday, Aug. 2, 1965 at O'Keefe
Theatre, Toronto, and closed Nov. 18, 1965
at Fisher Theatre, Detroit.

† Succeeded on tour by: 1. Patricia Welting.
2. Patricia Morison. Richard Grayson and
Willard Keefe were respectively company
manager and press representative for tour.
Original production with Alfred Drake, Doret-
ta Morrow, and Joan Diener opened Dec. 3,
1953 and played 583 performances. See
THEATRE WORLD, Vol. 10.

Anne Jeffreys, Alfred Drake
in
"KISMET"

NEW YORK STATE THEATER

Opened Tuesday, August 10, 1965.°
The Music Theater of Lincoln Center,
Richard Rodgers President and Producing
Director, presents:

CAROUSEL

Music by Richard Rodgers; Book and Lyrics,
Oscar Hammerstein 2nd; Based on Molnar's
Play "Liliom" as adapted by Benjamin F.
Glazer; Directed by Edward Greenberg;
Choreography, Agnes de Mille; Designed by
Paul C. McGuire; Costumes, Stanley Simmons;
Lighting, Peter Hunt; Orchestrations, Don
Walker; Musical Director, Franz Allers; Hair
Styles, Ronald DeMann; Costume Coordinator,
Steven Blumberg.

CAST

Carrie Pipperidge	Susan Watson†1
Julie Jordan	Eileen Christy
Mrs. Mullin	Benay Venuta
Billy Bigelow	John Raitt†2
Policeman	Thomas Barry
Mr. Bascombe	Ralston Hill
Nettie Fowler	Katherine Hilgenberg
Enoch Snow	Reid Shelton
Jigger Craigin	Jerry Orbach
Hannah	Jenny Workman
Boatswain	Birl Jonns
Arminy	Dixie Carter
Captain	John Dorrin
Heavenly Friend	Gwyllum Evans
Starkeeper	Edward Everett Horton
Louise	Linda Howe
Carnival Boy	Birl Jonns
Enoch Snow, Jr.	Richard Oliver
Principal	John Dorrin

SINGERS: Lynn Carroll, Ronn Carroll, Dixie
Carter, Cathy Corkill, Gene Davis, Audrey
Dearden, John Dorrin, Dorothy Emmerson,
Cleo Fry, Ben Laney, Terry Marone, Laried
Montgomery, Bob Neukum, Lucille Perret, Jo-
seph Pichette, Philip Rash, Sean Walsh, Peggy
Wathen

DANCERS: Bonnie Gene Card, Dennis Cole,
Richard Cousins, Victor Duntiere, Lois Etel-
man, Frank Hoopman, Anita Jones, Linda Keel-
er, Lucia Lamber, Arnott Mader, Richard
Oliver, Carol Perea, J. Hunter Ross, Terry
Ryland, Eva Marie Sage, Melissa Stoneburn,
Kathy Wilson, Toodie Wittmer

UNDERSTUDIES: Billy, Jerry Orbach; Julie,
Dorothy Emmerson; Carrie, Dixie Carter;
Enoch, Philip Rash; Nettie, Cleo Fry; Jigger,
Thomas Barry; Starkeeper, Gwyllum Evans;
Heavenly Friend, Ralston Hill; Bascombe, John
Dorrin; Policeman, Ronn Carroll

MUSICAL NUMBERS: "Waltz Suite," "You're
A Queer One, Julie Jordan," "When I Marry
Mr. Snow," "If I Loved You," "June Is
Bustin' Out All Over," "When The Children
Are Asleep," "Blow High, Blow Low," "Soli-
loquy," "This Was A Real Nice Clambake,"
"Geraniums In The Winter," "There's Nothin'
So Bad For A Woman," "What's The Use Of
Wond'rin'," "You'll Never Walk Alone," "The
Highest Judge Of All," Ballet.

A Musical Play in two acts and nine scenes
with a prelude. The action takes place on the
coast of Maine between 1873 and 1888.

Company Managers: Charles Mooney,
Ronald Brugiere
Press: Richard Maney
Stage Managers: Bill Ross, George Quick,
Robert Keegan

° Closed Sept. 18, 1965 after limited engagement of 47 performances. Opened national
tour Monday, Sept. 20, 1965 at the Shubert
in Cincinnati, and closed Feb. 5, 1966 at
the Shubert in Boston.

† Succeeded on tour by: 1. Dran Seitz, 2.
Harve Presnell. John L. Toohey was press
agent for tour.

Original production with John Raitt and
Jan Clayton opened April 19, 1945 and
ran for 881 performances. See THEATRE
WORLD, Vol. 1.

Linda Howe, Harve Presnell
Above: Edward Everett Horton, John Raitt
Top: John Raitt, Benay Venuta
Below: Eileen Christy, John Raitt, Jerry Orbach

Text running vertically: Mydtskov Photos

Opened Tuesday, November 23, 1965.°
S. Hurok presents under the patronage of His Majesty King Frederik IX of Denmark:

THE ROYAL DANISH BALLET

General Administrator, Henning A. Brondsted; General Manager, Jens Louis Petersen; Ballet Director, Niels Bjorn Larsen; Conductors, Poul Jorgensen, Robert Blot, Arthur Lief.

GUEST ARTISTS: Erik Bruhn, Flemming Flindt

SOLO DANCERS: Ruth Andersen, Verner Andersen, Fredbjorn Bjornsson, Eske Holm, Svend Erik Jensen, Niels Kehlet, Henning Kronstam, Anna Laerkesen, Jorn Madsen, Margrethe Schanne, Frank Schaufuss, Kirsten Simone, Solveig Ostergaard

DANCERS: Arne Bech, Jens Brenaa, Lotte Cornelius-Knudsen, Lise la Cour, Elisabeth Enevoldsen, Ole Fatum, Liselotte Frimann, Tommy Frishoi, Vivi Gelker, Ingrid Glindemann, Flemming Halby, Nina Herlov, Mette Honningen, Inge Jensen, Lillian Jensen, Ulla Skow Jensen, Vita Johansen, Annelise Johnsen, Iben Kehlet, Mona Kiil, Frantz Kjaerulff, Eva Kloborg, Hans Jacob Kolgaard, Dinna Bjorn Larsen, Peter Martins, Kjeld Noack, Inge Olafsen, Annemette Petersen, Aage Poulsen, Benny Poulsen, Lizzie Rode, Vibeke Roland, Mogens Rud, Flemming Ryberg, Viveka Segerskog, Ole Suhr, Palle Sorensen, Anne Marie Vessel, Annemari Vingaard, Arlette Weinrich, Tage Wendt

REPERTOIRE: "Romeo and Juliet," "Fanfare," "Carmen," "Napoli," "Coppelia," "Konservatoriet," "Miss Julie," "Whims Of Cupid," "The Private Lesson," "La Sylphide," "Moon Reindeer."

Company Manager: Edward A. Perper
Press: Martin Feinstein, Michael Sweeley, Edward Parkinson
Stage Managers: Poul Vessel, Knud Hogenhaven

° Closed Sunday, December 19, 1965.
(32 performances)

Kirsten Simone, Henning Kronstam
in "Romeo and Juliet"
Above: "Konservatoriet (Dancing School)
108 Top: Kirsten Simone, Erik Bruhn in "Carmen"
Right: Margrethe Schanne in "La Sylphide"

NEW YORK STATE THEATER

Opened Tuesday, January 18, 1966.°
Ballet Theatre Foundation, Inc. (Harold Taylor, President) presents:

AMERICAN BALLET THEATRE

Lucia Chase and Oliver Smith, Directors; Assistant to the Directors, John Kriza; Regisseur, Dimitri Romanoff; Ballet Master, Enrique Martinez; Conductor, Walter Hagen; Guest Conductor, Kenneth Schermerhorn.

PRINCIPAL DANCERS: Lupe Serrano, Royes Fernandez, Toni Lander, Scott Douglas, John Kriza, Ruth Ann Koesun, Bruce Marks, Sallie Wilson, Eleanor D'Antuono, Gayle Young.

GUEST ARTISTS: Carmen deLavallade, Mary Hinkson

DANCERS: Susan Borree, Veronika Mlakar, Basil Thompson, Paul Sutherland, Janet Mitchell, Joseph Carow, Karen Krych, Ted Kivitt, Victoria Leigh, Edward Verso, Jeanne Armin, William Glassman, Judith Lerner, Eliot Feld, Erin Martin, Tom Adair, Diane Anthony, Amy Blaisdell, Karena Brock, Susan Casey, Camille Crosby, Ellen Everett, Cynthia Gregory, Virginia Griffee, Judi Griffler, Alaine Haubert, Reese Haworth, Terry Hilton, Rosamond Lynn, Ray Morgan, Gilda Mullett, Alexandra Nadal, Paul Nickel, Terry Orr, Marcos Paredes, Christine Sarry, Gretchen Schumacher, Rosanna Seravalli, John Sowinski, Burton Taylor, Carol Todd, Diana Weber, Kasana Wojcik, Richard Zelens

REPERTOIRE: Theme and Variations, Dark Elegies, Jardin Aux Lilas, The Wind In The Mountains, The Combat, The Four Marys, Pillar of Fire, Balladen Der Liebe, Grand Pas-Glazounov, Fall River Legend, Sargasso, La Ville Mal Gardee, Billy The Kid, Kontraste, Ricercare, Etudes, Peter and The Wolf, Giselle, Les Sylphides, Swan Lake, Interplay, Pas De Deux, Miss Julie, Les Noces, Esmeralda Pas De Deux, Fancy Free, Don Quixote Pas De Deux, Caprichos.

Production Manager: Daryl Dodson
Press: Samuel Lurie, Stanley F. Kaminsky
Stage Managers: Tom Porter,
Joseph Carow

° Closed Sunday, February 13, 1966, after a limited engagement of 32 performances.

Jack Mitchell, Fred Fehls Photos

Toni Lander, Royes Fernandez in "La Sylphide"

Lupe Serrano, Royes Fernandez in "Giselle"
Above: "Theme and Variations" Top: "Les Noces"

109

NEW YORK STATE THEATER

Opened Tuesday, May 31, 1966.°
Music Theater of Lincoln Center (Richard Rodgers, President and Producing Director) presents:

ANNIE GET YOUR GUN

Music and Lyrics, Irving Berlin; Book, Herbert and Dorothy Fields; Director, Jack Sydow; Dances and Production Numbers Staged by Danny Daniels; Designed by Paul McGuire; Costumes, Frank Thompson; Lighting, Peter Hunt; Musical Director, Franz Allers; Orchestrations, Robert Russell Bennett; Dance Arrangements, Richard De Benedictis; Associate Conductor, Jonathan Anderson; Hair Styles, Ronald De Mann.

CAST

Little Boy	Jeffrey Scott
Little Girl	Deanna Melody
Charlie Davenport	Jerry Orbach
Dolly Tate	Benay Venuta
Iron Tail	Brynar Mehl
Yellow Foot	Gary Jendell
Mac	John Dorrin
Foster Wilson	Ronn Carroll
Frank Butler	Bruce Yarnell
Shy Girl	Diana Banks
Annie Oakley	Ethel Merman
Little Jake	David Manning
Nellie	Donna Conforti
Jessie	Jeanne Tanzy
Minnie	Holly Sherwood
Col. William F. Cody (Buffalo Bill)	Rufus Smith
Mrs. Little Horse	Mary Falconer
Mrs. Black Tooth	Jaclynn Villamil
Mrs. Yellow Foot	Kuniko Narai
Indian Boy	Jeffrey Scott
Conductor	Jim Lynn
Porter	Beno Foster
Waiter	David Forssen
Maj. Gordon Lillie (Pawnee Bill)	Jack Dabdoub
Chief Sitting Bull	Harry Bellaver
The Wild Horse	Jaime Rogers
Pawnee's Messenger	Walt Hunter
Major Domo	Ben Laney
Schuyler Adams	Ronn Carroll
Mrs. Schuyler Adams	Patricia Hall
Dr. Ferguson	Marc Rowan
Mrs. Ferguson	Bobbi Baird
Mr. T. L. C. Keefer	Walt Hunter
Ernest Henderson	Grant Spradling
Mrs. Ernest Henderson	Lynn Carroll
Mrs. Sylvia Potter-Porter	Mary Falconer
Mr. Clay	John Dorrin

SINGERS: Bobbi Baird, Vicki Belmonte, Chrysten Caroll, Lynn Carroll, Audrey Dearden, Lynn Dovel, Mary Falconer, Patricia Hall, Florence Mercer, Susan Terry, Kenny Adams, Ronn Carroll, John Dorrin, David Forssen, Beno Foster, Walt Hunter, Ben Laney, Jim Lynn, Marc Rowan, Grant Spradling

DANCERS: Diane Banks, Joanne DiVito, Rozann Ford, Barbara Hancock, Ruth Lawrence, Kuniko Narai, Eva Marie Sage, Evelyn Taylor, Jaclynn Villamil, Anne Wallace, Gjarne Buchtrup, Tony Catanzaro, Frank Derbas, Ronn Forella, Marcelo Gamboa, Jeremy Ives, Gary Jendell, Daniel Joel, Brynar Mehl, Gene Myers

UNDERSTUDIES: Annie, Eileen Rodgers; Frank, Jack Dabdoub; Sitting Bull, Ronn Carroll; Dolly, Iris O'Connor; Charlie, Jim Lynn; Pawnee, Walter Hunter; Buffalo Bill, John Dorrin; Wild Horse, Tony Catanzaro; Little Jake, Jeffrey Scott; Minnie, Joanne DiVito; Jessie, Nellie, Deanna Melody; Foster, Messenger, David Forssen; Mac, Ben Laney; Porter, Grant Spradling; Waiter, Major Domo, Marc Rowan; Conductor, Kenny Adams; Mrs. Potter-Porter, Mrs. Adams, Susan Terry

MUSICAL NUMBERS: "Colonel Buffalo Bill," "I'm A Bad Bad Man," "Doin' What Comes Naturally," "The Girl That I Marry," "You Can't Get A Man With A Gun," "There's No Business Like Show Business," "They Say It's Wonderful," "Moonshine Lullaby," "Wild West Pitch Dance," "My Defenses Are Down," "Wild Horse Ceremonial Dance," "I'm An Indian Too," "Adoption Dance," "Lost In His Arms," "I Got The Sun In The Morning and The Moon At Night," "Old Fashioned Wedding," "Anything You Can Do," Finale.

A Musical in two acts and seven scenes.

General Manager: Henry Guettel
Company Manager: Ronald Bruguiere
Press: Richard Maney
Stage Managers: William Ross, Charles Blackwell, J. P. Regan, Iris O'Connor

° For original production (May 16, 1946) with Ethel Merman and Ray Middleton, see THEATRE WORLD, Vol. 2.

Bruce Yarnell, Ethel Merman

Bruce Yarnell, Ethel Merman, Rufus Smith
Above: Jerry Orbach, Benay Venuta, Harry Bellav

Ethel Merman
in
"ANNIE GET YOUR GUN"

111

Peter Daness Photos

VIVIAN BEAUMONT THEATER

Opened Thursday, October 21, 1965.°
The Repertory Theater of Lincoln Center
under the direction of Herbert Blau and
Jules Irving presents:

DANTON'S DEATH

By Georg Buechner; Directed in a new ver-
sion by Herbert Blau; Scene Design and
Lighting, Jo Mielziner; Costumes, James Hart
Stearns; Supervised by John Boyt; Electronic
Music and Songs, Morton Subotnick; Technical
Director, Jose Sevilla; Hair Stylist, Jan La-
timer.

CAST

Young Man	David Sullivan
Women	Erica Yohn, Kate Wilkinson, Elizabeth Huddle, Ruth Attaway
Herault-Sechelles	Michael Granger
Ladies	Beatrice Manley, Priscilla Pointer
George Danton	Alan Bergmann
Julie, Danton's wife	Claudette Nevins
Philippeau	James Earl Jones
Camille Desmoulins	Robert Stattel
Lacroix	David J. Stewart
Simon	Ray Fry
Simon's wife	Shirley Jac Wagner
Citizen	Tom Rosqui
Cutler	Stacy Keach
Young Gentleman	Edward Cicciarelli
Billaud	Louis Zorich
Robespierre	Robert Symonds
Deputy from Lyons	Edward Winter
Legendre	Ronald Weyand
Collot D'Herbois	Paul Mann
Marion	Marcie Hubert
Rosalie	Diane Shalet
Adelaide	Erica Yohn
St. Just	Roscoe Lee Browne
Robespierre's Servant	Mariclare Costello
Beggar	Lincoln Kilpatrick
Madame	Kate Wilkinson
Eugenie	Elizabeth Huddle
Puppeteer	Carlo Mazzone-Clementi
Young Man with balloon	Frank Bayer
Gentleman	David Sullivan
Husband	James Greene
Wife	Beatrice Manley
Soldiers	Edward Cicciarelli, Edward Winter
Dumas	James Dukas
Morel	Ray Fry
Lucille, Camille's wife	Gail Fisher
Fouquier	Glenn Mazen
Jailer	Edward Winter
General Dillon	Robert Haswell
Laflotte	Robert Phalen
Barere	Tom Rosqui
Turnkey	Stacy Keach
Executioners	Ronald Weyand, Stanley Beck
Citizens in Public Square	Lincoln Kilpatrick, Jack Waltzer, James Greene
Women at Scaffold	Priscilla Pointer, Ruth Attaway, Edith Gresham
Children	Eileen Dolphin, Matthew Pryor, Paul Dwyer

Alternates: Barry Symonds, Victoria Symonds
UNDERSTUDIES: Danton, Tom Rosqui;
Herault, Glenn Mazen; Philippeau, David Sul-
livan; Camille, Robert Phalen; St. Just, Lincoln
Kilpatrick; Robespierre, Legendre, Stacy Keach;
Billaud, Fouquier, Barere, James Greene; Col-
lot, Robert Haswell; Lacroix, Ray Fry; Laflotte,
Edward Cicciarelli; Dillon, Ronald Weyand;
Simon, James Dukas; Julie, Lucille, Mariclare
Costello; Marion, Eugenie, Priscilla Pointer;
Rosalie, Adelaide, Elizabeth Huddle; Others,
Frank Bayer, Stanley Beck, Howard Fischer,
Edith Gresham, Shirley Jac Wagner, Jack
Waltzer, Timothy Ward

A Drama presented in two parts. The action
takes place between March 24 and April 5,
1794.

General Manager: Stanley Gilkey
Managing Director: Alan Mandell
Press: Barry Hyams, Susan Bloch
Stage Managers: Frederick de Wilde,
James Kershaw, Howard Fischer,
Timothy Ward, Frank Bayer

° Closed November 27, 1965. (46 performances)

Priscilla Pointer, Beatrice Manley,
James Earl Jones, Michael Granger, Robert Stattel
Above: Alan Bergmann, (also above) Robert Stattel

VIVIAN BEAUMONT THEATER

Opened Thursday, February 3, 1966.*
The Repertory Theater of Lincoln Center
(Herbert Blau, Jules Irving, Directors)
presents the American premiere of:

THE CONDEMNED OF ALTONA

By Jean-Paul Sartre; Adapted by Justin
O'Brien; Directed by Herbert Blau; Scene De-
sign, Robin Wagner; Costumes, Deidre Cartier;
Lighting, Martin Aronstein; Sound, Charles
Gross; Technical Director, Jose Sevilla.

CAST

Johanna _____ Carolyn Coates
Werner _____ Edward Winter
Leni _____ Priscilla Pointer
The Father _____ George Coulouris
Frantz _____ Tom Rosqui
The S.S. _____ James Dukas
Assistant S.S. _____ Louis Zorich
Heinrich _____ Robert Haswell
Klages _____ David Sullivan

UNDERSTUDIES: Johanna, Beatrice Manley;
Werner, Robert Stattel; Leni, Erica Yohn;
Father, Robert Haswell; Frantz, Stacy Keach;
S.S., Heinrich, Louis Zorich; Klages, Robert
Phalen

A Drama in three acts and five scenes. The
action takes place in 1959 in the Gerlach
House in Altona.

General Manager: Stanley Gilkey
Managing Director: Alan Mandell
Press: Barry Hyams, Susan Bloch
Stage Managers: James Kershaw,
Russell McGrath, Timothy Ward,
David Sullivan

* Closed Sunday, March 13, 1966.
(46 performances)

Opened Thursday, December 9, 1965.*
The Repertory Theater of Lincoln Center
under the direction of Herbert Blau and
Jules Irving presents:

THE COUNTRY WIFE

By William Wycherley; Directed by Robert
Symonds; Settings and Costumes, James Hart
Stearns; Associate Designer, James F. Gohl;
Costumes Supervised by Deidre Cartier; Light-
ing, Jean Rosenthal; Music and Songs, Stanley
Silverman; Technical Director, Jose Sevilla;
Assistant Director, Timothy Ward; Choreo-
graphy, David Sullivan.

CAST

Mr. Horner _____ Stacy Keach
Matou, Horner's Servant _____ Frank Bayer
A Quack _____ Michael Granger
Sir Jasper Fidget _____ Ray Fry
Lady Fidget _____ Priscilla Pointer
Mrs. Dainty Fidget _____ Shirley Jac Wagner
Mr. Harcourt _____ Robert Stattel
Mr. Dorilant _____ Edward Winter
Mr. Sparkish _____ Robert Symonds
Mr. Pinchwife _____ Robert Haswell
Miss Alithea _____ Carolyn Coates
Lucy _____ Marcie Hubert
Mrs. Squeamish _____ Beatrice Manley
Old Lady Squeamish _____ Edith Gresham
Alternates for children: David and Lara Speyer
MERCHANTS, THIEVES, PIMPS, AND
BAWDS: Ruth Attaway, Stanley Beck, Ed-
ward Cicciarelli, Mariclare Costello, Jeff David,
James Dukas, Paul Dwyer, Elaine Eldridge,
Amy Irving, Lincoln Kilpatrick, Richard Levy,
Glenn Maze, Carlo Mazzone-Clementi, Robert
Phalen, Tom Rosqui, David Sullivan, Barry
Symonds, Victoria Symonds, Jack Waltzer, Craig
Ward, Angela Wood, Erica Yohn, Louis
Zorich
UNDERSTUDIES: Mariclare Costello, James
Dukas, Elaine Eldridge, Glenn Mazen, Robert
Phalen, David Sullivan, Jack Waltzer, Angela
Wood, Erica Yohn
MUSICIANS: Martha Gerhart, Howard Col-
lins, Jeffrey Levine, Richard Fitz

A Comedy presented in two parts. The
action takes place in London the latter half of
the seventeenth century.

General Manager: Stanley Gilkey
Managing Director: Alan Mandell
Press: Barry Hyams, Susan Bloch
Stage Managers: James Kershaw,
Howard Fischer, Jeff David,
Stanley Beck, Jack Waltzer

* Closed Sunday, January 23, 1966. (46 performances) Last revival was Nov. 27, 1957
with Julie Harris and Laurence Harvey,
and ran for 45 performances. See THEATRE
WORLD, Vol. 14.

**Carolyn Coates, Tom Rosqui in "Condemned"
Top Left: Robert Haswell, Elizabeth Huddle,
Stacy Keach, Robert Stattel in "The Country Wife"
Below: Carolyn Coates, Elizabeth Huddle**

Beatrice Manley, Ronnie Misa,
Robert Symonds, Elizabeth Huddle

VIVIAN BEAUMONT THEATER
Opened Thursday, March 24, 1966.°
Repertory Theater of Lincoln Center presents:

THE CAUCASIAN CHALK CIRCLE

By Bertolt Brecht; English version by Eric
Bentley; Directed by Jules Irving; Sets, Costumes, and Masks, James Hart Stearns; Associate Designer, James F. Gohl; Lighting, Richard Nelson; Music and Songs composed by
Morton Subotnick; Music Director, Stanley Silverman; Production Assistant, Alfred Levinson;
Technical Director, Jose Sevilla.

CAST

ACT I:

The Prologue:
Delegates from goat-breeding farm:
Aleko Bereshwili _____ Boris Tumarin
Makina Abakidse _____ Shirley Jac Wagner
Young Peasants _____ Frank Bayer,
Edith Gresham
Delegates from fruit-growing farm:
Surab _____ Leonardo Cimino
His Wife _____ Elizabeth Huddle
Girl Tractorist _____ Marcie Hubert
Kato Wachtang,
agriculturist _____ Marketa Kimbrell
Wounded Soldier _____ Robert Phalen
Peasants _____ William Haddock, Judith Lowry
Delegate from Capitol _____ Ray Fry
Arkadi Tscheidse, Storyteller _____ Brock Peters
The Nobel Child:
Georgi Abashwili, governor _____ Glenn Mazen
Natella Abashwili, his wife ____ Beatrice Manley
Shalva Tzereteli, adjutant _____ John Devlin
Arsen Kazbeki, Fat Prince _____ Paul Mann
Bizergan Kazbeki, his nephew _____ Oliver Clark
Major Domo _____ Robert Haswell
Maro, the nurse _____ Ruth Attaway
Niko Mikadze, a doctor _____ James Dukas
Mika Loladze, a doctor _____ Earl Montgomery
Asja, lady in waiting _____ Carolyn Coates
Nina, lady in waiting _____ Erica Yohn
Masha, lady in waiting _____ Judith Propper
Suliko, lady in waiting _____ Marcie Hubert
Servants _____ David Sullivan,
Robert Stattel
A Judge _____ Robert Symonds
Messenger from Capitol _____ Edward Cicciarelli
Simon Shashava,
Palace guard _____ Edward Winter
The Corporal _____ Murvyn Vye
Grusha Vashnadze,
Palace kitchen maid _____ Elizabeth Huddle
Architects _____ Leonardo Cimino, Ray Fry
Cooks _____ Doris Rich, John Carpenter
Grooms _____ William Haddock, Stacy Keach
Kitchen Maids _____ Shirley Jac Wagner,
Priscilla Pointer, Edith Gresham
Private "Blockhead" _____ James Dukas
Ironshirts _____ Stanley Beck,
Edward Cicciarelli, Jeff David,
Michael Granger, Robert Phalen
Beggars _____ Elaine Eldridge, Richard Levy,
Carlo Mazzone-Clementi,
Priscilla Pointer, Judith Propper,
Tom Rosqui, Shirley Jac Wagner,
Ronald Weyand

ACT II:

Flight To The Northern Mountains:
Old Peasant with milk _____ Boris Tumarin
Peasant woman _____ Erica Yohn
Her husband _____ Ronald Weyand
Three Merchants _____ Carolyn Coates,
Ray Fry, John Carpenter
The Northern Mountains:
Lavrenti, Grusha's brother _____ Michael Granger
Aniko, his wife _____ Priscilla Pointer
Sasso, a servant _____ Oliver Clark
Peasant woman, Grusha's
mother-in-law _____ Shirley Jac Wagner
Jussup, her son _____ Glenn Mazen
Michael _____ Ronnie Misa
Brother Anastasias, a monk _____ Ray Fry
Drunken peasant _____ Stanley Beck
Two Musicians _____ David Sullivan,
Stacy Keach
Villagers _____ Ruth Attaway, John Carpenter,
Carolyn Coates, Elaine Eldridge, Edith
Gresham, Marcie Hubert, Carlo Mazzone-
Clementi, Robert Phalen, Priscilla Pointer,
Judith Propper, Ronald Weyand, Erica Yohn
Children _____ Steven Chall, Buster Davis
Alternates _____ Scooter Jolley, Barry Symonds

ACT III:

The Story of The Judge:
Azdak, village scrivener _____ Robert Symonds
Fugitive Grand Duke _____ Earl Montgomery
Shauwa, policeman _____ Ronald Weyand
The invalid _____ Ray Fry
His servant _____ David Sullivan
Limping man _____ Tom Rosqui
Doctor _____ John Carpenter
Blackmailer _____ Earl Montgomery
Innkeeper _____ Murvyn Vye
Ludovica, his daughter-in-law _____ Erica Yohn
Stableboy _____ Frank Bayer
Rich farmers _____ Leonardo Cimino,
Robert Haswell, John Carpenter
Irakli, a bandit _____ Lincoln Kilpatrick
Granny Grusinia _____ Shirley Jac Wagner
The Chalk Circle:
Illo Shuboladze, a lawyer _____ Earl Montgomery
Sandro Oboladze, a lawyer ____ Boris Tumarin
Messenger from Grand Duke ____ Robert Stattel
Very old couple _____ Judith Lowry,
William Haddock
Soloist _____ Marketa Kimbrell
Chorus _____ Elizabeth Cole, Barbara Smith
Conrad, Elizabeth S. Corrigan,
Mary Delson
Musicians _____ Jacob Glick, Richard Fitz,
Martha Gerhart, Elizabeth S. Corrigan
UNDERSTUDIES: Storyteller, John Carpenter;
Natella, Carolyn Coates; Shalva, Tom Rosqui;
Arsen, Earl Montgomery; Simon, Robert Phalen;
Corporal, Ronald Weyand; Grusha, Marcie
Hubert; Jussup, David Sullivan; Azdak, Ray
Fry; Shauwa, Tom Rosqui; Illo, Sandro, Glenn
Mazen

General Manager: Stanley Gilkey
Managing Director: Alan Mandell
Press: Barry Hyams, Susan Bloch
Stage Managers: Timothy Ward,
Russell McGrath, Frank Bayer,
Richard Levy

° Still playing May 31, 1966.

Sam Siegel Photos

OFF-BROADWAY

SULLIVAN STREET PLAYHOUSE
Opened Tuesday, May 3, 1960.°
Lore Noto presents:

THE FANTASTICKS

Book and Lyrics, Tom Jones; Music, Harvey Schmidt; Suggested by Edmund Rostand's Play "Les Romantiques;" Director, Word Baker; Musical Direction and Arrangements, Julian Stein; Designed by Ed Wittstein; Associate Producers, Sheldon Baron, Dorothy Olim, Robert Alan Gold; Assistant to Producer, David Harper; Original Cast Album by M-G-M Records.

CAST
The Narrator	John Boni†1
The Girl	B. J. Ward†2
The Boy	Bob Spencer
The Boy's Father	David Sabin†3
The Girl's Father	John J. Martin
The Actor	Lowry Miller†4
The Man Who Dies	Curt Williams†5
The Mute	Richard Barrie†6
The Handyman	Richard Drake

Pianist: Ronald Clairmont
Harpist: Sally Foster

UNDERSTUDIES: Narrator, George Ogee; Boy, Richard Rothbard; Girl, Sybil Lamb; Girl's Father, Curt Williams; Actor, Don Pomes; Boy's Father, Ed Garrabrandt

MUSICAL NUMBERS: Overture, "Try To Remember," "Much More," "Metaphor," "Never Say No," "It Depends On What You Pay," "Soon It's Gonna Rain," "Rape Ballet," "Happy Ending," "This Plum Is Too Ripe," "I Can See It," "Plant A Radish," "Round and Round," "They Were You," Finale.

A Musical in two acts.

Press: Harvey B. Sabinson, David Powers
Stage Managers: Geoffry Brown, Edward Garrabrandt, Elissa Lane

° Still playing May 31, 1966. For original production, see THEATRE WORLD, Vol. 16.
† Succeeded by: 1. Jack Mette, Keith Charles, 2. Leta Anderson, 3. Donald Babcock, 4. Curt Williams, 5. Don Pomes, 6. James Cook, Richard Barrie.

Front Row: Curt Williams, Leta Anderson, Don Pomes
Standing: Richard Barrie, John J. Martin, Bob Spencer, Keith Charles, Donald Babcock
Above: Keith Charles, Richard Barrie
Top: Leta Anderson, Bob Spencer

SHERIDAN SQUARE PLAYHOUSE

Opened Thursday, January 28, 1965.°
Ulu Grosbard, Joseph E. Levine, and
Katzka-Berne Corp. present:

A VIEW FROM THE BRIDGE

By Arthur Miller; Director, Ulu Grosbard;
Set, Robin Wagner; Lighting, John McLain;
Costumes, Doreen Ackerman; Sound, Gigi Cas-
cio; Production Assistant, Dean Delk.

CAST

Louis	Richard Castellano†1
Mike	Carmine Caridi†2
Alfieri	Val Bioglio†3
Eddie	Robert Duvall†4
Catherine	Susan Anspach†5
Beatrice	Jeanne Kaplan
Marco	Ramon Bieri†6
Tony	Gino Morra
Rodolpho	Jon Voight†7
1st Immigration Officer	Dan Priest
2nd Immigration Officer	Curt Dempster†8
Mr. Lipari	William Corio†9
Mrs. Lipari	Bea Brooks†10
"Submarines"	Noel Parente†11, Constantine Katsanos†12

UNDERSTUDIES: Marco, Louis Basile; Ro-
dolpho, Don Barshay; Beatrice, Maria Di Giovanni; Catherine, Emily Prager; Alfieri, Louis
Basile; Eddie, Joseph Mascolo

A Drama in two acts. The action takes
place at the present time.

General Manager: Joseph Beruh
Company Manager: Jewel Howard
Press: Dorothy Ross, Richard O'Brien,
Mike Gershman, Harold Rand
Stage Manager: Curt Dempster

° Still playing May 31, 1966. For original
production, see THEATRE WORLD, Vol. 21,
and original Broadway production, Vol. 12.

† Succeeded by: 1. Tony Pizzarusso, 2. Louis
Basile, 3. Mitchell Jason, 4. Richard Castel-
lano, 5. Susan Kapilow, 6. Joseph Mascolo,
7. Wayne Geis, 8. Griff Caine, 9. Henry
Ferrentino, 10. Maria Di Giovanni, 11. Don
Barshay, 12. Jack Minhinick.

Werner J. Kuhn Photos

Wayne Geis, Susan Kapilow
Above: Dan Priest, Joseph Mascolo,
Richard Castellano, Jeanne Kaplan

GATE THEATRE

Opened Thursday, June 3, 1965.°
Apex Productions presents:

TROUBLED WATERS
or
The Brother Who Protects And Loves

By Ugo Betti; Translated by Gino Rizzo and William Meriwether; Directed and Designed by Eric Salmon; Lighting, Roger Morgan; Technical Director, Skip Rognlien; Produced in association with Memphis State University.

CAST

The Two Men	Sal Caruso, Raymond Purcell
Giacomo	William Countryman
Alda, his sister	Mary Ann Hoxworth
Gabriele	Harris Yulin
Edvige, Giacomo's wife	Yolanda Childress
Aglae, Gabriele's wife	Dina Paisner
Madame Inez	Dina Paisner

A Drama in three acts. The action takes place in our own times in a small town in an unspecified country.

General Manager: Krone-Olin Management
Press: Howard Atlee, Warren Pincus, David Roggensack
Stage Managers; Mary Porter, Price Broughton

° Closed Sunday, June 6, 1965. (5 performances)

William Countryman, Mary Ann Hoxworth, Harris Yulin, and top with Yolanda Childress

ACTORS' PLAYHOUSE

Opened Monday, June 7, 1965.°
Theodore Mann and Howard J. Zuker
in association with Frank Cassidy present:

LIVE LIKE PIGS

By John Arden; with the Theatre Company
of Boston; Directed by David Wheeler; Set,
Robert Allen; Lighting, Neville Powers; Music
for Songs by Ervin Henning; Associate Producers, William Coltin, David E. Dick; Production Associate, Neville Powers.

CAST

Official	Stan Moore
Rachel	Josephine Lane†1
Rosie Sawney	Naomi Thornton†2
Sally	Anne Gordon
Sailor Sawney	Paul Benedict
Col	Joseph Maher
Mrs. Jackson	Audrey Ward†3
Doreen	Roberta Collinge
Mr. Jackson	Will Hare
Blackmouth	Robert Fields
Daffodil	Jane Lee Parker
Old Croaker	Harriet Rogers
Doctor	Betty Harmon
Policeman	Roger Hamilton

A Comedy in three acts. The action takes
place at the present time over a period of
a month in a housing development in the
North of England.

Press: Ben Kornzweig, Reginald Denenholz
Stage Manager: Michael Sinclair

° Closed Sunday, September 26, 1965.
(128 performances)

† Succeeded by: 1. Tresa Hughes, 2. Avra
Petrides, 3. Paddy Croft.

Harriet Rogers, Josephine Lane, Anne Gordon
Above: Robert Fields, Anne Gordon,
Naomi Thornton
118 Top: Joseph Maher, Roberta Collinge, Audrey Ward
Right: Paul Benedict, Janet Lee Parker

CHERRY LANE THEATER

Opened Tuesday, June 8, 1965.°
(Moved September 12, 1965 to Village
South Theater)
Theater 1965 presents:

THE ZOO STORY

By Edward Albee; Directed by Alan
Schneider; Designed by William Ritman.

CAST

Jerry --- Ben Piazza
Peter ---------------------------------- George Bartenieff

The action takes place at the present time
on a Sunday afternoon in Central Park, New
York City.

with

KRAPP'S LAST TAPE

By Samuel Beckett; Directed by Alan
Schneider; Designed by William Ritman.

CAST

Krapp ---------------------------------- George Bartenieff

The action takes place in Krapp's den late
on an evening in the future.

Administrative Director: Barry Plaxen
Press: Howard Atlee, Warren Pincus,
David Roggensack
Stage Manager: Charles Kindl

° Closed Sunday, October 31, 1965.
(168 performances)

George Bartenieff, Ben Piazza in "The Zoo Story"
Above: George Bartenieff in "Krapp's Last Tape"

THEATRE DE LYS

Opened Monday, June 28, 1965.°
Judith Rutherford Marechal, Josephine
Forrestal, and Seymour Litvinoff present:

LEONARD BERNSTEIN'S
THEATRE SONGS

Music by Leonard Bernstein; Lyrics by Mr.
Bernstein, Betty Comden, Adolph Green, Lillian Hellman, Stephen Sondheim, and Richard
Wilbur; Conceived and Directed by Will Holt;
Lighting, Jules Fisher; Orchestrations, Fred
Werner; Presented by arrangement with Lucille Lortel Productions, Inc.; Production Associates, Larry Goossen, Susan Richardson; Production Assistant, Dean Delk.

CAST

Trude Adams†1
Don Francks†2
Micki Grant

A musical evening of songs from "On
The Town," "Trouble In Tahiti," "Wonderful
Town," "Candide," and "West Side Story,"
presented in two parts.

Company Manager: Paul B. Berkowsky
Press: Max Eisen, Samuel J. Friedman,
Jane Friedman
Stage Manager: Dale E. Whitt

° Closed Sunday, September 12, 1965.
(88 performances)

† Succeeded by: 1. Lee Berry, 2. Will Holt.

Friedman-Abeles Photos

Don Francks
Above: Micki Grant, Don Francks, Trude Adams

CHERRY LANE THEATER

Opened Tuesday, September 14, 1965.°
Theater 1966 (Richard Barr, Clinton
Wilder, Edward Albee) presents:

HAPPY DAYS

By Samuel Beckett; Directed by Roger Blin;
Decor by Matias.

CAST

Winnie _____ Madeleine Renaud†1
Willie _____ Jean-Louis Barrault†2

A Play in two acts.

Administrative Director: Barry Plaxen
Press: Howard Atlee, Robert Larkin,
David Roggensack
Stage Manager: Richard d'Anjou

° Closed Sunday, October 10, 1965.
(32 performances)

† Succeeded by: 1. Ruth White, 2. Wyman
Pendleton.

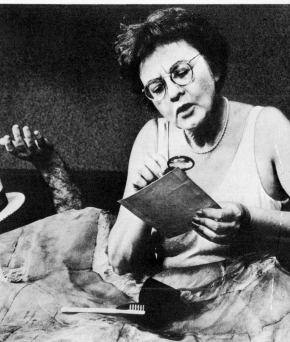

Ruth White
Above: Madeleine Renaud

Ruth White
Above: Madeleine Renaud

Eli Mintz, Danny Fortus in "Friends"
Top: Eli Mintz, Jay Barney in "Enemies"

THEATRE EAST

Opened Thursday, September 16, 1965.°
The Red Barn Theatre Limited presents:

FRIENDS
and
ENEMIES

Two plays by Arkady Leokum; Directed by
William Hunt; Sets and Lighting, Dafs, Inc.;
Costumes, Stephanie Kovanda.

"Enemies"
CAST

Gittleman _____ Eli Mintz
Miller _____ Jay Barney

The action takes place at the present time
in a corner of Selig's Restaurant.

"Friends"
CAST

The Tutor _____ Eli Mintz
The Pupil _____ Danny Fortus
Delivery Boy _____ David Roya

The action takes place at the present time
in the tutor's apartment overlooking the harbor
of a small city.

General Manager: Joseph Leberman
Press: Saul Richman
Stage Managers: Kay C. Coulthard,
Jay Hershkowitz

° Closed Sunday, January 23, 1966.
(139 performances)

FORTY-FIRST STREET THEATRE

Opened Tuesday, September 28, 1965.°
Al Jordan presents:

SWIM LOW LITTLE GOLDFISH

By Ronald Collier; Directed by Al Jordan; Art Direction, Howard Deutscher; Lighting, James Dwyer; Title Song, by Norman Brooks and Al Jordan, sung on record by Peter George.

CAST

Joan Watson	Carol Gutenberg
Mike Watson	Jack Aaron
Joe Darnell	Peter George
The Doctor	Eben Richards
Mrs. Prather	Lisa Mayo
Laura	JoAnn Hamilton
Richard	Himself

A Comedy in three acts. The action takes place in and around the fish bowl home of Richard, located in a New York apartment.

Company Manager: Bary Golden
Press: Richard Falk
Stage Manager: Robert Monroe

° Closed Tuesday, September 28, 1965.
(1 performance)

Top Right: Carol Gutenberg,
JoAnn Hamilton, Peter George

THE BLACKFRIARS' THEATRE

Opened Wednesday, October 6, 1965.°
The Blackfriars' Guild presents:

MACKEY OF APPALACHIA

Book, Music, Lyrics, and Direction by Walter Cool; Settings and Lighting, Allen Edward Klein; Costumes, Alice Merrigal; Musical Numbers Staged by Robert Charles.

CAST

Mackey	James Bormann
Jake	James Batch, George Patelis
Deardra	Frances Beck, Virginia Ellyn Haynes
Odd	Michael Murray, Christopher Smith
Emmey	Tish Yousef, Barbara Coggin
Weltha	Kay Preston, Elizabeth Ferraro
Happy Jack	Frank Johnson, Martin McHale
Loney	Mary W. O'Malley, Rosemary Gallo
Buck	John Beyer, Sonny Chriss
Ezria	Allister C. Whitman, Jerry Pearlman
Alice	Jacqueline Page, Laura Taylor
Maude	Kathryn Martin, E. Bette Pardee
Zeke	Bob Charles

MUSICAL NUMBERS: "Mackey of Appalachia," "Appalachia & Mackey," "Judging Song," "I Wonder Why," "Love Me Too," "You're Too Smart," "There Goes My Gal," "Love Will Come Your Way," "It's Sad To Be Lonesome," "Slatey Fork," "How We Would Like Our Man," "Lonely Voice," "My Love, My Love," "Blue and Troubled," "My Little Girl," "We're Having A Party," "Polka A La Appalachia," "Go Up To The Mountain," "There's Got To Be Love," "We Got Troubles," "Gotta Pay," "Only A Day Dream," "Things Ain't As Nice," "Everybody Loves A Tree," "We Are Friends," Finale.

A Musical Comedy in two acts and ten scenes. The action takes place in Slatey Fork, West Virginia, in October of 1900.

Press: Rev. Thomas F. Carey
Stage Managers: Robert Charles,
Marie Stuart, Judy Smith

° Closed Tuesday, November 23, 1965.
(48 performances)

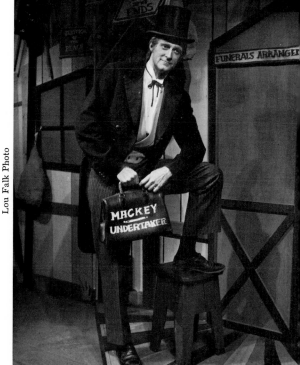

Mary O'Malley, Bob Charles, Kathryn Martin, Frank Johnson, Tish Yousef, John Beyer, Len Hall, Jacqueline Page, Michael Murray, Kay Preston, Allister Whitman, Frances Beck, John Batch **123**
Above: James Bormann

ORPHEUM THEATRE

Opened Friday, October 8, 1965.°
The Greater New York Chapter Inc. of
ANTA present the Claude Giroux-Orrin
Christy, Jr.-Frank Carrington production
of:

THE WORLD OF RAY BRADBURY

By Ray Bradbury; Directed by Charles Rome
Smith; Scenery and Lighting, Eldon Elder;
Costumes, Arnold Scaasi; Graphics, Joe Mug-
naini; Pendulum Sound, John Whitney.

"The Pedestrian"

CAST

Mead .... Paul Sparer
Stockwell .... George Voskovec
Police Voice .... Stewart Bradley

The time is in the 1990's, and the action
takes place in Stockwell's livingroom and on
the Night Street.

"The Veldt"

CAST

Technician .... Stewart Bradley
George .... Henry Madden
Lydia .... Gretchen Kanne
Peter .... John Zizak
Wendy .... Denise Stevens
David MacLean .... Paul Sparer

The action takes place in the playroom
and living quarters of the George Hadley home
in the 1990's.

"To The Chicago Abyss"

CAST

The Young Man .... Henry Madden
The Old Man .... George Voskovec
The Stranger .... Paul Sparer
The Wife .... Gretchen Kanne
The Policeman .... Stewart Bradley
The Boy .... John Zizak

The action takes place in the park, the
Stranger's house, and on the train in the
1990's.

UNDERSTUDIES: Policeman, Technician,
Nicholas Lewis; Mead, David MacLean, Stranger, Stewart Bradley

General Manager: Norman Kean
Press: John Springer Associates,
Walter Alford, Warren Pincus
Stage Managers: Terry Shank,
Nicholas Lewis

° Closed Sunday, October 10, 1965.
(5 performances)

**George Voskovec. Top: Denise Stevens,
John Zizak, Henry Madden, Gretchen Kanne
in "The Veldt"**

124

**George Voskovec, John Zizak
in "To The Chicago Abyss"**

STAGE 73

Opened Saturday, October 9, 1965.°
Arthur Cantor presents:

THE TRIGON

By James Broom Lynne; Directed by Arthur
Cantor; Scenery and Costumes, Richard Bi-
anchi; Associate Producer, Carl A. Gottlieb;
Production Assistants, Walter Russell, Martha
Knight.

CAST

Arthur	Jeremy Geidt
Basil	Geoffrey Webb
Charles	Michael Lipton
Mabel	Veronica Castang

Standby for Miss Castang: Jessica Rains

A Drama in three acts and five scenes. The
action takes place in a top-floor flat somewhere in London in the early 1950's.

General Manager: Carl A. Gottlieb
Press: Artie Solomon, Donna Silberberg
Stage Managers: David Rosenbaum,
Jessica Rains

° Closed Sunday, December 5, 1965.
(70 performances)

Veronica Castang, Michael Lipton
Michael Lipton, Geoffrey Webb, Jeremy Geidt

125

Werner J. Kuhn Photos

THEATRE DE LYS

Opened Monday, October 11, 1965.°
Judith Rutherford Marechal Productions,
Inc., & Konrad Matthaei in association
with Jay Stanwyck present The University
of Michigan Professional Theatre Program production of:

AN EVENING'S FROST

By Donald Hall; Conceived and Directed
by Marcella Cisney; Music Composed by
Richard Peaslee; Setting, Robin Wagner; Lighting, Gary Harris; Production Assistant, Tom
Woodard.

CAST

Jacqueline Brookes†1   Will Geer
Donald Davis†2   John Randolph
    Flutist: Margaret Strum

The prose, poetry, and letters of Robert
Frost presented in two parts.

General Manager: Paul B. Berkowsky
Press: Dorothy Ross, Richard O'Brien,
Susan Richardson, Larry Goossen
Stage Manager: William Weaver

° Closed Sunday, February 13, 1966.
(132 performances)

† Succeeded by: 1. Patricia O'Connell, 2. William Weaver.

**Will Geer, and above with Donald Davis,
Jacqueline Brookes, John Randolph**

ENATA THEATRE

Opened Thursday, October 14, 1965.°
Gilbert Bledsoe and Maxwell Silverman
present:

PLAY THAT ON YOUR OLD PIANO

By Dan Blue; Directed by John Gerstad;
oduction Designed by William Ritman; Cos-
mes, Noel Taylor; Lighting, Roger Johnson,
; Choreographic Consultant, Joan Gainer;
he Sidewalk Piano Rag" by Gaylord C.
ason; Title Song by Eddy Chalfin and Mike
oberman; Incidental Music Arranged by Gay-
rd C. Mason; Performed by Mr. Mason and
ndy Rasbury.

CAST

yra Scott	Parker McCormick
enry Scott	Dennis Scott
alvin Scott	Martin Rudy
eil Figaro	Richard Barrie
ike Figaro	Alfred Dennis
Wind	Gaylord C. Mason
olly Wind	Sylvia Miles
lian Heifetz	Sy Travers
ary Melody	Viola Swayne
r. Glick	Harold Herman

A Comedy in three acts. The action takes
ace in September of 1934 in the living
om and part of the bedroom in a flat on
e West Side of Chicago. Some of the
ents take place in different parts of that
idwestern mecca.

usiness Manager: Lawrence E. Orlando, Jr.
Press: David Rothenberg, Peter Bogart
Stage Manager: Andy Rasbury
Closed Sunday, October 17, 1965.
(6 performances)

Alix Jeffry Photos

Right: Dennis Scott, Sylvia Miles

er McCormick, Richard Barrie, Martin Rudy

Gaylord Mason, Sylvia Miles

CHERRY LANE THEATER

Opened Monday, October 18, 1965.°
Charles Gnys and Peter Harron present:

GOOD DAY

By Emanuel Peluso; Directed by Ben Skakt-
man; Designed by Peter Harvey; Lighting,
V. C. Fuqua.

CAST

The Young Man .... Frank Langella
The Old Lady .... Nancy Marchand
Bianco .... Joel Stuart

The action takes place at the present time
in a room in a large house.

THE EXHAUSTION OF
OUR SON'S LOVE

By Jerome Max; Directed by Walt Witcover;
Designed by Peter Harvey; Lighting, V. C.
Fuqua.

CAST

Sara Calendar .... Clarice Blackburn
Celia .... Betty Lou Holland
Sam Calendar .... Albert M. Ottenheimer
Raymond Calendar .... Stephen Strimpell

The action takes place on a summer morning on the back porch of a house in a suburban Pennsylvania community on the way to
Scranton.

Administrative Director: Barry Plaxen
Press: Howard Atlee, Michael Alpert,
David Roggensack
Stage Manager: Charles Kindl

° Closed Sunday, December 12, 1965.
(64 performances)

Frank Langella, Nancy Marchand in
"Good Day." Top: Clarice Blackburn, Betty L
Holland, Albert M. Ottenheimer, Stephen Strim
in "The Exhaustion Of Our Son's Love"

PROVINCETOWN PLAYHOUSE

Opened Wednesday, October 20, 1965.°
Iliad-Europa Productions in association
with Russell Allen Jacobsen presents:

KILL THE ONE-EYED MAN!

By Herb Schapiro; Based on Story by
Nikolai Gogol; Directed by Tom Competello;
Sets, James Washinton, Stephen Shea, E. Su-
san Reiner; Lighting, Earl Eidman; Music,
Gary William Friedman; Assistant Director,
Fred Carrion.

CAST

Popritchchine .... Michael Twain
Sophie, Mavra .... Rozanne Ritch
Supervisor, Director, Soldier,
   Attendant .... Hector Elizondo

A Drama in two acts and nine scenes. The
action takes place in Czarist Russia in the
1840's.

   Press: Ben Kornzweig, Reginald Denenholz
     Stage Manager: Fred Carrion
° Closed Tuesday, October 26, 1965.
  (8 performances)

**Left: Hector Elizondo, Michael Twain
Below: Michael Twain, Rozanne Ritch**

GRAMERCY ARTS THEATRE

Opened Wednesday, October 20, 1965.°
Dina and Alexander E. Racolin present:

WOMAN

An evening of dramatic readings from plays
by Congreve, Ibsen, Houghton, Sierra, and
Corwin; Directed by Herbert Biberman.

By

Gale Sondergaard

The emergence of Woman into fuller status
as a human being in relation to her man.
Dramatized from climaxes in five famous plays.
PART I: Congreve's "The Way Of The
World," and Ibsen's "A Doll's House."
PART II: Houghton's "Hindle Wakes," Mar-
tinez-Sierra's "Wife To A Famous Man," and
Norman Corwin's "To Tim—At Twenty."

   General Manager: Lily Turner
    Press: Max Eisen, Carl Samrock
   Stage Manager: James Nisbet Clark
° Closed Sunday, October 24, 1965.
  (7 performances)

Gale Sondergaard

EAST SEVENTY-FOURTH
STREET THEATRE

Opened Friday, October 22, 1965.°
Slade Brown presents:

HOTEL PASSIONATO

Book by Jerome J. Schwartz; Music,
Philip Springer; Lyrics, Joan Javits; Directed
by Michael Ross; Set and Lighting, Paul
Barnes; Costumes, Robert Mackintosh; Musical
Direction and Orchestrations, Gershon Kings-
ley; Incidental Dances, Bradford Craig.

CAST

Benoit Pinglet	Phil Leeds
Angelique Pinglet	Jo Anne Worley
Marcelle Paillardin	Marian Mercer
Henri Paillardin	Lee Cass
Victoire	Linda Lavin
Maxime	Paul Sand
Matthieu	Ned Wertimer
Yvette	Lucille Kane
Georgette	Jean Kane
Suzette	Maureen Kane
Flower Lady	Lois Zetter
Sandwich-board Man	Paul Sand
Concierge	Art Wallace
Bellboy	Robert Rovin
Tart	Lois Zetter
Sailor	Peter Maloney
Enrico	Adam Petroski
Baroness	Jean Kane
Inspector Boucard	Roger Hamilton
Policeman	Dutch Miller
Street Performers	Linda Lavin, Paul Sand

MUSICAL NUMBERS: "Not Getting Any
Younger," "What A Curious Girl," "We'll Suf-
fer Together," "A Perfectly Charming Visit,"
"You Gay Dog You!," "Hotel Passionato,"
"Don't," "What Is This Sensation?," "Tea-
Tea-Tea," "Hot Water Bottles," "Good, Good,
Good," "Tomorrow When The World Comes
Crashing Down Around Our Ears," "Marry
Me," "What A Night!," "The Confrontation,"
"We Saw Everybody There," Finale.

A Musical Comedy in two acts and five
scenes. The action takes place in and around
Paris in 1912.

Press: Shirley Herz

° Closed Sunday, October 31, 1965.
(11 performances)

The Kane Triplets, Ned Wertimer, Jo Anne Worley
Top: Marian Mercer, Phil Leeds

Paul Sand, Linda Lavin

Friedman-Abeles Photos

Jack Eddleman, Charlotte Jones
Top: (L & R) Joleen Fodor, Allan Bruce

THEATRE FOUR

Opened Wednesday, November 10, 1965.°
Scotia Productions in association with
Edward H. Davis present:

GREAT SCOT!

Book, Mark Conradt and Gregory Dawson;
Music, Don McAfee; Lyrics, Nancy Leeds;
Directed by Charles Tate; Scenery, Herbert
Senn, Helen Pond; Costumes, Patton Campbell;
Musical Direction, Joseph Raposo; Orchestra-
tions, Stephen Lawrence; Lighting, Theda Tay-
lor; Additional Orchestrations, Joseph Raposo,
Gershon Kingsley; Musical Staging, Joyce
Trisler; Production Assistants, Anita Berman,
Robert Essex.

CAST

Robert Burns	Allan Bruce
Jean Armour	Joleen Fodor
McGurk, Creech	Jack Eddleman
Heather, Duchess of Montrose, Fish Monger	Charlotte Jones
Gilbert, Rev. Dillingham, Duke of Montrose	Cash Baxter
James Armour, Duffy	Charles Hudson
Jamie	Arthur Whitfield
MacCohen, Constable, Bishop	Thomas Boyd
MacIntosh, Sailor, Town Elder	Charles Burks
Maggie, Mackerel, Lady Louise Glenpatrick	Shirley Caballero
Agnes McGurk, Lady Cynthia	Ginger Gerlach
Allison, Lucy	Mary Jo Gillis
Clarinda	Anita Maye
Lorna, Salmon	Lois Ann Saunders
Jock, Town Elder	Dale Westerman
Jennie	Camelot Guinevere

MUSICAL NUMBERS: "You're The Only
One," "Great Scot!," "I'll Find A Dream
Somewhere," "He's Not For Me," "She's Not
For Me," "Dance," "That Special Day,"
"Brandy In Your Champagne," "I'm Gonna
Have A Baby," "Original Sin," "I'll Still
Love Jean," "Where Is That Rainbow," "Prin-
ces' Street," "Happy New Year," "The Big-
bellied Bottle," "He Knows Where To Find
Me," "Where Does A Man Begin?," "What
A Shame," "I Left A Dream Somewhere,"
"We're Gonna Have A Wedding."

A Musical in two acts and twenty scenes.
The action takes place in Scotland in 1783-4.

General Manager: Edward H. Davis
Company Manager: Oscar Abraham
Press: David Rothenberg, Peter Bogart
Stage Managers: Fred Reinglas, Steve Wright

° Closed Sunday, December 12, 1965.
(38 performances)

Martha Holmes Photos

Tresa Hughes, Barnard Hughes, Agnes Young
Above: Faye Dunaway, Tom Ahearne

THE AMERICAN PLACE THEATRE

Opened Thursday, November 11, 1965.* (Moved January 7, 1966 to East 74th Street Theatre)
The American Place Theatre (Sidney Lanier, President; Wynn Handman, Artistic Director) in association with Norman Kean presents:

HOGAN'S GOAT

By William Alfred; Directed by Frederick Rolf; Scenery, Lighting, and Costumes by Kert Lundell; Music Consultant, Chan Daniels; Technical Director, Joseph Guadagni; Production Assistant, Irene Galombos.

CAST

Matthew Stanton ---------- Ralph Waite†1
Kathleen Stanton ---------- Faye Dunaway†2
John "Black Jack" Haggerty ---- Roland Wood
Petey Boyle ---------- Cliff Gorman
Bessie Legg ---------- Michaele Myers†3
Maria Haggerty ---------- Grania O'Malley
Father Stanislaus Coyne ---------- Barnard Hughes
Father Maloney ---------- John Dorman
Edward Quinn ---------- Tom Ahearne
James "Palsy" Murphy ---------- Conrad Bain
Bill ---------- Luke Wymbs†4
Ann Mulcahy ---------- Agnes Young†5
Josephine Finn ---------- Tresa Hughes
Boylan ---------- Tom Crane
Doctor ---------- David Dawson
Constituents: Eileen Fitzpatrick, Jack Fogarty, John Hoffmeister, Monica MacCormack, Michael Murray, Bruce Waite, Albert Shipley, Francis Ireland
Piano ---------- Stan Sussman†6

UNDERSTUDIES: Matthew, Arlen Dean Snyder; Kathleen, Bessie, Lilyan Wilder; Quinn, Murphy, Coyne, John Haggerty, Dan Morgan; Maria, Ann, Josephine, Paddy Crift

A Drama in two acts and nine scenes. The action takes place in the City of Brooklyn in April of 1890.

General Manager: Norman Kean
Company Manager: Max Gendel
Press: Phillip Bloom, Betty Lee Hunt, Fred Weterick
Stage Managers: Peter Galambos, William Tynan, Owen Ryan, Smith Lawrence

* Still playing May 31, 1966.

† Succeeded by: 1. Richard Mulligan, 2. Kay Chevalier, Karen McCrary, 3. Betty Oakes, 4. James Cashman, 5. Sheila Coonan, 6. David Schoming.

Ralph Waite, Faye Dunaway. Above: (L) Kay Chevalier,
Richard Mulligan, (R) Tom Ahearne, Tresa Hughes

ST. MARK'S PLAYHOUSE

Opened Monday, November 15, 1965.°
Robert Hooks Inc. presents:

HAPPY ENDING
and
DAY OF ABSENCE

By Douglas Turner Ward; Directed by
Philip Meister; Associate Producers, Juanita
Poitier, Doris Kuller; Sets and Lighting, Richard
Seger; Costumes, Whitney Blausen; Assistant
Director, Hal De Windt; Makeup, Raseac;
Assistant to the Producers, Cliff Frazier.

"Happy Ending"
CAST

Ellie	Esther Rolle
Vi	Frances Foster
Junie	Robert Hooks[1]
Arthur	Douglas Turner

A Comedy in one act. The action takes
place at the present time in the kitchen of
a Harlem tenement.

"Day Of Absence"
CAST

Clem	Lonne Elder
Luke	Arthur French
John	Robert Hooks[1]
Mary	Barbara Ann Teer[2]
First Operator	Hattie Winston
Second Operator	Maxine Griffith
Third Operator	Pamela Jones
Supervisor	Frances Foster[3]
Jackson	Adolph Caesar[4]
Mayor	Douglas Turner
First Citizen	Moses Gunn[5]
Second Citizen	Lonne Elder
Third Citizen	Arthur French
Industrialist	Moses Gunn[5]
Businessman	Lonne Elder
Clubwoman	Esther Rolle
Courier	Bostic Van Felton
Announcer	Mark Shapiro
Clan	Douglas Turner
Aide	Frances Foster
Pious	Moses Gunn[5]
Doll Woman	Hattie Winston
Brush Man	Robert Hooks[1]
Mop Man	Arthur French
Rastus	Moses Gunn[5]

A Comedy in one act. The action takes
place at the present time in an unnamed
Southern town.

General Management: Krone-Olim Management
Press: Howard Atlee, Michael Alpert,
David Roggensack
Stage Manager: Hal De Windt

° Still playing May 31, 1966.

† Succeeded by: 1. Billy Dee Williams, 2.
Frances Foster, 3. Tina Nurse, 4. L. Errol
Jaye, 5. Joseph Attles.

Bert Andrews Photos

Douglas Turner, Arthur French, Lonne Elder
Top: Robert Hooks, Frances Foster, Douglas Turner
Ward, Esther Rolle in "Happy Ending"
Left: Robert Hooks, Barbara Ann Teer in
"Day Of Absence"

POCKET THEATRE

Opened Thursday, November 18, 1965.°
CAM Productions present:

BUGS
and
VERONICA

By John White; Directed by Anna Sokolow;
Designed by Koski-Long; Original Music, Teo
Macero.

"Bugs"
CAST

Mrs. Rounce .... Alice Scudder
George Rounce .... Dylan Green
Millicent Marsh .... Joan Tyson
Mr. Rounce .... Jess Osuna
A Social Worker .... Lorraine Serabian

A Drama in one act. The action takes
place at the present time in the living room
of a tired frame house in industrial America.
Though in need of a paint job, it is, none-
theless, immaculate.

"Veronica"
CAST

Lou Long .... Bernard Grant
Leo Lane .... Ralph Bell
Plug .... Dylan Green
Liz .... Lorraine Serabian
Freck .... Jess Osuna

A Comedy in one act. The action takes
place at the present time in the choice suite
of a second-rate hotel on upper Broadway in
New York City.

Press: Arthur Cantor, Artie Solomon,
Donna Silberberg
Stage Manager: Art Wolff

° Closed Sunday, January 30, 1966.
(75 performances)

Dylan Green, Lorraine Serabian, Ralph Bell,
Bernard Grant in "Veronica". Above: Joan Tyson,
Dylan Green, Alice Scudder in "Bugs"

EAST SEVENTY-FOURTH
STREET THEATRE

Opened Thursday, November 18, 1965.°
Norman Kean presents:

THE BERNARD SHAW STORY

Compiled and Arranged by Bramwell Fletcher; As presented at the Gate Theatre, Dublin, under the Direction of Hilton Edwards; Lighting, Owen Ryan; Assistant to the Producer, Marilyn S. Miller; Technical Director, Jene Youtt; Production Assistant, Maggie Grynastyl.

with
BRAMWELL FLETCHER

A Dramatic Portrait as drawn by Mr. Fletcher from Shaw's own words, and presented in two parts.

Press: Ben Kornzweig, Reginald Denenholz, Anne Woll
Stage Manager: Gary Peterson

° Closed Sunday, January 2, 1966 after a limited engagement of 54 performances.

Friedman-Abeles Photo

Bramwell Fletcher as Bernard Shaw

THEATRE 62

Opened Saturday, November 20, 1965.*
The Theatre of The Zanies presents:

AN IMPUDENT WOLF

Written and directed by J. I. Rodale; Setting, J. I. Rodale; Lighting, Norman Blumenfeld.

CAST

Little Red .... Elaine Laurence
D. A. .... Barry Jay
Grandma .... Marcia Lewis
Clerk .... Liliane Simonet
Wolf .... Alvin Cohen
Judge .... Ed Lauter
Coffee House Poet .... Antony Tenuta
Bus Driver .... Rusty Dore
Mad Hatter .... Rusty Dore
The Proustian .... Roseanne Conte
Balloon Seller .... Antony Tenuta
Understudy .... Peter Freund

A Comedy in two acts.

Company Manager: Michael Gough
Press: Max Eisen, Carl Samrock
Stage Managers: Georgette C. Spelvin,
Roseanne Conte

* Closed Sunday, November 28, 1965.
(13 performances)

Alvin Cohen, Ed Lauter, Roseanne Conte. Above:
Elaine Laurence, Antony Tenuta, Marcia Lewis

Richard Kiley

Richard Kiley, Joan Diener, Irving Jacobson,
Ray Middleton, Robert Rounseville
Right: Richard Kiley, Irving Jacobson

ANTA WASHINGTON SQUARE THEATRE

Opened Monday, November 22, 1965.°
Albert W. Selden and Hal James present:

MAN OF LA MANCHA

Musical Play by Dale Wasserman; Book and Musical Staging, Albert Marre; Music, Mitch Leigh; Lyrics, Joe Darion; Choreography, Jack Cole; Settings and Lighting, Howard Bay; Costumes, Howard Bay and Patton Campbell; Musical Directions and Dance Arrangements, Neil Warner; Musical Arrangements, Music Makers, Inc.; An ANTA-Goodspeed Presentation; Production Assistant, Dwight Frye; Assistant Conductor, Robert Montesi; Original Cast Album by Kapp Records.

CAST

Don Quixote (Cervantes)	Richard Kiley†1
Sancho	Irving Jacobson
Aldonza	Joan Diener†2
The Innkeeper	Ray Middleton
The Padre	Robert Rounseville
Dr. Carrasco	Jon Cypher
Antonia	Mimi Turque
The Barber	Gino Conforti
Pedro, Head Muleteer	Shev Rodgers
Anselmo, a Muleteer	Harry Theyard
The Housekeeper	Eleanore Knapp
Jose, a Muleteer	Eddie Roll
Juan, a Muleteer	John Aristedes
Paco, a Muleteer	Antony De Vecchi
Tenorio, a Muleteer	Fernando Grahal
Maria, the innkeeper's wife	Marceline Decker
Fermina, a slavey	Gerrianne Raphael
Captain of The Inquisition	Renato Cibelli
Guitarist	David Serva

A Musical Play suggested by the life and works of Miguel de Cervantes y Saavedra and presented without intermission. All the characters in the play are imprisoned in a dungeon in Seville at the end of the sixteenth century. The entire action takes place there and in various other places in the imagination of Miguel de Cervantes.

General Manager: Walter Fried
Company Manager: Gino Giglio
Press: Arthur Cantor, Artie Solomon
Stage Managers: Mariel Sumner,
Michael Turque, Renato Cibelli

° Still playing May 31, 1966. Winner of Drama Critics Circle Award.

† Succeeded for two weeks by: 1. Jose Ferrer, 2. Gerrianne Raphael.

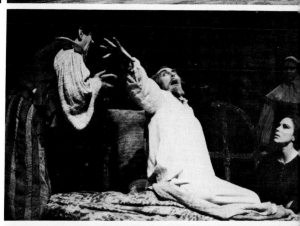

Bob Golby Photos

Ray Middleton, Richard Kiley, Irving Jacobson
Above: Irving Jacobson, Richard Kiley, Joan Diener   **139**

Adger Cowans Photos

MARTINIQUE THEATRE

Opened Sunday, November 28, 1965.°
Judith Rutherford Marechal, Paul Libin,
Jay Stanwyck present:

MEDEA

By Robinson Jeffers; Directed by Cyril
Simon; Setting, David Mitchell; Costumes,
Clifford Capone; Lighting, Roger Morgan; Pro-
duction Associates, Larry Goossen, Susan
Richardson; Production Assistant, John
Froscher.

CAST

The Nurse	Helen Craig†1
The Tutor	Paul B. Price
The Children	Tony Di Caprio†2,
	Paul Rufo
First Woman of Corinth	Rosemary Tory
Second Woman of Corinth	Annette Hunt
Third Woman of Corinth	Brenda Lesley
Medea	Gloria Foster
Creon	David Hooks†3
Jason	Michael Higgins†4
Aegeus	Mervyn Williams
Jason's Slave	Reno Roop
Attendants to Medea	Frances Siegal,
	Linda Simon
Soldier	Frank Savino

UNDERSTUDIES: Nurse, Rosemary Tory;
Creon, Jason, Frank Savino; Aegeus, Tutor,
Wil Albert

A Drama in two acts. The action takes
place before Medea's house in Corinth.

Press: Ben Kornzweig, Reginald Denenholz,
Anne Woll
Stage Manager: John Froscher

° Closed Sunday, February 13, 1966.
(77 performances)

† Succeeded by: 1. Virginia Downing, 2. Michael Rait, 3. John O'Shaughnessy, 4.
Frank Savino.

Gloria Foster, also above with Helen Craig

Tony Di Caprio, Gloria Foster, Paul Rufo

CIRCLE IN THE SQUARE

Opened Monday, December 6, 1965.°
Theodore Mann presents:

THE WHITE DEVIL

By John Webster; Directed by Jack Landau;
Setting, Peter Wexler; Lighting, Jules Fisher;
Costumes, Noel Taylor; Music, Herbert Harris;
Technical Assistant, Viktor Allen.

CAST

Count Lodovico	Paul Vincent
Gasparo	Ed Rombola
Vittoria Corombona	Carrie Nye†1
Duke of Brachiano	Paul Stevens†2
Flamineo	Frank Langella†3
Camillo	Frederic Warriner
Zanche	Terri Turner
Cornelia	Christine Pickles
Francisco De Medicis, Duke of Florence	Robert Burr†4
Cardinal Monticelso	Eric Berry†5
Isabella	Maria Tucci†6
Giovanni	Robert Benson Ross Burr, Peter Miner
Marcello	Peter Jacob
Doctor Julio	Al Corbin
A Lawyer	Ed Rombola
Matron	Jacqueline Britton
Carlo	Michael Boccio
Hortensio	Ralph Maurer
Silvio	John Culjak

A Drama presented in two parts. The action takes place in Rome and Padua.

Production Manager: Charles Hamilton
Press: Merle Debuskey, Violet Welles, Lawrence Belling
Stage Manager: Mark D. Healy

° Closed Sunday, April 17, 1966.
(152 performances)

† Succeeded by: 1. Maria Tucci, then Joyce Ebert, 2. Robert Milli, 3. Dino Narizzano, 4. Ramon Bieri, 5. Herbert Nelson, 6. Anna Shaler.

Friedman-Abeles Photos

Paul Stevens, Carrie Nye
Above: Maria Tucci, Paul Stevens
Top: Robert Burr, Carrie Nye, Eric Berry
Left: Frank Langella, Carrie Nye

RENATA THEATRE

Opened Thursday, December 16, 1965.°
Al Jordan presents:

THE PARASITE

By Robert N. Summers; Directed by Robert
N. Summers and Al Jordan; Art Direction,
Chester Delacruz; Lighting, Donald Gaymond.

CAST

Willie	Joseph R. Sicari
George Masters II	Peter Stuart
Dora Purvis	Ardyth Kaiser
Arthur Winslow	Louis Vuolo
Mathilde Stapler	Carole Ann Lewis
Selena Flood	Sheila Gary
Louise Delshaye	Joan Kroschell
George Masters, Jr.	Jay Barney

A Comedy in three acts and nine scenes.
The action takes place in a second floor room
in a Philadelphia rooming house.

Press: Richard Falk
Stage Manager: Lisa Mayo

° Closed Friday, December 17, 1965.
(2 performances)

SQUARE EAST

Opened Wednesday, December 22, 1965.°
Square East presents:

NEW COLE PORTER REVUE

Cast and Material Assembled and Directed
by Ben Bagley; Staged and Choreographed by
Buddy Schwab; Continuity, Special Vocal Arrangements, and Grand Finale written by Bud
McCreery; Musical Direction, Everett Gordon; Collage Paintings, Shirley Kaplan; Projections, Wallace Litwin; Costumes and Gowns,
Charles Fatone; Lighting, Jules Fisher; Per-
cussionist, Andrew Cyrille.

CAST

Dody Goodman	Danny Meehan
Bobby Short	Jane Manning
Carol Arthur	Virginia Vestoff

Standby: Al De Sio

A Revue in two parts using the songs of
Cole Porter.

Press: Merle Debuskey, Lawrence Belling
Stage Manager: John Molthen

° Closed Sunday, February 27, 1966.
(76 performances)

Friedman-Abeles, Avery Willard Photos

Danny Meehan, Dody Goodman, Bobby Short
Above: Carol Arthur, Bobby Short, Dody Goodman,
Jane Manning, Virginia Vestoff, Danny Meehan
Top: Sheila Gary in "The Parasite"

ACTORS PLAYHOUSE

Opened Wednesday, January 5, 1966.°
(Moved February 15, 1966 to Mermaid
Theatre)
The New Playwrights Productions Co., Inc.,
presents:

THE POCKET WATCH

By Alvin Aronson; Directed by Sherwood
Arthur; Set Design, Quinton Raines; Lighting,
Barbara Nollman.

CAST

Rachel Goldman	Rita Karin
Freda Goldman	Estelle Omens†1
Harold Schwartz	Daniel T. Frankel
Sophie Schwartz	Mimi Randolph†2
Chaim Goldman	Michael Gorrin
Sam Schwartz	Hy Anzell
Irving Friedman	C. M. Gampel

A Drama in three acts and nine scenes. The
action takes place during the summer of 1953
in Chaim Goldman's two-family house in a
run-down neighborhood of a small suburb
of Boston.

Press: David Lipsky, Marian Graham
Stage Managers: Paul Niven,
Quinton Raines, Thomas Lamon

° Still playing May 31, 1966.

† Succeeded by: 1. Mae Marmy, 2. Lucille
Hauser.

Right: Rita Karin, Daniel T. Frankel

Avery Willard Photos

Seated: Daniel T. Frankel, Rita Karin, Michael Gorrin. Standing: Mimi Randolph, Estelle Omens

Bert Andrews Photos

THE NEW THEATRE

Opened Sunday, January 9, 1966.°
Ivor David Balding for The Establishment Theatre Co., Inc. presents:

THE MAD SHOW

Book by Larry Siegel and Stan Hart; Based on MAD Magazine; Music, Mary Rodgers; Lyrics, Marshall Barer, Larry Siegel, Steven Vinaver; Scenery and Costumes, Peter Harvey; Lighting, V. C. Fuqua; Musical Director, Sam Pottle; Assistant to the Director, Rhoda Levine; Production Conceived and Directed by Alfred E. Neuman; Musical Consultant, John Anderson; Technical Assistant, Robert Drean.

CAST

Linda Lavin†1   Paul Sand†2
MacIntyre Dixon   Dick Libertini
Jo Anne Worley

ACT I: "Opening," "Academy Awards," "You Never Can Tell," "Getting To Know You," "Eccch," "Handle With Care," "The Real Thing," "Babysitter," "Primers," "Well It Ain't," "Misery Is," "Football In Depth," "Hate Song."

ACT II: "Kiddie T.V.," "Looking For Someone," "Zoom," "The Gift of Maggie (and others)," "Interview," "Snappy Answers," "T.V. Nik," "Transistors," "The Boy From," "The Irving Irving Story."

A Musical Revue in two acts and twenty-three scenes.

Executive Producer: Ivor David Balding
Company Manager: Thomas B. Burrows
Press: John Springer Associates, Walter Alford, Warren Pincus
Stage Managers: Gerald Simon, Dale Whitt
° Still playing May 31, 1966.
† Succeeded by: 1. Carol Morley, Mitzi McCall, 2. Charlie Brill.

Paul Sand, Linda Lavin, Jo Anne Worley. Above: MacIntyre Dixon, Dick Libertini

CHERRY LANE THEATER

Opened Thursday, January 27, 1966.°
Gene Persson, Edwin Wilson and Hy
Silverman present:

ROOMS

By Stanley Mann; Directed by George
Keathley; Sets and Lighting, C. Murawski;
Associate Producer, Margaret T. Barker; Pro-
duction Assistant, Melinda Page.

"Better Luck Next Time"
CAST

Bellhop _____ Charles Davisson
William Foster _____ James Broderick
Jenny Zubitsky _____ Shirley Knight
Potter _____ Charles Davisson
Miss Quincey _____ Irene Dailey

The action takes place in three scenes in
a suite on the twentieth floor of a New York
hotel.

"A Walk In Dark Places"
CAST

Dr. Robert Palmer _____ James Broderick
Mrs. Levene _____ Dorothy Raymond
Mrs. Henry _____ Irene Dailey
Helen Windsor _____ Shirley Knight

The action, in three scenes, takes place in
Dr. Palmer's office on the twentieth floor of a
building in Manhattan.

General Manager: John J. Miller
Press: John Springer Associates,
Walter Alford, Warren Pincus
Stage Managers: Dennis Eubanks,
Charles Davisson

° Closed Sunday, March 13, 1966. (54 performances)

Friedman-Abeles Photos

Irene Dailey, James Broderick, Shirley Knight
in "Better Luck Next Time". Above: Shirley Knight
James Broderick, Irene Dailey in
"A Walk In Dark Places"

146

JAN HUS PLAYHOUSE

Opened Wednesday, February 9, 1966.°
The American Revival Company (John Marqusee, Amnon Kabatchnik, Lewis Murray) presents:

WINTERSET

By Maxwell Anderson; Directed by Amnon Kabatchnik; Setting, Richard Bianchi; Costumes, Dina Harris; Lighting, Barbara Nollman; Sound, Paul John Austin; Production Assistant, Lee Beltzer; Violin Solos, H. W. Frankel.

CAST

Man in Blue	Buck Anderson
Man in Grey	Michael Talcott
Shadow	Robert Kya-Hill
Trock	Lester Rawlins
Lucio	Dominic Chianese
Piny	Virgilia Chew
Garth	Nick Padula
Miriamne	Patricia McAneny
Esdras	Sol Serlin
The Hobo	Leib Lensky
Streetwalker	Caroline Faulkner
First Girl	Carol Florence
Second Girl	Joyce Lee
Judge Gaunt	Warren Wade
Mio	Joseph Hindy
Carr	Joel Stuart
Herman	James Adrian Cohen
A Sailor	Tom Krichbaum
Radical	Kermit Brown
Policeman	Irwin Rosen
Sergeant	Paul John Austin

A Drama in three acts. The action takes place on the bank of a river, and in a cellar apartment in the early 1930's.

General Manager: Derek Mali
Press: Howard Atlee, David Roggensack
Stage Manager: Robert Stevenson

° Closed Sunday, March 6, 1966. (30 performances)

...tricia McAneny, Joseph Hindy. Top: Warren Wade,
...Sol Serlin, Patricia McAneny, Paul John Austin,
...vin Rosen, Joseph Hindy, Nick Padula, Leib Lensky

James Pritchett, Mildred Dunnock
Above: (Left and Right) Beatrice Straight, Mildred Dunnock

Friedman-Abeles Photos

GREENWICH MEWS THEATRE

Opened Thursday, February 10, 1966.°
IASTA presents:

PHÈDRE

By Jean Racine; English Version by William Packard; Directed by Paul-Emile Deiber; Sets, Geri Davis; Costumes, Sylvia Kalegi; Lighting, David Arkin; Hair Styles, Daniel C. Romanello; Music, Jean-Baptiste Moreau.

CAST

Hippolyte	Michael Durrell
Theramene	Sam Haigler Henry
Oenone	Mildred Dunnock†
Phedre	Beatrice Straight
Panope	Valerie von Volz
Aricie	Anne Draper
Theseus	James Pritchett
Ismene	Marguerite Hunt

A Drama presented in two parts. The action takes place in Trezene, a city in the Peloponnesos.

Company Manager: C. George Willard
Press: Merle Debuskey, Lawrence Belling, Violet Welles, Mae S. Hong
Stage Managers: Aida Alvarez, Tom Keo

° Closed Sunday, May 8, 1966 after a record-breaking 100 performances.

† Succeeded by Dorothy Hatch, then Dorothy Sands.

Beatrice Straight, Dorothy Sands
Top: Sam Haigler Henry, Dorothy Sands,
Michael Durrell

Beatrice Straight, James Pritchett

BLACKFRIARS' THEATRE

Opened Tuesday, February 1, 1966.°
The Blackfriars' Guild of New York, Inc.
presents:

CONSIDER THE LILIES

By Rev. Edward A. Molloy; Directed by
Walter Cool; Settings, T. Fabian; Costumes,
Alice Merrigal; Lighting, Marvin Gingold;
Decor, Robert Charles.

CAST

Pietro, Member of Catherine's
  company _____ Duke Howze,
                                   Len Schropfer
Father Raymond,
  Confessor to Catherine _____ Roy J. Lenahan,
                                   Steven Parris
Catherine of Siena _____ Barbara Coggin,
                                   Ruth Ballew
Count William de Beaufort, Father of
  Pope Gregory XI _____ Karl E. Williams,
                           Lawrence J. Buckley
Pierre Cardinal d'Estaing of
  Papal Court _____ William H. Cox,
                                    John Rush
Lady Elys de Turenne, Wife of
  Pope Gregory's nephew _____ Joan Lake,
                               Ann D'Andrea
Pope Gregory XI, the 200th
  Pontiff _____ Christopher Smith,
                                 A. J. Embie
Louis, Duke of Anjou, Brother of
  King Charles V of France ____ Gerald Denning,
                                 Bryan Hull

A Drama in two acts and seven scenes.
The entire action takes place between mid-
June and mid-September of 1376.

Press: Rev. Thomas F. Carey
Stage Managers: Robert Charles,
Marie Stuart, Judy Smith

° Closed Saturday, April 30, 1966.
(82 performances)

Joan Lake, Barbara Coggin
Above: Christopher Smith, Gerald Denning

Opened Sunday, February 13, 1966.°
Alton Wilkes and Jim Mendenhall Productions present:

THE DEADLY GAME

By James Yaffe; Director by Alton Wilkes;
Sets and Lighting, Richard Jackson; Executive
Technical Director, Ben Wampler; Technical
Director, Bryan Sheedy.

CAST

Emile Carpeau	Albert M. Ottenheimer
Bernard Laroque	Rudolf Weiss
Joseph Pillet	Lance Cunard
Nicole	Jana Klenburg[1]
Howard Trapp	Chet London[2]
Gustave Kummer	Roger De Koven[4]
Pierre	Michael O'Dowd
A Visitor	Paula Shaw[3]

A Drama in two acts and three scenes. The
entire action takes place in the house of Emile
Carpeau in the Swiss Alps at the present
time.

Press: David P. Rothenberg, Louise Weiner,
Larry Schneider
Stage Manager: Jim Hall

° Closed Sunday, May 15, 1966. (105 performances) Original production opened Feb. 2,
1960 and ran for 39 performances. See
THEATRE WORLD, Vol. 16.

† Succeeded by: 1. Paula Shaw, 2. Jim
Mendenhall, 3. Charlotte Glenn, 4. Drew
Eliot.

Friedman-Abeles Photos

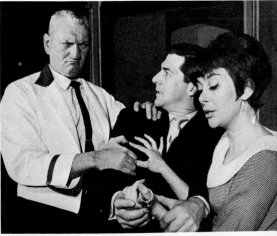

Roger De Koven, Paula Shaw, Rudolf Weiss
Above: Lance Cunard, Chet London

Rudolf Weiss, Roger De Koven, Jana Klenburg,
Albert M. Ottenheimer, Lance Cunard
Above: Michael O'Dowd, Chet London, Jana Klenburg

THE AMERICAN PLACE THEATRE

Opened Tuesday, February 15, 1966.°
The American Place Theatre (Sidney Lanier, President; Wynn Handman, Artistic Director) at St. Clement's Church presents:

JONAH

By Paul Goodman; Directed by Lawrence Kornfeld; Sets, Costumes, and Choreography, Remy Charlip; Music, Meyer Kupferman; Lighting, Roger Morgan; Technical Director, Stanley Rosenberg; Production Coordinator, Julia Miles.

CAST

Angel	Earle Hyman
Hephzibah	Ruth Jaroslow
Jonah	Sorrell Booke
Captain	John A. Coe
A Sailor	Jamil Zakkai
Sailors	Burt Supree, Jay Fletcher
Passengers	Richard Frisch, William Shorr, Stephanie Turash, Yolande Bavan
Angel Helpers	Larrio Ekson, Carl Wilson
Peasant	William Shorr
Guide	John A. Coe
Ninevites	Jay Fletcher, Carl Wilson, Pamela Jones, Larrio Ekson, Stephanie Turash, Richard Frisch
Cow	Ruth Jaroslow
Singer	Yolande Bavan
Courtier	Jeff Rock
Duchess	Marcia Kurtz
Lady	Gretchen MacLane
Duke	Jamil Zakkai
King	Robert Frink
Martial Singer	Richard Frisch
Coloratura	Stephanie Turash
Heavenly Counselors	Aileen Passloff, Marcia Kurtz, Burt Supree, Jay Fletcher, Gretchen MacLane
Worm	Yolande Bavan
Harpsichord	Robert Shattuck
Oboe, Recorder	Cary Karp

MUSICAL NUMBERS: "Leviathan," "Hey What's This?," "Sailor's Round," "Evocation," "Jonah's Melodrama," "I'll Carry You An Inch," "Puppet Dream," "Sleep Little Mouse," "I Cried For My Troubles," "My God, Why Hast Thou Forsaken Me?," "Forty Days," "There's Nothing New Under The Sun," "Miserere," "Day After Day," "The Suns That Daily Rise," "Angel's Ballet," "Madrigal," "I Am A Little Worm," "Paradise Quintet."

A Play with Music in two acts and nine scenes.

General Manager: Arthur Waxman
Press: John Springer Associates, Walter Alford, Warren Pincus
Stage Managers: Peter Galambos, William Tynan

° Closed Sunday, March 6, 1966.
(24 performances)

Martha Holmes Photos

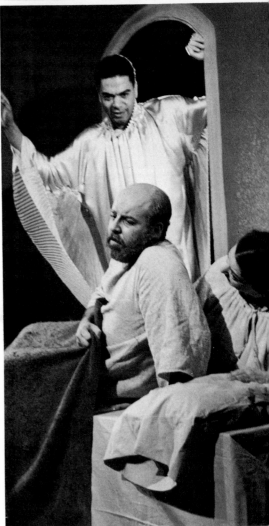

Earl Hyman, Sorrell Booke, Ruth Jaroslow
Top: Sorrell Booke, Robert Frink

ACTORS PLAYHOUSE
Opened Tuesday, March 1, 1966.°
The Loft presents:

THE COOP

By Ralph S. Arzoomanian; Directed by Martin Fried; Setting, Quinton Raines; Lighting, Barbara Nollman; Production Manager, Charles Gray; Producers, Lyn Austin, Ann McIntosh, Janet Coleman.

CAST
Danny .... Clifton James
Bazakis .... Andreas Voutsinas
Chicken .... Ron Van Lieu
Toby .... James Spruill
Sylvester .... William LeMassena
Peggy .... Patricia Fay

Standby: William Bush

A Drama presented without intermission. The action takes place in a prison cell.

Company Manager: James Walsh
Press: Samuel Lurie, Stanley F. Kaminsky
Stage Managers: Charles Gray,
Theresa Hill, Timothy Gordon,
Timothy Reynolds

° Closed Sunday, March 20, 1966.
(24 performances)

Bert Andrews Photo

BOUWERIE LANE THEATRE
Opened Tuesday, March 1, 1966.°
Cliff James presents:

LAUGHWIND

By Tom Waters; Directed by Mr. Waters; Sets, Elmon Webb; Lighting, Carl Seltzer; Assistant to the Producer, Karen Phillips.

CAST
Nell O'Shaunnessy .... Judith Younger
Jim O'Shaunnessy .... Donald Hylan
Morgan O'Shaunnessy .... Eugene Roche
John Hogan .... Walter Flanagan
Martina Lesko .... Vanda Barra

A Comedy in three acts and five scenes. The action takes place at the present time in the kitchen of the O'Shaunnessy family on Manhattan's West Side near the docks, and in Hogan's Bar.

General Management: Krone-Olim Management
Press: Howard Atlee, Michael Alpert,
David Roggensack
Stage Manager: Richard Hamilton

° Closed Sunday, March 6, 1966.
(7 performances)

William LeMassena. Above: Clifton James, ...mes Spruill, William LeMassena in "The Coop"
Right: Judith Younger, Eugene Roche, Donald Hylan in "Laughwind"

STAGE 73

Opened Saturday, March 5, 1966.°
The Establishment Theatre Co., Inc.
(Directors: Ivor David Balding, Peter
Cook, Joseph E. Levine) presents:

MONOPOLY

Four Plays by Peter Kass; Directed by
Daniel Petrie; Settings, Alan Kimmel; Costumes, Patricia Quinn Stuart; Lighting, Jules
Fisher; Executive Producer, Ivor David Balding; Production Associate, Peter L. Bellwood

"Make Like A Dog"

CAST

Elvira Miller ---------------------- Carolan Daniels
Stanley Miller ------------------------- Jess Osuna

The action takes place on a Sunday afternoon in a suburban New York home at the
present time.

"Suburban Tragedy"

CAST

Mr. Stein ---------------------------- John Karlen
Barbara Lang ---------------------- Deborah White
Mrs. Goldman ---------------------- Estelle Parsons

The action takes place on a Friday afternoon in a college classroom outside New York
at the end of summer.

"Princess Rebecca Birnbaum"

CAST

Elsie -------------------------------- Francine Beer
Shirley ----------------------------- Estelle Parsons
Helen ------------------------------ Carolan Daniels
Rebecca ---------------------------- Deborah White
Maury ------------------------------ Roy London

The action takes place on a Friday evening
early in June in a Bronx living room at the
present time.

"Young Marrieds Play
Monopoly"

CAST

Ruth -------------------------------- Avra Petrides
Joe ---------------------------------- John Karlen
Adam -------------------------------- Jess Osuna
Ava ---------------------------------- Carolan Daniels

The action takes place at the present time
late on a Saturday evening in the livingroom
of a Bronx luxury apartment.

UNDERSTUDIES: For Misses Daniels and
Petrides, Kathy Shawn; for Messrs. Karlen and
Osuna, John Mahon; for Miss White, Carol
MacCormack

General Manager: Thomas B. Burrows
Company Manager: James Walsh
Press: Walter Alford, Louise Weiner,
Paul Solomon, John Springer Associates
Stage Manager: Tom Iannicelli

° Closed Sunday, April 17, 1966. (51 performances)

Jess Osuna, Carolan Daniels in "Make Like A Dog"
Above: Roy London, Deborah White in "Princess
Rebecca Birnbaum". Top: Estelle Parsons,
John Karlen in "Suburban Tragedy". Right: John
Karlen, Avra Petrides in
"Young Marrieds Play Monopoly"

John Colicos, Jeanne Hepple
in
"SERJEANT MUSGRAVE'S DANCE"

155

THEATRE DE LYS

Opened Tuesday, March 8, 1966.°
Ivor David Balding for The Establishment Co., Inc. (Directors: Ivor David
Balding, Peter Cook, Joseph E. Levine)
by arrangement with Lucille Lortel Productions, Inc. presents:

SERJEANT MUSGRAVE'S
DANCE

By John Arden; Directed by Stuart Burge;
Scenery, Ed Wittstein; Costumes, Theoni V.
Aldredge; Lighting, Jules Fisher; Music, Dud-
ley Moore; Dances, Rhoda Levine; Production
Manager, Charles Maryan; Associate Producers,
Peter L. Bellwood, Thomas Burrows, Jay
Stanwyck.

CAST

Private Sparky	Terry Lomax
Private Hurst	Roy R. Scheider
Private Attercliffe	Leigh Wharton
Bludgeon, a bargee	David Doyle
Serjeant Musgrave	John Colicos†1
The Parson	Thomas Barbour
Mrs. Hitchcock	Charlotte Jones†2
Annie	Jeanne Hepple
The Constable	John P. Ryan
The Mayor	Dan Durning
A slow collier	Simm Landres
A pugnacious collier	Paul Hecht†3
Walsh, an earnest collier	W. B. Brydon†4
Trooper of Dragoons	Walter Hadler
Officer of Dragoons	Roger Hamilton
Colliers	Guy Bon Giovanni, James Davis, Jerry Hopkins

A Drama in three acts and eight scenes.
The action takes place in a mining town in the
north of England in the middle of the last
century during winter.

General Manager: Thomas B. Burrows
Company Manager: Paul B. Berkowsky
Press: John Springer Associates,
Walter Alford, Louise Weiner,
Paul Solomon
Stage Manager: Bernie Passeltiner

° Still playing May 31, 1966.

† Succeeded by: 1. W. B. Brydon, 2. Joan
White, Louise Larabee, 3. Walter Hadler, 4.
Paul Hecht.

156

Friedman-Abeles Photos

David Doyle, John Colicos, Terry Lomax
Above: W. B. Brydon, Roy R. Scheider,
Leigh Wharton, John Colicos
Top: Terry Lomax, Jeanne Hepple
Left: John Colicos

THEATRE FOUR

Opened Wednesday, March 9, 1966.°
Jeff Britton presents:

HOORAY! IT'S A GLORIOUS DAY . . . AND ALL THAT

Book, Maurice Teitelbaum, Charles Grodin; Music, Arthur Gordon; Lyrics, Ethel Bieber, Maurice Teitelbaum, Charles Grodin; Directed by Charles Grodin; Choreographed by Sandra Devlin; Scenery and Costumes, Peter Harvey; Lighting, Jules Fisher; Musical Direction and Vocal Arrangements, Peter Fuchs; Dance Arrangements, Lannie Meyers; Orchestrations, Gershon Kingsley; Production Assistants, Willard Bond, Gene Warner; Technical Director, Stanley Rosenberg.

CAST

J. K. Pfeffer	Daniel Keyes
Russell Underhand	Lou David
Maggie Martyr	Lois Holmes
Miss Blossom	Laverne Burden
Carl Strong	Ronald Holgate
Fuggsy	Louis Criscuolo
Villie	John Kane
Rose Pfeffer	Joan Eastman
Betty Plain	Mina Kolb
Kitty Sweetness	Joan Kroschell
Tap Dancer	Benny Smith
Nick	Raymond Allen
Customer	Don Emmons
Willard Gerard Ryan	Raymond Allen

SINGERS: Charles Burks, Joy Franz, Rosemary McNamara, Wilson Robey, William Wendt.

DANCERS: Pat Cope, Wilson Robey, Michael Maurer, Ann McKinley, Terry Nicholson, Lynn Simonson, Benny Smith, Jaclynn Villamil

UNDERSTUDIES: Carl, William Wendt; Kitty, Rosemary McNamara; Rose, Joy Franz

MUSICAL NUMBERS: "He's A Comin'," "I Hope He's Not Ashamed Of Me," "Happy," "What's A Gang Without A Guy Named Fuggsy?," "I Wish I Knew," "Love Was A Stranger To Me," "Tap Dance," "Nasality," "The Wonderland of Love," "Dear Diary, For Example," "It's A Glorious Day," "Panic Ballet," "Inspirational Song," "You're Gorgeous, You're Fantastic," "Everything Happens For The Best."

A Musical Comedy in two acts and ten scenes. The action takes place in New York City.

General Manager: Jeff Britton
Press: Frank Goodman, Martin Shwartz, Ruth Cage
Stage Manager: Fred Reinglas

Closed Sunday, March 20, 1966. (15 performances)

Alan Grossman Photos

Joan Kroschell, Mina Kolb

Ronald Holgate, Joan Kroschell, Mina Kolb
Above: Joan Eastman
Top: Benny Smith, Jaclynn Villamil, Lynn Simonson, Ann McKinley, Joan Eastman

157

William Mooney

PLAYERS THEATRE

Opened Sunday, March 13, 1966.°
Yvette Schumer and Ronald Much
present:

HALF HORSE, HALF ALLIGATOR

Material arranged by William Moo
Lighting, Roger Morgan.

CAST
William Mooney

An interpretation in regional dialects
nineteenth century American humor in
works of Mark Twain, James Russell Lo
Seba Smith, James Kirke Paulding, Ge
Washington Harris, Sol Smith, David Cro
and others.

Press: David Rothenberg
Stage Manager: John Swearingen

° Closed Sunday, April 10, 1966. (32
formances) First presented at Vien
English Theatre on September 4, 196

Opened Tuesday, March 22, 1966.°
Red Barn Theatre Ltd. presents:

LUDLOW FAIR
and
THE MADNESS OF LADY BRIGHT

By Lanford Wilson; Directed by William Hunt; Sets and Lighting, David F. Segal; Costume Supervision, Kapi Reith; Assistant to the Producer, Cynthia Zeger; Production Assistant, Bobbie Wood.

CAST
"Ludlow Fair"

Rachel ⸻ Ann Wedgeworth
Agnes ⸻ Sasha von Scherler

The action takes place at the present time on an evening in February about 11:30 P.M. in an East Side apartment in the 80's in Manhattan.

"The Madness Of Lady Bright"

Leslie Bright ⸻ Cris Alexander
Voices: Joanne Marsic, Barry Woloski

The action takes place at the present time on a Saturday afternoon in summer in Leslie Bright's West Side apartment in the 80's in Manhattan.

Company Manager: Joseph Leberman
Press: Saul Richman, Eleanor McCann

° Closed Sunday, April 3, 1966.
(15 performances)

Avery Willard Photos

Sasha von Scherler, Ann Wedgeworth in "Ludlow Fair"
Above: Cris Alexander in
"The Madness Of Lady Bright"

MARTINIQUE THEATRE

Opened Monday and Tuesday, April 11 and 12, 1966.°
Circle In The Square (Theodore Mann and Paul Libin) present:

6 FROM LA MAMA

Directed by Tom O'Horgan; Lighting, Jose Sevilla; Music, Tom O'Horgan; Artistic Coordinator, Tania Leontov.

Bill One

"Thank You, Miss Victoria"
by William Hoffman

Harry Judson .... Michael Warren Powell
Miss Genovese .... Jacque Lynn Colton
Office Boy .... Kevin O'Connor
Second Office Boy .... Victor LiPari

"This Is The Rill Speaking"
by Lanford Wilson

Jacque Lynn Colton, Michael Warren Powell, Mari-Claire Charba, Victor LiPari, Kevin O'Connor

"Birdbath"
by Leonard Melfi

Velma Sparrow .... Mari-Claire Charba
Frankie Basta .... Kevin O'Connor

Bill Two

"War"
by Jean-Claude van Itallie

Older Actor .... Michael Warren Powell
Younger Actor .... Kevin O'Connor
The Lady .... Mari-Claire Charba

"The Recluse"
by Paul Foster

The Recluse .... Jacque Lynn Colton
Jezebel .... Mari-Claire Charba

"Chicago"
by Sam Shepard

Stu .... Kevin O'Connor
Joy............................ Mari-Claire Charba
Myra .... Jacque Lynn Colton
Joe .... Victor LiPari
Sally .... Stephanie Gordon
Jim .... Michael Warren Powell

Production Manager: Charles Hamilton
Press: Merle Debuskey, Lawrence Belling, Violet Welles, Mae S. Hong
Stage Manager: Tom O'Horgan

° Closed Sunday, April 24, 1966. (16 performances) Program was reduced April 13 to "This Is The Rill Speaking," "Chicago," and "Birdbath," and title changed to "3 From La Mama."

James D. Gossage Photos

160

Michael Warren Powell in "Thank You, Miss Victo
Above: Kevin O'Connor, Mari-Claire
Charba in "Birdbath". Top: Jacque Lynn Colto
Mari-Claire Charba in "This Is The Rill Speaking

MASQUE THEATRE
Opened Monday, April 18, 1966.°
Gregory Reardon presents:

WHEN WE DEAD AWAKEN

By Henrik Ibsen; Director, Henry Calvert; Production Designer, Edward Haynes; Lighting, Fred Allison; Production Assistant, Mandy Evans.

CAST

Maia Rubek	Roslyn Valero
Professor Rubek	Peter Murphy
Inspector	George Axler
Irene	Rosemary Tory
Sister of Mercy	Pat McAndrew
Ulfheim	Jack Ramage

UNDERSTUDIES: George Axler, Pat McAndrew

A Drama in three acts. The action takes place at the Hotel Baths, in a region near a mountain health resort, and on a wind-driven mountainside, at anytime.

Press: David Lipsky, Marian Graham
Stage Manager: Edmund Williams

° Closed Sunday, April 24, 1966.
(9 performances)

Left: Rosemary Tory, Peter Murphy

Bob Klein, Sandra Caron, Fred Willard

SQUARE EAST
Opened Thursday, April 21, 1966.°
Bernard Sahlins presents:

THE RETURN OF THE SECOND CITY
in
"20,000 Frozen Grenadiers"

Directed by Sheldon Patinkin; Music Composed by William Mathieu and Will Holt; Musical Director, William Mathieu; Artistic Director, Sheldon Patinkin; Lighting, Ken Glickfeld.

CAST

Sandra Caron	Bob Klein
Judy Graubart	David Steinberg

Fred Willard

An evening of songs and sketches.

General Manager: Felice Rose
Assistant Manager: Marilyn Jones
Press: Merle Debuskey, Lawrence Belling

° Closed Sunday, May 15, 1966.
(29 performances)

161

AMERICAN PLACE THEATRE

Opened Thursday, April 21, 1966.°
The American Place Theatre (Sidney Lanier, President; Wynn Handman, Artistic Director) of St. Clement's Church presents:

THE JOURNEY OF THE FIFTH HORSE

By Ronald Ribman; Drawn in part from "Diary Of Superfluous Man" by Ivan Turgenev; Directed by Larry Arrick; Scenery and Costumes, Kert Lundell; Lighting, Roger Morgan; Musical Incidents, Sandra Lee; Technical Directors, James Dwyer, Charles Fichman; Production Coordinator, Julia Miles.

CAST

Terentievna	Mary Hayden
Zoditch	Dustin Hoffman
Sergey	Christopher Strater
Rubin (also Capt. Ivan Petrovich Narvinsky)	William H. Bassett
Miss Grubov (also Elizaveta Kirillovna Ozhogin)	Susan Anspach
Pandalevski (also Bizimionkov)	Lee Wallace
Katerina Prolomnaya	Catherine Gaffigan
Nikolai Alexeevich Chulkaturin	Michael Tolan
Dr. Korvin	Mark Hammer
Lawyer Levinov	Harry Miller
Feathers (also Volobrina)	Susan Lipton
Kirilla Matveich Ozhogin	Allan Rich
Anna Nikitishna Ozhogin	Martha Greenhouse
Gregory	Jack Aaron
Tania	Jane Buchanan
Lt. Zimin	Jim Doerr
Officers	Brian Turkington, Ron Seka

A Drama in two acts and three scenes. The action takes place in Petersburg, Russia, late in the nineteenth century, in the Grubov Publishing House, and the apartment of Mitkin Zoditch.

General Manager: Arthur Waxman
Stage Managers: Peter Galambos, Miskit Airth
Press: John Springer Associates, Walter Alford, Louise Weiner

° Closed April 30, 1966. (22 performances)

Martha Holmes Photos

Dustin Hoffman, Alan Rich, Lee Wallace
Above: Dustin Hoffman, Michael Tolan
Left: Michael Tolan, Susan Anspach

162

Philip Baker Hall, Judith Granite, Charles Durning

POCKET THEATRE

Opened Tuesday, April 26, 1966.°
Arthur Cantor, Ninon Tallon Karlweis and
Martin Rubin present:

THE WORLD OF GÜNTER GRASS

Adapted and Directed by Dennis Rosa;
Based on an arrangement by Sandra Hochman;
Literary Adviser, A. Leslie Willson; Original
Music, Ryan Edwards; Based on themes by
Richard Wagner; Designed by Richard Seger;
Lighting, Roger Morgan; Graphics Consultant,
Shirley Kaplan; Produced in association with
Santa Fe Productions, Inc.; Assistant to Pro-
ducers, Jon Froscher; Sound Technician, Dale
Soules.

ACT I: The Flood

The Poet _____ Richard Morse
Oskar (The Dwarf) _____ Joe Servello
Prinz (The Dog) _____ Philip Baker Hall
Point (A Rat) _____ Charles Durning
Pearl (A Rat) _____ Judith Granite

ACT II: After The Flood?

The Poet _____ Richard Morse
Oskar _____ Joe Servello
The Discussion Leader _____ Charles Durning
The Assistant to the Chair ____ Judith Granite
The Topic Under Discussion __ Philip Baker Hall

An evening of selections from the works
of Günter Grass, dramatist, novelist, poet,
sculptor, graphic artist, and jazz musician.

Press: Artie Solomon, Arthur Cantor,
Irene Pinn
Stage Manager: Yon Koski

° Still playing May 31, 1966. **163**

Opened Thursday, April 28, 1966.°
Patrick Baldauff, Frank Boone, Gillian
Crowe presents:

BOHIKEE CREEK

By Robert Unger; Directed by Donald Moreland; Designed by Tad Gesek; Music, Don
Moreland; Lyrics, Robert Unger.

CAST

Folk Singer		Richard Havens
I. Arnie		James Earl Jones
Aunty Mom		Georgia Burke
Able		Moses Gunn

A sandbar at dawn

II. Tinch		Wayne Grice
Halfbeak		Dennis Tate

A clay mudbank at midnoon

III. Reba		Billie Allen
Coke		Moses Gunn

A clearing at the water's edge at forenoon

IV. Bo		James Earl Jones
Harold		Julius Harris

A wharf deep inland at dusk

General Manager: Derek Mali
Press: Max Eisen, Carl Samrock
Stage Manager: George Cavey

° Closed Sunday, May 22, 1966. (30 performances)

Moses Gunn, Billie Allen

James Earl Jones, Georgia Burke, Moses Gunn
Above: James Earl Jones, Julius Harris

EIGHTY-FIRST STREET THEATRE
Opened Thursday, May 12, 1966.°
Transcenics, Inc., presents:

SUNSET

By Isaac Babel; Translated by Mirra Ginsburg and Raymond Rosenthal; Director, Aldo Bruzzichelli; Scenery, Kim Swados; Costumes, Evelyn Thompson; Lighting and Sound, Gary Harris; Music, Leo Smit; Technical Director, Tec Crans; Associate Producers, Rita Fredericks, Van Wolf; An Aldana Theatre Production; Production Assistant, Bill Knisly.

CAST

Arye Leib, Shamus of Teamster's Synagogue	Sol Serlin
Levka Krick, Mendel's son, a Hussar	Richard Anders
Dvoira Krick, Mendel's daughter	Geraldine Teagarden
Nechama Krick, wife of Mendel	Sylvia Mann
Benya Krick, Mendel's son	Michael Wager
Monsieur Boyarski, proprietor of clothing factory	Don Potter
Mendel Krick, proprietor of carting establishment	Martin Rudy
Nikifor, head driver	Henry Ferrentino
"Major" Popyatnik, a flutist	David Somerset
Mitya, a waiter	Ed Rombola
Ourussov, confidential solicitor	Marc Victor
Ryabtzov, tavern keeper	Roberts Blossom
Potapovna, vender of poultry	Madlyn Cates
Pyatirubel, a blacksmith	Mel Haynes
Fomin, a contractor	George Birimisa
A Turk	George Stauch
Potapovna's neighbors	Beth Porter, Donna Pizzi
Marusia, Potapovna's daughter	Patricia Hyland
Cantor Zweiback	Marc Victor
Senka Topun, a hood	Ralph Maurer
Boy	Martin Broms
Brobinetz, a noisy rich merchant	George Stauch
Semen, a peasant	John Ramsey
Madame Popyatnik, a gossip	Beatrice Pons
Klasha, a pregnant girl	Beth Porter
A young fellow	Rick Rotante
A cattle merchant	John Ramsey
Rabbi Ben Zacharia	Roberts Blossom

TAVERN GIRLS, SINGERS, SAILORS, NEIGHBORS: Beth Porter, Donna Pizzi, Irene Grumman, Bevya Rosen, Ralph Maurer, John Ramsey, Henry Ferrentino, George Stauch, Ed Rombola, Rick Rotante, Bill Knisly, Chuck Pauley

A Drama in eight scenes presented without intermission. The action takes place in The Moldavanka, the Jewish section of Odessa.

General Manager: James Walsh
Company Manager: Larry Alpert
Press: Dorothy Ross, Richard O'Brien, Carol A. Toy
Stage Manager: Ed Cambridge

° Closed Sunday, May 22, 1966.
(14 performances)

Michael Wager in "Sunset"

CIRCLE IN THE SQUARE
Opened Monday, May 16, 1966.°
Eli Ask and Andy Blue present:

FITZ
and
BISCUIT

By Maxime Furlaud; Director, Frank Corsaro; Designer, Eugene Lee; Music and Sound, Teiji Ito; Production Manager, Brooks Fountain; Production Assistant, Michael Walker; An Elan Production.

CAST

"Fitz"

Woodfin	Sam Waterston
Fitz	Sally Kirkland

"Biscuit"

Biscuit	John Harkins
Philip	Jeff Siggins

Standby: Peta Hargarther

The action of both plays takes place at the end of summer on the New England coast.

Press: Arthur Cantor, Artie Solomon
Stage Manager: Brooks Fountain

° Closed Sunday, May 22, 1966.
(8 performances)

Sally Kirkland, Sam Waterston in "Fitz"

Jeff Siggins, John Harkins in "Biscuit"

GREENWICH MEWS THEATRE

Opened Thursday, May 19, 1966.°
IASTA (Institute For Advanced Studies In
The Theatre Arts) presents:

THE BUTTERFLY DREAM

A Chinese Classical Comedy; English Version, A. C. Scott; Director, Hu Hung-Yen; Scenic Adaptation, Richard Foreman; Costumes, Fran Brassard; Production Design, James Gore; Traditional Chinese Music recorded in Hong Kong; Executive Producer, Jack Ward Mitchell; Technician, John Weeks.

CAST

T'ien Shih, wife of Ch'uang Tzu __ Natalie Ross
Servant Boy _____ Eric Tavares
Ch'uang Tzu, Taoist scholar and
    sorcerer _____ Reid Shelton
Chien Ch'ang,
    stage property man _____ Sam Haigler Henry
Two Hundred and Fifty, a
    paper boy used as funeral effigy ____ Tom Keo
A Girl, paper funeral effigy _____ Anne Draper
Hua Shen, spirit of Ch'uang Tzu
    transformed into handsome
    young scholar _____ Michael Durrell

Presented in two acts, the action takes place outside Ch'uang Tzu's house, in the living quarters of the house, and in the funeral chamber.

Company Manager: C. George Willard
Press: Merle Debuskey, Lawrence Belling,
Violet Welles
Stage Managers: Fred Reinglas,
Willard Bond

° Closed May 28, 1966. (14 performances)

Reid Shelton, Tom Keo
Above: Eric Tavares, Natalie Ross

Michael Durell, Tom Keo

CHERRY LANE THEATRE

Opened Thursday, May 19, 1966.°

Gene Persson presents:

BIG MAN

By Lawrence Weinberg; Director, Alex Horn; rs and Lighting, C. Murawski; Sound Editor, n Batiste; "Duet For Three" Director, An-ony May; Assistant to Producer, Joanne Wait.

CAST

Pecter	Rudy Bond
nny Grossman	Lou Gilbert
rse	Rue McClanahan
tendant	John McCurry
y Pecter	Barbara Hayes

The action takes place at the present time a hospital room.

DUET FOR THREE

CAST

m	Martin Priest
n	John P. Ryan
se	Maya Kenin

The action takes place in 1946 in a furnished m in New York City.

General Manager: Barry Plaxen

ess: David Rothenberg, Lawrence Schneider

Stage Managers: John Starkweather, John McCurry

Closed Sun., May 29, 1966. (14 perform-ances)

Friedman-Abeles Photos

Lou Gilbert, Rudy Bond
Above: John P. Ryan, Maya Kenin, Martin Priest
Left: Barbara Hayes, Lou Gilbert, Rudy Bond

JAN HUS PLAYHOUSE
Opened Monday, May 23, 1966.°
American Gilbert & Sullivan Presentations,
Inc. (Jeff G. Britton, Managing Director;
Dorothy Raedler, Artistic Director) pre-
sents:

THE AMERICAN SAVOYARDS

Libretto, W. S. Gilbert; Music, Arthur Sullivan; Staged by Dorothy Raedler; Musical Direction, Judith Somogi; Settings, Henry Heyman; Lighting, David Bamberger; Assistant
Musical Director, Kenneth Bowen; Associate
Producer, Dorothy Marie Robinson; At the
Hammond Organ, Kenneth Bowen; At the Piano, Judith Somogi.

THE PIRATES OF PENZANCE

CAST

Major-General Stanley ＿＿＿＿＿ Robert Brink
The Pirate King ＿＿＿＿＿＿ Richard Best
Samuel (his lieutenant) ＿＿＿ William Copeland
Frederick (Pirate Apprentice) ＿ Theodore Morrill
Sergeant of Police ＿＿＿＿＿ Ron Armstrong
Mabel ＿＿＿＿＿＿＿＿＿ Sandra Darling
Edith ＿＿＿＿＿＿＿ Arden Anderson-Broecking
Kate ＿＿＿＿＿＿＿＿＿ Helene Andreu
Isabel ＿＿＿＿＿＿＿＿＿ Naomi Robin
Ruth (Pirate Maid of All Works) ＿ Nell Evans
PIRATES, POLICE, DAUGHTERS: Dennis
Carpenter, Dick Cerasini, Donald Chapman,
Sheila Coleman, Bill Collins, Nina Gervais,
Bill Gibbens, Carl John, Karl Patrick Krause,
Dorothy Lancaster, Jack Lines, Regina Lynn,
Craig Palmer, Naomi Robin, William Tost, Joyce
Weibel

Opened Thursday, May 26, 1966.°

PRINCESS IDA

CAST

King Hildebrand ＿＿＿＿＿＿ Don Yule
Hilarion, his son ＿＿＿＿＿ Theodore Morrill
Cyril ＿＿＿＿＿＿＿＿＿ Don Junod
Florian ＿＿＿＿＿＿＿ William Copeland
King Gama ＿＿＿＿＿＿＿ Robert Brink
Arac ＿＿＿＿＿＿＿＿＿ Richard Best
Guron ＿＿＿＿＿＿＿＿ Donald Chapman
Scynthius ＿＿＿＿＿＿＿ Ron Armstrong
Princess Ida, Gama's daughter ＿ Donna Curtis
Lady Blanche ＿＿＿＿＿＿＿ Nell Evans
Lady Psyche ＿＿＿＿＿＿ Sandra Darling
Melissa ＿＿＿＿＿ Arden Anderson-Broecking
Sacharissa ＿＿＿＿＿＿＿ Joyce Weibel
Chloe ＿＿＿＿＿＿＿＿＿ Naomi Robin
Ada ＿＿＿＿＿＿＿＿＿ Helene Andreu
SOLDIERS, COURTIERS, GRADUATES: He-
lene Andreu, Dick Cerasini, Sheila Coleman,
Bill Collins, Nina Gervais, Bill Gibbens, Carl
John, Karl Patrick Krause, Dorothy Lancaster,
Jack Lines, Regina Lynn, Naomi Robin, Wil-
liam Tost, Joyce Weibel
  Press: Ben Kornzweig, Reginald Denenholz
  Stage Manager: David Bamberger
° Still playing in repertory May 31, 1966.

Donna Curtis, Don Yule, Nell Evans in "Princess Ida"
Above: Richard Best. Right: Richard Best,
Robert Brink, William Copeland in
"The Pirates Of Penzance"

Arden Anderson-Broecking, Don Yule, Sandra Darling,
Theodore Morrill, William Copeland in "Princess Ida"

OFF-BROADWAY PLAYS FROM OTHER SEASONS
THAT CLOSED DURING THIS SEASON

Play	Opened	Closed	Performances
The Knack	May 27, 1964	Jan. 9, 1966	685
The Trojan Women	Dec. 23, 1963	Oct. 10, 1965	640
New Pinter Plays (The Room, A Slight Ache)	Dec. 9, 1964	Oct. 3, 1965	342
Association of Producing Artists (in repertory)	Dec. 6, 1964	Sept. 5, 1965	281
The Decline and Fall of The Entire World As Seen Through The Eyes of Cole Porter Revisited	March 30, 1965	Nov. 28, 1965	273
American Savoyards in Gilbert and Sullivan (in repertory)	May 18, 1965	Jan. 2, 1966	263
Othello (in repertory with "Baal")	Oct. 12, 1964	July 4, 1965	216
The Exception and The Rule, The Prodigal Son	May 20, 1965	Sept. 19, 1965	141
Baal (in repertory with "Othello")	May 13, 1965	Sept. 18, 1965	59
The Wives	May 17, 1965	June 13, 1965	33
In White America	May 18, 1965	June 13, 1965	32
Square In The Eye	May 19, 1965	June 13, 1965	31

NEW YORK SHAKESPEARE FESTIVAL
Delacorte Theater, Central Park, New York
June 9 through August 28, 1965
Produced by Joseph Papp

DELACORTE THEATER

Opened Wednesday, June 9, 1965.°
Joseph Papp in cooperation with the City
of New York presents:

LOVE'S LABOR'S LOST

By William Shakespeare; Directed by Gerald Freedman; Setting by Ming Cho Lee;
Lighting, Martin Aronstein; Costumes, Theoni
V. Aldredge; Songs and Music, John Morris; Associate Producer, Bernard Gersten; Dance
by Robert Joffrey; Production Coordinator, Andrew Mihok.

CAST

Ferdinand, King of Navarre	James Ray
Longaville	Michael Moriarty
Dumaine	William Bogert
Berowne	Richard Jordan
Anthony Dull	Dan Durning
Costard	Joseph Bova
Don Adriano De Armado	Paul Stevens
Moth	John Pleshette
Jaquenetta	Alexandra Berlin
Boyet	Tom Aldredge
Princess of France	Jane White
Maria	Nancy Reardon
Katharine	Margaret Linn
Rosaline	Rae Allen
A Forester	Robert Burgess
Sir Nathaniel	Gerald E. McGonagill
Holofernes	Robert Ronan
Marcade	Oliver Dixon
Singer	Keith Baker
Dancer	Gerald Teijelo
Lady-in-Waiting	Betty Hellman

ATTENDANTS AND LORDS: Keith Baker,
Robert Burgess, Burke Byrnes, Oliver Dixon,
John Hoffmeister, Peter Jacob, Bruce Monette,
John Vidette.

UNDERSTUDIES: Ferdinand, William Bo-
gert; Princess, Rosaline, Betty Hellman.

FESTIVAL LINE SINGERS: Alexander Demas, Carole Demas, Debby Kooperman, Paula
Lani Rosen, Jonathan David Rosen

A Comedy presented in two parts. The action takes place in Navarre.

General Manager: Hilmar Sallee
Press: Merle Debuskey, Seymour Krawitz
Stage Managers: John Fenn, David Smith

° Closed July 3, 1965 after a limited engagement of 22 performances.

Friedman-Abeles Photos

Tom Aldredge, James Ray, Richard Jordan,
Jane White, Rae Allen, Paul Stevens

James Ray, Jane White. Above: Joseph Bova,
Alexandra Berlin. Top: Jane White, James Ray,
Rae Allen, Richard Jordan

DELACORTE THEATER
Opened Wednesday, July 7, 1965.°
Joseph Papp in cooperation with the City
of New York presents:

CORIOLANUS

By William Shakespeare; Directed by Gladys
Vaughan; Setting, Ming Cho Lee; Lighting,
Martin Aronstein; Music, David Amram; Stage
Dueling Choreography, Christopher Tanner; As-
sociate Producer, Bernard Gersten; Production
Coordinator, Andrew Mihok; Production As-
sistant, Amy Saltz.

CAST

First Citizen	Morris Erby
Second Citizen	Brad Sullivan
Menenius Agrippa	Staats Cotsworth
Caius Marcius Coriolanus	Robert Burr
Roman Senator	Leonard Hicks
Cominius	Michael McGuire
Titus Lartius	Herbert Nelson
Sicinius Velutus	Alan Ansara
Junius Brutus	James Earl Jones
Volscian Senator	Seymour Penzner
Tullus Aufidius	Mitchell Ryan
Volumnia	Jane White
Virgilia	Kate Sullivan
Valeria	Marcie Hubert
Lieutenant to Aufidius	Beeson Carroll
First Roman Officer	Ed Setrakian
Second Roman Officer	James Antonio
First Roman Citizen	Leonard Jackson
Second Roman Citizen	Morris Erby
Third Roman Citizen	Douglas Turner
Patrician	Humbert Alan Astredo
Aedile	Maury Cooper
Decanor	Ed Setrakian
Adrian	Humbert Alan Astredo
First Servingman	Maury Cooper
Second Servingman	James Antonio
Third Servingman	William Devane
First Volscian Watch	M. M. Streicher
Second Volscian Watch	Beeson Carroll
Young Marcius	Robert Ross Burr

CITIZENS, SOLDIERS, ATTENDANTS: James
Arnold, Robert Burgess, Burke Byrnes, Festus
Collier, Oliver Dixon, John Genke, Alec Healy,
Laura Hicks, John Hoffmeister, Anna Hors-
ford, James Howard, Peter Jacob, Leonard
Jackson, Ronald Johnson, Philip Kroopf, George
McGrath, George Muschamp, Nat Simmons,
John L. Starrs, John Vidette, Lisle Wilson,
Peter Yoshida

UNDERSTUDIES: Menenius, Seymour Penz-
ner; Volumnia, Virgilia, Marcie Hubert; Young
Marcius, Edward Britton Burr

FESTIVAL LINE SINGERS: Paula Rosen,
Nathan Rosen, Carole Demas, Alex Demas,
Thomas Ludlow

A Drama presented in two parts. The action takes place in Rome, and the Territories
of the Volscians and Antiates.

General Manager: Hilmar Sallee
Press: Merle Debuskey, Seymour Krawitz
Stage Manager: David Bishop

Closed Saturday, July 31, 1965 after a limited engagement of 23 performances.

Friedman-Abeles, George E. Joseph Photos

**Robert Burr, Jane White,
Staats Cotsworth, Mitchell Ryan**

**Staats Cotsworth, Jane White, Robert Burr,
Kate Sullivan. Above: Robert Burr**

Opened Wednesday, August 4, 1965.°
Joseph Papp in association with the City
of New York presents:

TROILUS AND CRESSIDA

By William Shakespeare; Directed by Joseph
Papp; Setting, Ming Cho Lee; Lighting, Mar-
tin Aronstein; Costumes, Theoni V. Aldredge;
Music, David Amram; Swordplay, James J.
Sloyan; Associate Producer, Bernard Gersten;
Production Coordinator, Andrew Mihok; Pro-
duction Assistant, Amy Saltz.

CAST

Priam, King of Troy	Leonard Hicks
Hector	Paul Stevens
Troilus	Richard Jordan
Paris	Humbert Alan Astredo
Deiphobus	Peter Jacob
Helenus	Michael Moriarty
Margarelon	James Howard
Aeneas	Jack Ryland
Antenor	Morris Erby
Calchas	John Hetherington
Pandarus	Frank Schofield
Agamemnon	Gerald E. McGonagill
Menelaus	Michael McGuire
Achilles	John Vernon
Ajax	James Earl Jones
Ulysses	Roscoe Lee Browne
Nestor	Tom Aldredge
Diomedes	Al Freeman, Jr.
Patroclus	Bill Gunn
Thersites	Joseph Bova
Helen	Jane White
Cassandra	Tobi Weinberg
Andromache	Chase Crosley
Cressida	Flora Elkins
Alexander	Seymour Penzner
Servant to Troilus	James Arnold
Servant to Paris	Robert Ronan
Servant to Diomedes	Peter Yoshida
Myrmidon	Ronald Johnson

SOLDIERS AND ATTENDANTS: Burke Byr-
nes, Festus Collier, Oliver Dixon, John Genke,
Alex Healy, John Hoffmeister, Leonard Jack-
son, Philip Kroopf, George McGrath, George
Muschamp, Nat Simmons, John Starr, John
Vidette, Lisle Wilson.

MUSICIANS: Andrew J. Baron, Richard Berg,
Henry J. Nowak.

FESTIVAL LINE SINGERS: Paula Rosen,
Jonathan Rosen, Carole Demas, Alex Demas.

UNDERSTUDIES: Priam, John Hetherington;
Hector, Leonard Hicks; Troilus, Michael Mori-
arty; Pandarus, Robert Ronan; Ajax, Diomed-
es, Morris Erby; Ulysses, Michael McGuire;
Helen, Cressida, Andromache, Cassandra, Betty
Hellman.

A Drama presented in two parts. The action takes place in Troy, and the Greek Camp.

General Manager: Hilmar Sallee
Press: Merle Debuskey, Seymour Krawitz
Stage Managers: Russell McGrath,
David Watrous

° Closed Saturday, August 28, 1965 after a
limited engagement of 23 performances.

Friedman-Abeles, George E. Joseph Photos

Frank Schofield, Flora Elkins, Richard Jordan

Tom Aldredge, Roscoe Lee Brown
Above: Richard Jordan, Flora Elkins

DELACORTE MOBILE THEATER

Opened Saturday, June 26, 1965.°
Joseph Papp in cooperation with the City
of New York presents:

KING HENRY V

By William Shakespeare; Directed by Jo-
seph Papp; Setting, Ming Cho Lee; Lighting,
Martin Aronstein; Costumes, Sonia Lowenstein;
Music, David Amram; Technical Director, Tec
Crans; Associate Producer, Bernard Gersten.

CAST

Chorus	Roy Shuman
King Henry V	Robert Hooks
Duke of Exeter	Drew Eliot
Earl of Westmoreland	Richard Nettum
Archbishop of Canterbury	Wayne Wilson
Duke of Orleans	Norman MacDonald
Bardolph	John Tyranos
Nym	William Duell
Pistol	Charles Durning
Hostess Quickly	Terri Turner
Duke of Bedford	Jon Renn McDonald
Lord Scroop	Arthur Berwick
Earl of Cambridge	Ray Stubbs
Sir Thomas Grey	Howard Honig
Charles VI	Lance Cunard
Lewis	Frank Groseclose
Constable of France	Albert Quinton
Montjoy	Bill Fletcher
Fluellen	George Stauch
Gower	Joseph Palmieri
Governor of Harfleur	Norman MacDonald
Katherine	Ellen Holly
Alice	Lynn Hamilton
Duke of Britaine	Howard Honig
Rambures	Jack Gianino
Sir Thomas Erpingham	Wayne Wilson
Duke of Gloucester	Joe Miller
Alexander Court	Patrick Gorman
John Bates	Ray Stubbs
Michael Williams	Ernie McClintock
Earl of Salisbury	Richard Marshall
Monsieur Le Fer	Arthur Berwick
Boy	Bill Egan
Isabel	Gladys Riddle
Duke of Burgundy	Bill Fletcher
King's Master-at-Arms	James J. Sloyan

SOLDIERS AND ATTENDANTS: Stephen
Cooke, John Garfield, Jr., Walter Hadler, Harold
Miller, Ed Rombola, Tony Thomas, Theodore
Wiechers, R. Victor Goff, Owen Levy.

UNDERSTUDIES: Chorus, Harold Miller;
Henry V, Jon Renn McDonald; Exeter, Rich-
ard Nettum; Westmoreland, Patrick Gorman;
Bardolph, Walter Hadler; Quickly, Gladys
Riddle; Katherine, Terri Turner; Gloucester,
Tony Thomas; Bates, Patrick Gorman; Wil-
iams, Ray Stubbs; Salisbury, Theodore Wie-
chers; Boy, Owen Levy.

A Drama presented in two parts. The action
takes place in England and France.

General Manager: Hilmar Sallee
Tour Director: Richard L. Robbins
Press: Merle Debuskey, Seymour Krawitz
Stage Managers: Donald Wesley,
Hal DeWindt, Arthur Berwick,
Patrick Gorman, James J. Sloyan

° Presented in repertory with "The Taming of
The Shrew" through August 22, 1965.
(54 performances)

Friedman-Abeles Photos

Lance Cunard, Ellen Holly, Robert Hooks
Above: Robert Hooks

173

DELACORTE MOBILE THEATER

Opened Monday, June 28, 1965.°
Joseph Papp in cooperation with the City of New York presents:

THE TAMING OF THE SHREW

By William Shakespeare; Directed by Joseph Papp; Setting, Ming Cho Lee; Lighting, Martin Aronstein; Costumes, Theoni V. Aldredge; Music, David Amram; Choreography, Anthony Weber; Associate Producer, Bernard Gersten; Technical Director, Tec Crans.

CAST

Grumio	Charles Durning
Madcaps, Strolling Players	William Duell, Frank Groseclose, Ray Stubbs, Ernie McClintock, Arthur Berwick, Patrick Gorman, Walter Hadler, Ed Rombola, James J. Sloyan, Joseph Palmieri
Petruchio	Roy Shuman
Hostess of Tavern	Gladys Riddle
Townswoman	Lynn Hamilton
Policeman	Harold Miller
Duke Charles	Drew Eliot
His Servants	John Garfield, Jr., Owen Levy, R. Victor Goff, Theodore Wiechers, Joe Miller, Jon Renn McDonald
First Lord	Bill Fletcher
Second Lord	Richard Nettum
Bartholomew	Bill Egan
Lucentio	Richard Marshall
Tranio	Jack Gianino
Biondello	William Duell
Hortensio	George Stauch
Gremio	Lance Cunard
Baptista Minola	Albert Quinton
Katherine	Ellen Holly
Bianca	Terri Turner
Curtis	Frank Groseclose
Madcap Haberdasher	Arthur Berwick
Madcap Tailor	Ray Stubbs
Bill Collector	Norman MacDonald
Vincentio	Wayne Wilson
Widow	Lynn Hamilton
Servants	Howard Honig, Stephen Cooke, Tony Thomas

UNDERSTUDIES: Grumio, William Duell; Lucentio, John Garfield, Jr.; Tranio, Ed Rombola; Hortensio, Joseph Palmieri; Baptista, Drew Eliot; Kate, Lynn Hamilton; Bianca, Gladys Riddle; Tailor, Joe Miller.

A Comedy presented in two parts.

General Manager: Hilmar Sallee
Tour Director: Richard L. Robbins
Press: Merle Debuskey, Seymour Krawitz
Stage Managers: Donald Wesley,
Hal DeWindt, Arthur Berwick,
Patrick Gorman, James J. Sloyan

° Closed August 22, 1965 after playing 53 performances in repertory with "Henry V."

Friedman-Abeles Photos

Roy Shuman

Ellen Holly
Above: Roy Shuman, Ellen Holly

Friedman-Abeles Photos

AMERICAN SHAKESPEARE FESTIVAL
Stratford, Connecticut
June 19 through September 12, 1965
Eleventh Season

THE TRAGEDY OF CORIOLANUS

By William Shakespeare; Directed by Allen Fletcher; Scenery and Costumes, Will Steven Armstrong; Lighting, Tharon Musser; Music, Conrad Susa; Musical Director, Jose Serebrier; Duels Staged by Christopher Tanner.

CAST

Menenius Agrippa	Patrick Hines
	John Carpenter
Caius Marcius Coriolanus	Philip Bosco
	Stephen Joyce
Cominius	Josef Sommer
Titus Lartius	Richard Kuss
Volumnia	Aline MacMahon
	Mary Hara
Virgilia	Maria Tucci
Valeria	Patricia Hamilton
Young Marcius	Vincent Aurelia
First Senator	John Carpenter
First Roman Officer	Robert Benedict
Second Roman Officer	David Grimm
Messenger	Deveren Bookwalter
Aedile	Edwin Owens
Junius Brutus	Rex Everhart
	Richard Mathews
Sicinius Velutus	Frederic Warriner
	Thomas Ruisinger
First Roman Citizen	Theodore Sorel
Second Roman Citizen	Richard Mathews
Third Roman Citizen	Richard Morse
Fourth Roman Citizen	Ted Graeber
Fifth Roman Citizen	Dennis Jones
Tullus Aufidius	John Cunningham
	Nick Smith
Volscian Lords	Todd Drexel,
	Thomas Ruisinger
Volscian Lieutenants	Terence Scammell,
	Ted Graeber, Robert Benedict
Servants to Aufidius	Dennis Jones,
	David Grimm, Thomas Ruisinger
Volscian Guards	Dennis Jones, Nick Smith

CITIZENS, SOLDIERS, SERVANTS: Dennis Aarons, Stephen Bernstein, Lawrence Block, Olivia Cole, Dimo Condos, Robert Cremonini, Mona Feit, James Haire, John Hamilton, William Jackson, Linda Kampley, Michael Parish, Suzanne Pred, Marvin Reedy, Jack Rice, Stanley Soble, Julius Sulmonetti, David Thompson, William Vines, Norton Wettstein

Patrick Hines, Philip Bosco, Josef Sommer, Aline MacMahon, Maria Tucci
Above: Philip Bosco, Aline MacMahon
Top: Maria Tucci, Patricia Hamilton, Aline MacMahon, Terence Scammell, Philip Bosco, John Cunningham

John Cunningham (with dagger raised) Philip Bosco (on floor)

175

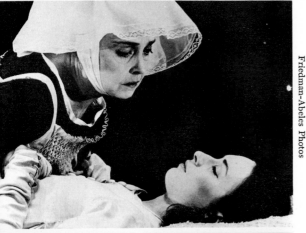

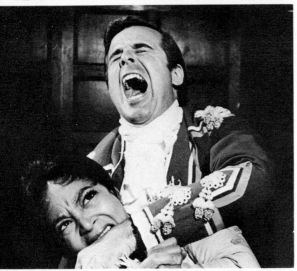

THE TRAGEDY OF ROMEO AND JULIET

By William Shakespeare; Directed by Allen Fletcher; Scenery, Will Steven Armstrong; Lighting, Tharon Musser; Costumes, Ann Roth; Songs and Music, Conrad Susa; Musical Director, Jose Serebrier; Choreography, William Burdick; Duels Staged by Christopher Tanner.

CAST

Chorus	Robert Benedict
Sampson	Nick Smith
Gregory	Richard Kuss
Abram	Edwin Owens
Balthasar	Richard Morse
Benvolio	Theodore Sorel, Dennis Jones
Tybalt	Ted Graeber, Richard Mathews
Lord Capulet	Josef Sommer, Nick Smith
Lady Capulet	Patricia Hamilton
Lord Montague	John Carpenter
Lady Montague	Mona Feit
Escalus	Todd Drexel
Romeo	Terence Scammell, Robert Benedict
Paris	DeVeren Bookwalter
Peter	David Grimm
Nurse	Lillian Gish, Mary Hara
Juliet	Maria Tucci, Geneva Bugbee
Mercutio	John Cunningham, Richard Mathews
Friar Lawrence	Patrick Hines, Thomas Ruisinger
Apothecary	Dennis Jones
Friar John	Richard Kuss
Chief Officer of the Watch	Nick Smith

CITIZENS, GUARDS, LADIES, ETC.: Dennis Aarons, Stephen Bernstein, Lawrence Block, Olivia Cole, Dimo Condos, Robert Cremonini, Mona Feit, James Haire, John Hamilton, William Jackson, Linda Kampley, Michael Parish, Suzanne Pred, Marvin Reedy, Jack Rice, Stanley Soble, Julius Sulmonetti, David Thompson, Norton Wettstein

THE TAMING OF THE SHREW

By William Shakespeare; Directed by Joseph Anthony; Original production concept by Don Driver; Scenery, William Pitkin; Lighting, Tharon Musser; Costumes, Hal George; Songs and Music, John Duffy; Musical Director, Jose Serebrier.

CAST

Lucentio	Robert Benedict, Deveren Bookwalter
Tranio	Richard Morse, Dennis Jones
Baptista Minola	Thomas Ruisinger, Edwin Owens
Hortensio	Todd Drexel
Gremio	Frederic Warriner, David Grimm
Katherina	Ruby Dee, Patricia Hamilton
Bianca	Geneva Bugbee
Biondello	Theodore Sorel
Petruchio	John Cunningham
Grumio	Rex Everhart
Curtis	David Grimm
A Pedant	Nick Smith
A Tailor	Ted Graeber
Vincentio	John Carpenter
Widow	Mary Hara

SERVANTS, LADIES, PRIESTS, ETC.: Dennis Aarons, Stephen Bernstein, Lawrence Block, Olivia Cole, Dimo Condos, Robert Cremonini, Mona Feit, James Haire, John Hamilton, William Jackson, Linda Kampley, Michael Parish, Suzanne Pred, Marvin Reedy, Jack Rice, Stanley Soble, Julius Sulmonetti, David Thompson, Norton Wettstein

Ruby Dee, John Cunningham in "The Taming Of The Shrew." Above: Lillian Gish, Maria Tucci Top: Terence Scammell, Maria Tucci in "Romeo and Juliet"

THE TRAGEDY OF KING LEAR

By William Shakespeare; Directed by Allen Fletcher; Scenery and Costumes, Will Steven Armstrong; Lighting, Tharon Musser; Songs and Music, Conrad Susa; Musical Director, Jose Serebrier; Duels Staged by Christopher Tanner.

CAST

Earl of Kent	Roy Poole
Earl of Gloucester	Patrick Hines
Edmund	John Cunningham
Lear, King of Britain	Morris Carnovsky
Goneril	Patricia Hamilton
Regan	Mary Hara
Cordelia	Ruby Dee
Duke of Albany	Josef Sommer
Duke of Cornwall	Theodore Sorel
Duke of Burgundy	Deveren Bookwalter
King of France	Robert Benedict
Edgar	Stephen Joyce
Oswald	Ted Graeber
Knights to Lear	Dennis Jones, Richard Kuss, John Carpenter, Richard Morse
Fool	Richard Mathews
Servant to Cromwell	David Grimm
Old Man	Thomas Ruisinger
Knight to Regan	Edwin Owens
French Captain	Todd Drexel
Doctor	John Carpenter
Officer to Goneril and Edmund	Nick Smith
A Herald	Richard Kuss

KNIGHTS AND SERVANTS: Dennis Aarons, Stephen Bernstein, Lawrence Block, Dimo Condos, Robert Cremonini, James Haire, John Hamilton, William Jackson, Michael Parish, Marvin Reedy, Jack Rice, Stanley Soble, Julius Sulmonetti, David Thompson, Norton Wettstein.

Producer: Joseph Verner Reed
Artistic Director: Allen Fletcher
Associate Producer: Berenice Weiler
Press: Shirley Herz, William Casstevens, Milan Stitt, David Welsh
Stage Managers: John Seig, Lo Hardin, Mort Siegel, Meribeth Meacham

Friedman-Abeles Photos

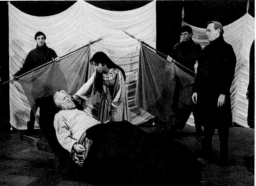

Morris Carnovsky, Mary Hara, Patrick Hines, John Cunningham, Patricia Hamilton, Josef Sommer, Ruby Dee. Above: Morris Carnovsky, Ruby Dee

Stephen Joyce, Morris Carnovsky, Richard Matthews Above: Morris Carnovsky, Ruby Dee

177

THE MERRY WIVES OF WINDSOR

By William Shakespeare; Staged by Mel Shapiro; Setting and Costumes, Peggy Kellner; Music and Songs, Conrad Susa; Lighting, Daniel Dugan; Special Projections, Joseph J. Krysiak.

CAST

Shallow	Michael O'Sullivan
Abraham Slender	Nicholas Martin
Sir Hugh Evans	Anthony Zerbe
Page	James Gallery
Sir John Falstaff	Will Geer
Bardolph	Stephen D. Newman
Pistol	Philip Minor
Nym	Joseph J. Krysiak
Anne Page	Jackie Coslow
Mistress Ford	Patricia O'Connell
Mistress Page	Jacqueline Brookes
Simple	Robert Teuscher
Robin	Byron Smith
Host of Garter Inn	Terrence Evans
Mistress Quickly	Janice Fuller
Fenton	Donald Gantry
Jack Rugby	Robert Moriarty
Doctor Caius	Jerome Raphel
Ford	Ramon Bieri
Servants to Ford	Leroy Logan, Alan Fudge
William Page	Nathan S. Haas
Policeman	Wayne Maunder

FAIRIES, ELVES, OUPHS, IMPS: Ann Marie Halstead, April Ann Reyna, Brenda Riner, Linda Marie Riner, Nathan S. Haas, Jeff McLellan, Joseph Orlando, Matthew Raymond Sinor, Bruce Toker, George Turner.

Patricia O'Connell, Will Geer, Jacqueline Brookes
Above: Michael O'Sullivan, Nicholas Martin

KING HENRY VIII

By William Shakespeare; Staged by Philip Minor; Setting, Peggy Kellner; Costumes, Douglas Russell; Music and Songs, Conrad Susa; Lighting, Daniel Dugan.

CAST

Prologue	Nicholas Martin
Henry VIII	Ramon Bieri
Cardinal Wolsey	Michael O'Sullivan
Cardinal Campeius	Robert Colonna
Cranmer	Alan Fudge
Duke of Buckingham	Jerome Raphel
Duke of Suffolk	Anthony Zerbe
Duke of Norfolk	Terrence Evans
Lord Chamberlain	Alan Stambusky
Earl of Surrey	Donald Gantry
Gardiner	James Storm
Lord Sands	Robert Teuscher
Sir Thomas Lovell	Wayne Maunder
Sir Henry Guildford	Marshall Wright
Cromwell	Leroy Logan
Griffith	Stephen D. Newman
Capucius	Michael Montel
Queen Katharine	Jacqueline Brookes
Anne Bullen	Jackie Coslow
Old Lady	Patricia O'Connell
Patience	Janice Fuller
Gentlemen	Robert Moriarty, Brandwell Teuscher, Nicholas Martin
Surveyor	James Gallery
Porter	James Gallery
Porter's Man	Nicholas Martin
Sergeant-at-arms	Joseph J. Krysiak
Guards	Charles Newman, John Herring
Pages	Ned Newman, Byron Smith
Servant	J. Phillip Babb
Ladies	Renee Hobbs, Christie Virtue, Gabrielle DaPeer, Lisa Cilley

CORIOLANUS

By William Shakespeare; Staged by Milton Katselas; Setting and Costumes, Peggy Kellner; Music and Songs, Conrad Susa; Lighting, Daniel Dugan.

CAST

First Citizen	Terrence Evans
Second Citizen	Joseph J. Krysiak
Third Citizen	Stephen D. Newman
Menenius Agrippa	Michael O'Sullivan
Caius Marcius Coriolanus	Anthony Zerbe
Aediles	Scott Thomas, Wayne Maunder
Cominius	Will Geer
Titus Lartius	James Gallery
Junius Brutus	Jerome Raphel
Sicinius Velutus	Philip Minor
Tullus Aufidius	Ramon Bieri
Lieutenant to Aufidius	Alan Fudge
Volscian Senators	Leroy Logan, Robert Teuscher
Volumnia	Jacqueline Brookes
Virgilia	Jackie Coslow
Valeria	Patricia O'Connell
Young Marcius	Nathan S. Haas, Matthew Raymond Sinor
Messenger	James Storm
Gentlewomen	Lillian Herzberg, Idy Minihan
Soothsayer	J. Phillip Babb
First Servingman	J. Phillip Babb
Second Servingman	Alan Stambusky
Third Servingman	Robert Colonna
First Roman Senator	Alan Stambusky
Second Roman Senator	Michael Montel
Third Roman Senator	Vince Vitale

SOLDIERS AND CITIZENS: Robert Moriarty, Byron Smith, James Storm, John Herring, Wayne Maunder, Charles Newman, Terrence Evans, Joseph J. Krysiak, Stephen D. Newman, Alan Stambusky, Robert Teuscher, Marshall Wright, J. Phillip Babb, Leroy Logan, Robert Colonna, Brandwell Teuscher, Alan Fudge, Bill Ross, Michael Montel, Lisa Cilley, Nancy Breitenbach, Janice Fuller, Harriet Buffington, Idy Minihan, Vince Vitale, Lillian Herzberg, Jacquellyne Garner, Nancy Crawford, Michael Ross, Gerald Nawrocki

Press: William B. Eaton
Stage Managers: Dorothy Fowler, Nikos Kafkalis, Nicholas Martin, Bill Ross
Technical Director: William C. Roberts

Anthony Zerbe, Jacqueline Brookes
Above: Anthony Zerbe, Michael O'Sullivan in "Coriolanus"
Top: Ramon Bieri, Michael O'Sullivan, Jacqueline Brookes in "King Henry VIII"

THE STRATFORD FESTIVAL OF CANADA

Stratford, Ontario
Michael Langham, Artistic Director
June 14 through October 2, 1965
Thirteenth Season

HENRY IV, PART ONE

By William Shakespeare; Directed by Stuart
Burge; Designed by Desmond Heeley; Fights
arranged by Patrick Crean; Music by John
Cook. Opened Monday, June 14, 1965, and
played 39 performances in repertory.

CAST

King Henry IV	Leo Ciceri
Henry, Prince of Wales	Douglas Rain
Lord John of Lancaster	J. C. Juliani
Earl of Westmoreland	Max Helpmann
Sir Walter Blunt	Claude Bede
Henry Percy, Earl of Northumberland	Mervyn Blake
Henry Percy, called Hotspur	Douglas Campbell
Lady Percy, wife to Hotspur	Martha Henry
Edmund Mortimer	Paul Massie
Lady Mortimer	Joan Karasevich
Owen Glendower	Powys Thomas
Earl of Worcester	William Needles
Earl of Douglas	Hugh Webster
Sir Richard Vernon	Bruno Gerussi
Richard Scroop	Joseph Shaw
Sir Michael	Lewis Gordon
Sir John Falstaff	Tony Van Bridge
Poins	Heath Lamberts
Bardolph	Eric Christmas
Gadshill	Bruno Gerussi
Peto	J. C. Juliani
Mistress Quickly	Mary Savidge
Sheriff	Mervyn Blake
Francis	Lewis Gordon
First Carrier	Hugh Webster
Second Carrier	Kenneth Pogue
Traveller	Patrick Crean
Chamberlain	Joseph Shaw
Vintner	Paul Massie
Ostler	Al Kozlik
Hotspur's servant	Briain Petchey
Messenger	Leon Pownall

ATTENDANTS, MONKS, SERVANTS, ETC.:
David Anderson, Larry Aubrey, Guy Bannerman, Peter Cheyne, Tim Davisson, Mike Fletcher, Mark Gilliland, Roland Hewgill, Henry Hovenkamp, Ken James, Krysia Jarmicki, Karen Madsen, Richard Monette, Janet Murray, Michael O'Regan, David Pape, Donna Peerless, Gregory Reid, Edward Rudney, Gordon Thomson

UNDERSTUDIES: Falstaff, Ken James; Henry IV, J. C. Juliani; Glendower, Al Kozlik; Hal, Paul Massie; Worcester, Briain Petchey; Northumberland, Kenneth Pogue; Hotspur, Edward Rudney

Peter Smith Photos

Leo Ciceri, J. C. Juliani, Douglas Rain,
Claude Bede, Tony Van Bridge

Douglas Rain, Douglas Campbell
Above: Douglas Rain (L), Tony Van Bridge (R)
Top: Douglas Campbell, Leo Ciceri

FALSTAFF
(Henry IV, Part Two)

By William Shakespeare; Directed by Stuart Burge; Designed by Desmond Heeley; Music by John Cook. Opened Tuesday, June 15, 1965, and played 30 performances.

CAST

Rumour	Ken James
King Henry IV	Leo Ciceri
Prince Hal (later Henry V)	Douglas Rain
Prince John of Lancaster	J. C. Juliani
Prince Humphrey of Gloucester	Dan MacDonald
Prince Thomas of Clarence	Paul Massie
Earl of Warwick	Claude Bede
Earl of Westmoreland	Max Helpmann
Earl of Surrey	Henry Hovenkamp
Harcourt	Richard Monette
Lord Chief Justice	William Needles
Gower	Leon Pownall
Lord Biddulph	Claude Bede
Earl of Northumberland	Mervyn Blake
Scroop	Joseph Shaw
Lord Mowbray	Kenneth Pogue
Lord Hastings	Roland Hewgill
Lady Percy	Martha Henry
Lady Northumberland	Maureen Fitzgerald
Sir John Coleville	Edward Rudney
Porter	Lewis Gordon
Travers	Paul Massie
Morton	Patrick Crean
Sir John Falstaff	Tony van Bridge
His Page	Benedict Campbell
Poins	Heath Lamberts
Bardolph	Eric Christmas
Pistol	Peter Donat
Peto	J. C. Juliani
Mistress Quickly	Mary Savidge
Doll Tearsheet	Frances Hyland
Francis	Lewis Gordon
Fang	Al Kozlik
Snare	Briain Petchey
Shallow	William Hutt
Silence	Mervyn Blake
Davy	Roland Hewgill
Mouldy	William Needles
Shadow	Briain Petchey
Wart	Heath Lamberts
Feeble	Al Kozlik
Bullcalf	Ken James
Musicians	Robert Comber, Earl Reiner, Ron Laurie

SERVANTS, MONKS, CITIZENS, ETC.: David Anderson, Larry Aubrey, Guy Bannerman, Peter Cheyne, Tim Davisson, Mike Fletcher, Mark Gilliland, Henry Hovenkamp, Ken James, Krysia Jarmicki, Joan Karasevich, Dan Mac-Donald, Karen Madsen, Janet Murray, Michael O'Regan, David Pape, Donna Peerless, Leon Pownall, Gregory Reid, Gordon Thomson

UNDERSTUDIES: Silence, Lewis Gordon; Falstaff, Ken James; Henry IV, J. C. Juliani; Pistol, Al Kozlik; Hal, Paul Massie; Shallow, Briain Petchey; Northumberland, Kenneth Pogue; Tearsheet, Joan Karasevich

Peter Smith Photos

Douglas Rain, Leo Ciceri

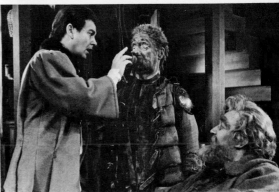

Douglas Rain, Eric Christmas, Tony Van Bridge
Above: Al Kozlik, William Needles, Eric Christmas, Mary Savidge, Briain Petchey, Tony Van Bridge, Benedict Campbell. Top: Mary Savidge, Tony Van Bridge, Frances Hyland

181

JULIUS CAESAR

By William Shakespeare; Directed by Douglas Campbell; Designed by Leslie Hurry; Fights arranged by Patrick Crean. Opened Wednesday, June 16, 1965, and played 45 performances.

CAST

Julius Caesar	Joseph Shaw
Octavius Caesar	Paul Massie
Marcus Antonius	Bruno Gerussi
M. Aemil Lepidus	Kenneth Pogue
Cicero	Claude Bede
Publius	Roland Hewgill
Popilius Lena	Eric Christmas
Marcus Brutus	William Hutt
Cassius	Peter Donat
Casca	Max Helpmann
Trebonius	J. C. Juliani
Decius Brutus	Dan MacDonald
Ligarius	Powys Thomas
Metellus Cimber	Edward Rudney
Cinna	Henry Hovenkamp
Flavius	Patrick Crean
Marullus	Leo Ciceri
Artemidorus	Briain Petchey
Soothsayer	Al Kozlik
Antony's servant	Kenneth Pogue
Caesar's servant	Leon Pownall
Cinna the Poet	Powys Thomas
Octavius' officer	Patrick Crean
Poet	Roland Hewgill
Lucilius	J. C. Juliani
Titinius	Dan MacDonald
Messala	Leo Ciceri
Young Cato	Leon Pownall
Volumnius	Roland Hewgill
Pindarus	Briain Petchey
Varro	Al Kozlik
Clitus	Henry Hovenkamp
Claudius	Gregory Reid
Strato	Edward Rudney
Lucius	Heath Lamberts
Dardanius	Richard Monette
A Cobbler	Hugh Webster
A Carpenter	Ken James
Calpurnia	Frances Hyland
Portia	Kate Reid
Lady-in-Waiting to Calpurnia	Maureen Fitzgerald

SENATORS, SOLDIERS, CITIZENS: David Anderson, Larry Aubrey, Guy Bannerman, Peter Cheyne, Tim Davisson, Mike Fletcher, Mark Gilliland, Krysia Jarmicki, Joan Karasevich, Karen Madsen, Richard Monette, Janet Murray, Michael O'Regan, David Pape, Donna Peerless, Gregory Reid, Gordon Thomson

UNDERSTUDIES: Caesar, Henry Hovenkamp; Antony, Dan MacDonald; Cassius, Briain Petchey; Brutus, Kenneth Pogue; Casca, Edward Rudney; Portia, Maureen Fitzgerald; Calpurnia, Joan Karasevich

Peter Smith Photos

William Hutt, Paul Massie, Peter Donat, Bruno Gerussi

Center: Bruno Gerussi, Joseph Shaw
Top: Frances Hyland, Joseph Shaw

182

Peter Smith Photos

William Hutt, Kate Reid
Above: Kate Reid, Frances Hyland, Hugh Webster

THE CHERRY ORCHARD

By Anton Chekhov; Translated by Tyrone Guthrie and Leonid Kipnis; Directed by John Hirsch; Designed by Brian Jackson; Music by Louis Applebaum. Opened Monday, July 26, 1965, and played 15 performances.

CAST

Ranevskaya,	
Lyubov Andreyevna	Kate Reid
Anya	Susan Ringwood
Varya	Frances Hyland
Gaev, Leonid Andreyevich	William Hutt
Lopahin,	
Yermolai Alexeyevich	Douglas Campbell
Trofimov, Pyotr Sergeyevich	Hugh Webster
Simeonoff-Pishchik	Mervyn Blake
Charlotta Ivanovna	Mary Savidge
Yepihodov	William Needles
Dunyasha	Martha Henry
Firs	Powys Thomas
Yasha	Bruno Gerussi
A Passer-by	Dan MacDonald
Station Master	Al Kozlik
Post Office Clerk	Briain Petchey

SERVANTS AND GUESTS: Maureen Fitzgerald, Lewis Gordon, J. C. Juliani, Joan Karasevich, Michael O'Regan, Leon Pownall, Edward Rudney, Gordon Thomson

UNDERSTUDIES: Trofimov, Lewis Gordon; Yasha, J. C. Juliani; Firs, Al Kozlik; Gaev, Dan MacDonald; Yepihodov, Richard Monette; Pishchik, Leon Pownall; Lopahin, Edward Rudney; Ranevskaya, Charlotta, Maureen Fitzgerald

Administrative Director: Victor Polley
Company Manager: Bruce Swerdfager
Press: Jack Karr, Barbara Reid
Stage Managers: Thomas Bohdanetzky,
Bill Kearns, Ronald Pollock,
Alan Wallis, William Webster

183

Mary Martin
in
"HELLO, DOLLY!"
Toured Armed Forces Installations overseas and opened in London production

HELLO, DOLLY!

Book, Michael Stewart; Based on Play "The Matchmaker" by Thornton Wilder; Music and Lyrics, Jerry Herman; Directed and Choreographed by Gower Champion; Settings, Oliver Smith; Costumes, Freddy Wittop; Lighting, Jean Rosenthal; Dance and Incidental Music Arrangements, Peter Howard; Musical Direction, Myron Roman; Orchestrations, Philip J. Lang; Vocal Arrangements, Shepard Coleman; A David Merrick-Champion Five, Inc. Production; Presented by David Merrick. Opened Tuesday, Sept. 7, 1965 in Community Concourse, San Diego, Calif., and still playing May 31, 1966 at Shubert in Chicago.

CAST

Mrs. Dolly Gallagher Levi	Carol Channing†1
Ernestina	Barbara Shannon
Ambrose Kemper	Edward Miller†2
Horse	Georgeanna Paxton, Dean Taliaferro
Horace Vandergelder	Milo Boulton
Ermengarde	Mary Jane Conte
Cornelius Hackl	Garrett Lewis†3
Barnaby Tucker	Harvey Evans
Irene Molloy	Joanne Horne
Minnie Fay	Barbara Doherty
Mrs. Rose	Betty Madison†4
Rudolph	James Beard
Judge	Henry Sutton
Court Clerk	Dugan Miller

TOWNSPEOPLE, WAITERS, ETC.: Betty Budzak, Leslie Daniel, Dodie Foland, Melodi Null, Lorri Kemp, Lois LaBonte, Barbara Logan, Linda Lowell, Betty Madison, Paula Martin, Dorothy McPherson, Donni Meyer, Georgeanna Paxton, Nancy Roman, Judy Shaw, Dean Taliaferro, Judy Berke, Andy Bew, Jack Bray, Gerard Brentte, Blake Brown, Chris Calkins, Danny Cartegena, Terry De Mari, Les Edwards, Craig Fine, Doug Hinshaw, Tony Juliano, David McCorkle, Dugan Miller, Don Minter, Bill Richards, Jim Sanderson, Charles Scott, Bill Sisson

UNDERSTUDIES: Dolly, Lisa Carroll; Ernestina, Barbara Logan; Ambrose, Jim Sanderson; Ermengarde, Paula Martin; Cornelius, David McCorkle; Barnaby, Chris Calkins; Irene, Lorri Kemp; Vandergelder, Henry Sutton; Mrs. Rose, Leslie Daniel; Rudolph, Charles Scott; Judge, Bill Sisson

A Musical in two acts and fifteen scenes. The action takes place in Yonkers and Manhattan.

General Manager: Jack Schlissel
Company Manager: Herb Carlin
Press: Lee Solters, Harvey B. Sabinson, David Powers, Gertrude Bromberg
Stage Managers: Pat Tolson, Lee Murray, Mary Porter, Henry Sutton

† Succeeded by: 1. Eve Arden, 2. Jim Sanderson, 3. Carlton Carpenter, Rex Robbins, 4. Leslie Daniel.

For original New York production, see THEATRE WORLD, Vol. 20.

Carol Channing (C) in "Hello, Dolly" number, also above, and top (C) in "Before The Parade Passes By" number

Betty Grable

HELLO, DOLLY!

Book by Michael Stewart; Based on Play "The Matchmaker" by Thornton Wilder; Music and Lyrics by Jerry Herman; Directed and Choreographed by Gower Champion; Settings, Oliver Smith; Costumes, Freddy Wittop; Lighting, Jean Rosenthal; Dance and Incidental Music Arrangements by Peter Howard; Musical Direction, Jay Blackton; Orchestrations, Philip J. Lang; Vocal Arrangements, Shepard Coleman; A David Merrick and Champion-Five Production. Opened at the Tivoli Theatre, Chattanooga, Tenn., Wednesday, November 3, 1965, and still playing May 31, 1966.

CAST

Mrs. Dolly Gallagher Levi	Betty Grable
Ernestina	Patricia Sauers
Ambrose Kemper	Richard Hernany
Horse	Eileen Barbaris, Debra Lyman
Horace Vandergelder	Max Showalter
Ermengarde	Judy Jenson
Cornelius Hackl	Arthur Bartow
Barnaby Tucker	Danny Lockin
Irene Molloy	June Helmers
Minnie Fay	Billie Hayes
Mrs. Rose	Charlise Mallory
Rudolph	Duane Morris
Judge	Eddie Hanley
Court Clerk	Alexander Orfaly

TOWNSPEOPLE, ETC.: Eileen Barbaris, Alberta Barry, Eileen Casey, Polly Dawson, Susan Freeman, Barbara Gregory, Caryl Hinchee, Kathryn Humphreys, Debra Lyman, Charlise Mallory, Ellen Mitchell, Susan Mora, Diane Nels, Anne Leslie, Janyce Nyman, Julie Sargent, Robert Avian, Alvin Beam, Edmund Belson, Wayne Boyd, Gene Cooper, Byron Craig, Norman Fredericks, Richard Gingrich, Ed Goldsmid, Mickey Hinton, Jim Hovis, Robert L. Hultman, Robert Lenn, Alexander Orfaly, Rudy Rajkovich, Bob Remick, Rec Russell, Leslie Kimble, Charles Vick, Lou Zeldis

UNDERSTUDIES: Dolly, Anne Russell; Vandergelder, Eddie Hanley; Mrs. Molloy, Julie Sargent; Minnie Fay, Debra Lyman; Barnaby, Ed Goldsmid; Ambrose, Robert Lenn; Ernestina, Barbara Gregory; Mrs. Rose, Polly Dawson; Ermengarde, Alberta Barry; Rudolph, Alexander Orfaly; Judge, Norman Fredericks

MUSICAL NUMBERS: "I Put My Hand In," "It Takes A Woman," "Put On Your Sunday Clothes," "Ribbons Down My Back," "Motherhood," "Dancing," "Before The Parade Passes By," "Elegance," "The Waiters' Gallop," "Hello, Dolly!," "It Only Takes A Moment," "So Long, Dearie," Finale.

A Musical in two acts and fifteen scenes. The action takes place in Yonkers and Manhattan in the past.

General Manager: Jack Schlissel
Company Manager: Fred Cuneo
Press: Harvey B. Sabinson, Lee Solters, David Powers, Gertrude Bromberg
Stage Managers: Jose Vega, Jack Timmers, Bruce Laffey

For original New York production, see THEATRE WORLD, Vol. 20.

THE ABSENCE OF A CELLO

By Ira Wallach; Directed by Charles Olsen; Scenery and Lighting, William Ritman; Presented by The Producing Managers' Co. Opened Tuesday, January 4, 1966, and closed June 11, 1966 at the Huntington Hartford Theatre, Los Angeles. (138 performances)

CAST

Celia Pilgrim	Florida Friebus
Andrew Pilgrim	Hans Conried
Marian Jellicoe	Michaele Myers
Emma Littlewood	Ruth McDevitt
Perry Littlewood	Eldon Quick
Joanna Pilgrim	Nancy Priddy
Otis Clifton	Donald Buka

A Comedy in three acts. The action takes place at the present time in the living room of Andrew Pilgrim's New York apartment.

Company Manager: Seth Schapiro
Press: Bernard Simon, Herbert Carlin
Stage Managers: Carl Benson, Lynn Statten

For original New York production, see THEATRE WORLD, Vol. 21.

Left: Hans Conreid, Eldon Quick, Nancy Priddy, Florida Friebus. Below: Hans Conried, Ruth McDevitt. Right: Hans Conried, Donald Buka, Michaele Myers

THE GAME OF HEROES
(An Anthology of Italian Theatre)

Producer, Teatro Populare Italiano; Director, Vittorio Gassman; Costumes, Enrico Savelli; Music, Florenzo Carpi; Special effects, Koski-Long; Presented by Jay K. Hoffman. Opened Monday, February 21, 1966 at the Vivian Beaumont Theater, Lincoln Center, New York, and closed March 5, 1966 at the U.C.L.A. Auditorium in Los Angeles.

CAST

Vittorio Gassman
Edmonda Aldini   Carlo Montagna
David Sigel, Narrator

PROGRAM

PART I: Scenes from "Il Parlamento," "La Locandiera," "Oreste."
PART II: Scenes from "The Man With A Flower In His Mouth," "The Queen and The Rebels," "An Airfield Too Far Away," "Waste."

Company Manager: Memo Ambrosi

Carlo Montagna, Edmonda Aldini, Vittorio Gassman

Marilyn Michaels, Anthony George
Above: Lillian Roth, Anthony George,
Marilyn Michaels, Danny Corroll

Top: Marilyn Michaels, Anthony George, Lillian Roth

FUNNY GIRL

Book by Isobel Lennart; Music, Jule Styne;
Lyrics, Bob Merrill; From an original story
by Miss Lennart; Directed by Lawrence Kasha;
Musical Numbers Created by Carol Haney;
Choreographed by Larry Fuller; Scenery and
Lighting, Robert Randolph; Costumes, Stan-
ley Simmons; Music Director, Jack Lee; Or-
chestrations, Ralph Burns; Vocal Arrangements,
Buster Davis; Dance Orchestrations, Luther
Henderson; Presented by Martin Tahse by ar-
rangement with Ray Stark in association with
Seven Arts Productions. Opened Friday, Oc-
tober 8, 1965 at the Dallas, Texas, State
Fair, and still touring May 31, 1966.

CAST

Fanny Brice	Marilyn Michaels
John, Stage Manager	Michael Harrison
Emma	Isabell Sanford
Mrs. Brice	Lillian Roth†1
Mrs. Strakosh	Dena Dietrich
Mrs. Meeker	Carole Love
Mrs. O'Malley	Peggy Cooper
Tom Keeney	Sam Kressen
Eddie Ryan	Danny Carroll
Heckie	Glenn Stetson
Trombone Smitty	Frank De Sal
Five Finger Finney	Clifford Allen
Bubbles	Mary Jane Houdina
Polly	Marybeth Kurdock
Maude	Joyce Driscoll
Nick Arnstein	Anthony George
Stage Director	Charles Cagle
Florenz Ziegfeld, Jr.	Richard Buck
Mimsey	Gail Ziegler
Ziegfeld Tenor	Ray Rocknak†2
Ziegfeld Lead Dancer	Frank De Sal
Adolph	Ray Rocknak
Mrs. Nadler	Eleanor Shaw
Paul	Ron L. Steinbeck
Vera	Sandra O'Neill
Jenny	Suzanne Crumpler
Mr. Renaldi	Charles Cagle

SHOWGIRLS: Suzanne Crumpler, Susan Kennedy, Shay Lundberg, Sandra O'Neill, Gail
Ziegler

SINGERS: Joe Bellomo, Joan Bryant, Charles
Cagle, Peggy Cooper, Michael Harrison, Carole
Love, Carol Marraccini, Ray Rocknak, Eleanor
Shaw, Glenn Stetson

DANCERS: Clifford Allen, Frank De Sal,
Joyce Driscoll, Mary Jane Houdina, J. J. Jep-
son, Marybeth Kurdock, David Moffat, Cynthia
Riffle, Ron L. Steinbeck, Ron Tassone, Sandra
West, Linda Wiles

UNDERSTUDIES: Fanny, Sandra O'Neill;
Mrs. Brice, Dena Dietrich; Nick, Joe Bellomo;
Ziegfeld, Charles Cagle; Tom, Charles Cagle;
Emma, Joan Bryant; Eddie, Frank De Sal;
Mrs. Strakosh, Carole Love; Mrs. O'Malley,
Mrs. Meeker, Eleanor Shaw; Rinaldi, Joe Bel-
lomo

MUSICAL NUMBERS: "If A Girl Isn't
Pretty," "I'm The Greatest Star," "Cornet
Man," "Who Taught Her Everything She
Knows?," "His Love Makes Me Beautiful,"
"I Want To Be Seen With You Tonight,"
"Henry Street," "People," "You Are Woman,"
"Don't Rain On My Parade," "Sadie, Sadie,"
"Find Yourself A Man," "A Temporary Ar-
rangement," "Rat-Tat-Tat-Tat," "Who Are You
Now?," "Rehearsal," "The Music That Makes
Me Dance."

A Musical in two acts. The action takes
place in various theatres, onstage and backstage, on New York's lower East Side, in
Baltimore, and on Long Island.

General Manager: Elizabeth McCann
Company Manager: Emmett Callahan
Press: Morton Langbord, Ken Hinaman
Stage Managers: Thelma Chandler,
Henry Garrard, Christopher Scott

† Succeeded by: 1. Nancy Andrews, 2. Michael
Harrison.

For original New York production, see
THEATRE WORLD, Vol. 20.

Friedman-Abeles Photos

THE ODD COUPLE

By Neil Simon; Directed by Harvey Medlinsky; Scenery, Oliver Smith; Lighting, Jean Rosenthal; Costumes, Ann Roth; Presented by Saint Subber. Opened Monday, December 27, 1965, and still touring May 31, 1966.

CAST

Speed	William Pierson
Murray	Peter Boyle
Roy	Rik Colitti
Vinnie	Harry Eno
Oscar Madison	Dan Dailey
Felix Unger	Richard Benjamin
Gwendolyn Pigeon	Barbara Evans
Cecily Pigeon	Diane Aubrey

UNDERSTUDIES: Oscar, Peter Boyle; Felix, William Pierson; Murray, Speed, Roy, Carmine Caridi; Gwendolyn, Cecily, Diane Eden; Vinnie, Bud Schweich

A Comedy in three acts and four scenes. The action takes place at the present time in an apartment on Riverside Drive in New York City.

General Manager: C. Edwin Knill
Company Manager: Morry Efron
Press: Harvey B. Sabinson, Lee Solters, Robert Reud
Stage Managers: Scott Jackson, Bud Schweich

For original New York production, see THEATRE WORLD, Vol. 21.

Richard Benjamin, Harry Eno, Peter Boyle, Dan Dailey, William Pierson, Rik Coletti
Above: Richard Benjamin, Dan Dailey, Diane Aubrey, Barbara Evans

NATIONAL REPERTORY THEATRE

Michael Dewell and Frances Ann Dougherty, Producers; Directors, Jack Sydow and Margaret Webster; Set Designer, Will Steven Armstrong; Costumes, Alvin Colt, Edith Lutyens Bel Geddes; Lighting, Tharon Musser; Production Supervisor, Robert Calhoun; Assistant Producer, Gina Shield; Musical Director, Dean Fuller; Presented by The American National Theatre and Academy. Opened Monday, November 8, 1965, and closed in Los Angeles March 26, 1966.

THE MADWOMAN OF CHAILLOT

By Jean Giraudoux; In a version by Maurice Valency; Directed by Margaret Webster; Scenery, Will Steven Armstrong; Costumes, Edith Lutyens Bel Geddes.

CAST

The Waiter	Geddeth Smith
The President	G. Wood
The Baron	John Eames
The Street Singer	Gerardine Douglas
The Flower Girl	Marcia LaBelle
The Ragpicker	Alan Oppenheimer
The Deaf Mute	Vincent Baggetta
Irma	Patricia Guinan
The Peddler	Gabrielle Strasun
The Broker	Ted Graeber
The Accordion Player	Peter Dompe
A Little Man	James B. Douglas
Man with a Newspaper	Ronald Feinberg
The Prospector	John Straub
Aurelia, The Madwoman of Chaillot	Eva LeGallienne
The Page Boy	Jerry Zafer
Dr. Jadin	Joseph Palmieri
The Policeman	Herbert Foster
Pierre	John Garfield, Jr.
The Police Sergeant	Arn Weiner
The Sewer Man	James B. Douglas
Constance, The Madwoman of Passy	Sylvia Sidney
Gabrielle, The Madwoman of St. Sulpice	Leora Dana
Josephine, The Madwoman of La Concorde	Sloane Shelton
The Presidents	G. Wood, John Eames, Geddeth Smith
The Prospectors	John Straub, Ted Graeber, James Haire
The Press Agents	Ronald Feinberg, James B. Douglas, Joseph Palmieri
The Ladies	Diana Frothingham, Laura Stuart, Elizabeth Davison
The Adolph Bertauts	John Eames, Herbert Foster, James Haire
Customers of the Cafe	Elizabeth Davison, Marsha Sheiness, Joseph Palmieri, James Haire, Diana Frothingham, Laura Stuart

THE RIVALS

By Richard Brinsley Sheridan; With a New Epilogue by Marya Mannes; Directed by Jack Sydow; Scenery, Will Steven Armstrong; Costumes, Alvin Colt.

CAST

Lucy	Leora Dana
Thomas	Joseph Palmieri
Fag	John Eames
Lydia Languish	Diana Frothingham
Julia	Patricia Guinan
Mrs. Malaprop	Sylvia Sidney
Sir Anthony Absolute	G. Wood
Boy	Jerry Zafer
Captain Absolute	James B. Douglas
Faulkland	Ted Graeber
Bob Acres	Herbert Foster
Sir Lucius O'Trigger	Alan Oppenheimer
David	Geddeth Smith
Julia's Maid	Gerardine Douglas

Van Williams Photos

Sylvia Sidney, G. Wood, Leora Dana
Above: Sylvia Sidney, Eva LeGallienne, Leora Dana
Top: Vincent Baggetta, John Garfield, Jr.,
Eva LeGallienne, Arn Weiner

THE TROJAN WOMEN

By Euripides; Based on the version by
Gilbert Murray; Directed by Margaret Webster;
Scenery, Will Steven Armstrong; Costumes, Alvin Colt.

CAST

The God Poseidon ---------------------- G. Wood
The Goddess Pallas Athena .. Gabrielle Strasun
Hecuba, Queen of Troy ------- Eva LeGallienne
Cassandra ------------------------------ Sloane Shelton
Andromache ------------------------------ Leora Dana
Helen -------------------------- Diana Frothingham
Talthybius ------------------ Alan Oppenheimer
King Menelaus ------------------------ John Straub
Women of Troy --------- Laura Stuart (Leader),
　　Elizabeth Davison, Gerardine Douglas,
　　Patricia Guinan, Marcia LaBelle, Marsha
　　Sheiness, Gabrielle Strasun
Soldiers of Talthybius --------- Vincent Baggetta,
　　　　Ronald Feinberg, John
　　　　Garfield, Jr., Arn Weiner
Soldiers of Menelaus ----------------- Peter Dompe,
　　　　　　　James Haire
Officer -------------------------------- Geddeth Smith

　　General Manager: Hugh Southern
　　Company Manager: Boris Bernardi
Press: Mary Bryant, Robert W. Jennings
　Stage Managers: William Armitage,
Greg Adams, Ronald Feinberg, James Haire

Van Williams Photos

Eva LeGallienne, Leora Dana
Above: John Straub, Diane Frothingham

Eva LeGallienne

191

BAREFOOT IN THE PARK

By Neil Simon; Director, Mike Nichols; Settings, Oliver Smith; Lighting, Jean Rosenthal; Costumes, Donald Brooks; Presented by Saint Subber. Opened Monday, July 27, 1964 in Central City, Colo., Opera House, and still touring May 31, 1966.

CAST

Corie Bratter	Joan Van Ark[1]
Telephone Man	Lou Tiano
Delivery Man	Paul Haney
Paul Bratter	Richard Benjamin[2]
Mrs. Banks	Myrna Loy
Victor Velasco	Sandor Szabo

UNDERSTUDIES: Mrs. Banks, Carolyn Brenner; Paul, Jerry Mickey; Corie, Millee Taggart; Victor, Paul Haney.

A Comedy in three acts and four scenes. The action takes place at the present time in the Bratters' apartment on East 48th Street in New York.

General Manager: C. Edwin Knill
Company Manager: Morry Efron
Press: Harvey B. Sabinson,
Robert Reud, Alan Edelson
Stage Managers: Scott Jackson, Paul Haney

† Succeeded by: 1. Beverly Penberthy, 2. Phillip Clark. For original New York production, see THEATRE WORLD, Vol. 20.

Left: Sandor Szabo, Beverly Penberthy, Myrna Loy, Phillip Clark (also below)

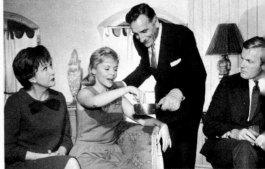

BAREFOOT IN THE PARK

By Neil Simon; Directed by Harvey Medlinsky; Setting, Oliver Smith; Costumes, Donald Brooks; Lighting, Jean Rosenthal; Production Assistant, James Turner; Presented by Saint Subber. Opened Friday, September 24, 1965, at the Masonic Auditorium, Scranton, Pa., and closed May 1, 1966 at Place Des Arts, Montreal, Canada.

CAST

Corie Bratter	Joan McCall
Telephone Man	Alan North
Delivery Man	Don Fenwick
Paul Bratter	Joel Crothers†
Mrs. Banks	Lynn Bari
Victor Velasco	Woody Romoff

UNDERSTUDIES: Corie, Pamela Grey; Mrs. Banks, Edythe Wood; Velasco, Alan North; Paul, Telephone Man, Don Fenwick.

A Comedy in three acts and four scenes. The action takes place at the present time in the Bratters' apartment on East 48th Street in New York.

General Manager: C. Edwin Knill
Company Manager: James O'Neil
Press: Bernard Simon, Joe Shea
Stage Managers: Victor Straus,
Don Fenwick

† Played by Tab Hunter for six weeks. (Jan. 11-Feb. 20, 1966)

For original New York production, see THEATRE WORLD, Vol. 20.

Friedman-Abeles Photos

Lynn Bari, Joan McCall, Joel Crothers Above: Lynn Bari, Joan McCall, Woody Romoff Tab Hunter

FIDDLER ON THE ROOF

Book, Joseph Stein; Music, Jerry Bock; Lyrics, Sheldon Harnick; Based on Sholom Aleichem's stories; Directed and Choreographed by Jerome Robbins; Settings, Boris Aronson; Costumes, Patricia Zipprodt; Lighting, Jean Rosenthal; Orchestrations, Don Walker; Musical Director, Joseph D. Lewis; Dance Music Arranged by Betty Walberg; Vocal Arrangements, Milton Greene; Assistant Conductor, Norman Freeman; Presented by Harold Prince. Opened Tuesday, April 19, 1966 at The Music Center, Los Angeles, and still touring May 31, 1966.°

CAST

Tevye, the dairyman	Luther Adler
Golde, his wife	Dolores Wilson
Tzeitel	Felice Camargo
Hodel	Royce Lenelle
Chava	Kelly Wood
Shprintze	Renee Tetro
Bielke	Maureen Polye
Yente, the matchmaker	Ruth Jaroslow
Motel, the tailor	David Garfield
Perchik, the student	Joseph Masiell
Lazar Wolf, the butcher	Paul Marin
Mordcha, the innkeeper	Fyv Finkel
Rabbi	Baruch Lumet
Mendel, his son	Stanley Soble
Avram, the bookseller	Maurice Brenner
Nachum, the beggar	Herb Corben
Grandma Tzeitel	Tanny McDonald
Fruma-Sarah	Ann Davies
Constable	Clarence Hoffman
Fyedka	Louis Waldon
Shandel, Motel's mother	Charlet Oberley
The Fiddler	Al DeSio

VILLAGERS: Michael Gray, James Spann, Michael Maurer, Michael Aubrey, Violet Lane, Charles Burks, Harry Endicott, Ralph Vucci, James McArdle, Tanny McDonald, Oskar Sobron, Enid Hart, Marsha Meyers, Lynn Archer, Martha Pollak, Kathleen Noser, Leo Postrel, Judith Doren, Ross DiVito, Steve Bohm, Jerry Wyatt

UNDERSTUDIES: Tevye, Paul Marin; Golde, Lynn Archer; Lazar, Maurice Brenner; Tzeitel, Kathleen Noser; Hodel, Tanny McDonald; Chava, Marsha Meyers; Motel, Stanley Soble; Perchik, Michael Maurer; Yente, Violet Lane; Fyedka, Jerry Wyatt; Shprintze, Bielke, Judith Doren; Mordcha, Leo Postrel; Avram, Rabbi, Ralph Vucci; Mendel, James Spann; Fiddler, Michael Aubrey; Constable, Charles Burks

MUSICAL NUMBERS: "Tradition," "Matchmaker," "If I Were A Rich Man," "Sabbath Prayer," "To Life," "Miracle of Miracles," "The Tailor, Motel Kamzoil," "Sunrise, Sunset," "Bottle Dance," "Wedding Dance," "Now I Have Everything," "Do You Love Me?," "I Just Heard," "Anatevka," Epilogue.

General Manager: Carl Fisher
Company Manager: Abe Cohen
Press: Sol Jacobson, Lewis Harmon, Hal Wiener
Stage Managers: Ruth Mitchell, Robert Currie, Anne Sullivan

° For original New York production, see THEATRE WORLD, Vol. 21.

Dolores Wilson, Luther Adler, Tanny McDonald
Above: Al DeSio, Luther Adler
Top: Royce Lenelle, Luther Adler, Dolores Wilson, Felice Camargo, Maureen Polye, Renee Tetro, Kelly Wood

DIAL 'M' FOR MURDER

By Frederick Knott; Director, Eric Berry; Setting, Robert Conley; Lighting, Karl Nielsen; Assistant and Advance Director, Karl Nielsen; Presented by The Producing Managers. Opened Monday, Jan. 24, 1966 in Municipal Theatre, Atlanta, Ga., and closed Sunday, April 3, 1966 in Paramus, N. J., Theatre.

CAST

Margot Wendice	Joan Fontaine
Max Halliday	Jeffrey Lynn
Tony Wendice	Richard Clarke
Capt. Lesgate	Richard Waring
Inspector Hubbard	Eric Berry
Thompson	Karl Nielsen

A Melodrama in three acts and six scenes. The action takes place at the present time in the livingroom of the Wendices' apartment in London.

Stage Manager: Karl Nielsen

For original Broadway production, see THEATRE WORLD, Vol. 9.

Bob Davidoff Photo

Top Right: Eric Bentley, Jeffrey Lynn, Joan Fontaine, Richard Clarke, Richard Waring

THE SUBJECT WAS ROSES

By Frank D. Gilroy; Director, Ulu Grosbard; Scenery, Edgar Lansbury; Lighting, Jules Fisher; Costumes, Donald Foote; Original Cast Recording on Columbia Records; Presented by Edgar Lansbury. Opened at Huntington Hartford Theatre, Los Angeles, Sept. 13, 1965, and still touring, May 31, 1966.

CAST

John Cleary	Jack Albertson
Nettie Cleary	Martha Scott[1]
Timmy Cleary	Martin Sheen

UNDERSTUDIES: John, Wallace Rooney; Nettie, Bella Jarrett; Timmy, Mike Scanlon.

A Drama in two acts and seven scenes. The action takes place in a middle class apartment in May of 1946.

General Manager: Joseph Beruh
Company Manager: James Miller[2]
Press: Samuel J. Friedman
Stage Managers: Paul Leaf, Ci Herzog, Mike Scanlon

† Succeeded by: 1. Bella Jarrett for two weeks' vacation, 2. William Wilson.

For original New York production, see THEATRE WORLD, Vol. 20.

Jack Albertson, Martha Scott, Martin Sheen (also above). Left: Jack Albertson, Martha Scott

LUV

By Murray Schisgal; Directed by Jack Sydow; Designed by Oliver Smith; Lighting, Jean Rosenthal; Costumes, Theoni V. Aldredge; Song, Irving Joseph; Presented by Claire Nichtern. Opened Monday, September 6, 1965 at The Playhouse in Wilmington, Del., and still touring May 31, 1966.

CAST

Harry Berlin _____ Herbert Edelman
Milt Manville _____ Tom Bosley
Ellen Manville _____ Dorothy Loudon
UNDERSTUDIES: Milt, Robert Murray; Ellen, Jennie Ventriss; Harry, Jack Heller

A Comedy in two acts. The action takes place on a bridge at the present time.

General Manager: Robert Kamlot
Company Manager: James Preston
Press: Ben Kornzweig, Reginald Denenholz, Bev Kelley
Stage Managers: Frank Hamilton, Robert Murray, Jack Heller

For original New York production, see THEATRE WORLD, Vol. 21.

Left: Tom Bosley, Dorothy Loudon, Herbert Edelman. Above: Dorothy Loudon, Tom Bosley

THE OWL AND THE PUSSYCAT

By Bill Manhoff; Director, Leonard Auerbach; Scenery and Lighting, Jo Mielziner; Costumes, Florence Klotz; Projections, Anatole Kovarsky; Music, Mark Lawrence; Music Arranged by Norman Paris; Presented by Philip Rose, Pat Fowler, and Seven Arts Productions. Opened Wednesday, Sept. 15, 1965 at the Shubert in New Haven, and closed at the National in Washington, May 21, 1966.

CAST

F. Sherman _____ Russell Nype
Doris W. _____ Eartha Kitt
Standbys: Cherry Davis, Steven Meyer

A Comedy in three acts and eight scenes. The action takes place at the present time in an apartment in San Francisco.

General Manager: Walter Fried
Company Manager: William Orton
Press: Merle Debuskey, George Deber
Stage Managers: Bert Wood, Steven Meyer

For original Broadway production, see THEATRE WORLD, Vol. 21.

Russell Nype, Eartha Kitt

ANY WEDNESDAY

By Muriel Resnik; Director, Howard Erskine; Scenery, Robert Randolph; Costumes, Vilma Ault; Lighting, James M. Riley; Production Assistant, Kevin Sullivan; Presented by Zev Bufman. Opened Monday, Feb. 28, 1966 at the Hanna Theatre, Cleveland, and still touring May 31, 1966.

CAST

John Cleves .... John Dutra
Ellen Gordon .... June Wilkinson
Cass Henderson .... Frank Farmer
Dorothy Cleves .... Patricia Jenkins

Understudies: Doris Ingraham, George Gitto

A Comedy in two acts and four scenes. The action takes place at the present time in a garden apartment in the East Sixties in Manhattan.

Company Manager: Irving Cone
Press: Maurice Turet
Stage Managers: Eddie Dimond,
George Gitto

For original Broadway production, see THEATRE WORLD, Vol. 20.

June Wilkinson, Frank Farmer
**Above: Patricia Jenkins, June Wilkinson,
Frank Farmer**

John Dutra, June Wilkinson

THE LOVING COUCH

By Ray Allen; Director, Ray Montgomery; Presented by Stan Seiden in association with Jack Yonchar. Opened Monday, May 9, 1966 at Penn Theatre, Pittsburgh, and still touring May 31, 1966.

CAST

Miriam Corday	Virginia Mayo
Gil Corday	Terry Phillips
Dave Clark	Gene Shane
Ruth Crecilius	Sabrina
The Blessed Martha Crecilius	Reni Riano

A Comedy in two acts and six scenes. The action takes place at the present time in Gil Corday's New York apartment.

Company Manager: Boris Bernardi
General Manager: Rand Barker
Press: Bill Tostevin, Ed Howe
Stage Manager: Don McArt

Left: Virginia Mayo

HELEN HAYES REPERTORY COMPANY

Director, Jack Manning; Scenery, William and Jean Eckart; Costumes, Patton Campbell and Costume Associates; Co-Producers, Helen Hayes, Jack Manning; Associate Producer, Frances Ann Smith; Production Coordinator, Barry Hoffman; Lighting, Roscoe Farmer. Opened April 8, 1966 at Brown Theatre, Louisville, Ky., and closed in Hartford, May 15, 1966.

LOVERS, VILLAINS AND FOOLS

Scenes from Shakespeare (Hamlet, Henry V, Two Gentlemen From Verona, King John, Henry IV, Julius Caesar, As You Like It, Twelfth Night, The Taming Of The Shrew, Sonnets, Merchant Of Venice, Richard II, The Tempest, Macbeth, Antony and Cleopatra, narrated by Helen Hayes with Jack Manning, Larry Swanson, d. j. sullivan, Eric Berry, Jack Davidson, Eric Nord, Martha Galphin, Aviva, Cynthia Latham.

THE CIRCLE

by Somerset Maugham

CAST

Arnold Champion-Cheney	d. j. sullivan
Butler	Eric Nord
Mrs. Shenstone	Cynthia Latham
Elizabeth	Martha Galphin
Edward Luton	Jack Davidson
Clive Champion-Cheney	Larry Swanson
Lady Catherine Champion-Cheney	Helen Hayes
Lord Porteous	Eric Berry

UNDERSTUDIES: Elizabeth, Mrs. Shenstone, Aviva; Arnold, Edward, Clive, Eric Nord

A Drama in three acts. The action takes place in the drawing-room of Aston-Aday, Arnold Champion-Cheney's house in Dorset, England in 1921.

Company Manager: Marshall Young
Press: Fred Weterick,
Betty Lee Hunt Associates
Stage Managers: Frances Ann Smith, Aviva

Right Center: Helen Hayes, Larry Swanson
in "The Circle"

Eric Nord Photos

D. J. Sullivan, Cynthia Latham, Jack Davidson,
Martha Galphin, Helen Hayes, Eric Berry
in "The Circle"

197

Friedman-Abeles Photos

HOT SEPTEMBER

Book by Paul Osborn; Based on Play "Picnic" by William Inge; Music, Kenneth Jacobson; Lyrics, Rhoda Roberts; Staged by Joshua Logan; Choreography, Danny Daniels; Scenery, Oliver Smith; Musical Staging, Joshua Logan, Danny Daniels; Costumes, Theoni V. Aldredge; Lighting, Jean Rosenthal; Musical Direction and Vocal Arrangements, Milton Rosenstock; Orchestrations, Philip J. Lang; Dance Music and Dance Orchestrations, Robert Prince; Presented by Leland Hayward and David Merrick. Opened Tuesday, September 14, 1965 at the Shubert Theatre, Boston, and closed there October 9, 1965.

CAST

Millie Owens	Lee Lawson
Bomber	Richard Granat
Beano	Don Slaton
Binky	Michael Scotlin
Rubberneck	Les Freed
Poopdeck	Gene Lindsey
Spider	Gene Castle
Corky	Brown Bradley
Madge Owens	Kathryn Hays[1]
Flo Owens	Patricia Roe[2]
Hal Carter	Sean Garrison
Mrs. Potts	Paula Trueman
Rosemary Sydney	Lovelady Powell
Alan Seymour	John Stewart
Juanita Badger	Lada Edmund, Jr.
Ben	Ed Crowley
Jim	John Hallow
Howard Bevans	Eddie Bracken
Irma Kronkite	Evelyn Page
Christine Schoenwalder	Betty Lester
Selma	Alice Evans

SINGERS: Darrell J. Askey, Brown Bradley, Connie Danese, Gay Edmond, Judie Elkins, Les Freed, Renee Gorsey, Gene Lindsey, Marilyne Mason, Diane McAfee, Charles McKenna, Richard Nieves

DANCERS: Barbara Alexander, Gene Castle, Kay Cole, Barbara Douglas, Ronn Forella, Charles Kalan, Michele Karaty, Ray Morgan, Marie Patrice, Don Percassi, Michel Scotlin, Don Slaton, Geri Spinner, Anne Wallace

MUSICAL NUMBERS: "Another Crummy Day," "Hey, Delilah," "Whistle Of A Train," "Golden Moment," "Come On Strong," "Somethin' More," "Live," "What Do You Do?," "Tell Me The Truth," "Show Me Where The Good Times Are," "Frug," "This Town/A Guy Like Me," "Who Needs It?," "Hot September Dance," "Rosemary's Soliloquy," "You," "I Got It Made," "Goodbye, Girls," "I Blew It."

A Musical in two acts and eight scenes. The action takes place at the present time in a small Kansas town.

General Manager: Warren O'Hara
Press: Frank Goodman, Martin Shwartz, Louise Weiner
Stage Managers: Ross Bowman, Mitch Erickson, John Hallow

† Succeeded by: 1. Sheila Sullivan, 2. Betty Lester.

Top Left: Sean Garrison, Kathryn Hays
Below: Eddie Bracken, Lovelady Powell

Eddie Bracken, John Stewart, Paula Trueman,
Sean Garrison, Lee Lawson, Kathryn Hays
Above: Sean Garrison, John Stewart

LOVE IS A BALL!

Entire production Conceived, Directed and Choreographed by J Marks, Music of Henry Mancini, Stan Kenton, Dave Brubeck, John Lewis, Franz Waxman; Special Material and New Lyrics, James Thurber, Jules Feiffer, J Marks; Costumes and Wigs, James Croshaw; Scenery, Peter Girolami; Orpheus Setting, Jean Cocteau; Arrangements and Special Scoring, Stan Kenton, Lennie Niehaus, Jerry Cournoyer, Bill Popp; Musical Direction, Bob Ayres; Vocal Coaching, Richie Crabtree; Lighting, J Marks; Film Animations, Al Medoro; Presented by Robert T. Gaus in association with the San Francisco Contemporary Dancers Foundation. Opened Monday, September 27, 1965 in the Civic Auditorium, San Jose, Calif., and closed Monday, October 25, 1965 in the Civic Auditorium, Fort Worth, Texas.

CAST

Alice Ghostley	J Marks
Diana Russell	James Croshaw
Raymond Evans	Nancy Wolfe
Michele Sevryn	Gayle Howard
Mardi Van Winkle	Ingrid Anderson
Sandra Shea	Gary Pinley
Barbara Keeling	Pat Finnegan
Rudy Grau	Robert Crandall
Alan Viau	Sandra Viera

PROGRAM

PART I: "Dialogue Of The Clown," "Oom-Pah-Pah!," "I've Been Waiting For Your Phone Call," "Elegant Lovers," "Hello, Young Lovers," "First Love," "Blues In The Night," "The Blues," "Boogie," "Goddesses Of Love," "The Boston Beguine," "Naked Love," "If Ever I Would Leave You," "The Four Seasons," "Courtly Lovers."

PART II: "Ballad Of Lovers," "Orpheus," "Love For Sale," "Johnny Come Lately," "The Thurber Set," "Love Is A Ball!"

Company Manager: Trilby James
Press: Bernard Simon
Stage Managers: Bruce Mack, Bill Son

Right: Sandra Shea, Alice Ghostley (also top), Ingrid Anderson, Raymond Evans

Jayne Mansfield

THE RABBIT HABIT

By Rex Carlton; Director, Matt Cimber; Sets, Henry E. Lowenstein; Additional Dialogue, Ken Callender; Costume Supervisor, Marjorie Simon; Presented by Dick Randall and Lee Hewitt. Opened Wednesday, December 1, 1965 in the Denver, Colo., Auditorium, and closed December 18, 1965 in the Moore Theatre, Seattle, Wash.

CAST

Kate	Marjorie Bennett
Doris	Joan Shawlee
Jill	Jayne Mansfield
Dr. John Neilson	Hugh Marlowe
Prof. Hartoonian	Alex D'Arcy
Dr. Valerie Swanson	Jadeen Vaughn

Understudy: Gyan Loren

A Comedy in two acts and four scenes. The action takes place in the fashionable residence of Dr. Nielson near a missile base at Cape Kennedy, Florida at the present time.

General Manager: Lee Hewitt
Stage Manager: Richard B. Shull

THIS WINTER'S HOBBY

By Jack Finney; Director, Donald McWhinnie; Sets, Oliver Smith; Costumes, Florence Klotz; Lighting, Tharon Musser; Associate Producer, George Platt; Production Supervisor, Michael Thoma; An Epic Production presented by Hillard Elkins. Opened Monday, March 21, 1966 at the Shubert in New Haven, and closed April 9, 1966 at the Walnut in Philadelphia.

CAST

Charles Bishop	E. G. Marshall
Duffy Bishop	Nan Martin
Arnold	William Hickey
Tommy	Michael Beckett
Laura Amling	Martha Bundy
Sheriff McCarthy	Norman Bly

UNDERSTUDIES: Charles, Sheriff, Dan Rubinate; Duffy, Laura, Carolyn Judd; Arnold, Michael Beckett; Tommy, Clyde Burton

A Drama in three acts and six scenes. The action takes place at the present time in a house in Westchester.

General Manager: Bill Levine
Press: Jane Friedman
Stage Managers: Joseph Olney,
Dan Rubinate

Friedman-Abeles Photos

E. G. Marshall, Nan Martin
**Above: Michael Beckett, William Hickey,
E. G. Marshall, Nan Martin**

Norman Bly, E. G. Marshall, Michael Beckett,
Nan Martin, William Hickey
Above: E. G. Marshall

VENUS IS

By Chester Erskine; Directed by Word Baker; Designed and Lighted by Jo Mielziner; Costumes, Ramse Mostoller; Music, Sol Kaplan; Production Assistant, Dan Scott; Presented by Martin Lee. Opened Tuesday, April 5, 1966 at the Billy Rose Theatre in New York, and closed there on April 9, 1966, after 7 previews.

CAST

Chuck Woodruff	Jerry Strickler
Kathy Scofield	Pamela Toll
Sue Johnson	Avra Petrides
Mamie	Lois Kibbee
Brian Scofield	Jonathan Moore
Harry	George Bartenieff
Phil Johnson	George Robertson
Ted Brown	Michael Baseleon
Stan Williams	Ed Zimmermann
Doris Williams	Diane Kagan
Vincent Martin	Ernest Graves
Jack Lamont	Stratton Walling
Mara Lamont	Audra Lindley
Leslie Elgar	Ann Shropshire

RECORDED VOICES: Bernard Grant, Joyce Gordon, Gerry Matthews, Fredricka Weber
UNDERSTUDIES: Phil, Brian, George Robertson; Sue, Doris, Kathy, Margaret Linn; Mara, Leslie, Mamie, Natalie Priest; Jack, Vincent, Harry, Dalton Dearborn

A Comedy in three acts. The action takes place on a beach along the Pacific Coast at the present time.

Business Manager: Victor Samrock
Press: Bill Doll & Co., Midori Tsuji, Robert Ganshaw, Dick Spittel
Stage Managers: Ben Janney, Nelle Nugent

Impact Photo

George Robertson, Lois Kibbee, Michael Baseleon

Friedman-Abeles Photos

THE OFFICE

By Maria Irene Fornes; Director, Jerome Robbins; Scenery, Ed Wittstein; Costumes, Willa Kim; Lighting, Jules Fisher; Music, Robert Prince; Production Assistants, Janet O'Morrison, H. Kelly English; Produced by arrangement with The Establishment Theatre Co.; Presented by Joseph E. Levine and Ivor David Balding. Opened Thursday, April 21, 1966 at the Henry Miller's Theatre, NYC, and closed there April 30, 1966 after 10 previews.

CAST

Pfancoo	Jack Weston
Princess	Ruth White
Shirley	Elaine May
Lois	Marilyn Chris
Miss Punk	Doris Roberts
Joe	Clifford Arashi
Gucci	Tony Lo Bianco
Delivery Man	Bernard Passeltiner

A Comedy in two acts and four scenes. The action takes place at the present time in December in the office of Hinch, Inc.

General Manager: Richard Horner
Company Manager: Nicholas A. B. Gray
Press: Walter Alford, Louise Weiner, Richard Spittel, John Springer Associates
Stage Managers: Randall Brooks, Thomas Porter

Elaine May, Jack Weston,
and above with Doris Roberts

THE PORCELAIN YEAR

By Reginald Rose; Directed by Alex Segal; Scenery, Peter Larkin; Costumes, Theoni V. Aldredge; Lighting, John Gleason; Production Associate, Jessica Levy; Presented by Katzka-Berne in association with Defender Productions. Opened Monday, October 11, 1965 at the Locust Street Theatre in Philadelphia, and closed at the Shubert in New Haven on November 13, 1965.

CAST

Frederick Potter .... John Megna
Alice Potter .... Barbara Bel Geddes
Elizabeth Potter .... Kim Darby
Harold Potter .... Arthur Hill
Jules Walker .... Martin Balsam

UNDERSTUDIES: Alice, Loretta Leversee; Harold, Morgan Sterne; Elizabeth, Debby Paine; Fred, Michael McCormack

A Drama in three acts and four scenes. The action takes place at the present time in the living room of the Potter house in Brentwood, a suburb of Los Angeles.

General Manager: Joseph Beruh
Company Manager: Richard Osorio
Press: David Lipsky, Marian Graham
Stage Managers: Del Hughes, Gigi Cascio

Friedman-Abeles Photos

Martin Balsam, Arthur Hill, Barbara Bel Geddes

**Arthur Hill, John Megna, Barbara Bel Geddes
Above: Kim Darby, Arthur Hill**

PROFESSIONAL RESIDENT COMPANIES

(Failure to meet deadline unfortunately necessitated omission of several important companies)

Rebman, Ben Bliss Photos

Russell Collins, Myrna Kaye in "Tartuffe"
Above: Romana Portaro, Robert Snook, Richard
Halverson, Vaughn McBride, Dorothy Paxton,
Myrna Kaye, Robert Allman in
"You Can't Take It With You"

CLEVELAND PLAY HOUSE
Cleveland, Ohio
October 6, 1965 through May 15, 1966
Fiftieth Season
K. Elmo Lowe, Director

Coordinating Director, Kirk Willis; Assistant Director, William Peterson; Manager, Leonore Klewer; Scenic Director, Paul Rodgers; Associate, Ben Letter; Technical Suvervisor, Orison Bedell; Costumes, Edith Owen, Martha Braun, Phyllis Kress; Directors, K. Elmo Lowe, Kirk Willis, William Woodman, Chris Hamilton.

PRODUCTIONS

"Tartuffe" opened Oct. 6, 1965; "The Ballad Of The Sad Cafe" opened Oct. 20, 1965; "Slow Dance On The Killing Ground" opened Oct. 27, 1965; "Carved In Snow" opened Nov. 10, 1965; "Uncle Vanya" opened Nov. 24, 1965; "Never Too Late" opened Dec. 10, 1965; "You Can't Take It With You" opened Dec. 15, 1965; "Cinderella" opened Dec. 27, 1965; "Dylan" opened Jan. 19, 1966; "Poor Richard" opened Jan. 26, 1966; "You Never Can Tell" opened Feb. 16, 1966; "The Amorous Flea" opened March 2, 1966; "Who's Afraid Of Virginia Woolf?" opened March 16, 1966; "Twelfth Night" opened March 23, 1966; "Our Town" opened April 13, 1966; "The Absence Of A Cello" opened April 20, 1966; "Antigone" opened Dec. 5, 1965; "Brecht On Brecht" opened Dec. 12, 1965.

COMPANY

Michele Ackerman, Robert Allman, Peter Bartlett, June Cartwright, Timothy Clague, Russell Collins, Patricia Elliot, Marsha Gerson, James Gorgal, Richard Halverson, Edith Hathaway, William Howey, Philip Kerr, Allen Leatherman, Christine MacDonald, Keith Mackey, Sarah May, Bob Moak, Mary Moore, Richard Oberlin, Edith Owen, William Paterson, Dorothy Paxton, Bjorn Pernvik, James Ragan, Regena Reddik, Lorra Rose, Mary Patrice Shelley, Robert Snook, Susan Stirling, Suzanne Sullivan, Larry Tarrant, Kirk Willis.

Press: Rice Hershey, Ruth Fischer
Stage Managers: Richard Halverson, James Ragan, Paul Rodgers, Richard Oberlin, William Paterson, Robert Snook, Allen Leatherman, Vaughn McBride

203

MILWAUKEE REPERTORY THEATRE
Milwaukee, Wisconsin
October 28, 1965 through May 1, 1966
Eleventh Season
John A. McQuiggan, Producer

General Manager, Charles R. McCallum; Sets and Lighting, Charles Dox, Jr.; Costumes, John Lehmeyer; Music Director, Richard Cumming; Directors, Stephen Porter, Philip Minor, Tom Brennan, Adrian Hall, John A. McQuiggan, Rocco Bufano; Choreography, Jerry Grasse.

PRODUCTIONS

"Saint Joan" Oct. 28-Nov. 14, 1965; "The Diary Of A Scoundrel" Nov. 18-Dec. 5, 1965; "The Time Of Your Life" Dec. 9, 1965-Jan. 9, 1966; "Mother Courage" Jan. 13-30, 1966; "The Servant Of Two Masters" Feb. 3-20, 1966; "Henry IV, Part I," Feb. 24-March 13, 1966; "The Glass Menagerie" March 17-April 3, 1966; "Anatol" April 14-May 1, 1966.

COMPANY

Robert J. Colonna, Mary Doyle, Joseph Endes, Anne Francine, James Gallery, Stefan Gierasch, Jerry Grasse, Jill Heavenrich, Jeanne Helminiak, Kenneth Hill, Clinton Kimbrough, Tom Lacy, Nicholas Martin, Virginia Payne, Pamela Payton-Wright, Andrew Robinson, Roger M. Steffens, James Storm, Dilys Tosteson, Bennett Sargent, Rick Mitz, Donald Gantry, Richard Blanchard, Russell Gold, Thomas Keener, Steve Aronson, Milton Coleman, Ronnie Claire Edwards, Joanna Featherstone, Katy Hartnett, Deborah Harvey, George Kalland, David Logan, William Olsen, Carol Terry, Edmund Torrance, Ruth Young, Harley Rodd, Jeanne Feuerstenau, Michael Pederson, David F. Stecker, Sada Thompson, Ralph Williams, Kristina Callahan, David Daniels, Joleen Fodor, Faith Quabius, Lorinne Vozoff.

Business Manager: Peggy Rose
Press: Mary McDonald Welles, Margery Duke
Stage Managers: Richard Nesbitt, Jerry Grasse, David Logan

Gene of Aida Photos

James Gallery, Clinton Kimbrough, Stefan Gierasch in "Diary Of A Scoundrel"
Above: Sada Thompson, Ralph Williams in "The Glass Menagerie"

Stefan Gierasch, Russell Gold, James Storm, Kenneth Hill, Mary Doyle in "Saint Joan"
Above: Joleen Fodor, Tom Lacy, David Daniels in "Anatol"

Donald Gantry, Joseph Endes, James Gallery, James Storm in "Henry IV"
Above: James Gallery, Anne Francine in "Mother Courage"

Joseph C. Towler, Jr. Photos

THE CHARLES PLAYHOUSE
Boston, Massachusetts
Sept. 29, 1965 through
May 15, 1966
Ninth Season

Frank Sugrue, Managing Director; Michael Murray, Artistic Director; Robert Alexander, Children's Theatre Director; Newton Wayland, Musical Director; Assistant to Producers, Cynthia Mutti, Priscilla Wilson; Scenery and Costumes, William D. Roberts; Lighting, Hugh E. Lester.

PRODUCTIONS

"The Miser" opened Sept. 29, 1965, "Poor Bitos" opened Nov. 10, 1965, "Major Barbara" opened Dec. 15, 1965, "Galileo" opened Jan. 19, 1966, "Inspector General" opened March 2, 1966, "The Tiger" and "The Typists" opened April 6, 1966. (264 performances)

COMPANY

Lucy Martin, John Devlin, Lawrence Pressman, Peggy Pope, Ron Bishop, Terrence Currier, Joe Hardy, Lynn Milgrim, Lynn Martin, William Oransky, Orest Kinasewich, Barry Michlin, Joyce Bang, Frances Roth, Herb Katz, Richard Spiegel, Edward Znag.

General Manager: Hugh E. Lester
Press: Nance Movsesian, Marta Dennis
Stage Managers: Bob Alexander, Paul F. Pietz

ony Van Bridge, Lawrence Pressman in "Galileo"
**Above: Denise Fergusson, Eric House
in "Poor Bitos"**

**Lynn Milgrim, Edward Znag in "The Tiger"
Above: Gwyllum Evans, Lawrence Pressman
in "The Inspector General"**

**Edward Znag, Lucy Martin, Ronald Bishop
in "Major Barbara"
Above: Terrence Currier in "The Miser"**

THE THEATRE GROUP
University of California, Los Angeles
June 4, 1965 through February 20, 1966
Seventh Season
Gordon Davidson, Executive Coordinator

Executive Committee, Abbott Kaplan, William W. Melnitz, Lamont Johnson, Gordon Davidson; Administrative Assistant, Ditta Oliker; Scenery, Joseph A. Rubino, Jim Freiburger, Peter Wexler; Costumes, Mina Mittelman, Michael Travis, Peter Wexler, Dorothy Jeakins; Lighting, Myles Harmon, Arvid Nelson; Music, Naomi Caryl Hirshhorn, Salli Terri; Musical Director, Samuel Matlovsky; Directors, Alfred Ryder, Philip Abbott, John McLiam, Gordon Davidson, Paul Shyre, Edward Parone; Production Assistants, Jay Jacobson, Marily Meyer.

PRODUCTIONS
"An Evening of Tennessee Williams, Harold Pinter, Murray Schisgal," "Robert Frost: Promises To Keep," "The Deputy," "Yeats & Company: The Prose, Poetry, and Plays of W. B. Yeats," "Oh What A Lovely War."

COMPANY
Joyce Van Patten, Lee Philips, John Crowther, Mike Kellin, Nina Foch, Sharon Farrell, Wayne Ritter, Alfred Ryder, John Ragin, Anna Brown, Joel Miller, Jay Jacobson, Philip Abbott, Sandy Kenyon, Gail Kobe, John McLiam, James O'Reare, Joseph Ruskin, Robert Brown, Philip Cary Jones, Richard Carlyle, Walter Koenig, Mark Richman, William Wintersole, Alan Napier, Ronald Long, Andre Carpenter, Ian Wolfe, Walter Koenig, Lucian Baker, Richard S. Ramos, Philip Bourneuf, Teri Lee Robertson, Lois Newman, Don Spencer, Neil Elliot, John Rayner, Paul Schneider, Patricia Cutts, Brendan Dillon, Will Kuluva, Diana Maddox, Murray Matheson, Helene Winston, Susan Browning, Mary Donovan, Lola Fisher, Mitzi Hoag, Maria Lennard, George Blackman, Christopher Cary, Peter Church, Barry Dennen, Robert Fields, Martin Horsey, Nigel McKeand, John Orchard, Nicholas Simons.
Press: Richard E. Kitzrow, Ann Sumner
Stage Managers: Myles Harmon, Joel Miller, Jay Jacobson

Production of "The Deputy" was sent on national tour during this season. The Theatre Group has been signed for resident company at The Music Center, Los Angeles, starting in the fall of 1967.

Ivan Protheroe Photos

James O'Reare, John McLiam, Philip Abbott,
Gail Kobe, Sandy Kenyon in
"Robert Frost: Promises To Keep"
Above: Lee Philips, Joyce Van Patten in "The Love
Top: Nina Foch, Mike Kellin in "Windows"

Will Kuluva, Diana Maddox, John Crowther,
Helene Winston, Brendan Dillon, Patricia Cutts,
Murray Matheson in "Yeats & Co."
Above: "Oh What A Lovely War"
Lola Fisher (C)

Alan Napier, Philip Bourneuf, Ronald Long
in "The Deputy"

MINNESOTA THEATRE COMPANY
Tyrone Guthrie Theatre
Minneapolis, Minnesota
May 10 through Nov. 20, 1965
Third Season

Tyrone Guthrie, Artistic Director; Douglas Campbell, Associate Artistic Director; Edward Payson Call, Assistant Artistic Director; Tanya Moiseiwitsch, Principal Designer; Lewis Brown, Associate Designer; Herbert Pilhofer, Musical Director; Oliver Rea, Peter Zeisler, Managing Directors; Barton H. Emmet, Administrative Director.

PRODUCTIONS

"Richard III" opened May 10, "The Way Of The World" opened May 11, "The Cherry Orchard" opened June 15, "The Caucasian Chalk Circle" opened August 3, "The Miser" opened September 7, 1965. The company gave 214 regular performances and 28 special student performances.

COMPANY

Paul Ballantyne, Earl Boen, Graham Brown, Zoe Caldwell, Kristina Callahan, John Cappelletti, Charles Cioffi, John Cromwell, Hume Cronyn, Niki Flacks, Ed Flanders, Kenneth Frankel, Ellen Geer, Helen Harrelson, James Horswill, James J. Lawless, John Lewin, John MacKay, Sandy McCallum, Evie McElroy, Robert Milli, Ruth Nelson, Robert Pastene, Lee Richardson, Ken Ruta, Thomas Slater, Alvah Stanley, Jessica Tandy, Donald West, Ann Whiteside, Nancy Wickwire.

Press: Bradley G. Morison, Kay Fliehr, Richard Hinkie, Anne Richards, Bonnie Wilson
Stage Managers: Rex Partington, Ken Costigan, Gordon Smith
Technical Directors: Richard Borgen, James Bakkom

Ken Ruta, Zoe Caldwell, Ellen Geer, Robert Milli, Jessica Tandy, Paul Ballantyne, Nancy Wickwire, Ed Flanders in "The Way Of The World"
Above: Earl Boen, Alvah Stanley, Hume Cronyn in "Richard III"

Helen Harrelson, Matt Talberg, Ed Flanders, Zoe Caldwell in "Caucasian Chalk Circle"

Ed Flanders, Hume Cronyn, Thomas Slater in "The Miser"
Above: Ken Ruta, Kristina Callahan, Jessica Tandy, Nancy Wickwire, Sandy McCallum, Lee Richardson, Robert Pastene in "The Cherry Orchard"

THEATRE SAINT PAUL
St. Paul, Minnesota
October 16, 1965 through May 1, 1966
Tenth Season
Rex Henriot, Managing Director

Art Director, Robert D. Emeott; Children's Theatre Director, Zoaunne Henriot; Guest Director, Tom Roland; Playwright in Residence, Barry Pritchard; Costumes, Sara Gage; Lighting, Dan Goodwin.

PRODUCTIONS

"She Loves Me" opened Oct. 16, 1965; "The Typists" and "The Tiger" opened Oct. 28, 1965; "Androcles and The Lion" opened Jan. 6, 1966; "The Physicists" opened Feb. 10, 1966; "Blood, Sweat and Stanley Poole" opened March 3, 1966; "A New Play" opened March 24, 1966.

COMPANY

Gary Gage, Zoaunne Henriot, Gerald Hjert, Sandy McCallu, Tom Roland, James Weston, Janice Rittmaster, Jerry Sando, John Y. Harrington, Scott Johnston, Mary Marshall, Barry Pritchard, Peggy Brown, Diane Prindible, P! Morton, Brian Joyce, Sr.

Press: Judith Anderson
Stage Managers: Brian Joyce, Sr., Tom Atkins

Act Two Photos

Zoaunne Henriot, Tom Roland in "The Typists" and top right in "The Tiger"

Gerald Hjert, Scott Johnston, Gary Gage, Zoaunne Henriot, Jim Weston in "She Loves Me" Above: Gerald Hjert, Janice Rittmaster in "She Loves Me"

Walt Burton Photos

PLAYHOUSE IN THE PARK
Cincinnati, Ohio
April 7 through Sept. 12, 1965
Brooks Jones, Producer

Kent Paul, Associate Producer; Directors, Lloyd Richards, Brooks Jones, Stephen Porter, David Hooks, Douglas Seale, and Ty McConnell; Scenic Designers, Douglas W. Schmidt, Keith Brown; Costumes, Caley Summers; Lighting, Keith Brown, Douglas W. Schmidt, Eric Gertner.

PRODUCTIONS

"Ghosts" opened April 7, "The Collection" and "The Lover" opened April 28, "Major Barbara" opened May 19, "Summer Of The Seventeenth Doll" opened June 9, "She Stoops To Conquer" opened June 30, "The Blood Knot" opened July 21, "The Glass Menagerie" opened August 11, "The Fantasticks" opened September 1, 1965.

COMPANY

Eric Gertner, Betty Lou Holland, David Hooks, Brooks Jones, Dennis Longwell, Lloyd Richards, Leon Shaw, Douglas Schmidt, Mary Sinclair, Caley Summers, Jonathan Farwell, Dan Travanty, Richard Silverman, Robin Gammell, Paddy Croft, Estelle Parsons, Ruth Rosen, Paxton Whitehead, Patrick Tovatt, Robert Stevenson, Nina Kuhn, Donald Ewer, Karen Austin, John A. Coe, Eleanor Hazelton, Margaretta Warwick, Clifford A. Pellow, Douglas Seale, Oliver Clark, Sharon Laughlin, Donald Symington, Forrest Smith, Jon Reynolds, Albert J. Allen, Lee Dunholter, Bob Lipka, Jr., Richard Meibers, Marian Schmidt, Abe Dunsky, Jonathan Marks, Phelps Montgomery, Philip Hanson, Andre Womble, Eugenia Rawls, Max Jacobs, Fred Roth, Jack Davison, Alice Cannon, Ty McConnell, David Ringer, Steven Smith, Linda Wellbaum.

Business Manager: Jane Krause
Stage Managers: Robert Stevenson, Eric Gertner

Top Left: Paxton Whitehead, Estelle Parsons in "Major Barbara." Below: Betty Lou Holland in "The Lover"

Clifford A. Pellow, Estelle Parsons in "Summer Of The Seventeenth Doll" Above: Philip Hanson, Andre Womble in "Blood Knot"

Eugenia Rawls in "The Glass Menagerie"

ALLEY THEATRE
Houston, Texas
October 13, 1965 through May 8, 1966
Nina Vance, Producer-Director

Associate Director, John Wylie; Designer, Paul Owen; Technical Director, Stanley Crow; Lighting, Florine (Sissy) Pulley; Production Associates, Trent Jenkins, Jim Kleeman, Jerry Ballew, Al Smither; Administrative Director, Milton Moss; Executive Director, Iris Siff.

PRODUCTIONS
"The Devil's Disciple" Oct. 13-Nov. 20, 1965; "Ah, Wilderness!" Nov. 24, 1965-Jan. 1, 1966; "Right You Are If You Think You Are" Jan. 5-Feb. 12, 1966; "You Can't Take It With You" Feb. 16-March 26, 1966; "Duel Of Angels" March 30-May 8, 1966.

COMPANY
George Anderson, Jerry Ballew, Linda Brown, J. Robert Dietz, Lillian Evans, Betty Fitzpatrick, Jerry Hardin, William Hardy, Dale Helward, Diane Hill, Trent Jenkins, Jim Kleeman, Marie LeMaster, Lorraine Meyer, Joseph Ruskin, Beth Sanford, Johnny Simons, Aubrey Simons, Al Smither, Barry Snider, Tom Toner, Audrey Ward.

Press: Terry Thompson, Robert Feingold
Stage Managers: Bettye Fitzpatrick, Beth Sanford

Marc St. Gil Photos

J. Robert Dietz, Bettye Fitzpatrick, Barry Snider in "The Devil's Disciple"
Above: (C) Barry Snider in "The Devil's Disciple"

McCARTER THEATRE
Princeton, New Jersey
October 8, 1965 through April 17, 1966
Arthur W. Lithgow, Executive Director

Associate Director, Mario Siletti; Guest Directors, Morton Siegel, Jan Moerel, Donald Moffat; Settings, Clyde W. Blakeley, Barbara C. Miller, Myles Smith; Costumes, Charles Blackburn; Lighting, Clyde W. Blakeley, Myles Smith; Music Coordinator, Gerald Warfield; Technical Directors, Myles Smith, John C. Schenck III; Administrative Assistant, John Condon.

PRODUCTIONS
"Mother Courage," "Coriolanus," "Major Barbara," "An Enemy Of The People," "Lady Windermere's Fan," "A Midsummer Night's Dream," "Miss Julie," "Candida," "Arrah-na-pogue" (Arrah of The Kiss).

COMPANY
Gregory Abels, Emery Battis, Ed Bordo, Anne Gee Byrd, David Byrd, Ralph Drischell, Charlotte Glenn, Ruby Holbrook, Duncan Hoxworth, Larry Linville, David Little, Judy London, Morton Siegel, Mario Siletti, Clarence Felder, Martha Knight, Penny Larsen, Anne Murray, Tony Musante, Frederic O'Brady, James Tripp.

General Manager: Nancy Shannon
Press: John V. McKenna, Penny Larsen, Martha H. Balkeley
Stage Managers: Jan Moerel, Martha Knight, John Merensky, Marcy Williams

Anne Gee Byrd, Gregory Abels, David Byrd
in "Candida"
ve: Anne Murray, Tony Musante in "Miss Julie"

David Byrd, Tony Musante,
and Above: Anne Gee Byrd in "Arrah-Na-Pouge"

ACTOR'S WORKSHOP
San Francisco, California
October 22, 1965 through April 9, 1966

Ken Kitch, Managing Director; John Hancock, Artistic Director; Associate Directors, Kenneth Margolis, Mark Estrin, Tom Gruenewald; Sets and Costumes, Ian Strasfogel, William Stewart Jones, Joan Larkey, Robert LaVigne, Jim Dine, Donald J. Childs, Warren Travis; Lighting, Donald J. Childs, Jim Rynning, Joan Larkey, Al Jutzi, F. Leon Leake, Kenneth Margolis, J. Thompson Poynter; Music, Morton Subotnik, Paul Gemignani, Ramon Sender; Choreography, Jane Lapiner; Technical Director, Donald J. Childs.

PRODUCTIONS

"The Milk Train Doesn't Stop Here Anymore" opened July 23, 1965; "Edward II" opened Oct. 22, 1965; "The Last Analysis" opened Nov. 26, 1965; "The Cage" and "Point Conception" opened Dec. 11, 1965; "Don Juan" opened Dec. 31, 1965; "The Father" opened Feb. 4, 1966; "The Empire Builders" opened Feb. 18, 1966; "A Midsummer Night's Dream" opened March 11, 1966.

COMPANY

Winifred Mann, Robert Benson, Sally Kemp, Joyce Lancaster, Robert Skundberg, Lindsay Moller, Nancy Bond, Tom Tarpey, Barton Heyman, Laurie Israel, Harold Keith, Joe Weiner, C. David Colson, Milt Kogan, Abe Vigoda, Daniel Ades, Alfred Leberfeld, Eric Feldman, Anthony Smith, Joe Brotherton, David Stiers, Richard Bright, Aaron Friedley, Jr., Bert Brauer, John Thibault, Hal Landon, Jr., V. L. McNally, Gary Capshaw, Jan M. Wagoner, Kjell Rostad, Peter Cohon, Myron Ruderman, Don Pedro Colley, Samuel Hitchcock, John Hart, Frank Silvey, Paul Shippee, Alison Gundlefinger, Kathleen Heflin, Maurice Argent, Bonnie Beecher, Rhoda Gemignani, Russell R. Husted, Fanny Lubritsky, Marshall Efron, Gary Capshaw, Billie Dixon, Hal Landon, Jr., Shelagh Hyner, Judi Quick, Wendy Wasdahl, Patricia Bokhari, Wendy Bohle, Joseph Miksak, Doug Von Koss, Susan Tanner, Ann Arensberg, Carol Feigenbaum, Lizzie Raab.

Press: Marion Conrad Associates
Stage Managers: Douglas Von Koss, Jane S. Montgomery, Michael Allen, Craig C. Weir, Linda Teague

Spicer, Hank Kranzler Photos

Stefan Gierasch in "A Man's A Man"

Alfred Leberfeld, Daniel Ades in "A Midsummer Night's Dream"
Above: Michael Linenthal, Robert Skundberg, Jane Steckle in "The Empire Builders"

Dudley, Hardin & Yang Photos

SEATTLE REPERTORY THEATRE
Seattle, Washington
October 25, 1965 through
April 17, 1966
Third Season

Stuart Vaughan, Artistic Director; General Manager, Donald Foster; Assistant Artistic Director, Pirie MacDonald; Assistant General Manager, Peter Donnelly; Literary Adviser, David Wagoner; Scenic Designer, Samuel Ball; Lighting, Richard Nelson; Costumes, Allan Granstrom; Stage Manager, R. Derek Swire.

PRODUCTIONS

"Julius Caesar" opened Oct. 25, 1965; "Long Day's Journey Into Night" opened Oct. 26, 1965; "The Importance Of Being Earnest" opened Oct. 27, 1965; "Ah, Wilderness" opened Dec. 19, 1965; "Heartbreak House" opened Jan. 5, 1966; "Galileo" opened March 2, 1966.

COMPANY

Roy Clary, Gordon Coffey, Glenn O. Diehl, Kay Doubleday, Jonathan Farwell, Pauline Flanagan, Anne Gerety, John Gilbert, Allan Granstrom, Elizabeth MacDonald, Stillman Moss, William Myers, William Newman, Donald Perkins, Nina Polan, Archie Smith, Anne Thompson, George Vogel, Michael Goodwin, Bernard J. Frawley, Jack Smith.

Left: Nina Polan, William Myers in "Julius Caesar"

Don Perkins, Anne Gerety in
"Long Day's Journey Into Night"

Jonathan Farwell, Pauline Flanagan in
"The Importance Of Being Earnest"

213

FAYE DUNAWAY
of
"Hogan's Goat"

DAVID CARRADINE
of
"The Royal Hunt Of The Sun"

215

GLORIA FOSTER
of
"Medea"

JOHN DAVIDSON
of
"Oklahoma!"

JOHN CULLUM
of
"On A Clear Day You Can See Forever"

ZOE CALDWELL
in
"Slapstick Tragedy"

Friedman-Abeles Photo

219

LESLEY ANN WARREN
of
"Drat! The Cat!"

Friedman-Abeles Photo

JERRY LANNING
of
"Mame"

Friedman-Abeles Photo

221

ROBERT HOOKS
of
"Where's Daddy?" and "Day Of Absence"

APRIL SHAWHAN
of
"3 Bags Full"

RICHARD MULLIGAN
of
"Mating Dance" and "Hogan's Goat"

SANDRA SMITH
of
"Any Wednesday"

PROMISING PERSONALITIES
THEATRE WORLD AWARD WINNERS

1944-45
Richard Davis	John Lund	John Raitt	Richard Hart	Donald Murphy
Judy Holliday	Betty Comden	Margaret Phillips	Charles Lang	Nancy Noland
Bambi Linn				

1945-46
Burt Lancaster	Bill Callahan	Wendell Corey	Mary James	Paul Douglas
Patricia Marshall	Barbara Bel Geddes	Marlon Brando	Beatrice Pearson	

1946-47
Patricia Neal	David Wayne	Keith Andes	Dorothea	Ann Crowley
James Mitchell	Marion Bell	John Jordan	MacFarland	George Keane
Ellen Hanley	Peter Cookson			

1947-48
Douglas Watson	Valerie Bettis	Ralph Meeker	Edward Bryce	Mark Dawson
Meg Mundy	Whitfield Connor	Peggy Maley	June Lockhart	Estelle Loring
James Whitmore	Patrice Wymore			

1948-49
Carol Channing	Gene Nelson	Julie Harris	Doe Avedon	Jean Carson
Tod Andrews	Allyn Ann McLerie	Richard Derr	Cameron Mitchell	Bob Scheerer
Mary McCarty	Byron Palmer			

1949-50
Charlton Heston	Grace Kelly	Charles Nolte	Roger Price	Phil Arthur
Priscilla Gillette	Don Hanmer	Lydia Clarke	Nancy Andrews	Barbara Brady
Rick Jason	Marcia Henderson			

1950-51
Richard Burton	Maureen Stapleton	William Smithers	Martin Brooks	James Daly
Barbara Ashley	Eli Wallach	Jack Palance	Pat Crowley	Cloris Leachman
Russell Nype	Isabel Bigley	Marcia Van Dyke		

1951-52
Audrey Hepburn	Ronny Graham	Marian Winters	Diana Herbert	Helen Wood
Tony Bavaar	Virginia de Luce	Kim Stanley	Dick Kallman	Peter Conlow
Patricia Benoit	Charles Proctor	Conrad Janis	Eric Sinclair	

1952-53
Paul Newman	Geraldine Page	Rosemary Harris	Peter Kelley	Richard Kiley
Eileen Heckart	Ray Stricklyn	John Kerr	Penelope Munday	Gloria Marlowe
John Stewart	Edie Adams	Gwen Verdon	Sheree North	

1953-54
Eva Marie Saint	James Dean	Harry Belafonte	Jonathan Lucas	Joan Diener
Leo Penn	Kay Medford	Carol Haney	Ben Gazzara	Scott Merrill
Elizabeth Montgomery	Orson Bean			

1954-55
Anthony Perkins	Julie Andrews	Christopher Plummer	David Daniels	Jack Lord
Jacqueline Brookes	Dennis Patrick	Loretta Leversee	Barbara Cook	Mary Fickett
Page Johnson	Shirl Conway			

1955-56
Jayne Mansfield	Laurence Harvey	Al Hedison	Diane Cilento	Gaby Rodgers
Anthony Franciosa	Susan Johnson	Sarah Marshall	Dick Davalos	Earle Hyman
Susan Strasberg	John Michael King	Andy Griffith	Fritz Weaver	

1956-57
George Grizzard	Peggy Cass	Cliff Robertson	Jason Robards, Jr.	Sylvia Daneel
Carol Lynley	Peter Palmer	Pippa Scott	Bradford Dillman	Peter Donat
Sydney Chaplin	Inga Swenson			

1957-58
Anne Bancroft	Robert Morse	Carol Lawrence	Jacqueline McKeever	Wynne Miller
George C. Scott	Joan Hovis	Warren Berlinger	Timmy Everett	Richard Easton
Colleen Dewhurst	Eddie Hodges			

1958-59
Rip Torn	Paul Roebling	Pat Suzuki	Ina Balin	Susan Oliver
Dolores Hart	France Nuyen	Tammy Grimes	Richard Cross	Roger Mollien
Lou Antonio	Ben Piazza	William Shatner	Larry Hagman	

1959-60
Carol Burnett	Jane Fonda	Warren Beatty	Dick Van Dyke	Patty Duke
Donald Madden	John McMartin	Anita Gillette	George Maharis	Lauri Peters
Eileen Brennan	Elisa Loti			

1960-61
Robert Goulet	James MacArthur	Ron Husmann	Joan Hackett	Nancy Dussault
Joyce Bulifant	June Harding	Dennis Cooney	Bruce Yarnell	

1961-62
Barbara Harris	Peter Fonda	Janet Margolin	Elizabeth Ashley	James Earl Jones
John Stride	Karen Morrow	Sean Garrison	Robert Redford	Keith Baxter
Brenda Vaccaro	Don Galloway			

1962-63
Dorothy Loudon	Alan Arkin	Liza Minnelli	Diana Sands	Melinda Dillon
Stuart Damon	Estelle Parsons	Bob Gentry	Swen Swenson	Brandon Maggart
Julienne Marie	Robert Drivas			

1963-64
Gilbert Price	Barbara Loden	Gloria Bleezarde	Ketty Lester	Imelda De Martin
John Tracy	Philip Proctor	Alan Alda	Jennifer West	Lawrence Pressman
Claude Giraud				

1964-65
Michael O'Sullivan	Bea Richards	Clarence Williams III	Robert Walker	Luba Lisa
Carolyn Coates	Joanna Pettet	Linda Lavin	Joyce Jillson	Nicolas Surovy
Victor Spinetti	Jaime Sanchez			

| ‑ude Adams | Robert Alda | Elizabeth Allen | Victor Arnold | Carol Arthur |

BIOGRAPHIES
OF THIS SEASON'S CASTS

ADAMS, TRUDE. Born in Brooklyn, June 19, 1931. Attended public schools and American School of Design. Made Broadway debut in 1955 in "Catch A Star," followed by "She Loves Me," "Leonard Bernstein's Theatre Songs" (Off-Bdwy).

ADLER, LUTHER. Born in New York City, May 4, 1903. Attended Lewis Inst. Made first appearance in 1908 in "Schmendrick." Other performances include "Night Over Taos," "Success Story," "Alien Corn," "Men In White," "Gold Eagle Guy," "Awake And Sing," "Paradise Lost," "Johnny Johnson," "Golden Boy," "Rocket To The Moon," "The Russian People," "Two On An Island," "Common Ground," "Beggars Are Coming To Town," "Dunnigan's Daughter," "A Flag Is Born," "The Merchant of Venice," "A Month In The Country," "A Very Special Baby," "The Passion of Josef D," "The Three Sisters," "Fiddler On The Roof."

AHEARNE, TOM. Born in Boston in 1904. Made Broadway bow in 1922 in "The World We Live In." Among his many appearances are "Guys and Dolls," "Three Men On A Horse," "Broadway," "Carousel," "Bells Are Ringing," "Mr. Roberts," "The Unsinkable Molly Brown," "Hogan's Goat" (Off-Bdwy).

ALDA, ALAN. Born in New York City, Jan. 28, 1936. Attended Fordham Univ. and Cleveland Playhouse. Broadway credits include "Only In America," "Purlie Victorious," "Fair Game For Lovers" for which he won a THEATRE WORLD Award, and "Cafe Crown." Off-Broadway credits: "Darwin's Theories," "A Whisper In God's Ear," and "Second City" (1963 edition), "The Owl and The Pussycat."

ALDA, ROBERT. Born in New York City, Feb. 26, 1914. Attended New York U. Made many motion pictures and appeared in night clubs before making Broadway bow in 1950 in "Guys and Dolls." Has appeared since in "Harbor Lights," "What Makes Sammy Run."

ALDREDGE, TOM. Born in Dayton, Ohio, Feb. 28, 1928. Attended U. of Dayton, and Goodman Theatre. Made Broadway bow in 1959 in "The Nervous Set." Has appeared Off-Bdwy in "The Tempest," "Between Two Thieves," "Henry V," "The Premise," "Love's Labour's Lost," "Troilus and Cressida," and in "UTBU," "Slapstick Tragedy."

ALEXANDER, CRIS. Born in Tulsa, Okla., in 1920. Has appeared in "Liliom," "On The Town," "Present Laughter," "Wonderful Town," "Auntie Mame," and Off-Bdwy in "Parade," "The Madness of Lady Bright."

ALLEN, ELIZABETH. Born in Jersey City, N. J., Jan. 25, 1934. Attended Rutgers U. Made Broadway debut in 1957 in "Romanoff and Juliet," followed by "The Gay Life," "Do I Hear A Waltz?"

ALLEN, NORMAN. Born in London, Dec. 24, 1939. Attended Royal Academy of Dramatic Art. Played in English productions before making New York bow in 1963 in "Chips With Everything," followed by "Half A Sixpence."

ALLEN, RAE. Born in Brooklyn, July 3, 1926. Attended Hunter College, American Academy of Dramatic Arts. Has appeared in "Where's Charley?," "Alive and Kicking," "Call Me Madam," "Pajama Game," "Damn Yankees," "Pictures In The Hallway" and "I Knock At The Door" (Off-Bdwy), "Oliver!," "Traveller Without Luggage," "On A Clear Day You Can See Forever," APA.

ALLINSON, MICHAEL. Born in London. Attended Lausanne U. and Royal Academy of Dramatic Art. Made New York bow in 1960 in "My Fair Lady," followed by "The Importance of Being Earnest" (Off-Bdwy), "Hostile Witness."

ARKIN, ALAN. Born in NYC, March 26, 1934. Attended Los Angeles Junior College, and Bennington College. Won 5 acting scholarships, including Brandeis Arts Inst. Appeared Off-Bdwy in "Heloise," "Man Out Loud," and on Broadway in "From The Second City" (1962), and "Enter Laughing" for which he received a THEATRE WORLD Award, "Luv."

ARMUS, SIDNEY. Born in the Bronx, Dec. 19, 1924. Attended Brooklyn College. Has appeared in "South Pacific," "Wish You Were Here," "The Flowering Peach," "A Hole In The Head," "The Cold Wind and The Warm," "Harold," "A Thousand Clowns," "Never Live Over A Pretzel Factory," "The Odd Couple."

ARNOLD, VICTOR. Born July 1, 1936 in Herkimer, N. Y. Graduate of NYU. Made Broadway bow in 1964 in "The Deputy." Has appeared Off-Bdwy in "Shadow Of Heroes," "Merchant Of Venice," "3 X 3," and "Lovey," and in "Malcolm."

ARTHUR, BEATRICE. Born in NYC, May 13. Attended The New School. Has appeared in "Seventh Heaven" (1954), "Nature's Way," "The Threepenny Opera," "Shoestring Revue," "Ulysses in Nighttown," "The Gay Divorce," "Fiddler On The Roof," "Mame."

ARTHUR, CAROL. Born in Hackensack, N. J., August 4, 1935. Attended American Academy of Dramatic Arts. Made Broadway debut in 1964 in "High Spirits." Has appeared on tour or Off-Bdwy in "Once Upon A Mattress," "Kicks and Co.," "Oh, What A Lovely War!," "Quality Street," "On The Town," "I Can Get It For You Wholesale," "New Cole Porter Revue."

ATIENZA, EDWARD. Born in London, Jan. 27, 1924. Attended U. of London, and London Academy of Music and Dramatic Arts. Made New York bow in 1957 in "Romanoff and Juliet," followed by "Becket," Old Vic (CC) productions, "Andorra," "The Affair," "Ivanov."

BACALL, LAUREN. Born in NYC, Sept. 16, 1924. Attended American Academy of Dramatic Arts. Made Broadway debut in "Franklin Street." Went to Hollywood and appeared in many movies before returning to Broadway in 1959 in "Goodbye Charlie," followed by "The Cactus Flower."

BACCALA, DONNA. Born in Baltimore, Md., April 26, 1945. Attended Inst. of Notre Dame. Made Broadway debut in 1963 in "No Strings," followed by "Royal Flush," "The Impossible Years."

Donna Baccala   Kaye Ballard   Jay Barney   Sandy Baron   Bonnie Bede

BAIN, CONRAD. Born in Lethbridge, Can., Feb. 4, 1923. Attended American Academy of Dramatic Arts. Has appeared in "Sixth Finger In A Five Finger Glove," "Candide," "The Makropoulos Secret," "Hot Spot," "Advise and Consent," "The Queen and The Rebels" and "Hogan's Goat" (Off-Bdwy).

BAIRD, CLARIBEL. Born Dec. 9, 1904 in Van Alstyne, Tex. Attended Okla. College, U. of Mich. and U. of London. Made Broadway debut Nov. 23, 1965 in APA revival of "You Can't Take It With You."

BALLARD, KAYE. Born in Cleveland, Ohio, Nov. 20, 1926. Appeared in stock, vaudeville, and night clubs before making New York bow in "The Golden Apple," followed by "Carnival," "The Beast In Me," "Royal Flush," "Cole Porter Revisited" (Off-Bdwy).

BALSAM, MARTIN. Born in NYC, Nov. 4, 1919. Trained at Actors Studio. Has appeared in "Ghost For Sale," "The Closing Door," "Sundown Beach," "Macbeth," "The Rose Tattoo," "Camino Real," "Middle Of The Night," "The Porcelain Year."

BANCROFT, ANNE. Born in NYC, Sept. 17, 1931. Attended American Academy of Dramatic Arts. Made Broadway debut in 1958 in "Two For The Seesaw" for which she received a THEATRE WORLD Award, followed by "The Miracle Worker," "Mother Courage and Her Children," "The Devils."

BARAGREY, JOHN. Born in Haleyville, Ala., April 15, 1918. Attended U. of Ala. Has appeared in "Sons and Soldiers," "Twilight Bar," "The Enchanted," "Pride's Crossing," "The Royal Family" (revival), "The Crucible," "The Devils."

BARBOUR, THOMAS. Born in NYC, July 25, 1921. Graduate of Princeton and Harvard. Has appeared Off-Bdwy in "Twelfth Night," "The Merchant of Venice," "The Admirable Bashville," "The River Line," "The Lady's Not For Burning," "The Enchanted," "Antony and Cleopatra," "The Saintliness of Margery Kempe," "Dr. Willy Nilly," "Under The Sycamore Tree," "Epitaph For George Dillon," "The Thracian Horses," "The Old Glory," "Sergeant Musgrave's Dance."

BARNEY, JAY. Born in Chicago, March 14, 1918. Attended U. of Chi., American Theatre Wing, Actors Studio. Has appeared in "The Respectful Prostitute," "Hope's The Thing With Feathers," "Detective Story," "The Number," "The Grass Harp," "Richard III," "Stockade," "The Immoralist," "The Trial," "The Young and Beautiful," "Eugenia," "Enemies" (Off-Bdwy).

BARON, SANDY. Born in Brooklyn in 1938. Graduate of Brooklyn College. Has appeared in "Second City," "The Premise," "Tchin-Tchin," "One Flew Over The Cuckoo's Nest," "Arturo Ui," "Generation."

BARRS, NORMAN. Born in London, Nov. 6, 1917. Appeared with Dublin Gate Co. in "The Old Lady Says No!," and "Where Stars Walk," and in "Now I Lay Me Down To Sleep," "The Little Glass Clock," "The Apple Cart," "The Little Moon of Alban," "Kwamina," "Poor Bitos," "The Zulu and The Zayda," "Hostile Witness."

BARTENIEFF, GEORGE. Born in Berlin, Ger., Jan. 24, 1933. Made Broadway bow in 1947 in "The Whole World Over." Appeared this season in "Venus Is."

BASELEON, MICHAEL. Born in Tarkio, Mo. Attended Northwestern U. and Actors Studio. Has appeared in "Caligula," "Night Life," "Dear Me, The Sky Is Falling," Off-Bdwy in "Hamlet," "Henry IV," "Richard II," "Romeo and Juliet," "The Tempest," and "Journey To The Day," "Venus Is."

BATTLES, MARJORIE. Born in Philadelphia, June 5, 1939. Attended Brandeis U. Appeared in stock before making Broadway debut in 1965 in "The Cactus Flower."

BEDELIA, BONNIE. Born in NYC, March 25, 1948. Attended Hunter College. Made Broadway debut in 1962 in "Isle of Children," followed by "Enter Laughing," "The Playroom."

BEDFORD, PATRICK. Born in Dublin, Ire., May 30, 1932. Appeared with Dublin Gate Theatre before making Broadway bow in 1966 in "Philadelphia Here I Come."

BEL GEDDES, BARBARA. Born in NYC, Oct. 31, 1923. Has appeared in "Out Of The Frying Pan," "Little Darling," "Nine Girls," "Mrs. January and Mr. X," "Deep Are The Roots" for which she received a THEATRE WORLD Award, "Burning Bright," "The Moon Is Blue," "The Sleeping Prince," "Silent Night, Lonely Night," "Mary, Mary," "The Porcelain Year," "Luv."

BELLAVER, HARRY. Born Feb. 12, 1905 in Hillsboro, Ill. Attended Brookwood Labor College. Made Broadway bow in 1931 in "The House of Connelly," followed by "Night Over Taos," "Carry Nation," "We, The People," "The Threepenny Opera," "The Sellout," "Page Miss Glory," "Noah," "The Black Pit," "How Beautiful With Shoes," "Russet Mantle," "St. Helena," "To Quito and Back," "Tortilla Flat," "Johnny 2 X 4," "Mr. Sycamore," "The World's Full Of Girls," "Annie Get Your Gun" (original and LC revival).

BELLINI, CAL. Born in San Francisco. Attended Princeton U. Made Broadway bow in 1959 in "Cut Of The Axe," followed by Off-Bdwy productions of "Shakuntala," "Two By Saroyan," and "The Immoralist," and "Ross," "The Royal Hunt Of The Sun."

BERGMANN, ALAN. Born in Brooklyn, and attended Syracuse U. and Catholic U. Made Broadway bow in 1961 in "Gideon," followed by "Here Come The Clowns," "Portrait Of The Artist As A Young Man," "Barroom Monks," "Night Life," "Lorenzo," "Luther," "Danton's Death" (LC Rep. Co.).

BERRY, ERIC. Born in London, Jan. 9, 1913. Attended Royal Academy of Dramatic Arts. Made New York bow in 1954 in "The Boy Friend," followed by "Family Reunion," "The Power and The Glory," "Beaux Stratagem," "The Broken Jug," "Pictures In The Hallway," "Peer Gynt," "The Great God Brown," "Henry IV," "The White House," "The White Devil."

BETHENCOURT, FRANCIS. Born in London, Sept. 5, 1924. Attended Mayfield College. Trained with Melville Rep. Co. before making New York bow in 1948 in "Anne Of The Thousand Days," followed by "The Happy Time," "Dial 'M' For Murder," "A Visit To A Small Planet," "Ross," "The Right Honourable Gentleman."

BIKEL, THEODORE. Born in Vienna, May 2, 1924. Attended College Mikue, Israel, and Royal Academy of Dramatic Arts, London. Made Broadway bow in 1955 in "Tonight in Samarkand," followed by "The Lark," "The Rope Dancers," "The Sound Of Music," "Pousse-Cafe."

Cal Bellini	Alan Bergmann	Coral Browne	Peter Bull	Ruth Buzzi

BIRD, JOSEPH. Born in Pittsburgh, Sept. 22, 1926. Graduate of Penn State. Has appeared Off-Bdwy in "Moon In The Yellow River," "Electra," "Go Show Me A Dragon," and APA productions including their 1965 Broadway debut in "You Can't Take It With You."

BOLIN, SHANNON. Born in South Dakota, Jan. 1, 1917. Attended U. of Md. Has appeared in "Helen Goes To Troy," "The Golden Apple," "Regina," "Only In America," "Damn Yankees," "The Student Gypsy," "Xmas In Las Vegas."

BOND, SUDIE. Born July 13, 1928 in Louisville, Ky. Attended Intermont College, Rollins College, NYU. Has appeared Off-Bdwy in "Summer and Smoke," "Tovarich," "The American Dream," "The Sandbox," "Endgame," "Theatre Of The Absurd," "Home Movies," "Softly and Consider The Nearness," and in "Waltz Of The Toreadors," "Auntie Mame," "The Egg," "Harold," "My Mother, My Father and Me," "The Impossible Years."

BOSLEY, TOM. Born in Chicago, Oct. 1, 1927. Attended DePaul U. Made Broadway bow in 1959 in "Fiorello!," followed by "Nowhere To Go But Up," "Natural Affection," "A Murderer Among Us," "Catch Me If You Can," "Luv."

BOVASSO, JULIE. Born in Brooklyn, August 1, 1930. Attended CCNY. Appeared Off-Bdwy in "Naked," "The Maids," "The Lesson," and "The Typewriter" before making Broadway debut in 1957 in "Monique," followed by "Minor Miracle."

BRACKEN, EDDIE. Born in Astoria, N. Y., Feb. 7, 1920. Attended Professional Children's School. Made Broadway bow in 1931 in "The Man On Stilts," followed by "The Lady Refuses," "Life's Too Short," "The Iron Men," "Brother Rat," "What A Life," "Too Many Girls," "The Seven Year Itch," "The Teahouse Of The August Moon," "Shinbone Alley," "Beg, Borrow Or Steal," "The Odd Couple."

BRIDGES, BEAU. Born Dec. 9, 1941 in Los Angeles. Attended UCLA and U. of Hawaii. Appeared in West Coast productions and on TV before making Broadway bow in 1966 in "Where's Daddy?"

BRODERICK, JAMES. Born in Charlestown, N. H., March 7, 1928. Attended U. of N.H. and Neighborhood Playhouse. Made Broadway bow in 1953 in "Maggie," and has appeared Off-Bdwy in "View From The Bridge," "A Touch Of The Poet," "Two By Saroyan," "The Firebugs," "Rooms."

BROOKES, JACQUELINE. Born in Montclair, N. J., July 24, 1930. Attended U. of Iowa and Royal Academy of Dramatic Arts. Made Broadway debut in 1955 in "Tiger At The Gates," and appeared Off-Bdwy in "The Cretan Woman" for which she received a THEATRE WORLD Award, "The Clandestine Marriage," "Measure For Measure," "The Duchess of Malfi," "Ivanov," "Six Characters In Search Of An Author," "An Evening's Frost."

BROOKS, LAWRENCE. Born in Westbrook, Me., Aug. 7, 1912. Made Broadway bow in 1944 in "Song Of Norway," followed by "My Romance," "Anya."

BROUN, HEYWOOD HALE. Born in NYC, March 10, 1918. Graduate of Swarthmore. Has appeared in "Love Me Long," "The Bird Cage," "The Live Wire," "The Small Hours," "The Pink Elephant," "His and Hers," "Point Of No Return," "The Bells Are Ringing," "The Andersonville Trial," "Send Me No Flowers," "Take Her, She's Mine," "My Mother, My Father and Me," "The Old Glory" (Off-Bdwy), "Xmas In Las Vegas."

BROWN, WALTER P. Born in Newark, N. J., April 18, 1926. Attended Brooklyn Conservatory of Music. Made Broadway bow in "Porgy and Bess," followed by "Fiorello!," "The Advocate," at City Center in "Guys and Dolls" and "South Pacific," "Kelly."

BROWNE, CORAL. Born in Melbourne, Aust., July 23, 1913. Appeared on English stage before making Broadway debut in 1956 in "Tamburlaine," followed by "Troilus and Cressida," "The Rehearsal," "The Right Honourable Gentleman."

BRUCE, ALLAN. Born in Glasgow, Scot., Nov. 2, 1930. Appeared in Europe, and in U.S. night clubs before making New York bow Off-Bdwy in 1965 in "Great Scot!."

BRUCE, CAROL. Born in Great Neck, L. I., Nov. 15, 1919. Made Broadway debut in "George White's Scandals of 1939," followed by "Nice Goin'," "Louisiana Purchase," "Show Boat" (1946 revival), "Along Fifth Avenue," "A Family Affair," "Pal Joey" (City Center), "Do I Hear A Waltz?"

BUKA, DONALD. Born in 1921 in Cleveland, Ohio. Attended Carnegie Tech. Has appeared in "Twelfth Night," "The Corn Is Green," "Bright Boy," "Helen Goes To Troy," "Sophie," "Live Life Again," and toured in "The Cat and The Canary" and "The Absence Of a Cello."

BULL, PETER. Born in London, March 21, 1912. Attended Winchester College, Tours U. Has appeared on Broadway in "Escape Me Never," "The Lady's Not For Burning," "Luther," "Pickwick."

BURKE, GEORGIA. Born in LaGrange, Ga., Feb. 27, 1906. Attended Claflin U. and NYU. Made Broadway debut in "Lew Leslie's Blackbirds," followed by "Five Star Final," "Savage Rhythm," "In Abraham's Bosom," "Old Man Satan," "They Shall Not Die," "Mamba's Daughters," "Cabin In The Sky," "No Time For Comedy," "Sun Fields," "Decision," "Anna Lucasta," "The Wisteria Trees," "The Grass Harp," "Porgy and Bess" (revival), "Bohikee Creek" (Off-Bdwy).

BURNS, DAVID. Born in NYC, June 22, 1902. Has appeared in "Polly Preferred," "Wonder Boy," "Face The Music," "The Man Who Came To Dinner," "Pal Joey," "My Dear Public," "Billion Dollar Baby," "Make Mine Manhattan," "Out Of This World," "Two's Company," "Men Of Distinction," "A Hole In The Head," "The Music Man," "A Funny Thing Happened On The Way To The Forum," "Hello, Dolly!"

BURR, ROBERT. Born in Jersey City, N. J. Attended Colgate U. Has appeared in "The Cradle Will Rock," "Mister Roberts," "Romeo and Juliet," "Picnic," "The Lovers," "Anniversary Waltz," "Top Man," "Remains To Be Seen," "The Wall," "Andersonville Trial," "A Shot In The Dark," "A Man For All Seasons," "Luther," "Hamlet" (1964), "Bajour," "The White Devil," "The Royal Hunt Of The Sun."

BUZZI, RUTH. Born July 24, 1936 in Westerly, R. I. Attended Pasadena Playhouse School. Appeared Off-Bdwy in "Mis-Guided Tour," "A Man's A Man," "Babes In The Wood," "Baker's Dozen," and "The Game Is Up" before making Broadway debut in 1966 in "Sweet Charity."

William Callan   Helena Carroll   Roy Castle   Jordan Charney   James Coco

CALL, JOHN. Born in Philadelphia, Nov. 3, 1915. Attended U. of Pa. Has appeared in "Father Malachy's Miracle," "Merchant of Yonkers," "As You Like It," "Be So Kindly," "But For The Grace Of God," "The Flying Gerardos," "So Proudly We Hail," "Bet Your Live," "Bloomer Girl," "Pipe Dream," "A Touch Of The Poet," "Oliver!," "Pickwick," "A Time For Singing."

CALLAN, WILLIAM. Born Jan. 1, 1918 in Brooklyn. Graduate of NYU and Catholic U. Made Broadway bow in 1954 in "Anastasia," followed by "The Visit," "Many Loves" (Off-Bdwy), "Masquerade," "Midgie Purvis," "A Man For All Seasons," "After The Fall," "Malcolm."

CALVIN, HENRY. Born May 25, 1918 in Dallas, Tex. Appeared in concert and opera before making Broadway debut in 1947 in a revival of "The Chocolate Soldier," followed by revivals of "Sally" and "Kismet."

CARPENTER, CARLTON. Born in Bennington, Vt., July 10, 1926. Attended Northwestern U. Has appeared in "Bright Boy," "Career Angel," "Three To Make Ready," "Magic Touch," "John Murray Anderson's Almanac," "Hotel Paradiso," "Hello, Dolly!"

CARNEY, ART. Born in Mt. Vernon, N. Y., Nov. 4, 1918. Appeared in vaudeville, night clubs, stock and TV before making Broadway bow in 1957 in "The Rope Dancers," followed by "Take Her, She's Mine," "The Odd Couple."

CARR, KENNETH. Born May 3, 1943 in the Bronx, N. Y. Attended public schools and Max Slater Acting Academy. Made Broadway bow Oct. 13, 1965 in "The Impossible Years."

CARRADINE, DAVID. Born Dec. 8, 1940 in Hollywood, Calif. Attended San Francisco State College. After appearing in stock and films, made his Broadway bow in 1964 in "The Deputy," followed by "The Royal Hunt Of The Sun" for which he received a THEATRE WORLD Award.

CARROLL, DANNY. Born May 30, 1940 in Maspeth, L. I. Graduate of High School of Performing Arts. Made Broadway bow in 1957 in "The Music Man," followed by "The Boys From Syracuse," and "Babes In The Wood" Off-Bdwy, "Flora, The Red Menace," "Funny Girl."

CARROLL, HELENA. Born in Glasgow, Scot. Attended Webber-Douglas School of Drama, London. Came to U.S. with Dublin Players. Founded, produced, directed, and acted with the Irish Players Off-Bdwy. Made Broadway debut in 1956 in "Separate Tables," followed by "A Touch Of The Poet," "Happy As Larry," "Little Moon of Alban," "The Hostage," "Oliver!," "Pickwick."

CASSIDY, JACK. Born in Richmond Hills, L. I., March 5, 1927. Has appeared in "Something For The Boys," "Sadie Thompson," "Around The World," "Inside U.S.A.," "Small Wonder," "Music In My Heart," "Alive and Kicking," "Wish You Were Here," "Sandhog," "Shangri-La," "The Beggar's Opera," "She Loves Me," "Fade Out—Fade In," "It's A Bird . . . It's A Plane . . . It's Superman."

CASTLE, ROY. Born August 31, 1932 in England. Attended public schools, and appeared in vaudeville in England. Made Broadway debut Oct. 4, 1965 in "Pickwick."

CHANNING, CAROL. Born in Seattle, Wash., Jan. 31, 1921. Attended Bennington College. Made New York stage debut in 1941 in "No For An answer," followed by "Let's Face It," "Proof Through The Night," "Lend An Ear" for which she received a THEATRE WORLD Award, "Gentlemen Prefer Blondes," "Wonderful Town," "The Vamp," "Show Girl," "Hello, Dolly."

CHAPLIN, SYDNEY. Born in Los Angeles, March 31, 1926. Attended Lawrenceville School. Made several films before making Broadway bow in 1956 in "Bells Are Ringing" for which he received a THEATRE WORLD Award, followed by "Goodbye Charlie," "Subways Are For Sleeping," "In The Counting House," "Funny Girl."

CHARNEY, JORDAN. Born in NYC. Graduate of Brooklyn College. Appeared Off-Bdwy in "Harry, Noon and Night," "A Place For Chance," "Hang Down Your Head and Die," "The Pinter Plays," "Telemachus Clay," and "The Zoo Story." Made Broadway bow in 1966 in "Slapstick Tragedy."

CHASE, ILKA. Born April 8, 1900 in NYC. Attended private schools. Made Broadway debut in 1924 in "The Red Falcon," followed by "Shall We Join The Ladies?," "Antonia," "Embers," "The Happy Husband," "Animal Kingdom," "Forsaking All Others," "Days Without End," "While Parents Sleep," "Wife Insurance," "Small Miracle," "Revenge With Music," "Keep Off The Grass," "Beverly Hills," "The Women," "In Bed We Cry," "Barefoot In The Park."

COATES, CAROLYN. Born April 29, 1930 in Oklahoma City. Attended UCLA. Appeared in Natl. Co. of "Sweet Bird Of Youth," and Off-Bdwy in "The Innocents," "The Balcony," "Electra," "The Trojan Women" for which she received a THEATRE WORLD Award, and with Lincoln Center Rep. Co. in "The Country Wife," "The Condemned of Altona," and "The Caucasian Chalk Circle."

COCO, JAMES. Born in NYC on March 21, 1930. Has appeared Off-Bdwy in "The Moon In The Yellow River," "That 5 A.M. Jazz," "Lovey," "Squat Betty and The Sponge Room," "Salome." Made Broadway bow in 1957 in "Hotel Paradiso," followed by "Everybody Loves Opal," "A Passage To India," "Arturo Ui," "The Devils."

COLBY, BARBARA. Born July 2, 1940 in NYC. Attended Carnegie Tech, Bard College, and La Sorbonne, Paris. Appeared Off-Bdwy in "Under Milkwood" and "Six Characters In Search of An Author" before making Broadway debut in 1965 in "The Devils."

COLICOS, JOHN. Born in Toronto, Can., Dec. 10, 1928. Made Broadway bow in 1966 in "The Devils," and has appeared in Orson Welles' City Center "King Lear" (1956), and Off-Bdwy in "Sergeant Musgrave's Dance."

COLLINS, BLANCHE. Born in NYC, May 12, 1918. Attended Columbia. Has appeared in "Scarlet Sister Mary," "Strike Me Pink," "The Cradle Will Rock," "G.I. Hamlet," "On A Clear Day You Can See Forever."

COLLINS, PAUL. Born in London, July 25, 1937. Attended City and State College in Los Angeles, and Actors Studio. Appeared Off-Bdwy in "Say Nothing" and "Cambridge Circus" before making Broadway bow in 1965 in "The Royal Hunt Of The Sun."

hn Colicos   Paul Collins   Eve Collyer   Gino Conforti   Staats Cotsworth

COLLYER, EVE. Born in Pittsburgh, Nov. 26, 1927. Graduate of Carnegie Tech. Has appeared Off-Bdwy in "The Way of The World," "Morning's At Seven," "The Adding Machine," "Don Juan In Hell," and "Diversions," and Broadway debut was in 1959 in "The Music Man," followed by "Gideon," "Arturo Ui," "Right Honourable Gentleman."

CONFORTI, GINO. Born in Chicago, Jan. 30, 1932. Attended Catholic U. Off-Bdwy appeared in "The Fantasticks," "Smiling The Boy Fell Dead," and made Broadway bow in 1961 in "A Family Affair," followed by "She Loves Me," "Fiddler On The Roof," "Poor Bitos," "Never Live Over A Pretzel Factory," "Man Of La Mancha."

CONNELL, JANE. Born in Berkeley, Calif., Oct. 27, 1925. Attended U. of Calif. Appeared in night clubs before making New York debut in "Shoestring Revue." Has appeared since in "The Threepenny Opera," "New Faces of 1956," "Pieces of Eight," "Demi-Dozen," "Drat! The Cat!," "Mame."

CONNOLLY, THOMAS. Born in NYC. Attended Westchester College and NYU. Made New York bow Off-Bdwy in "The Moon In The Yellow River," followed by "The Miracle Worker," "The Riot Act," "Never Too Late," "Philadelphia, Here I Come!"

CONVY, BERT. Born July 23, 1935 in St. Louis, Mo. Graduate of UCLA. Made New York bow in "Billy Barnes Revue," followed by "Nowhere To Go But Up," "Morning Sun," "Love and Kisses," "Fiddler On The Roof," "The Impossible Years."

COOK, BARBARA. Born Oct. 25, 1927 in Atlanta, Ga. Made Broadway debut in 1951 in "Flahooley," followed by "Plain and Fancy" for which she received a THEATRE WORLD Award, "Candide," "The Music Man," City Center revivals of "Carousel," and "The King and I," "The Gay Life," "She Loves Me," "Something More," "Any Wednesday," "Show Boat" (LC revival).

COONEY, DENNIS. Born in NYC, Sept. 19, 1938. Attended Fordham U. Appeared Off-Bdwy in "Whisper To Me" and "Every Other Girl" for which he received a THEATRE WORLD Award, before making Broadway bow in 1961 in "Ross," followed by "Love and Kisses," "In A Summer House" (Off-Bdwy), "The Lion In Winter."

COOPER, ANTHONY KEMBLE. Born in London, Feb. 6, 1908. Made New York bow in 1925 in "Lass O' Laughter," followed by "The School For Scandal," "His Majesty's Car," "The Command To Love," "Quiet, Please," "Anne Of England," "Hay Fever," "Mary Of Scotland," "Age 26," "Sheppey," "Ten Little Indians," "Sweethearts," "Mr. Pickwick," "Foxy," "Hostile Witness."

COOPER, MELVILLE. Born in Birmingham, England, Oct. 15, 1896. Made New York bow in 1935 in "Laburnum Grove," followed by "Jubilee," "The Merry Widow," "While The Sun Shines," "Firebrand of Florence," "Pygmalion," "Gypsy Lady," "The Haven," "An Inspector Calls," "The Liar," "The Day After Tomorrow," "Make A Wish," "Much Ado About Nothing" (1952), "Escapade," "My Fair Lady," "Hostile Witness."

CORZATTE, CLAYTON. Born in Fairhope, Ala., March 4, 1927. Graduate of U. of Ala. Has appeared with American, San Diego, and Antioch Shakespeare Festivals, and with the APA since 1961 in such plays as "The Wild Duck," "The Lower Depths," "School For Scandal," "A Midsummer Night's Dream," "Ghosts," "The Sea Gull," "War and Peace," "You Can't Take It With You."

COTSWORTH, STAATS. Born in Oak Park, Ill., Feb. 17, 1908. Received training with Eva LeGallienne's Civic Repertory Theatre. Among his many roles are "Romeo and Juliet," "Alice In Wonderland," "Rain From Heaven," "Murder At The Vanities," "Madame Capet," "Macbeth," "She Stoops To Conquer," "Richard III," "Advise and Consent," "Hamlet," "I Knock At The Door," "Pictures In A Hallway," "Right Honourable Gentleman."

COULOURIS, GEORGE. Born in Manchester, Eng., Oct. 1, 1903. Made New York bow in 1929 in "The Novice and The Duke," followed by "The Apple Cart," "The Late Christopher Bean," "Best Sellers," "Mary Of Scotland," "Valley Forge," "Blind Alley," "Saint Joan," "Julius Caesar," "The Shoemaker's Holiday," "Madame Capet," "The White Steed," "Richard III," "The Alchemist," "The Insect Comedy," "Beekman Place," "The Condemned of Altona" (LC Rep.).

COWLES, MATTHEW. Born in NYC, Sept. 28, 1944. Attended King-Coit School and Neighborhood Playhouse. Has appeared in "The Rose and The Ring," "The Golden Fleecing," "No Time For Sergeants," "Our Town," "The Faraway Princess," "Malcolm."

CRAIG, HELEN. Born in San Antonio, Tex., May 13, 1914. Attended Scarborough School. Made Broadway debut in 1936 in "Russet Mantle," followed by "New Faces," "Julius Caesar," "Soliloquy," "Family Portrait," "The Unconquered," "Johnny Belinda," "As You Like It," "Lute Song," "Land's End," "The House of Bernarda Alba," "Maya," "Diamond Orchid," "Medea" (Off-Bdwy).

CRONIN, JANE. Born April 4, 1936 in Boston, Mass. Attended Boston U. School of Theatre. Appeared in "The Bald Soprano" (Off-Bdwy), and toured in "Desire Under The Elms" and "The Sign In Sidney Brustein's Window" before making Broadway debut November 1, 1965 in "Postmark Zero."

CRONYN, HUME. Born in London, Ont., Can., July 18, 1911. Attended Ridley College, McGill U., American Academy of Dramatic Arts. Has appeared in "Hipper's Holiday," "High Tor," "Escape This Night," "Three Men On A Horse," "Boy Meets Girl," "Room Service," "The Three Sisters," "Mr. Big," "Retreat To Pleasure," "The Fourposter," "The Honeys," "A Day By The Sea," "The Man In The Dog Suit," "Triple Play," "Big Fish, Little Fish," "Hamlet," "The Physicists," and with Minnesota Theatre Co.

CULLUM, JOHN. Born March 2, 1930 in Knoxville, Tenn. Graduate of U. of Tenn. Made Broadway bow in 1960 in "Camelot," followed by "Infidel Caesar," "The Rehearsal," "Hamlet," "On A Clear Day You Can See Forever."

CULVER, ROLAND. Born in London, Aug. 31, 1900. Attended Holgate College and Royal Academy of Dramatic Arts. Made Broadway bow in 1953 in "The Little Hut," followed by "Five Finger Exercise," "Ivanov."

231

Lance Cunard	Jon Cypher	Stuart Damon	Barbara Dana	Edgar Da

CUMMINGS, ROBERT. Born in Joplin, Mo., June 9, 1910. Attended Carnegie Tech. Made Broadway bow in 1931 in "The Roof" using name Blade Stanhope Conway. Changed it to Brice Hutchens and appeared in "Earl Carroll's Vanities," and "Ziegfeld Follies." As Robert C. Conway appeared in "Strange Orchestra," and went to Hollywood. After many films, returned to Broadway in 1951 in "Faithfully Yours," and in 1966 in "The Wayward Stork."

CUNARD, LANCE. Born March 20, 1910 in Collingswood, N. J. Attended Ursinus College. Made New York bow in 1945 with Fred Stone in "You Can't Take It With You," followed by "Legend Of Lizzie," "The Visit," "The Trial," "Alcestis," "Spring's Awakening," "Volpone," "Richard III," "Henry V," "Rules Of The Game," "As You Like It," "A Midsummer Night's Dream," "The Taming Of The Shrew," "Corruption In The Palace of Justice," "Colombe," "Sign Of Winter," "Orphee," "The Deadly Game."

CUNNINGHAM, SARAH. Born Sept. 8, 1918 in Greenville, S. C. Attended Furman U., New School, American Theatre Wing, Actors Studio. Made Broadway debut in 1948 in "The Respectful Prostitute" and "A Happy Journey," followed by "Blood Wedding," "The Young and Fair," "House of Bernarda Alba," "The World of Sholem Aleichem," "Fair Game," "The Visit," "Toys In The Attic," "Portrait of The Artist As A Young Man," "The Barroom Monks," "Christy," "The Zulu and The Zayda."

CUNNINGHAM, ZAMAH. Born in Portland, Ore. Has appeared in many New York productions, including "Post Road," "Are You Decent?," "Tanyard Street," "Gentlewoman," "The Trojan Women," "On The Town," "Shadow Of A Gunman," "Minor Miracle."

CURTIS, KEENE. Born in Salt Lake City, Feb. 15, 1923. Graduate U. of Utah. Made Broadway bow in 1949 in "The Shop At Sly Corner," followed by stage managing many productions. In 1960 he joined the APA as an actor and has appeared in such productions as "The School For Scandal," "The Tavern," "Anatole," "Scapin," "Right You Are," "The Importance Of Being Earnest," "Twelfth Night," "King Lear," "The Seagull," "Lower Depths," "Man and Superman," "Judith," "War and Peace," "You Can't Take It With You."

CUSHMAN, NANCY. Born in Brooklyn, April 26, 1913. Graduate of Rollins College. Has appeared in "White Man," "Storm Over Patsy," "Gloriana," "Janie," "Be Your Age," "J. B.," "Little Me," Off-Bdwy in "The American Dream" and "The Child Buyer," "Skyscraper."

CUTTS, PATRICIA. Born in London, July 20, 1931. Attended Royal Academy of Dramatic Arts. Made New York debut in 1955 in "The Matchmaker," followed by "Kean," "Any Wednesday."

CYPHER, JON. Born Jan. 13, 1932 in Brooklyn. Graduate of U. of Vermont. Made Broadway bow in 1958 in "The Disenchanted," followed by "The Wives" and "The Great Western Union" Off-Bdwy, "Jennie," "Night of The Iguana," "Man of La Mancha."

DAILEY, DAN. Born NYC. In minstrel show as a child. On Broadway in "Babes In Arms," "Stars In Your Eyes," "I Married An Angel," "Catch Me If You Can," "The Odd Couple."

DAILEY, IRENE. Born Sept. 12, 1920 in NYC. Attended Sacred Heart Convent. After stock and touring, made Broadway debut in "Nine Girls" in 1943, followed by "Truckline Cafe," "Idiot's Delight" (CC 1951), "The Good Woman of Setzuan," "Miss Lonelyhearts," "Andorra," "The Subject Was Roses," "Rooms" (Off-Bdwy).

DAINE, LOIS. Born Dec. 5, 1941 in Bolton, Lancashire, Eng. After successful career on British stage, made Broadway debut Nov. 31, 1965 in "Inadmissible Evidence."

DALE, GROVER. Born in Harrisburg, Pa., July 22, 1935. After teaching dancing, made Broadway bow in "Li'l Abner," followed by "West Side Story," "Greenwillow," Off-Bdwy in "Fallout" and "Too Much Johnson," "Sail Away," "Half A Sixpence."

DAMON, CATHRYN. Born Sept. 11 in Seattle, Wash. Studied at Met Opera Ballet School. Made Broadway debut in 1954 in "By The Beautiful Sea," followed by "The Vamp," "Shinbone Alley," "A Family Affair," "Foxy," Off-Bdwy in "The Boys From Syracuse" and "The Secret Life of Walter Mitty," "Flora, The Red Menace," "UTBU."

DAMON, STUART. Born in Brooklyn, Feb. 5, 1937. Graduate of Brandeis U. Made Broadway bow in 1959 in "First Impressions," followed by "From A To Z," "Entertain A Ghost," Off-Bdwy revival of "The Boys From Syracuse" for which he received a THEATRE WORLD Award, "Do I Hear A Waltz?"

DANA, BARBARA. Born Dec. 28, 1940 in NYC. Appeared Off-Bdwy in "A Clearing In The Woods," "A Worm In The Horseradish," "Angels of Anadarko," "Second City," and made Broadway debut in 1963 in "Enter Laughing" followed by "Who's Afraid Of Virginia Woolf?," "Where's Daddy?"

DANA, LEORA. Born April 1, 1923 in NYC. Attended Barnard College and Royal Academy of Dramatic Arts. Made Broadway debut in 1947 in "The Madwoman of Chaillot," followed by "The Happy Time," "Point Of No Return," "Sabrina Fair," "The Best Man," "In The Summer House" (Off-Bdwy), "Beekman Place," National Repertory Theatre productions.

DANIELS, CAROLAN. Born May 16, 1940 in Fullerton, Calif. Graduate of USC. Appeared Off-Bdwy in "Telemachus Clay" before making Broadway debut in 1964 in "Slow Dance On The Killing Ground," followed by "Me and Thee," "Monopoly" (Off-Bdwy).

DANIELS, EDGAR. Born in Raleigh, N. C., June 3, 1932. Attended UNC. Has appeared in "New Girl In Town," "La Plume De Ma Tante," "Caligula," "The Affair," "A Man For All Seasons," "Hostile Witness."

DANIELS, WILLIAM. Born in Brooklyn, March 31, 1927. Graduate of Northwestern U. Made Broadway bow in 1943 in "Life With Father," followed by "Richard II," "Seagulls Over Sorrento," "Legend of Lizzie," "Cat On A Hot Tin Roof," "A Thousand Clowns," Off-Bdwy in "The Zoo Story," "The Iceman Cometh," and "Look Back In Anger," "Dear Me, The Sky Is Falling," "One Flew Over The Cuckoo's Nest," "On A Clear Day You Can See Forever."

D'ANTONAKIS, FLEURY. Born in Athens, Greece, May 11, 1939. Graduate of Brandeis U. and Neighborhood Playhouse. Made Broadway debut in 1965 in "Do I Hear A Waltz?"

232

ny Davis, Jr.   MacIntyre Dixon   Stephen Douglass   M'el Dowd   James Dukas

DAVID, CLIFFORD. Born in Toledo, O., June 30, 1932. Attended Toledo U. and Actors Studio. Made Broadway bow in 1960 in "Caligula," followed by "Wildcat," "The Aspern Papers," "The Boys From Syracuse" (Off-Bdwy), "On A Clear Day You Can See Forever."

DAVID, THAYER. Born March 4, 1927, in Medford, Mass. Graduate of Harvard. Has appeared in "The Relapse," "King Lear" (CC), "The Carefree Tree" and "The White Devil" at the Phoenix, "Mister Johnson," "Protective Custody," "Oscar Wilde" (OB), "A Man For All Seasons," "Andorra," NRT revivals of "The Seagull" and "The Crucible," "The Royal Hunt Of The Sun."

DAVIDSON, JOHN. Born in Pittsburgh, Dec. 13, 1941. Graduate of Denison U. Made Broadway bow in 1963 in "Foxy," followed by City Center revival of "Oklahoma!" for which he received a THEATRE WORLD Award.

DAVIS, OSSIE. Born in Cogdell, Ga., in 1917. Attended Howard U. Made Broadway debut in 1946 in "Jeb," followed by "Anna Lucasta," "The Leading Lady," "The Smile Of The World," "The Wisteria Trees," "The Royal Family" (CC), "The Green Pastures" (1951), "Remains To Be Seen," "Touchstone," "No Time For Sergeants," "Jamaica," "A Raisin In The Sun," "Purlie Victorious" which he wrote, "Ballad of Bimshire" (Off-Bdwy), "The Zulu and The Zayda."

DAVIS, SAMMY, JR. Born Dec. 8, 1925 in NYC. Played in vaudeville, burlesque, and night clubs before making Broadway bow in 1956 in "Mr. Wonderful," followed by "Golden Boy."

DeANDA, PETER. Born in Pittsburgh, March 10, 1940. Attended Actors Workshop and Pittsburgh Playhouse. Appeared Off-Bdwy in "The Blacks," "Dutchman," and "Sound Of Silence" before making Broadway bow in 1965 in "The Zulu and The Zayda."

DEKKER, ALBERT. Born Dec. 20, 1905 in Brooklyn. Graduate of Bowdoin College. Made Broadway bow in 1928 in "Marco Millions," followed by "Volpone," "Conflict," "Troika," "Sisters of The Chorus," "Grand Hotel," "Napi," "Brittle Heaven," "Fly Away Home," "Johnny Johnson," "An Enemy of The People," "Death of A Salesman," "Gertie," "The Andersonville Trial," "Face of A Hero," "A Man For All Seasons," "The Devils."

DeKOVEN, ROGER. Born in Chicago, Oct. 22, 1907. Attended U. of Chi., Northwestern, and Columbia. Made Broadway bow in 1926 in "Juarez and Maximilian," followed by "The Mystery Man," "Once In A Lifetime," "Counsellor-at-Law," "Murder In The Cathedral," "The Eternal Road," "Brooklyn, U.S.A.," "The Assassins," "Joan of Lorraine," "Abie's Irish Rose" (1954), "The Lark," "The Hidden River," "Compulsion," "The Miracle Worker," "The Fighting Cock," "Tovarich" (1963), "Arturo Ui," "Funny Girl," and Off-Bdwy in "The Deadly Game."

DELL, GABRIEL. Born in Barbados, B.W.I., Oct. 7, 1930. Has appeared in "Dead End," "Tickets, Please," "Ankles Aweigh," "Fortuna," City Center revivals of "Can-Can," "Wonderful Town," and "Oklahoma!," "Marathon '33," "Anyone Can Whistle," "The Sign In Sidney Brustein's Window," "Luv."

DeWOLFE, BILLY. Born in Wollaston, Mass., Feb. 18. Appeared in vaudeville, night clubs, and movies before making Broadway bow in 1953 in "John Murray Anderson's Almanac," followed by "Ziegfeld Follies," "How To Succeed In Business Without Really Trying" (1966 CC).

DIENER, JOAN. Born Feb. 24, 1934 in Cleveland, O. Attended Sarah Lawrence College. Made Broadway debut in 1948 in "Small Wonder," followed by "Season In The Sun," "Kismet" for which she received a THEATRE WORLD Award, "Man of La Mancha."

DILWORTH, GORDON. Born May 29, 1913 in Brooklyn. Attended Miami, Ohio, U., Juilliard School of Music. Made Broadway bow in 1937 in "Babes In Arms," followed by "Sunny River," "The Fair At Sorochinsk," "Queen of Spades," "Helen Goes To Troy," City Center revivals of "The Merry Widow," "Pagliacci," and "The Gypsy Baron," "Paint Your Wagon," "Sandhog," "My Fair Lady," "The Unsinkable Molly Brown," "On A Clear Day You Can See Forever."

DIXON, MacINTYRE. Born Dec. 22, 1931 in Everett, Mass. Graduate of Emerson College. Appeared Off-Bdwy in "Quare Fellow," "Plays For Bleecker Street," "Stewed Prunes," "Cat's Pajamas," "Three Sisters," "Three By Three," "Second City," "Upstairs At The Downstairs," and "The Mad Show." Made Broadway debut in 1965 in "Xmas In Las Vegas."

DORMAN, JOHN. Born in Boise, Idaho, July 19, 1922. Attended Iowa State College, Seattle Repertory Playhouse. Has appeared in "Peter Pan" (1951), "The Skin Of Our Teeth," "Requiem For A Nun," "Hogan's Goat" (Off-Bdwy).

DOUGLASS, STEPHEN. Born in Mt. Vernon, Ohio, Sept. 27, 1921. Made Broadway debut in "Carousel," followed by "Arms and The Girl," "Make A Wish," "The Golden Apple," "The Pajama Game," "Damn Yankees," "Rumple," City Center "Brigadoon," "110 In The Shade," "Show Boat" (LC revival).

DOWD, M'EL. Born Feb. 2 in Chicago. Studied at Goodman Theatre. Appeared Off-Bdwy in "Macbeth," "A Midsummer Night's Dream," "Romeo and Juliet," and "Julius Caesar" before making Broadway debut in 1958 in "Methuselah," followed by "Royal Gambit," "Sweet Bird Of Youth," "Camelot," "The Emperor," "A Case of Libel," "Right Honourable Gentleman."

DRAKE, ALFRED. Born Oct. 7, 1914 in NYC. Graduate of Brooklyn College. Made Broadway bow in 1935 in chorus of "The Mikado," followed by "White Horse Inn," "Babes In Arms," "The Two Bouquets," "One For The Money," "The Straw Hat Revue," "Two For The Show," "Out Of The Frying Pan," "As You Like It" (1941), "Yesterday's Magic," "Oklahoma!," "Sing Out, Sweet Land," "Beggar's Holiday," "The Cradle Will Rock," "Joy To The World," "Kiss Me, Kate," "The Liar," "The Gambler," "The King and I," "Kismet," "Kean," "Lorenzo," "Hamlet" (1964), 1965 LC revival of "Kismet."

DRUMMOND, ALICE. Born in Pawtucket, R. I., May 21, 1929. Attended Pembroke College. Made Broadway debut in 1963 in "The Ballad of The Sad Cafe" after appearing with the Phoenix Co., and Off-Bdwy in "Royal Gambit," "Go Show Me A Dragon," "Sweet Of You To Say So," "Gallows Humor," "The American Dream," and "The Giants' Dance." Appeared this season in "Malcolm."

DUKAS, JAMES. Born in Portsmouth, O., June 6, 1926. Graduate of W. Va. U. Studied at American Theatre Wing. Made New York bow Off-Bdwy in 1956 in "The Man With The Golden Arm," followed by "Brothers Karamazov," and "The Threepenny Opera," Broadway debut in 1960 in "The Visit," and subsequently "The Last Analysis," with LC Rep. Co. in "Incident At Vichy," "After The Fall," "The Condemned of Altona."

| Nancy Dussault | Alvin Epstein | Rex Everhart | Patte Finley | Gail Fishe |

DUNAWAY, FAYE. Born Jan. 14, 1941 in Tallahassee, Fla. Attended U. Fla., Boston U. Made Broadway debut in 1962 in "A Man For All Seasons," followed by LC Rep. Co. productions of "After The Fall," "But For Whom Charlie" and "Tartuffe," Off-Bdwy in "Hogan's Goat" for which she received a THEATRE WORLD Award.

DUNNOCK, MILDRED. Born Jan. 25 in Baltimore, Md. Graduate of Goucher College and Columbia. Made New York debut in 1932 in "Life Begins," followed by "The Corn Is Green," "Richard III," "Only The Heart," "Foolish Notion," "Lute Song," "Another Part of The Forest," "The Hallams," "Death of A Salesman," "Pride's Crossing," "The Wild Duck," "In The Summer House," "Cat On A Hot Tin Roof," "Child of Fortune," "The Milk Train Doesn't Stop Here Anymore," "Traveller Without Luggage," and Off-Bdwy in "The Trojan Women" and "Phedre."

DUSSAULT, NANCY. Born in Pensacola, Fla., June 30, 1936. Graduate of Northwestern U. Made New York bow Off-Bdwy in "Diversions," followed by "Street Scene" (CC), "Dr. Willy Nilly," "The Cradle Will Rock," "No For An Answer," "Do Re Mi" for which she received a THEATRE WORLD Award, "The Sound of Music," "Bajour."

DYBAS, JAMES. Born Feb. 7, 1944 in Chicago. Had experience in stock before making Broadway debut in 1965 in "Do I Hear A Waltz?"

EDDLEMAN, JACK. Born Sept. 7, 1933 in Weatherford, Tex. Attended U. of Okla., U. of Mo. and Northwestern. Made Broadway bow in 1957 in "Shinbone Alley," followed by "Carousel" (CC), "Oh, Captain!," "Camelot," "Hot Spot," "The Girl Who Came To Supper," "Oh, What A Lovely War!," "My Fair Lady" (CC), and Off-Bdwy in "Diversions," "Lend An Ear," and "Great Scot!."

ELLIOT, JANE. Born in NYC on Jan. 17, 1947. Attended the Dalton School. Made Broadway debut Oct. 13, 1965 in "The Impossible Years."

ENSERRO, MICHAEL. Born in Soldier, Pa., Oct. 5, 1918. Attended Allegheny College and Pasadena Playhouse. Has appeared in "Molly and Me," "The Passion of Josef D," and Off-Bdwy in "Penny Change," "The Fantasticks," and "The Miracle."

EPSTEIN, ALVIN. Born May 14, 1925 in NYC. Attended Queens College, Etienne Decroux School of Mime, and Habimah Theatre, Tel Aviv. Has appeared with Marcel Marceau, and in "King Lear," "Waiting For Godot," "From A To Z," Off-Bdwy in "Purple Dust," "Pictures In A Hallway," "Clerambard" and "Endgame," "No Strings," "The Passion of Josef D," "Postmark Zero."

EVERHART, REX. Born June 13, 1920 in Watseka, Ill. Graduate of U. of Mo. and NYU. Studied at Pasadena Playhouse. Made Broadway bow in 1955 in "No Time For Sergeants," followed by "Tall Story," "Moonbirds," "Tenderloin," "Matter of Position," "Rainy Day In Newark," "Skyscraper," 1960-1 season with Phoenix Theatre, and 5 seasons with American Shakespeare Theatre.

EWELL, TOM. Born April 29, 1909 in Owensboro, Ky. Attended U. of Wisc. Made New York bow in 1934 in "They Shall Not Die," followed by "Sunny River," "Ethan Frome," "Family Portrait," "Merchant of Yonkers," "Liberty Jones," "Tobacco Road," "Brother Rat," "Apple of His Eye," "John Loves Mary," "Small Wonder," "The Seven Year Itch," "Tunnel of Love," "Thurber Carnival," "Xmas In Las Vegas."

FAIRMAN, MICHAEL. Born Feb. 25, 1934 in NYC. Appeared in stock before making New York bow Off-Bdwy in "Red Roses For Me," and Broadway debut Dec., 1965 in "The Cactus Flower."

FELLOWS, DON. Born Dec. 2, 1922 in Salt Lake City. Attended U. of Wisc. Has appeared in "Mister Roberts," "South Pacific," "Only In America," "Marathon '33," "Friday Night" (Off-Bdwy), "Generation."

FIEDLER, JOHN. Born in Plateville, Wisc., Feb. 3, 1925. Studied at Neighborhood Playhouse. Made New York bow in 1954 Phoenix revival of "The Seagull," followed by "Sing Me No Lullaby," "One Eye Closed," "The Terrible Swift Sword," "Howie," "A Raisin In The Sun," "Harold," "The Odd Couple."

FIELD, BETTY. Born Feb. 8, 1918 in Boston. Attended American Academy of Dramatic Arts. Made Broadway debut in 1934 in "Page Miss Glory," followed by "Three Men On A Horse," "Room Service," "What A Life," "Primrose Path," "Two On An Island," "Flight To The West," "A New Life," "The Voice of The Turtle," "Dream Girl," "The Rat Race," "Not For Children," "The Fourposter," "Ladies of The Corridor," "Festival," "Waltz of The Toreadors," "A Touch of The Poet," "A Loss of Roses," "Strange Interlude" (1963), "Where's Daddy?"

FINLEY, PATTE. Born in Asheville, N. C., reared in Seattle, Wash. Attended U. of Wash. Appeared Off-Bdwy in "The Boy Friend" and "Greenwich Village U.S.A." before making Broadway debut in 1965 in "Hello, Dolly!"

FISHER, GAIL. Born Aug. 18, 1939 in Orange, N. J. Attended American Academy of Dramatic Arts. Made Broadway debut in 1961 in "Purlie Victorious," followed by Off-Bdwy performances in "Simply Heavenly," "Susan Slept Here," and "Danton's Death" (LC Rep.).

FLETCHER, BRAMWELL. Born in Bradford, Yorkshire, Eng., Feb. 20, 1904. Made New York bow in 1929 in "Scotland Yard," followed by "Ten Minute Alibi," "Lady Precious Stream," "Within The Gates," "Storm Operation," "Rebecca," "The Day After Tomorrow," "Maggie," "The Little Glass Clock," "The Lovers," "Candida," "Misalliance," "The Wisteria Trees," "My Fair Lady," and Off-Bdwy in "The Cherry Orchard" and "The Bernard Shaw Story."

FLETCHER, JACK. Born in Forest Hills, L. I., April 21, 1921. Attended Yale. Has appeared in "Trial Honeymoon," "She Stoops To Conquer," "Romeo and Juliet," CC revivals of "Can-Can," "Wonderful Town," and "Cyrano de Bergerac," Off-Bdwy in "Comic Strip," "Upstairs At The Downstairs," "The Way of The World," "Thieves' Carnival," and "The Amorous Flea," "Ben Franklin In Paris," "Drat! The Cat!"

FODOR, JOLEEN. Born Nov. 12, 1939 in Medina, O. Attended Denison U. and U. of Colo. Appeared Off-Bdwy in "Leave It To Jane," "Little Mary Sunshine" and "Riverwind" before Broadway debut in 1963 in "The Student Gypsy," followed by "A Funny Thing Happened On The Way To The Forum," OB in "Babes In The Wood" and "Great Scot!"

tance Ford   Henderson Forsythe   Don Francks   Arny Freeman   Valerie French

FONDA, HENRY. Born in Grand Island, Neb., May 16, 1905. Attended U. of Minn. Made Broadway bow in 1929 in "The Game of Love and Death," followed by "I Loved You Wednesday," "Forsaking All Others," "New Faces of 1934," "The Farmer Takes A Wife," "Mister Roberts," "Point of No Return," "The Caine Mutiny Court Martial," "Two For The Seesaw," "Silent Night, Lonely Night," "Critic's Choice," "A Gift of Time," "Generation."

FORD, CONSTANCE. Born in the Bronx, N.Y. Attended Hunter College. Made Broadway debut in 1949 in "Death of A Salesman," followed by "See The Jaguar," "Say, Darling," "Golden Fleecing," "Nobody Loves An Albatross," "UTBU."

FORD, PAUL. Born Nov. 2, 1901 in Baltimore. Attended Dartmouth. Made Broadway bow in 1944 in "Decision," followed by "Lower North," "Kiss Them For Me," "Flamingo Road," "On Whitman Avenue," "Another Part of The Forest," "Command Decision," "The Teahouse of The August Moon," "Whoop-Up," "The Music Man," "Thurber Carnival," "Never Too Late," "3 Bags Full."

FORSTER, ROBERT. Born July 13, 1941 in Rochester, N. Y. Attended Heidelberg College, Alfred U., U. of Rochester. Made Broadway debut Sept. 22, 1965 in "Mrs. Dally."

FORSYTHE, HENDERSON. Born Sept. 11, 1917 in Macon, Mo. Attended Iowa U. Has appeared in "The Cellar and The Well," "Miss Lonelyhearts," "The Iceman Cometh" (OB), "Who's Afraid of Virginia Woolf?," OB in "The Collection," "The Room" and "A Slight Ache," "Malcolm," "Right Honourable Gentleman."

FOSTER, GLORIA. Born Nov. 15, 1936 in Chicago. Attended Ill. State U., Chicago Teachers College, Goodman Theatre. Has appeared Off-Bdwy in "In White America" and "Medea" for which she received a THEATRE WORLD Award.

FRANCE, RICHARD. Born Jan. 6, 1930 in Chicago. Began career at 8. Made New York bow in 1951 in "Seventeen," followed by "Wish You Were Here," "Pal Joey," "By The Beautiful Sea," "What Makes Sammy Run?," and CC revivals of "Kiss Me, Kate," "The Pajama Game," "Annie Get Your Gun," "Show Boat," "Fiorello!," and "Oklahoma!"

FRANCIS, ARLENE. Born Oct. 20, 1908 in Boston. Attended Finch College and Theatre Guild Drama School. Made New York debut in 1936 in "Horse Eats Hat," followed by "The Women," "All That Glitters," "Michael Drops In," "Journey To Jerusalem," "The Doughgirls," "The Overtons," "The French Touch," "The Cup of Trembling," "My Name Is Aquilon," "Metropole," "The Little Blue Light," "Late Love," "Once More, With Feeling," "Beekman Place," "Mrs. Dally."

FRANCKS, DON. Born Feb. 28, 1932 in Vancouver, Can. Made Broadway debut Feb. 6, 1965 in "Kelly," followed by "Leonard Bernstein's Theatre Songs" Off-Bdwy.

FRANKLIN, HUGH. Born Aug. 24, 1916 in Muskogee, Okla. Attended Northwestern. Made Broadway bow in 1938 in "Gloriana," followed by "Harriet," "Alice In Wonderland," "Medea," "The Best Man," "Luther," "A Shot In The Dark," "Arturo Ui," "The Devils."

FREEMAN, ARNY. Born Aug. 28, 1908 in Chicago. Made Broadway bow in 1949 in "A Streetcar Named Desire," followed by CC revivals of "Dream Girl" and "The Shrike," "The Great Sebastians," "Tall Story," "Hot Spot," "The Gay Divorcee" (OB), "What Makes Sammy Run?," "Cactus Flower."

FRENCH, VALERIE. Born in London, Eng. Attended Malvern Girls' College. Made Broadway debut Nov. 30, 1965 in "Inadmissible Evidence."

FREY, NATHANIEL. Born Aug. 3, 1918 in NYC. Attended NYU and American Theatre Wing. Made Broadway bow in 1947 in "Barefoot Boy With Cheek," followed by "High Button Shoes," "Touch and Go," "Call Me Madam," "A Tree Grows In Brooklyn," "Wonderful Town," "Damn Yankees," "Goldilocks," "Harold," "She Loves Me," "The Odd Couple."

FRIEBUS, FLORIDA. Born Oct. 10, 1909 in Auburndale, Mass. Attended Wellesley College, and Theatre Guild School. Made Broadway debut in 1927 in "Triple Crossed," followed by "The Ivory Door," "The Lady From The Sea," with Civic Rep. Theatre Co., "Pride and Prejudice," "The Primrose Path," OB in "Church Street" and "The Victors," "Come Back, Little Sheba," "Collector's Item," "Tea and Sympathy," "Absence of A Cello."

GALLAGHER, HELEN. Born in Brooklyn in 1926. Studied at American Ballet School. Made Broadway debut in 1947 in "Seven Lively Arts," followed by "Mr. Strauss Goes To Boston," "Billion Dollar Baby," "Brigadoon," "High Button Shoes," "Touch and Go," "Make A Wish," "Pal Joey," "Hazel Flagg," CC revivals of "Guys and Dolls," "Finian's Rainbow," and "Oklahoma!," "The Pajama Game," "Bus Stop," "Portofino," "Sweet Charity."

GARRISON, SEAN. Born Oct. 19, 1937 in NYC. After films and TV made Broadway bow in 1960 in "There Was A Little Girl," followed by "Half-Past Wednesday" (OB) for which he received a THEATRE WORLD Award, "Like Other People," "The Beauty Part," "The Pleasure of His Company," "Camelot," "Hot September."

GAYNES, GEORGE. Born in Helsinki, Fin., May 3, 1917. Studied at Milan Conservatory. Sang opera in Europe and CC. Has appeared in "The Consul," "Out Of This World," "Wonderful Town," "Beggar's Opera," "Can-Can" (CC), "Lady of The Camellias," "Dynamite Tonight" (OB), CC Gilbert and Sullivan Co., "Any Wednesday."

GEER, WILL. Born March 9, 1902, in Frankfort, Ind. Attended Chicago U., Columbia, and Oxford U., Eng. Played in stock and tent shows before making New York bow in 1924 in "Uncle Tom's Cabin," followed by "The Merry Wives of Windsor," "Let Freedom Ring," "Snickering Horses," "Bury The Dead," "200 Were Chosen," "A House In The Country," "Of Mice and Men," "Steel," "Freedom of The Press," "The Cradle Will Rock," "Journeymen," "Sing Out The News," "Tobacco Road," "The More The Merrier," "Johnny On The Spot," "My Maryland," "Moon Vine," "Sophie," "Flamingo Road," "On Whitman Avenue," "Hope Is The Thing With Feathers," Phoenix Theatre Co. APA, and American Shakespeare Festival productions, "The Vamp," "The Ponder Heart," "No Time For Sergeants," "110 In The Shade," "An Evening's Frost" (OB).

Mark Gordon

Gordon Gould

Micki Grant

James Greene

William G

GHOSTLEY, ALICE. Born Aug. 14, 1926 in Eve, Mo. Attended Okla. U. Made Broadway debut in "New Faces of 1952" followed by "Sandhog," "Livin' The Life," "Trouble In Tahiti," "Shangri-La," "Maybe Tuesday," "Thurber Carnival," "The Beauty Part," "The Sign In Sidney Brustein's Window," "Love Is a Ball."

GIELGUD, JOHN. Born April 14, 1904 in London. Attended Royal Academy of Dramatic Arts. After great success in Eng., made Broadway bow in 1928 in "The Patriot," followed by "Hamlet," "The Importance of Being Earnest," "Love For Love," "Crime and Punishment," "The Lady's Not For Burning," "Medea," "Ages of Man," "School For Scandal," "Homage To Shakespeare," "Tiny Alice," "Ivanov."

GISH, LILLIAN. Born Oct. 14, 1896 in Springfield, O. Stage debut at 6. After eminent career in films, came to Broadway in 1930 in "Uncle Vanya," followed by "Camille," "Nine Pine Street," "The Joyous Season," "Hamlet," "The Star Wagon," "Dear Octopus," "Life With Father," "Mr. Sycamore," "Crime and Punishment," "The Curious Savage," "The Trip To Bountiful," "Family Reunion," "All The Way Home," "Too True To Be Good," "American Shakespeare Festival 1965," "Anya."

GLENN, SCOTT. Born Jan. 26, 1942 in Pittsburgh. Graduate of William & Mary College. Made Broadway debut Oct. 13, 1965 in "The Impossible Years."

GOODMAN, DODY. Born Oct. 28 in Columbus, O. Studied at Met Opera Ballet School. Made Broadway debut in 1947 in "High Button Shoes," followed by "Miss Liberty," "Call Me Madam," "Wonderful Town," Off-Bdwy in "Shoestring Revue," "Shoestring '57," "Parade," "Fiorello!" (CC), "A Rainy Day In Newark," "New Cole Porter Revue" (OB).

GORDON, MARK. Born in NYC. Studied at American Theatre Wing. Appeared Off-Bdwy in "Desire Under The Elms," "Man Who Never Died," "The Iceman Cometh," "Deep Are The Roots," "The Caretaker," "The Third Ear," and "Conerico Was Here To Stay," on Broadway in "Moon Besieged," "Compulsion," and "The Devils."

GORDON, RUTH. Born Oct. 30, 1896 in Wollaston, Mass. Attended American Academy of Dramatic Arts. Made Broadway debut in 1915 in "Peter Pan," followed by "Seventeen," "Clarence," "Saturday's Children," "Serena Blandish," "Hotel Universe," "A Church Mouse," "Three Cornered Moon," "Ethan Frome," "The Country Wife," "A Doll's House," "The Three Sisters," "Over 21," "The Leading Lady," "The Smile of The World," "The Matchmaker," "The Good Soup," "My Mother, My Father, and Me," "A Very Rich Woman."

GOSSETT, LOUIS. Born May 27, 1936 in Brooklyn. Graduate of NYU. Made Broadway bow in 1953 in "Take A Giant Step," followed by "The Desk Set," "Lost In The Stars" (CC), "A Raisin In The Sun," "Tambourines To Glory," Off-Bdwy in "The Blacks," "Telemachus Clay," and "The Bloodknot," "The Zulu and The Zayda."

GOULD, ELLIOTT. Born Aug. 29, 1938 in Brooklyn. Attended Columbia. Made Broadway bow in 1957 in "Rumple," followed by "Say, Darling," "Irma La Douce," "I Can Get It For You Wholesale," "Drat! The Cat!"

GOULD, GORDON. Born May 4, 1930 in Chicago. Graduate of Yale and Cambridge U., Eng. Has appeared with APA in "Right You Are," "The Tavern," "Scapin," "Impromptu At Versailles," "The Lower Depths," "War and Peace," "Man and Superman," "Judith," and in their Broadway debut of "You Can't Take It With You."

GRABLE, BETTY. Born Dec. 18, 1916 in St. Louis, Mo. Graduate of Hollywood Professional School. Made Broadway debut in 1939 in "DuBarry Was A Lady." After many films, returned to stage in touring company of "Hello, Dolly!"

GRANT, MICKI. Born June 30 in Chicago. Attended U. of Ill. and Geller School of Theatre. Made Broadway debut in 1963 in "Tambourines To Glory," and played Off-Bdwy in "Fly Blackbird," "The Blacks," "Brecht On Brecht," "Jerico Jim-Crow," "The Cradle Will Rock," "Leonard Bernstein's Theatre Songs."

GRAVES, ERNEST. Born May 5, 1919 in Chicago. Studied at Goodman Theatre School. Made Broadway bow in 1941 in "Macbeth," followed by "The Russian People," "Cyrano de Bergerac," "Eastward In Eden," "Venus Is."

GRAY, CHARLES D. Born August 29, 1928 in Hampshire, Eng. Appeared with Old Vic before making New York bow with them in 1956 in "Romeo and Juliet," "Macbeth," "Richard II" and "Troilus and Cressida," followed by "Kean," "Poor Bitos," "Right Honourable Gentleman."

GREENE, JAMES. Born Dec. 1, 1926 in Lawrence, Mass. Graduate of Emerson College. Made Broadway bow in 1951 in "Romeo and Juliet," followed by OB productions of "The Iceman Cometh," "American Gothic," "The King and The Duke," "The Hostage," "Plays For Bleecker Street," "Moon In The Yellow River," "Misalliance," LC Rep. Co. for 2 years, and on Broadway in "Girl On The Via Flaminia," "Compulsion," "Inherit The Wind," "Shadow Of A Gunman," "Andersonville Trial," "Night Life," APA's "You Can't Take It With You."

GREGORY, WILL. Born Nov. 18, 1928 in Glasgow, Scot. Attended Western Reserve U. and Cleveland Playhouse. Appeared Off-Bdwy in "Orpheus Descending," "Summer and Smoke," "A Streetcar Named Desire," "Eclipse Day," "Psalm For Fat Tuesdays" before making Broadway bow in 1965 in "Cactus Flower."

GRESHAM, EDITH. Born in NYC. Attended Pelham Hall. Made Broadway debut in 1919 in "39 East," followed by "Whispering Friends," "Hamlet," "Frederika," "The Women," "Sing Out The News," "Run, Sheep, Run," "Three's A Family," "Oklahoma!" LC Repertory Co.

GRIFFIES, ETHEL. Born April 26, 1878 in Sheffield, Eng. Attended George Green College. Made stage debut as a child, and appeared in many plays and films in England before making Broadway debut in 1924 in "Havoc," followed by "Interference," "Pygmalion," "Amriners," "Loose Ends," "The Criminal Code," "Old English," "The Druid Circle," "The Hallams," "The Shop At Sly Corner," "The Leading Lady," "Miss Liberty," "Legend of Sarah," "The Royal Family," "The Autumn Garden," "Billy Liar" (OB), "Write Me A Murder," "A Very Rich Woman," "Ivanov."

ael Hadge   A. Larry Haines   Sheila Hancock   Daniel P. Hannafin   Robert H. Harris

GRIFFIS, WILLIAM. Born July 12, 1917 in Hollywood, Calif. Made Broadway bow in 1953 in "A Pin To See The Peepshow," followed by OB productions of "The Corn Is Green," "Major Barbara," "Capacity For Wings," and "No Trifling With Love," "Look After Lulu," "Here's Love," "The Cradle Will Rock," "Never Too Late," "Philadelphia, Here I Come!"

GRIZZARD, GEORGE. Born April 1, 1928 in Roanoke Rapids, N. C. Graduate of U. of N. C. Made Broadway bow in 1954 in "All Summer Long," followed by "The Desperate Hours," "The Happiest Millionaire" for which he received a THEATRE WORLD Award, "The Disenchanted," "Big Fish, Little Fish," 'PA Repertory 1961-2, "Who's Afraid Of Virginia Woolf?," "The Glass Menagerie" (1965).

GROSSMANN, SUZANNE. Born in Switzerland. Graduate of McGill U. in Canada. Appeared in Stratford (Can.) Shakespeare Festival before making Broadway debut March 3, 1966 in "The Lion In Winter."

GROVER, EDWARD. Born Oct. 23, 1932 in Los Angeles. Graduate of U. of Toledo, U. of Texas. Made Broadway bow Nov. 1, 1965 in "Postmark Zero" after Off-Bdwy performances in "Ivanov," "A Trip To Bountiful," "Six Characters In Search of An Author," "Misalliance," and "The Alchemist." Toured in "The Hostage" and "Spoon River."

HACKETT, BUDDY. Born Aug. 31, 1924 in Brooklyn. Appeared in night clubs, films, and TV before making Broadway debut in 1954 in "Lunatics and Lovers," followed by "I Had A Ball."

HADGE, MICHAEL. Born June 6, 1932 in Greensboro, N. C. Made Broadway debut in 1958 in "The Cold Wind and The Warm," followed by "Lady of The Camellias," "The Impossible Years."

HAINES, A. LARRY. Born Aug. 3, 1917 in Mt. Vernon, N. Y. Attended City College. Made Broadway debut in 1962 in "A Thousand Clowns," followed by "Generation."

HALL, ED. Born Jan. 11, 1931 in Roxbury, Mass. Attended Harvard. Has appeared in "The Climate of Eden," "No Time For Sergeants," "A Raisin In The Sun," Off-Bdwy in "The Death of Bessie Smith" and "Trumpets of The Lord," "The Zulu and The Zayda."

HALL, MARGARET. Born in Richmond, Va. Graduate of William & Mary College. Made Broadway debut in 1960 in "Becket," appeared OB in "The Boy Friend," "Fallout," "U.S.A.," "A Midsummer Night's Dream," and "Little Mary Sunshine," "High Spirits," "Mame."

HAMILTON, MARGARET. Born Dec. 9, 1902 in Cleveland, O. Attended Cleveland Playhouse. Made Broadway debut in 1932 in "Another Language," followed by "Dark Tower," "The Farmer Takes A Wife," "Outrageous Fortune," "The Men We Marry," "Fancy Meeting You Again," "Annie Get Your Gun" (CC), "Goldilocks," "UTBU."

HAMMER, BEN. Born Dec. 8, 1925 in Brooklyn. Graduate of Brooklyn College. Made Broadway bow in 1955 in "The Great Sebastians," followed by "The Diary of Anne Frank," "The Tenth Man," "Mother Courage," "The Deputy," "The Royal Hunt of The Sun."

HANCOCK, SHEILA. Born Feb. 22, 1933 on Isle of Wight, Eng. Attended Royal Academy of Dramatic Arts. Appeared in many revues and plays in England before making New York debut in "Entertaining Mr. Sloane."

HANNAFIN, DANIEL P. Born Feb. 8, 1933 in NYC. Attended Juilliard. Has appeared in CC revivals of "South Pacific," "Wonderful Town," "Brigadoon," "Oklahoma!," and in "Camelot," "Flora, The Red Menace," "Baker Street."

HARRIS, BARBARA. Born in Evanston, Ill. Made Broadway debut in 1961 in "From The Second City," followed Off-Bdwy by "Seacoast of Bohemia," "Alarums and Excursions," and "Oh, Dad, Poor Dad, Mamma's Hung You In The Closet and I'm Feeling So Sad" for which she received a THEATRE WORLD Award, "Mother Courage and Her Children," "Dynamite Tonight" (OB), "On A Clear Day You Can See Forever."

HARRIS, JULIE. Born Dec. 2, 1925 in Grosse Point, Mich. Attended Yale Drama School. Made Broadway debut in 1945 in "It's A Gift," followed by "Henry V," "Oedipus," "The Playboy of The Western World," "Alice In Wonderland," "Macbeth," "Sundown Beach" for which she received a THEATRE WORLD Award, "The Young and The Fair," "Magnolia Alley," "Montserrat," "The Member of The Wedding," "I Am A Camera," "Mlle. Colombe," "The Lark," "The Country Wife," "The Warm Peninsula," "The Little Moon of Alban," "A Shot In The Dark," "Marathon '33," "Ready When You Are, C. B.," "Skyscraper."

HARRIS, ROBERT H. Born July 15, 1911 in NYC. Appeared with Yiddish Art Theatre before making Broadway bow in 1938 in "Schoolhouse On The Lot," followed by "Richard III," "Look, Ma, I'm Dancin'," "My Sister Eileen," "Brooklyn, U.S.A.," "Herod and Miriamne," "Somewhere In France," "Foxy," "Minor Miracle," "Xmas In Las Vegas."

HARRIS, ROSEMARY. Born Sept. 19, 1930 in Ashby, Suffolk, Eng. Studied at Royal Academy of Dramatic Arts. Made Broadway debut in 1952 in "The Climate of Eden" for which she received a THEATRE WORLD Award, followed by "Troilus and Cressida," "Interlock," "The Disenchanted," "The Tumbler," many APA productions including "The Tavern," "School For Scandal," "The Seagull," "The Importance of Being Earnest," "War and Peace," "Man and Superman," "Judith," and "You Can't Take It With You," "The Lion In Winter."

HAYES, HELEN. Born Oct. 10, 1900, in Washington, D.C. Graduate of Sacred Heart Academy. Made Broadway debut in 1909 in "Old Dutch," followed by "The Summer Widowers," "Penrod," "Dear Brutus," "Clarence," "To The Ladies," "We Moderns," "Dancing Mothers," "Caesar and Cleopatra," "What Every Woman Knows," "Coquette," "Mary of Scotland," "Victoria Regina," "Twelfth Night," "Candle In The Wind," "Happy Birthday," "The Wisteria Trees," "Mrs. McThing," "The Glass Menagerie" (CC), "The Skin Of Our Teeth," "Time Remember'd," "A Touch of The Poet," "A Program For Two Players," "The White House," tour with Helen Hayes Repertory Co. and APA.

HECKART, EILEEN. Born March 29, 1919 in Columbus, O. Graduate of Ohio State U. Made New York debut in Off-Bdwy in 1943 in "Tinker's Dam," followed by "Our Town" (CC), "They Knew What They Wanted," "The Traitor," "Hilda Crane," "In Any Language," "Picnic" for which she received a THEATRE WORLD Award, "The Bad Seed," "A View From The Bridge," "The Dark At The Top Of The Stairs," "Invitation To A March," "Pal Joey" (CC), "Everybody Loves Opal," "A Family Affair," "Too True To Be Good," "And Things That Go Bump In The Night," "Barefoot In The Park."

Jack Hollander   Katharine Houghton   Elizabeth Huddle   Charles Hudson   Martin Hu

HEFFERNAN, JOHN. Born May 30, 1934 in NYC. Attended City College, Columbia, and Boston U. Made New York bow Off-Bdwy in "The Judge," followed by "Julius Caesar," "The Great God Brown," "Lysistrata," "Peer Gynt," "Henry IV," "The Taming of The Shrew," "She Stoops To Conquer," "The Plough and The Stars," "The Octoroon," "Hamlet," "Androcles and The Lion," "A Man's A Man," "The Winter's Tale," "Luther," "Tiny Alice," "Postmark Zero."

HELMORE, TOM. Born in London, Jan. 4, 1912. Attended Tonbridge School. Made Broadway bow in 1939 in "No Time For Comedy," followed by "The Day Before Spring," "Clutterbuck," "The Legend of Sarah," "Love and Let Love," "The High Ground," "The Winner," "One Eye Closed," "The Dark Is Light Enough," "Debut," "Mary, Mary," "The Playroom."

HEPPLE, JEANNE. Born Aug. 2, 1936 in London. Attended Guildhall School of Music and Drama. Member of Royal Shakespeare Co., and National Theatre Co. of Eng. Made Broadway debut Nov. 30, 1965 in "Inadmissible Evidence," and Off-Bdwy in "Sergeant Musgrave's Dance."

HEWITT, ROBERT. Born Aug. 12, 1922 in Sydney, Aust. Attended Danvers School of Speech and Drama in London. Member of Old Vic Co. Made Broadway bow in 1963 in "Chips With Everything" followed by "The Zulu and The Zayda."

HILL, ARTHUR. Born Aug. 1, 1922 in Melfort, Can. Attended U. of British Col. Made Broadway bow in 1955 in "The Matchmaker," followed by "Look Homeward, Angel," "The Gang's All Here," "All The Way Home," "Who's Afraid Of Virginia Woolf?," "Something More," "The Porcelain Year."

HINES, MIMI. Born July 17, 1933 in Vancouver, Can. Appeared with husband Phil Ford in night clubs and on television before making Broadway debut Dec. 27, 1965 succeeding Barbra Streisand in "Funny Girl."

HINES, PATRICK. Born March 17, 1930 in Burkeville, Tex. Graduate of Tex. U. Made New York bow with Phoenix Theatre Co. in "Duchess of Malfi," "Lysistrata," "Peer Gynt," "Henry IV" and "The Great God Brown" which was moved to Broadway in 1959. Has appeared with American Shakespeare Festival since 1956, and in "A Passage To India," "The Devils."

HINGLE, PAT. Born July 19, 1923 in Denver, Colo. Graduate of Tex. U., member of Actors Studio. Made Broadway bow in 1953 in "End As A Man," followed by "Festival," "Cat On A Hot Tin Roof," "Girls Of Summer," "The Dark At The Top Of The Stairs," "J.B.," "The Deadly Game," "Strange Interlude" (1963), "Blues For Mr. Charlie," "A Girl Could Get Lucky," "The Glass Menagerie" (1965).

HOLBROOK, HAL. Born Feb. 17, 1925 in Cleveland, O. Graduate of Denison U. Made Broadway debut in 1961 in "Do You Know The Milky Way?," followed by "Abe Lincoln In Illinois" (OB), and LC Rep. Co. productions of "Marco Millions," "Incident At Vichy," "Tartuffe." Toured world in his one-man show "Mark Twain Tonight!," presented it Off-Bdwy in 1959, and on Broadway in 1966.

HOLGATE, RONALD. Born May 26, 1937 in Aberdeen, S. D. Attended Northwestern, and New Eng. Conservatory. Made New York bow in 1961 Off-Bdwy in "Hobo," followed by "A Funny Thing Happened On The Way To The Forum," "Milk and Honey," "Hooray! It's A Glorious Day . . . And All That" (OB).

HOLLIDAY, BOB. Born Nov. 12, 1932 in Brooklyn. Appeared in night clubs before making Broadway debut in 1959 in "Fiorello!," followed by "It's A Bird . . . It's A Plane . . . It's Superman!"

HOLLANDER, JACK. Born Jan. 29, 1918 in Chicago. Graduate of Goodman Memorial Theatre School. Made Broadway bow in 1959 in "The Miracle Worker," followed by "All The Way Home," "Gideon," OB in "Girl Of The Golden West," "The Dybbuk," and "Journey To The Day," "The Impossible Years."

HOLM, JOHN CECIL. Born Nov. 4, 1904 in Philadelphia. Attended U. of Pa. Made Broadway debut in 1929 in "The Front Page," followed by "Whirlpool," "Penal Law 2010," "The Up and Up," "Wonder Boy," "Bloodstream," "Dangerous Corner," "Mary of Scotland," "Midgie Purvis," "Gramercy Ghost," "Mr. President," "The Advocate," "A Mighty Man Is He," "Philadelphia, Here I Come!"

HOOKS, ROBERT. Born in Philadelphia. Attended Temple U. Made Broadway bow in "A Raisin In The Sun," followed by "A Taste of Honey," "Tiger, Tiger Burning Bright," "Arturo Ui," "The Milk Train Doesn't Stop Here Anymore," Off-Bdwy in "Henry V," "Ballad Of Bimshire," "The Blacks," "The Dutchman," "Happy Ending" and "Day Of Absence," "Where's Daddy?"

HORTON, EDWARD EVERETT. Born March 18, 1886 in Brooklyn. Attended Oberlin College and Columbia. Made Broadway bow in 1908 in "The Man Who Stood Still," followed by "The Cheater," "Elevating A Husband," "Springtime For Henry," "A Funny Thing Happened On The Way To The Forum," "Carousel" (LC).

HOUGHTON, KATHARINE. Born March 10, 1945 in Hartford, Conn. Graduate of Sarah Lawrence College. Made Broadway debut Sept. 30, 1965 in "A Very Rich Woman."

HOWARD, ALAN. Born March 21, 1951 in Rockville Centre, L. I. Attended Professional Children's School. Made Broadway debut in 1960 in "The Wall," followed by "Garden Of Sweets," "A Gift Of Time," Off-Bdwy in "King Of The Whole Damn World" and "Square In The Eye," "The Playroom."

HUDDLE, ELIZABETH. Born Jan. 20, 1940 in Redding, Calif. Attended Sacramento State College, U. of Pacific. Made New York debut with Lincoln Center Repertory Theater in "Danton's Death," "The Country Wife," "Condemned of Altona," "The Caucasian Chalk Circle."

HUDSON, CHARLES. Born March 29, 1931 in Thorpsprings, Tex. Attended American Academy of Dramatic Arts, American Theatre Wing. Made Broadway bow in 1951 in "Billy Budd," followed by roles Off-Bdwy in "The Streets Of New York," "The Summer Of Daisy Miller," "Great Scot!"

HUGHES, TRESA. Born Sept. 17, 1929 in Washington, D. C. Attended Wayne U. Has appeared Off-Bdwy in "Electra" and "The Crucible," and in "The Miracle Worker," "The Devil's Advocate," "Dear Me, The Sky Is Falling," "The Last Analysis," "Hogan's Goat" (OB).

rle Hyman   **Max William Jacobs**   **Page Johnson**   **Charlotte Jones**   **John Kane**

HUMPHREY, CAVADA. Born June 17 in Atlantic City, N. J. Graduate of Smith College. Made New York debut Off-Bdwy in "A Man's House," followed by "The House In Paris," "The Cherry Orchard," "The Song of Bernadette," "As The Girls Go," "The Devil's Disciple," "Moon In Capricorn," "Richard II," "The Taming Of The Shrew," "Love's Labour's Lost," "Richard III," "Othello," "Henry IV," "Girl Of The Golden West," "Time Remember'd," "Dear Liar," "Life Is A Dream," APA revival of "You Can't Take It With You."

HUSTON, MARTIN. Born Feb. 8, 1941 in Lexington, Ky. Attended Columbia. Made Broadway debut in 1959 in "Only In America," followed by "Take Her, She's Mine," "Come Blow Your Horn," "A Race Of Hairy Men."

HYMAN, EARLE. Born Oct. 11, 1926 in Rocky Mt., N. C. Studied at American Theatre Wing, and New School. Made Broadway debut in 1943 in "Run, Little Chillun," followed by "Anna Lucasta," "The Climate of Eden," "The Merchant of Venice," "Othello," "Julius Caesar," "The Tempest," "No Time For Sergeants," "Mr. Johnson" for which he received a THEATRE WORLD Award, "St. Joan," "Hamlet," "Waiting For Godot," American Shakespeare Festival productions, Off-Bdwy in "The Duchess of Malfi," "The White Rose and The Red," "The Worlds Of Shakespeare," "Jonah."

IRVING, GEORGE S. Born Nov. 1, 1922 in Springfield, Mass. Attended Leland Powers School. Made Broadway bow in 1943 in "Oklahoma!," followed by "Call Me Mister," "Along Fifth Avenue," "Two's Company," "Me and Juliet," "Can-Can," "Shinbone Alley," "Bells Are Ringing," "The Good Soup," "Tovarich," "A Murderer Among Us," "Alfie," "Anya."

JACKSON, ANNE. Born Sept. 3, 1926 in Alleghany, Pa. Attended Neighborhood Playhouse, New School, Actors Studio. Made Broadway debut in 1945 in "Signature," followed by "Yellow Jack," "John Gabriel Borkman," "The Last Dance," "Summer and Smoke," "Magnolia Alley," "Love Me Long," "The Lady From The Sea," "Never Say Never," "Oh, Men! Oh, Women!," "Rhinoceros," Off-Bdwy in "Brecht On Brecht," "The Tiger" and "The Typists," "Luv."

JACOBS, MAX WILLIAM. Born April 28, 1937 in Buffalo, N. Y. Graduate of Ariz. U. Made Broadway debut in 1965 in "The Zulu and The Zayda."

JAMES, CLIFTON. Born May 29, 1921 in Spokane, Wash. Attended Ore. U. and Actors Studio. Has appeared in "The Time Of Your Life" (CC), "The Cave Dwellers," "Great Day In The Morning," "Andorra," "And Things That Go Bump In The Night," "The Coop" (OB).

JAMESON, HOUSE. Born Dec. 17, 1902 in Austin, Tex. Graduate of Columbia. Made Broadway debut in 1923 in "Saint Joan," followed by "Goat Song," "Grand Street Follies," "Garrick Gaieties," "An American Tragedy," "The Dark Hours," "We, The People," "Judgement Day," "In Time To Come," "The Patriots," "Requiem For A Nun," "Never Too Late," "The Great Indoors."

JASON, HARVEY. Born Feb. 29, 1940 in London. Attended Carnegie Tech. Appeared Off-Bdwy in "An Enemy Of The People," "The Saving Grace," "Electra," "Henry V," "Measure For Measure," "The Establishment." Made Broadway debut in 1966 in "Hostile Witness."

JEFFREYS, ANNE. Born Jan. 26, 1928 in Goldsboro, N. C. Attended Anderson College. Made Broadway debut in 1947 musical version of "Street Scene," followed by "My Romance," "Kiss Me, Kate," "Three Wishes For Jamie," "Camelot," "Kismet" (LC).

JILLSON, JOYCE. Born Dec. 26, 1946 in Cranston, R. I. Attended Harvard, Boston U., New England Conservatory. Made Broadway debut in "The Sound Of Music," followed by "Route 1" (Off-Bdwy), "The Roar Of The Greasepaint, The Smell Of The Crowd" for which she received a THEATRE WORLD Award, "La Grosse Valise."

JOHNSON, PAGE. Born Aug. 25, 1930 in Welch, W. Va. Graduate of Ithaca College. Made Broadway bow in 1951 in DeHavilland's "Romeo and Juliet," followed by "Electra," "Oedipus," "Camino Real," "In April Once" for which he received a THEATRE WORLD Award, "Red Roses For Me," "The Lovers," Off-Bdwy in "Military Taps," "The Enchanted," "Guitar," "4 In 1," "Journey of The Fifth Horse."

JOHNSON, VAN. Born Aug. 25, 1916 in Newport, R. I. Made Broadway debut in "New Faces of 1936," followed by "Too Many Girls," "Pal Joey" (1940), "Come On Strong," "Mating Dance."

JOHNSON, JUSTINE. Born June 13 in Evanston, Ill. Attended Chicago U. and Goodman Theatre School. Made New York debut Off-Bdwy in "The Chair," followed by "The Time Of Your Life" (CC), "The Pajama Game," "Milk and Honey," "How To Succeed In Business Without Really Trying" (CC).

JONES, CHARLOTTE. Born Jan. 1 in Chicago. Attended Loyola, and DePaul U. Has appeared Off-Bdwy in "False Confessions," "Sign Of Jonah," "Girl On The Via Flaminia," "Red Roses For Me," "Night Is Black Bottles," "Camino Real," "Plays For Bleecker Street," "Pigeons," "Great Scot!," and "Sergeant Musgrave's Dance," on Broadway in "Camino Real," "Buttrio Square," "Mame."

JONES, JAMES EARL. Born Jan. 17, 1931 in Tate County, Miss. Graduate of Mich. U. Made Broadway bow in 1957 in "The Egghead," followed by "Sunrise At Campobello," "The Cool World," Off-Bdwy in "The Pretender," "The Blacks," "Clandestine On The Morning Line," "The Apple," "A Midsummer Night's Dream," "Moon On A Rainbow Shawl" for which he received a THEATRE WORLD Award, "P.S. 193," "The Last Minstrel," "The Love Nest," "The Bloodknot," "Othello," "Baal," "Danton's Death" (LC).

JONES, NEIL. Born May 6, 1942 in Boston. Attended Boston Conservatory of Music. Has appeared in "The Music Man," "Hello, Dolly!"

JORDAN, RICHARD. Born July 19, 1938 in NYC. Attended Harvard. Made Broadway bow in 1961 in "Take Her, She's Mine," followed by New York Shakespeare Festival productions, "Bicycle Ride To Nevada," APA's "War and Peace" and "Judith," "Generation."

KANE, JOHN. Born Aug. 29, 1920 in Davenport, Iowa. Attended St. Ambrose College. Broadway debut in 1944 in "Three's A Family," followed by "Marcus In The High Grass," "Ding Dong Bell," "Uncle Willie," "The Visit," "Hooray! It's A Glorious Day . . . And All That" (Off-Bdwy).

| Karnilova, Maria | Daniel Keyes | Tom Klunis | Ruth Kobart | Yaphet Ko |

KARNILOVA, MARIA. Born Aug. 3, 1920 in Hartford, Conn. Attended Met Opera Ballet School. Appeared with Ballet Theatre before making Broadway debut in 1938 in "Stars In Your Eyes," followed by "Call Me Mister," "High Button Shoes," "Two's Company," "Hollywood Pinafore," "Beggar's Opera" (CC), "Kaleidoscope" (OB), "Ballets U.S.A.," "Gypsy," "Miss Liberty," "Out Of This World," "Bravo Giovanni," "Fiddler On The Roof."

KASZNAR, KURT. Born Aug. 12, 1913 in Vienna. Studied with Max Reinhardt. Made New York bow in "The Eternal Road," followed by "The Army Play By Play," "Joy To The World," "Make Way For Lucia," "Montserrat," "The Happy Time," "Waiting For Godot," "Seventh Heaven," "Six Characters In Search Of An Author" (OB), "Look After Lulu," "The Sound Of Music," "Barefoot In The Park."

KATES, BERNARD. Born Dec. 26, 1922 in Boston. Attended American Academy of Dramatic Arts. Has appeared in "At War With The Army," "Billy Budd," "Inherit The Wind," "The Disenchanted," "Have I Got A Girl For You," "The Devils."

KENNEDY, MADGE. Born April 19, 1894 in Chicago. Attended Art Students League. Made Broadway debut in 1912 in "Little Miss Brown," followed by "Twin Beds," "Fair and Warmer," "Cornered," "Love In A Mist," "Badges," "Spite Corner," "Poppy," "Paris Bound," "Private Lives," after many years in films, returned to Broadway in "A Very Rich Woman."

KERMOYAN, MICHAEL. Born Nov. 29, 1925 in Fresno, Calif. Attended Stanford, USC, Los Angeles Conservatory. Made Broadway debut in 1954 in "The Girl In Pink Tights," followed by "Sandhog," "Whoop-Up," "Happy Town," "Camelot," "The Happiest Girl In The World," "Fly Blackbird," "Ross," "Angels of Anadarko," "Tovarich," "Anya."

KEYES, DANIEL. Born March 6, 1914 in Concord, Mass. Attended Exeter, Harvard, and American Theatre Wing. Made Broadway bow in 1954 in "The Remarkable Mr. Pennypacker," followed by "Bus Stop," "Our Town" (OB), "Only In America," "Christine," "First Love," "Epitaph For George Dillon" (OB), "Take Her, She's Mine," "Plays For Bleecker Street," "Six Characters In Search of An Author" (OB), "Baker Street," "Hooray! It's A Glorious Day . . . And All That," and "Serjeant Musgrave's Dance" (OB).

KILEY, RICHARD. Born March 31, 1922 in Chicago. Attended Loyola U. and Barnum Dramatic School. Toured in "A Streetcar Named Desire" before making Broadway bow in 1953 in "Misalliance" for which he received a THEATRE WORLD Award, followed by "Kismet," "Sing Me No Lullaby," "Time Limit!," "Redhead," "Advise and Consent," "No Strings," "Here's Love," "I Had A Ball," "Man of La Mancha."

KING, DENNIS. Born Nov. 2, 1897 in Coventry, Eng. Made Broadway bow in 1921 in "Claire De Lune," followed by "Romeo and Juliet," "Antony and Cleopatra," "The Vagabond King," "The Three Musketeers," "I Married An Angel," "A Doll's House," "The Three Sisters," "Dunnigan's Daughter," "He Who Gets Slapped," "Medea," "Edward, My Son," "The Devil's Disciple," "Billy Budd," "Music In The Air," "The Strong Are Lonely," "Lunatics and Lovers," "A Day By The Sea," "Affair Of Honor," "Shangri-La," "The Hidden River," "The Greatest Man Alive," "Love and Libel," "Photo Finish," "Minor Miracle."

KING, JOHN MICHAEL. Born May 13, 1926 in NYC. Attended American Academy of Dramatic Arts. Has appeared in "Inside U.S.A.," "Courtin' Time," "Music In The Air," "Of Thee I Sing," "Buttrio Square," "Me and Juliet," "Ankles Aweigh," "Hit The Trail," "Fanny," "My Fair Lady" for which he received a THEATRE WORLD Award, "Anya."

KLUGMAN, JACK. Attended Carnegie Tech, American Theatre Wing. Made Broadway bow in 1952 in "Golden Boy," followed by "Coriolanus" (OB), "A Very Special Baby," "Gypsy," "Tchin-Tchin," "The Odd Couple."

KLUNIS, TOM. Born in San Francisco where he became a member of the actor's Workshop. Appeared Off-Bdwy in "The Immoralist," "Hamlet," "Arms and The Man," "Measure For Measure," "Henry V," "Romeo and Juliet," "The Balcony," "Our Town," "The Man Who Never Died," "God Is My Ram," and on Broadway in "Gideon," "The Devils."

KNIGHT, SHIRLEY. Born July 5 in Goessel, Kan. Attended Phillips U., Wichita U. Made Broadway debut in 1964 in "The Three Sisters," followed by Off-Bdwy roles in "Journey To The Day" and "Rooms."

KOBART, RUTH. Born April 24, 1924 in Des Moines, Iowa. Graduate of Chicago Am. Conservatory, and Hunter College. Made Broadway debut in 1955 in "Pipe Dream," followed by "Maria Golovin," "How To Succeed In Business Without Really Trying," "A Funny Thing Happened On The Way To The Forum," "Oklahoma!" (CC). Has also appeared with Lemonade Opera Co., and NYC Opera Co.

KORVIN, CHARLES. Born Nov. 21, 1912 in Postyen, Hun. Attended Sorbonne, and Ecole du Louvre. Made Broadway debut in 1943 in "Dark Eyes," followed by many films in Hollywood. Returned to Broadway in 1965 in "Barefoot In The Park."

KOTTO, YAPHET. Born Nov. 15, 1937 in NYC. Made Broadway bow in 1965 in "The Zulu and The Zayda" after Off-Bdwy roles in "Bloodknot," "In White America," "Black Monday," "Great Western Union," "Cyrano de Bergerac."

KROSCHELL, JOAN. Born March 3 in Chicago. Attended Bennington College. Has appeared Off-Bdwy in "Leave It To Jane," "The Streets of New York," with American Savoyards, "Down In The Valley," "The Parasite," "Hooray! It's A Glorious Day . . . And All That."

KRUGER, HARDY. Born in Berlin, Ger., April 12, 1928. Appeared on stage and in films in Europe before making Broadway debut Nov. 1, 1965 in "Postmark Zero."

LADD, MARGARET. Born Nov. 8, 1942 in Providence, R. I. Graduate of Bard College. Appeared Off-Bdwy in "The Knack," and "Free, Free, Free," before making Broadway debut Feb. 1, 1966 in "The Great Indoors."

LAMPERT, ZOHRA. Born May 13, 1936 in NYC. Attended Chicago U. Appeared Off-Bdwy in "Venus Observed" and "Diary Of A Scoundrel" before making Broadway debut in 1956 in "Major Barbara," followed by "Maybe Tuesday," "Look: We've Come Through," "First Love," "Mother Courage and Her Children," "After The Fall" and "Marco Millions" with LC Rep. Co., "Nathan Weinstein, Mystic, Conn."

LANGELLA, FRANK. Graduate of Syracuse U. Has appeared Off-Bdwy in "The Immoralist," "Good Day," "The Old Glory," "The White Devil."

n Kroschell   Frank Langella   Loi Leabo   Sondra Lee   Michael Lewis

LANSBURY, ANGELA. Born Oct. 16, 1925 in London. Attended Webber-Douglas School, Feagin School of Drama. Made Broadway debut in 1957 in "Hotel Paradiso," followed by "A Taste Of Honey," "Anyone Can Whistle," "Mame."

LARABEE, LOUISE. Born April 9 in Bremerton, Wash. Has appeared in "Angel Island," "The Land Is Bright," "Guest In The House," "Junior Miss," "Sleep No More," "The Number," "A Date With April," "Picnic," "Right Honourable Gentleman."

LAURENCE, PAULA. Born Jan. 25 in Brooklyn. Attended Our Lady of Lourdes School. Made Broadway debut in 1936 in "Horse Eats Hat," followed by "Dr. Faustus," "Junior Miss," "Something For The Boys," "One Touch of Venus," "Cyrano de Bergerac," "The Liar," "Season In The Sun," "Tovarich," "The Time Of Your Life," "The Beggar's Opera," "Hotel Paradiso," "Night Of The Iguana," "Have I Got A Girl For You," "Ivanov."

LAVIN, LINDA. Born Oct. 15, 1939 in Portland, Me. Graduate of William & Mary College. Made Broadway debut in 1962 in "A Family Affair," followed by "The Riot Act," "Wet Paint" (Off-Bdwy) for which she received a THEATRE WORLD Award, "The Game Is Up," "Hotel Passionato," "The Mad Show," "It's A Bird . . . It's A Plane . . . It's Superman!"

LEABO, LOI. Born Sept. 27, 1938 in Portland, Ore. Attended Reed College. Made Broadway debut in "The Music Man," followed by "110 In The Shade," and CC revivals of "Brigadoon," "The King and I," and "Oklahoma!"

LEE, SONDRA. Born Sept. 30, 1930 in Newark, N. J. Studied at Met Opera Ballet School. Made Broadway debut in 1947 in "High Button Shoes," followed by "Peter Pan," "Hotel Paradiso," "Sunday In New York," "Hello, Dolly!"

LeGALLIENNE, EVA. Born Jan. 11, 1899 in London. Attended Royal Academy of Dramatic Arts. Made Broadway debut in 1915 in "Mrs. Boltay's Daughters." Organized Civic Rep. Theatre in 1926 and presented many notable productions before disbanding in 1933. Has appeared in "Liliom," "The Swan," "The Master Builder," "L'Aiglon," "Madame Capet," "Uncle Harry," "The Cherry Orchard," "Therese," "What Every Woman Knows," "Alice In Wonderland," "Ghosts," "Hedda Gabler," "The Corn Is Green" (CC), "The Southwest Corner," "Mary Stuart," "Elizabeth The Queen," National Rep. Theatre revivals of "Ring Round The Moon," "The Seagull," "The Madwoman of Chaillot," "The Rivals" and "The Trojan Women."

LEIGH, VIVIEN. Born Nov. 5, 1913 in Darjeeling, India. Attended Comedie Francaise, and Royal Academy of Dramatic Arts. Made Broadway debut in 1940 in "Romeo and Juliet," followed by "Antony and Cleopatra," "Caesar and Cleopatra," "Duel of Angels," "Tovarich," "Ivanov."

LEIGHTON, MARGARET. Born Feb. 26, 1922 in Barnt Gree, Warwickshire, Eng. Attended Church of Eng. College. Made Broadway debut in 1946 with Old Vic Co. Has appeared since in "Separate Tables," "Much Ado About Nothing," "Night Of The Iguana," "Tchin-Tchin," "The Chinese Prime Minister," "Homage To Shakespeare," "Slapstick Tragedy."

LeMASSENA, WILLIAM. Born May 23, 1916 in Glen Ridge, N. J. Attended NYU. Made Broadway bow in 1940 in "The Taming Of The Shrew," followed by "There Shall Be No Night," "The Pirate," "Hamlet," "Call Me Mister," "Inside U.S.A.," "I Know My Love," "Dream Girl," "Nina," "Ondine," "Fallen Angels," "Redhead," "The Conquering Hero," "The Beauty Part," "The Coop" (OB).

LeNOIRE, ROSETTA. Born Aug. 8, 1911 in NYC. Studied at American Theatre Wing. Made Broadway debut in 1936 in "Macbeth," followed by "Bassa Moona," "The Hot Mikado," "Marching With Johnny," "Janie," "Decision," "Three's A Family," "Destry Rides Again," CC revivals of "Finian's Rainbow" and "South Pacific," Off-Bdwy in "The Bible Salesman," "Double Entry," "Clandestine On The Morning Line," and "Cabin In The Sky," "Sophie," "Tambourines To Glory," "Blues For Mr. Charlie," "The Great Indoors."

LESLIE, BETHEL. Born Aug. 3, 1929 in NYC. Attended Breaney School. Has appeared in "Snafu," "Years Ago," "The Wisteria Trees," "Mary Rose," "The Brass Ring," "Inherit The Wind," "Catch Me If You Can."

LEVINE, SAM. Born Aug. 28, 1905. Attended American Academy of Dramatic Arts. Made Broadway bow in 1927 in "Wall Street," followed by "Three Men On A Horse," "Dinner At Eight," "Room Service," "Margin For Error," "A Sound of Hunting," "Light Up The Sky," "Guys and Dolls," "The Hot Corner," "Fair Game," "Make A Million," "Heartbreak House," "The Good Soup," "The Devil's Advocate," "Let It Ride," "Seidman and Son," "Cafe Crown," "The Last Analysis," "Nathan Weinstein, Mystic, Conn."

LEVIN, MICHAEL. Born Dec. 8, 1932 in Minneapolis. Graduate of U. of Minn. Made Broadway debut Oct. 26, 1965 in "The Royal Hunt Of The Sun."

LEWIS, MICHAEL. Born June 20, 1930 in NYC. Attended Chicago U., and Royal Academy of Dramatic Arts. Made Broadway bow in 1954 in "Quadrille," followed by "Small War On Murray Hill," "Once There Was A Russian," "The Visit," "Little Moon Of Alban," "A Man For All Seasons," "On A Clear Day You Can See Forever."

LINDFORS, VIVECA. Born Dec. 29, 1920 in Upsala, Sweden. Attended Stockholm Royal Dramatic Theatre School. Made Broadway debut in 1952 in "I've Got Sixpence," followed by "Anastasia," "King Lear" (CC), "Miss Julie" (Phoenix), "The Golden Six" (OB), "Brecht On Brecht," "Pal Joey" (CC), "Postmark Zero."

LINDLEY, AUDRA. Born Sept. 24, 1918 in Los Angeles. Studied with Max Reinhardt. Has appeared in "Comes The Revolution," "Heads Or Tails," "Hear That Trumpet," "The Young and Fair," "Venus Is."

LIPTON, MICHAEL. Born April 27, 1925 in NYC. Attended Queens College. Has appeared in "Caesar and Cleopatra" (1949), "The Moon Is Blue," "Sing Me No Lullaby," "Wake Up, Darling," "The Tenth Man," "Separate Tables," Off-Bdwy in "The Lover" and "Trigon."

LISA, LUBA. Born in Brooklyn. Attended American Theatre Wing. Made Broadway debut in 1961 in "Carnival," followed by "I Can Get It For You Wholesale," "West Side Story," (CC), "I Had A Ball" for which she received a THEATRE WORLD Award.

| Michael Lombard | Chet London | Will Mackenzie | John Malcolm | Paul Man |

LOMBARD, MICHAEL. Born Aug. 8, 1934 in Brooklyn. Graduate of Brooklyn College and Boston U. Has appeared Off-Bdwy in "King Lear," "The Merchant Of Venice," "Cages," "The Pinter Plays," and on Broadway in "Poor Bitos," "The Devils."

LONDON, CHET. Born April 8, 1931 in Boston. Attended St. Alselm's College. Has been on Broadway in "First Love" and "Calculated Risk," Off-Bdwy in "The Shoemaker and The Peddler," "Romeo and Juliet," "A Midsummer Night's Dream," "Hamlet," "The Deadly Game."

LOWENS, CURT. Born Nov. 17, 1925 in Allenstein, Ger. Schooled in Germany and Holland. Made Broadway bow in 1951 in "Stalag 17" followed by "The Threepenny Opera" (CC), "The First Gentleman," "Postmark Zero."

LOY, MYRNA. Born Aug. 2, 1905 in Helena, Mont. Appeared in stage presentations in Hollywood's Grauman's Chinese Theatre before beginning a long, successful movie career. Returned to the stage in "Barefoot In The Park."

LUDWIG, KAREN. Born Oct. 19, 1942 in San Francisco. Studied at Berghof Studio. Appeared Off-Bdwy in "The Trojan Women," on Broadway in "The Deputy" (1964), "The Devils."

LUDWIG, SALEM. Born July 31, 1915 in Brooklyn. Attended Brooklyn College. Made Broadway bow in 1947 in "Miracle In The Mountains," followed by "Camino Real," "An Enemy Of The People," "All You Need Is One Good Break," Off-Bdwy in "The Brothers Karamazov," "The Victim," "The Troublemaker," and "Man Of Destiny," "Inherit The Wind," "The Disenchanted," "Rhinoceros," "The Three Sisters," "The Zulu and The Zayda."

LUISI, JAMES. Born Nov. 11, 1928 in NYC. Attended St. Francis College, and American Academy of Dramatic Arts. Appeared Off-Bdwy in "The Crucible," "The Threepenny Opera," "Between Two Thieves," and "Detective Story," on Broadway in "Alfie," "Do I Hear A Waltz?," "Sweet Charity."

LUMSDEN, GEOFFREY. Born Dec. 29, 1914 in London. Attended Royal Academy of Dramatic Arts. Made Broadway debut in 1962 in "The Affair," followed by "Hostile Witness."

LUND, ART. Born April 1, 1920 in Salt Lake City. Graduate of Eastern Ky. State College. Made Broadway bow in 1956 in "The Most Happy Fella," followed by "Of Mice and Men" (OB), "Destry Rides Agian," "Donnybrook!," "Sophie," CC revivals of "Fiorello!" and "Most Happy Fella."

LYNCH, RICHARD. Born Feb. 12, 1940 in Brooklyn. Studied at Berghof, and Actors Studio. Has appeared in "Live Like Pigs" (Off-Bdwy), "The Devils."

MACKENZIE, WILL. Born July 24, 1938 in Providence, R. I. Graduate of Brown U. Appeared with American Shakespeare Festival, Off-Bdwy in "Wonderful Town" (CC), "Put It In Writing," "Morning Sun," and "Brigadoon" (CC) before making Broadway bow in 1965 in "Half A Sixpence," followed by "Hello, Dolly!"

MALCOLM, JOHN. Born in London, July 4, 1906. Attended Stanford U. Made Broadway debut in 1930 in "Scarlet Sister Mary," followed by "Love Duel," "Kingdom of God," "Payment Deferred," "Come of Age," "Love Goes To Press," "The Living Room," "Witness For The Prosecution," "The Hasty Heart," "A Majority of One," "The Affair," "A Time For Singing."

MANN, PAUL. Born Dec. 2, 1913 in Toronto, Can. Studied at Neighborhood Playhouse, Group Theatre School. Made New York bow in 1935 in "Bitter Oleander," followed by "Johnny Johnson," "Flight To The West," "Macbeth," "The Whole World Over," "Flight Into Egypt," "Too Late The Phalarope," Lincoln Center Repertory Theater.

MANNING, JACK. Born June 3, 1916 in Cincinnati. Graduate of Cinn. U. Made Broadway bow in 1941 in "Junior Miss," followed by "The Great Big Doorstep," "Harriet," "Mermaids Singing," "Alice In Wonderland," "Man and Superman," "Billy Budd," "The Tender Trap," "Say, Darling," "Do I Hear A Waltz?," Helen Hayes Repertory Co.

MANSFIELD, JAYNE. Born April 19, 1933 in Bryn Mawr, Pa. Attended UCLA. Made Broadway debut in 1955 in "Will Success Spoil Rock Hunter?" for which she received a THEATRE WORLD Award, followed by "The Rabbit Habit."

MARAND, PATRICIA. Born Jan. 25, 1934 in Brooklyn. Attended American Academy of Dramatic Arts. Made Broadway debut in "South Pacific," followed by "Wish You Were Here," "It's A Bird . . . It's A Plane . . . It's Superman!"

MARCHAND, NANCY. Born June 19, 1928 in Buffalo, N. Y. Graduate of Carnegie Tech. Made New York debut in "The Taming Of The Shrew" (CC), followed by "Love's Labour's Lost," "The Merchant of Venice," American Shakespeare Festival, "Much Ado About Nothing," "The Balcony" (OB), APA Repertory Co., "Three Bags Full."

MARIE, JULIENNE. Born in 1943 in Toledo, O. Attended Juilliard. Has appeared in "The King and I," "Whoop-Up!," "Gypsy," "Foxy," and Off-Bdwy in "The Boys From Syracuse" for which she received a THEATRE WORLD Award, "Othello," (OB), "Do I Hear A Waltz?"

MARLOWE, HUGH. Born Jan. 30, 1911 in Philadelphia. Studied at Pasadena Playhouse. Made Broadway bow in 1936 in "Arrest That Woman," followed by "Kiss The Boys Goodbye," "Young Couple Wanted," "The Land Is Bright," "Lady In The Dark," "It Takes Two," "Laura," "Duet For Two Hands," "The Rabbit Habit."

MARSHALL, E. G. Born June 18, 1910 in Owatonna, Minn. Attended Minn. U. Made Broadway debut in 1938 in "Prelude To Glory," followed by "Jason," "The Skin Of Our Teeth," "The Petrified Forest," "Jacobowsky and The Colonel," "The Iceman Cometh," "Hope's The Thing," "The Survivors," "The Crucible," "Red Roses For Me," "Waiting For Godot," "The Gang's All Here," "This Winter's Hobby."

MARSHALL, PETER L. Born March 30, 1930 in Clarksburg, W. Va. Made Broadway debut in 1961 in "How To Make A Man," followed by "Skyscraper."

MARTIN, MARY. Born Dec. 1, 1913 in Weatherford, Tex. Attended Ward-Belmont School. Made Broadway debut in 1938 in "Leave It To Me," followed by "One Touch Of Venus," "Lute Song," "Annie Get Your Gun," "South Pacific," "Kind Sir," "Peter Pan," "The Skin Of Our Teeth," "The Sound Of Music," "Jennie," "Hello, Dolly!"

MARYE, DONALD. Born April 7, 1905 in Chicago. Graduate of Carnegie Tech. Made Broadway bow in 1953 in "The Crucible," followed by "Make A Million," "Luther," "Philadelphia, Here I Come!"

| k Manning | Dermot McNamara | Kay Medford | Marian Mercer | Alan Mixon |

MASSI, BERNICE. Born Aug. 23 in Camden, N. J. Made Broadway debut in 1952 in "South Pacific," followed by "Wish You Were Here," "Can-Can," "By The Beautiful Sea," "No Strings," "What Makes Sammy Run?"

MATHEWS, CARMEN. Born May 8, 1918 in Philadelphia. Graduate of Bennett College. Attended Royal Academy of Dramatic Arts. Made Broadway debut in 1938 in "Henry IV," followed by "Hamlet," "Richard II," "Harriet," "The Cherry Orchard," "The Assassin," "Man and Superman," "The Ivy Green," "Courtin' Time," "My Three Angels," "Holiday For Lovers," "Night Life," "Lorenzo," "The Yearling."

MATHEWS, GEORGE. Born Oct. 10, 1911 in NYC. Made Broadway bow in 1937 in "Professional," followed by "Life of Reilly," "Cuckoos On The Hearth," "Eve of St. Mark," "Kiss Them For Me," "Antigone," "Temper The Wind," "The Silver Whistle," "A Streetcar Named Desire," "Barefoot In Athens," "The Desperate Hours," "Holiday For Lovers," "The Shadow of A Gunman," "Triple Play," "Luther," "Catch Me If You Can," "A Time For Singing."

MATTHEWS, ART. Born in NYC. Attended Columbia and Northwestern. Made New York bow with American Savoyards, followed by "Leave It To Jane" (Off-Bdwy), "Mame."

McMARTIN, JOHN. Born in Warsaw, Ind. Attended Columbia. Made New York debut Off-Bdwy in "Little Mary Sunshine" for which he received a THEATRE WORLD Award, followed by Broadway bow in "The Conquering Hero," "Blood, Sweat and Stanley Poole," "Children From Their Games," "A Rainy Day In Newark," "Too Much Johnson" (OB), "Sweet Charity."

McNAMARA, DERMOT. Born Aug. 24, 1925 in Dublin, Ire. Attended St. Joseph's School. Made Broadway bow in 1959 in "A Touch Of The Poet," followed by Off-Bdwy roles in "The Wise Have Not Spoken," "Three By Synge," "The Playboy Of The Western World," "Shadow and Substance," "Happy As Larry," and "Sharon's Grave," "Philadelphia, Here I Come!"

McVEY, PATRICK. Born March 17, 1913 in Ft. Wayne, Ind. Graduate of Ind. Law School, and Pasadena Playhouse. Has appeared in "State Of The Union," "Detective Story," "Hold It," "Bus Stop," "Catch Me If You Can."

MEDFORD, KAY. Born Sept. 14, 1920 in NYC. Made Broadway debut in 1951 in "Paint Your Wagon," followed by "Two's Company," "John Murray Anderson's Almanac," "Lullaby" for which she received a THEATRE WORLD Award, "Black-Eyed Susan," "Almost Crazy," "Wake Up, Darling," "Mr. Wonderful," "A Hole In The Head," "Carousel" (CC), "Handful Of Fire," "Bye, Bye, Birdie," "In The Counting House," "The Heroine," "Pal Joey" (CC), "Funny Girl."

MEEHAN, DANNY. Born Feb. 17, 1933 in White Plains, N. Y. Attended American Academy of Dramatic Arts. Made Broadway bow in 1958 in "Whoop-Up!," followed by "Do Re Mi," "Funny Girl." Off-Bdwy in "Smiling The Boy Fell Dead," "The Thracian Horses," "O, Oysters," and "New Cole Porter Revue."

MEEKER, RALPH. Born Nov. 21, 1920 in Minneapolis. Attended Northwestern. Made Broadway bow in 1945 in "Strange Fruit," followed by "Cyrano de Bergerac," "Mister Roberts" for which he received a THEATRE WORLD Award, "A Streetcar Named Desire," "Picnic," "Cloud 7," "Rhinoceros," "Something About A Soldier," "After The Fall," "But For Whom Charlie," "Mrs. Dally."

MERCER, MARIAN. Born Nov. 26, 1935 in Akron, O. Graduate of Mich. U. Made New York debut in 1960 in "Greenwillow," followed by "Fiorello!," "Little Mary Sunshine" (OB), "New Faces of 1962," "Hotel Passionato" (OB).

MERIVALE, JOHN. Born Dec. 1, 1917 in Toronto, Can. Attended Oxford and Old Vic School. Made New York bow in 1938 in "Lorelei," followed by "Journey's End," "Romeo and Juliet," "Lady Windermere's Fan," "An Inspector Calls," "Anne Of The Thousand Days," "Day After Tomorrow," "Getting Married," "Venus Observed," "The Deep Blue Sea," "The Reluctant Debutante," "Duel Of Angels," "Ivanov."

MERMAN, ETHEL. Born Jan. 16, 1912 in Astoria, L. I. Appeared in vaudeville before Broadway debut in 1930 in "Girl Crazy," followed by "George White's Scandals," "Take A Chance," "Anything Goes," "Red, Hot and Blue," "Stars In Your Eyes," "Panama Hattie," "Something For The Boys," "Annie Get Your Gun" (also in 1966 revival), "Call Me Madam," "Happy Hunting," "Gypsy."

MIDDLETON, RAY. Born Feb. 8, 1907 in Chicago. Graduate of Ill. U. and Juilliard. Made Broadway bow in 1933 in "Roberta," followed by "Knickerbocker Holiday," "George White's Scandals," "Annie Get Your Gun," "Love Life," "South Pacific," "Too Good To Be True," "Man of La Mancha."

MILLAND, RAY. Born Jan. 3, 1908 in Neath, Wales. Attended King's College. After appearing in over 120 films, made Broadway debut Feb. 17, 1966 in "Hostile Witness."

MILLER, BETTY. Born March 27, 1925 in Boston. Attended CCLA and Dramatic Workshop. Appeared Off-Bdwy in "Summer and Smoke," "Cradle Song," "La Ronde," "Plays For Bleecker Street," "Desire Under The Elms," "The Balcony," "The Power and The Glory," "Beaux Stratagem," New York Shakespeare Festival. Made Broadway debut in 1954 in "Girl On The Via Flaminia," followed by APA revival of "You Can't Take It With You."

MILLER, BUZZ. Born Dec. 23, 1928 in Snowflake, Ariz. Graduate of Ariz. State College. Made Broadway bow in 1948 in "Magdalena," followed by "Pal Joey," "Two's Company," "Me and Juliet," "Pajama Game," "Bells Are Ringing," "Redhead," "Bravo Giovanni," "Hot Spot," "Funny Girl."

MILLIGAN, JOHN. Born in Vancouver, Can. Studied at Bristol Old Vic School. Has appeared in "The Matchmaker," "The First Gentleman," "Love and Libel," "Look Back In Anger," "Hilary," "The Devils."

MINTZ, ELI. Born Aug. 1, 1904 in what is now Poland. Appeared in European and American Yiddish theatres before Broadway debut in 1948 in "Me and Molly," followed by "The Fifth Season," "A Worm In The Horseradish" (OB), "The 49th Cousin," "I Was Dancing," "Catch Me If You Can," "Friends and Enemies" (OB).

Donald Moffat	Robert Moore	Karen Morrow	Margaret Mullen	Mary Ann N

MIXON, ALAN. Born March 15, 1933 in Miami, Fla. Attended Miami U. Off-Bdwy credits: "Suddenly Last Summer," "Desire Under The Elms," "The Trojan Women," "The Alchemist," and "The Child Buyer." Broadway bow in 1962 in "Something About A Soldier," followed by "The Sign In Sidney Brustein's Window," "The Devils."

MOFFAT, DONALD. Born Dec. 26, 1930 in Plymouth, Eng. Attended Royal Academy of Dramatic Arts. Made Broadway bow in 1957 in "Under Milk Wood," followed by "Much Ado About Nothing," "The Tumbler," "Duel Of Angels," "A Passage To India," "The Affair," Off-Bdwy in "The Bald Soprano," "Jack," "Misalliance," and APA Repertory, "You Can't Take It With You."

MONTAGUE, LEE. Born Oct. 16, 1927 in London. Studied at Old Vic School. Made Broadway debut in 1952 in "The Climate of Eden," followed by "Entertaining Mr. Sloane."

MONTGOMERY, EARL. Born April 17, 1921 in Memphis, Tenn. Graduate of Harvard. Made New York bow in 1947 in "Galileo," followed by "Summer and Smoke," "The Relapse," "Mr. Pickwick," "Love's Labour's Lost," "The Merchant of Venice," "The Strong Are Lonely," "The Heavenly Twins," "A Visit To A Small Planet," "Look After Lulu," "Lady of The Camellias," "Tovarich," "The Rehearsal," "The Caucasian Chalk Circle" (LC).

MOORE, ROBERT. Born Aug. 7, 1930 in Washington, D. C. Attended Catholic U. Made Broadway debut in 1948 in "Jenny Kissed Me," followed by "The Owl and The Pussycat," "Cactus Flower."

MORRIS, CHESTER. Born Feb. 16, 1901 in NYC. Made Broadway bow in 1918 in "The Copperhead," followed by "Thunder," "Extra," "The Home Towners," "Whispering Friends," "Yellow," "Crime," "Fast Life," "Blue Denim," "Advise and Consent," "The Subject Was Roses."

MORRISSEY, EAMON. Born Jan. 25, 1943 in Dublin, Ire. Attended Smith Academy of Acting, and Dublin Gate Theatre. Made Broadway debut Feb. 16, 1966 in "Philadelphia, Here I Come!"

MORROW, KAREN. Born Dec. 15, 1936 in Chicago. Attended Clarke College, and Workshop "M". Made New York debut Off-Bdwy in 1961 in "Sing, Muse!" for which she received THEATRE WORLD Award, followed by "The Boys From Syracuse" (OB), "I Had A Ball," "Oklahoma!" (CC), "The Most Happy Fella" (CC).

MULLEN, MARGARET. Born Aug. 28, 1910 in Portsmouth, N. H. Made Broadway debut in 1928 in "Straight Through The Door," followed by "Affair Of State," "Fata Morgana," "Ladies Money," "Three Men On A Horse," "Room Service," "Dead End," "Sweet River," "Red Harvest," "Yankee Point," "Mrs. O'Brien Entertains," "Anya."

MULLIGAN, RICHARD. Born Nov. 13, 1932 in the Bronx. Made Broadway debut in 1961 in "All The Way Home," followed by "Nobody Loves An Albatross," "Never Too Late," "Mating Dance," "Hogan's Goat" (OB).

MUNSHIN, JULES. Born Feb. 22, 1915 in NYC. Studied at Berghof Studio. Made Broadway debut in 1943 in "The Army Play-By-Play," followed by "Call Me Mister," "Bless You All," "Mrs. McThing," "The Good Soup," "Show Girl," "The Gay Life," "Oliver!" "Oklahoma!" (CC).

NAISMITH, LAURENCE. Born Dec. 14, 1908 in Thames-Ditton, Eng. Attended All Saints Choir School. After successful career in England, made Broadway debut in 1963 in "School For Scandal," followed by "Here's Love," "A Time For Singing."

NELSON, BARRY. Born in Oakland, Calif. Graduate of U. of Calif. Made Broadway debut in 1943 in "Winged Victory," followed by "Light Up The Sky," "The Moon Is Blue," "Wake Up, Darling," "The Rat Race," "Mary, Mary," "Nobody Loves An Albatross," "Cactus Flower."

NEWLEY, ANTHONY. Born Sept. 21, 1931 in London. Received training with Dewsbury Rep. Co. Made Broadway debut in 1956 in "Cranks," followed by "Stop The World—I Want To Get Off," "The Roar Of The Greasepaint—The Smell Of The Crowd" both of which he co-authored.

NILES, MARY ANN. Born May 2, 1933 in NYC. Attended Miss Finchley's School and Ballet Academy. Made Broadway debut in 1945 in "Girl From Nantucket," followed by "Dance Me A Song," "Call Me Mister," "Make Mine Manhattan," "La Plume de Ma Tante," "Carnival," Off-Bdwy in "The Boys From Syracuse" and "Your Sister Rose," "Flora, The Red Menace."

O'BRIEN, DAVID. Born Oct. 1, 1935 in Chicago. Graduate of Stanford, and Fulbright Scholar to London Academy of Music and Dramatic Art. Appeared Off-Bdwy in "Under Milk Wood" and "A Month In The Country" before making Broadway bow in 1962 in "A Passage To India," followed by "Arturo Ui," "A Time For Singing."

O'LOUGHLIN, GERALD S. Born Dec. 23, 1921 in NYC. Attended Rochester U., Lafayette College, Neighborhood Playhouse. Made Broadway bow in 1952 in "Golden Boy," followed by "The Flowering Peach," "A Streetcar Named Desire" (CC), "The Dark At The Top Of The Stairs," "Shadow Of A Gunman," "A Touch Of The Poet," "Machinal" (OB), "A Cook For Mr. General," "Calculated Risk," "One Flew Over The Cuckoo's Nest," "Happily Never After."

OLSON, JAMES. Born Oct. 8, 1930 in Evanston, Ill. Attended Northwestern, and Actors Studio. Made Broadway bow in 1955 in "The Young and The Beautiful," followed by "The Sin Of Pat Muldoon," "J. B.," "The Chinese Prime Minister," "The Three Sisters" (1964), "Slapstick Tragedy."

OLSON, KAY. Born April 2, 1942 in Chicago. Graduate of Ill. U. Made Broadway debut Oct. 6, 1965 in "The Roar Of The Greasepaint—The Smell Of The Crowd."

O'NEAL, FREDERICK. Born Aug. 27, 1905 in Brooksville, Miss. Attended New Theatre School, American Theatre Wing. Co-founded American Negro Theatre in 1940 and appeared in their productions before making Broadway bow in 1944 in "Anna Lucasta," followed by "Take A Giant Step," "The Winner," "House Of Flowers," Off-Bdwy in "The Man With The Golden Arm" and "Ballad Of Bimshire." Is president of Actors Equity.

O'NEILL, DICK. Born August 29, 1928 in the Bronx. Attended Utica College. Made Broadway bow in 1961 in "The Unsinkable Molly Brown," followed by "Skyscraper."

id O'Brien   Mairin D. O'Sullivan   Maurice Ottinger   James Patterson   Brock Peters

ORBACH, JERRY. Born Oct. 20, 1935 in NYC. Attended Ill. U., and Northwestern. Appeared Off-Bdwy in "The Threepenny Opera," "The Fantasticks," and "The Cradle Will Rock." Made Broadway debut in 1961 in "Carnival," followed by "Guys and Dolls" (CC), "Carousel" and "Annie Get Your Gun" at Lincoln Center.

ORCHARD, JULIAN D. C. Born March 3, 1930 in Wheatley, Oxford, Eng. Attended Guildhall School of Music and Drama, London. Made Broadway debut Oct. 4, 1965 in "Pickwick."

O'SHAUGHNESSY, JOHN. Born Sept. 20, 1907 in Spokane, Wash. Attended Wash. U., and Cornish School. Made New York bow in 1933 in "Six Miracle Plays," followed by "Parade," "Let Freedom Ring," "Bury The Dead," "200 Were Chosen," "Excursion," "Washington Jitters," "The Boys From Syracuse," Off-Bdwy in "The Hostage," and "Medea."

O'SHEA, TESSIE. Born March 13, 1918 in Caerdydd, G.B. Attended private schools. Made stage debut in 1923. Made Broadway bow in 1963 in "The Girl Who Came To Supper," followed by "A Time For Singing."

OSTRIN, ART. Born Aug. 30, 1937 in NYC. Has appeared in City Center revivals of "The Time Of Your Life," and "South Pacific," "Irma La Douce," "Around The World In 80 Days," "Slapstick Tragedy."

O'SULLIVAN, MAIRIN D. Born Jan. 1 in Ireland. Member of Abbey Theatre in Dublin before making Broadway debut Feb. 16, 1966 in "Philadelphia, Here I Come!"

O'SULLIVAN, MAUREEN. Born May 17 in Roscommon, Ire. Attended Sacred Heart Convent. After long film career, made Broadway debut in 1962 in "Never Too Late," followed by "The Subject Was Roses."

O'SULLIVAN, MICHAEL. Born March 4, 1934 in Phoenix, Ariz. Attended Regis College, Denver U., and Goodman Theatre School. Appeared Off-Bdwy in "Six Characters In Search Of An Author," "In White America," and with LC Rep. Co. in "Tartuffe" for which he received a THEATRE WORLD Award. Made Broadway bow in 1964 in "The White House," followed by "It's A Bird . . . It's A Plane . . . It's Superman!"

OTTENHEIMER, ALBERT M. Born Sept. 6, 1904 in Tacoma, Wash. Graduate of U. of Wash. Co-founder of Seattle Rep. Co. Made Broadway debut in 1946 in "Affair Of Honor," followed by "West Side Story," "The Deputy." Off-Bdwy credits: "Monday's Heroes," "Tiger," "Mother Riba," "A Christmas Carol," "Juno and the Paycock," "The Italian Straw Hat," "The Iceman Cometh," "Call It Virtue," "The Immoralist," "The Cat and The Canary," "The Exhaustion Of Our Son's Love," and "The Deadly Game."

OTTINGER, MAURICE. Born June 27 in Newport, Tenn. Graduate of East Tenn State U., and U. of Wisc. Appeared Off-Bdwy in "Dark Of The Moon," "The Crucible," and "Come Share My House." Made Broadway debut in 1963 in "Dear Me, The Sky Is Falling," followed by "Any Wednesday."

PAGAN, PETER. Born July 24, 1921 in Sydney, Aust. Attended Scots College. Has appeared in "Escapade," "Portrait Of A Lady," "The Dark Is Light Enough," "Child Of Fortune," "Hostile Witness."

PAGE, GERALDINE. Born Nov. 22, 1924 in Kirksville, Mo. Studied at Goodman Theatre School. Appeared in several Off-Bdwy plays before making Broadway debut in 1953 in "Mid-Summer" for which she received a THEATRE WORLD Award, followed by "The Immoralist," "The Rainmaker," "The Innkeepers," "Separate Tables," "Sweet Bird Of Youth," "Strange Interlude" (1963), "The Three Sisters" (1964), "P.S. I Love You," "The Great Indoors."

PARSONS, ESTELLE. Born Nov. 20, 1927 in Lynn, Mass. Attended Conn. College, Boston U. Law School, Actors Studio. Made Broadway debut in 1956 in "Happy Hunting," followed by "Whoop-Up!," "Beg, Borrow or Steal," Off-Bdwy in "The Threepenny Opera," "Automobile Graveyard," "Mrs. Dally Has A Lover" for which she received a THEATRE WORLD Award, "In The Summer House," and "Monopoly," "Ready When You Are, C. B.," "Malcolm."

PATTERSON, JAMES. Born June 29, 1932 in Derry, Pa. Appeared Off-Bdwy in "Brothers Karamazov," "Epitaph For George Dillon," "The Zoo Story," "The Collection," and "Benito Cereno." Made Broadway bow in 1964 in "Conversation At Midnight," followed by "Inadmissible Evidence."

PENDLETON, WYMAN. Born April 18, 1916 in Providence, R. I. Graduate of Brown U. Appeared Off-Bdwy in "Gallows Humor," "American Dream," "Zoo Story," "Corruption In The Palace of Justice," "The Giants' Dance," "The Child Buyer," "Happy Days," and in "Tiny Alice," "Malcolm."

PETERS, BROCK. Born July 2, 1927 in NYC. Attended Chicago U., CCNY. Made Broadway bow in 1943 in "Porgy and Bess," followed by "South Pacific," "Anna Lucasta," "My Darlin' Aida," "Mister Johnson," "Kwamina," "The Caucasian Chalk Circle" (LC).

PETINA, IRRA. Born April 18, 1900 in Petrograd, Russia. Studied at Curtis Inst. Sang with Met Opera Co. Made Broadway debut in 1944 in "Song Of Norway," followed by "The Chocolate Soldier," "Music In The Air," "The Gypsy Baron," "The Waltz King," "Magdalena," "Candide," "Anya."

PLESHETTE, JOHN. Born July 27, 1942 in NYC. Attended Brown U. Appeared Off-Bdwy in "A Sound Of Silence" and with New York Shakespeare Festival 1965, made Broadway debut in "The Zulu and The Zayda."

PLUMMER, CHRISTOPHER. Born Dec. 13, 1929 in Toronto, Can. Attended Jennings School. Made Broadway bow in 1954 in "The Starcross Story," followed by "Home Is The Hero," "The Dark Is Light Enough" for which he received a THEATRE WORLD Award, "Medea," "The Lark," "The Night Of The Auk," "J. B.," "Arturo Ui," "The Royal Hunt Of The Sun."

POINTER, PRISCILLA. Born in NYC. Graduate of Professional Children's School. With San Francisco Actor's Workshop from 1952-65, and Lincoln Center Rep. Theater Co. this season.

PONAZECKI, JOE. Born Jan. 7, 1934 in Rochester, N. Y. Attended Rochester U., Columbia. Made Broadway bow in 1959 in Gielgud's "Much Ado About Nothing," followed by "Send Me No Flowers," "A Call On Kuprin," "Take Her, She's Mine," "The Dragon" (OB), "Fiddler On The Roof," "Xmas In Las Vegas," "Three Bags Full."

245

| Philip Proctor | Mylo Quam | Ronald Radd | Dorothy Raymond | John Rand |

PRESNELL, HARVE. Born Sept. 14, 1933 in Modesto, Calif. Attended USC. Made Broadway bow Nov. 3, 1960 in "The Unsinkable Molly Brown," followed by revival of "Carousel."

PRESTON, ROBERT. Born June 8, 1918 in Newton Highland, Mass. Attended Pasadena Playhouse. After many films, made Broadway debut in 1951 in "Twentieth Century," followed by "The Male Animal," "Men Of Distinction," "His and Hers," "The Magic and The Loss," "The Tender Trap," "Janus," "The Hidden River," "The Music Man," "Too True To Be Good," "Nobody Loves An Albatross," "Ben Franklin In Paris," "The Lion In Winter."

PRICE, GILBERT. Born Sept. 10, 1942 in NYC. Studied at American Theatre Wing. Has appeared Off-Bdwy in "Kicks & Co.," "Fly Blackbird," and "Jerico Jim-Crow" for which he received a THEATRE WORLD Award. Made Broadway bow May 16, 1965 in "The Roar Of The Greasepaint—The Smell Of The Crowd."

PRIOLO, SUSAN. Born Aug. 15, 1957 in Brooklyn. Made Broadway debut Jan. 4, 1966 in "UTBU."

PROCTOR, PHILIP. Born July 28, 1940 in Goshen, Ind. Graduate of Yale. Made Broadway bow in "A Sound Of Music," followed by roles Off-Bdwy in "The Cherry Orchard," "Portrait Of The Artist," "Barroom Monks," "A Thistle In My Bed," and "The Amorous Flea" for which he received a THEATRE WORLD Award, "A Time For Singing."

QUAM, MYLO. Born June 1, 1942 in Fargo, N. Dak. Attended Brandeis, Boston, L. I. and New York Universities, and American Shakespeare Academy. Appeared Off-Bdwy in "Deathwatch," "The Killers," and "Picnic On The Battlefield," before making Broadway debut Oct. 26, 1965 in "The Royal Hunt Of The Sun."

QUITAK, OSCAR. Born March 10, 1926 in London. Attended Royal Academy of Dramatic Arts. Appeared in many English productions, including Old Vic, before making Broadway debut Oct. 4, 1965 in "Pickwick."

RADD, RONALD. Born in Sunderland Co., Durham, Eng., Jan. 22, 1929. After 7 years of repertory in Eng., made Broadway bow in 1957 in "Hotel Paradiso," followed by 4 years as Doolittle in "My Fair Lady," "Ivanov."

RAE, CHARLOTTE. Born April 22, 1926. Graduate of Northwestern. Made Broadway debut in 1952 in "Three Wishes For Jamie," followed by "The Threepenny Opera" (OB), "The Golden Apple," "The Littlest Revue" (OB), "Li'l Abner," "The Beauty Part," (OB) in "The Beggar's Opera," "The New Tenant," and "Victims Of Duty," "Pickwick."

RAITT, JOHN. Born Jan. 29, 1917 in Santa Ana, Calif. Graduate of Redlands U. Made Broadway bow in 1945 in "Carousel" for which he received a THEATRE WORLD Award, followed by "Magdalena," "Three Wishes For Jamie," "The Pajama Game," 1965 revival of "Carousel."

RAMSEY, LOGAN. Born March 21, 1921 in Long Beach, Calif. Graduate of St. Joseph's College. Made Broadway bow in 1950 in "The Devil's Disciple," followed by "The High Ground," "In The Summer House," "The Good Woman of Setzuan," (OB), "Sweet Bird Of Youth," "Marathon '33," "The Great Indoors."

RANDALL, TONY. Born Feb. 26, 1920 in Tulsa, Okla. Attended Northwestern, Columbia, Neighborhood Playhouse. Made Broadway debut in 1947 in "Antony and Cleopatra," followed by "To Tell You The Truth," "Caesar and Cleopatra," "Oh, Men! "Oh, Women!," "Inherit The Wind," "Oh, Captain!," "UTBU."

RANDOLPH, JOHN. Born June 1, 1915 in the Bronx. Attended CCNY, American Theatre Wing, Actors Studio. Made Broadway bow in 1937 in "Revolt Of The Beavers," followed by "The Emperor's New Clothes," "Capt. Jinks," "No More Peace," "Coriolanus," "Medicine Show," "Hold On To Your Hats," "Native Son," "Command Decision," "Come Back, Little Sheba," "The Golden State," "Peer Gynt," "Paint Your Wagon," "Seagulls Over Sorrento," "The Grey-Eyed People," "Room Service" (1953), "All Summer Long," "House Of Flowers," "The Visit," "Mother Courage and Her Children," "A Sound Of Music," "A Case of Libel," "Conversation At Midnight," "An Evening's Frost" (OB).

RAPHAEL, GERRIANNE. Born Feb. 23, 1935 in NYC. Attended New School and Columbia. Has appeared in "Solitaire," "Guest In The House," "Violet," "Goodbye, My Fancy," "Seventh Heaven," "Li'l Abner," "Saratoga," Off-Bdwy in "The Threepenny Opera," "The Boy Friend," "Ernest In Love," and "Man Of La Mancha."

RAWLINS, LESTER. Born Sept. 24, 1924 in Farrell, Pa. Attended Carnegie Tech. Has appeared in "Othello," "King Lear," "The Lovers," "A Man For All Seasons," Off-Bdwy in "Endgame," "The Quare Fellow," "Camino Real," "Hedda Gabler," "The Old Glory," "The Child Buyer," and "Winterset."

RAYMOND, DOROTHY. Born Nov. 21 in Pittsburgh. Graduate of Carnegie Tech. Made Broadway debut in 1925 in "The Jazz Singer," followed by "Eve's Leaves," "Iphigenia In Aulis," "Big Blow," "Broken Chain," "Dodsworth," "Calling All Stars," "Uncle Willie," "Compulsion," Off-Bdwy in "The Boy Friend," "Power Of Darkness," and "Rooms."

REID, KATE. Born Nov. 4, 1930 in London. Attended Toronto U. Appeared with Canadian Shakespeare Festival. Made Broadway debut in 1962 in "Who's Afraid Of Virginia Woolf?," followed by "Dylan," "Slapstick Tragedy."

REILLY, CHARLES NELSON. Born Jan. 13, 1931 in NYC. Attended Conn. U. Appeared Off-Bdwy in "Nightcar," "Fallout," "Lend An Ear," "Parade," "The Inspector General," "3 Times 3," and "Apollo of Bellac" before making Broadway debut in 1960 in "Bye, Bye, Birdie," followed by "How To Succeed In Business Without Really Trying," "Hello Dolly!," "Skyscraper."

REMICK, LEE. Born Dec. 14, 1935, in Boston. Attended Barnard College. Made Broadway debut in 1953 in "Be Your Age," followed by "Anyone Can Whistle," "Wait Until Dark."

RICH, DORIS. Born Aug. 14, 1905 in Boston. Attended American Academy of Dramatic Arts. Made Broadway debut in 1927 in "Getting In The Movies," followed by "The Mad Hopes," "The Taming Of The Shrew," "Sophie," "Flamingo Road," "Strange Bedfellows," "The Madwoman Of Chaillot," "Affair Of Honor," "Redhead," "The Physicists," "UTBU."

| William Roerick | Clifford Rose | Tom Rosqui | Jack Ryland | Peter Sallis |

RIPLEY, TRESCOTT (formerly Patricia). Born Aug. 15, 1926 in Evanston, Ill. Graduate of Bennington College. Has appeared Off-Bdwy in "The Hostage," "Garden District," "Threepenny Opera," "The Infernal Machine," and "The Ticklish Acrobat," on Broadway in "Be Your Age," "Major Barbara," "Great God Brown," "Sweet Bird Of Youth," "The Beauty Part," "Ballad Of The Sad Cafe," "The Physicists," "Half A Sixpence."

RITCHARD, CYRIL. Born Dec. 1, 1897 in Sydney, Aust. Attended Sydney U. Made Broadway bow in 1947 in "Love For Love," followed by "Make Way For Lucia," "The Relapse," "Peter Pan," "A Visit To A Small Planet," "The Pleasure Of His Company," "The Happiest Girl In The World," "Romulus," "Too True To Be Good," "The Irregular Verb To Love," "The Roar Of The Greasepaint—The Smell Of The Crowd."

RITTER, THELMA. Born Feb. 14, 1905 in Brooklyn. Attended American Academy of Dramatic Arts. Made Broadway debut in 1926 in "The Shelf," followed by "In Times Square," "New Girl In Town," "UTBU."

RIVERA, CHITA. Born Jan. 23, 1933 in Washington, D.C. Attended American School of Ballet. Made Broadway debut in 1950 in "Guys and Dolls," followed by "Call Me Madam," "Can-Can," "Shoestring Revue" (OB), "Seventh Heaven," "Mr. Wonderful," "West Side Story," "Bye Bye Birdie," "Bajour."

ROBARDS, JASON. Born July 26, 1922 in Chicago. Attended American Academy of Dramatic Arts. Made Broadway debut in 1947 with D'Oyly Carte Opera Co., followed by "Stalag 17," "The Chase," Off-Bdwy in "American Gothic," and "The Iceman Cometh," "Long Day's Journey Into Night" for which he received a THEATRE WORLD Award, "The Disenchanted," "Toys In The Attic," "Big Fish, Little Fish," "A Thousand Clowns," "After The Fall," and "But For Whom Charlie" with LC Rep. Co., "Hughie," "The Devils."

RODGERS, SHEV. Born April 9, 1928 in Hollister, Calif. Attended San Francisco State College. Made Broadway bow in 1959 in "Redhead," followed by "The Music Man," "Man Of La Mancha."

ROERICK, WILLIAM. Born Dec. 17, 1912 in NYC. Attended Hamilton College. Made Broadway bow in 1935 in "Romeo and Juliet," followed by "St. Joan," "Hamlet," "Our Town," "The Importance Of Being Earnest," "The Land Is Bright," "Autumn Hill," "This Is The Army," "The Magnificent Yankee," "Tonight At 8:30," "Madam, Will You Walk" (OB), "The Burning Glass," "The Right Honourable Gentleman."

ROGERS, GINGER. Born July 16, 1911 in Independence, Mo. Made Broadway debut in 1929 in "Top Speed," followed by "Girl Crazy" after which Hollywood claimed her for 71 movies. Returned to Broadway in 1951 in "Love and Let Love," then "Hello, Dolly!" in 1965.

ROLF, FREDERICK. Born Aug. 14, 1926 in Berlin, Ger. Toured in repertory before making Broadway bow in 1951 in "Saint Joan," followed by "Coriolanus" (OB), "The Strong Are Lonely," American Shakespeare Festival, "Time Remember'd," Off-Bdwy in "The Smokeweaver's Daughter," "Between Two Thieves," "Hedda Gabler," and "The Day The Whores Came Out To Play Tennis," "The Egg," "Hogan's Goat" (OB) which he directed.

ROLLE, ESTHER. Born Nov. 8 in Pompano Beach, Fla. Attended Hunter College. Made Broadway debut in 1964 in "Blues For Mr. Charlie," followed by "Purlie Victorious," "The Amen Corner," Off-Bdwy in "The Blacks," "Happy Ending" and "Day Of Absence."

ROSE, CLIFFORD. Born Oct. 24, 1929 in Hamnish, Herefordshire, Eng. Attended U. of London. Made Broadway bow with Royal Shakespeare Co. in 1964 in "King Lear" and "The Comedy Of Errors," followed by "Marat/Sade."

ROSE, GEORGE. Born Feb. 19, 1920 in Bicester, Eng. Attended London's Central School of Drama. Made New York debut with Old Vic Co. in 1946 in "Henry IV," followed by "Much Ado About Nothing," "A Man For All Seasons," "Hamlet" (1964), "A Royal Hunt Of The Sun."

ROSQUI, TOM. Born June 12, 1928 in Oakland, Calif. Graduate of College of Pacific. Member of San Francisco Actor's Workshop. Made New York bow in 1965-6 Lincoln Center Rep. Co. productions.

ROTH, LILLIAN. Born Dec. 13, 1910 in Boston. As a child, appeared in vaudeville with "The Roth Kids." Made Broadway debut in 1917 in "The Inner Man," followed by "Penrod," "The Betrothal," "Shavings," "Padlocks of 1927," "Earl Carroll's Vanities," "Midnight Frolics," "I Can Get It For You Wholesale," "Funny Girl."

ROUNSEVILLE, ROBERT. Born March 25, 1919 in Attleboro, Mass. Attended Tufts U. In addition to opera, has appeared on Broadway in "Babes In Arms" (1937 debut), "The Two Bouquets," "Knickerbocker Holiday," "Higher and Higher," "Up In Central Park," 1952 Gilbert & Sullivan revivals, "Show Boat" (1954), "The Merry Widow," "Candide," "Brigadoon" (CC), "Man Of La Mancha."

ROZAKIS, GREGORY. Born Jan. 30, 1943 in NYC. Attended NYU. Made Broadway debut in 1963 in "Natural Affection," followed by "The Royal Hunt Of The Sun."

RYLAND, JACK. Born July 2, 1935 in Lancaster, Pa. Attended American Foundation of Dramatic Arts, Phil. Has appeared Off-Bdwy in "Palm Tree In A Rose Garden," "Lysistrata," "The White Rose and The Red," "The Old Glory" and with New York Shakespeare Festival. Made Broadway bow in 1959 in "The World Of Suzie Wong," followed by "A Very Rich Woman."

SABOL, DICK. Born April 5, 1937 in Yonkers, New York. Appeared Off-Bdwy in "The Hostage" and "Leave It To Jane" before making Broadway bow March 6, 1966 in "3 Bags Full."

SALLIS, PETER. Born Feb. 1, 1921 in Twickenham, Eng. Attended Royal Academy of Dramatic Arts. Made Broadway debut in 1965 in "Baker Street," followed by "Inadmissible Evidence."

SANCHEZ, JAIME. Born Dec. 19, 1938 in Rincon, P. R. Attended Actors Studio. Made Broadway bow in 1957 in "West Side Story," followed by "Oh, Dad, Poor Dad, Momma's Hung You In The Closet and I Feel So Sad," New York Shakespeare Festival's "A Midsummer Night's Dream" and "Othello," Off-Bdwy in "The Toilet" and "Conerico Was Here To Stay" for which he received a THEATRE WORLD Award.

SAND, PAUL. Born March 5, 1935 in Santa Monica, Calif. Attended CCLA. Studied with Marcel Marceau. Made Broadway bow in 1961 in "From The Second City," followed by Off-Bdwy roles in "Journey To The Day," "Wet Paint," "Hotel Passionato," and "The Mad Show."

| Roy R. Scheider | Harry Secombe | Paula Shaw | P. Jay Sidney | Nat Simmo |

SANDS, DIANA. Born Aug. 22, 1934 in NYC. Has appeared in "A Raisin In The Sun," "Tiger, Tiger Burning Bright" for which she received a THEATRE WORLD Award, Off-Bdwy in "The World of Sholom Aleichem," "Major Barbara," "The Man With The Golden Arm," "Land Beyond The River," and "Brecht On Brecht," "Blues for Mr. Charlie," "The Owl and The Pussycat."

SAPPINGTON, FAY. Born May 22, 1906. Attended U. of Tex. and Pasadena Playhouse. Has appeared in "Southern Exposure," "The Cellar and The Well," "Glad Tidings," "The Yearling."

SCHEIDER, ROY R. Born Nov. 10, 1935 in Orange, N. J. Graduate of Franklin and Marshall College. Made Broadway debut in 1965 in "The Chinese Prime Minister," followed by "The Alchemist," "Sergeant Musgrave's Dance" (OB).

SCHNABEL, STEFAN. Born Feb. 2, 1912 in Berlin, Ger. Attended U. of Bonn, and Old Vic. Made New York bow in 1937 in "Julius Caesar," followed by "Shoemaker's Holiday," "Glamour Preferred," "Land Of Fame," "The Cherry Orchard," "Around The World," "Now I Lay Me Down To Sleep," "Idiot's Delight" (CC), "The Love Of Four Colonels," "Plain and Fancy," "Small War On Murray Hill," "A Very Rich Woman."

SCOTT, MARTHA. Born Sept. 22, 1914 in Jamesport, Mo. Graduate of U. of Mich. Made Broadway debut in 1938 in "Our Town," followed by "Foreigners," "The Willow and I," "Soldier's Wife," "The Voice of The Turtle," "It Takes Two," "Design For A Stained Glass Window," "The Remarkable Mr. Pennypacker," "Cloud 7," "A Distant Bell," "The Tumbler," "The 49th Cousin," "Never Too Late," "The Subject Was Roses."

SECOMBE, HARRY. Born Sept. 8, 1921 in Swansea, Wales. Made Broadway debut Oct. 4, 1965 in "Pickwick."

SHARPE, JOHN. Born Oct. 2, 1932 in Chicago. Attended Northwestern. Has appeared in "Seventeen," "Shoestring Revue" (OB), "The Most Happy Fella," "Sweet Charity."

SHAW, PAULA. Born July 17, 1941 in the Bronx. Graduate of Bard College. Has appeared Off-Bdwy in "Digging For Apples," "Wide Open Cage," "Legend of Charlie Parker," "Penelope," and "The Deadly Game."

SHEEN, MARTIN. Born Aug. 3, 1940 in Dayton, O. Appeared Off-Bdwy in "The Connection," "Many Loves" and "The Jungle of Cities," and made Broadway bow in 1964 in "Never Live Over A Pretzel Factory," followed by "The Subject Was Roses."

SHERMAN, HIRAM. Born Feb. 11, 1908 in Boston. Attended U. of Ill., and Goodman Theatre. Made Broadway bow in 1936 in "Horse Eats Hat," followed by "Shoemaker's Holiday," "Sing Out The News," "Very Warm For May," "The Talley Method," "Cyrano de Bergerac," "The Alchemist," "4 Twelves Are 48," "The Moon Is Blue," "Two's Company," "The Frogs Of Spring," "3 For Tonight," "Goodbye Again," "Measure For Measure," "International Soiree," "Mary, Mary," "Where's Daddy?"

SHERWOOD, MADELEINE. Born Nov. 13, 1926 in Montreal, Can. Attended Yale Drama School. Has appeared in "The Chase," "The Crucible," "Cat On A Hot Tin Roof," "Invitation To A March," "Camelot," "Arturo Ui," "Do I Hear A Waltz?," "Inadmissible Evidence."

SHOWALTER, MAX (Casey Adams). Born June 2, 1917 in Caldwell, Kan. Attended Pasadena Playhouse. Made Broadway bow in 1938 in "Knights Of Song," followed by "Very Warm For May," "My Sister Eileen," "Show Boat," "John Loves Mary," "Make Mine Manhattan," "Hello, Dolly!"

SIDNEY, P. JAY. Made Broadway debut in 1934 in "Dance With Your Gods," followed by "Twentieth Century," "Carmen Jones," "Green Pastures," "Run, Little Chillun," "Jeb," "The Cool World," "The Octoroon" (OB), "The Winner," "The Playroom."

SIDNEY, SYLVIA. Born Aug. 10, 1910 in NYC. Attended Theatre Guild School. Made Broadway debut in 1926 in "Prunella," followed by "The Squall," "Crime," "Mirrors," "The Breaks," "Nice Women," "Cross Roads," "Many A Slip," "Bad Girl," "To Quito and Back," "The Gentle People," "A Very Special Baby," "Auntie Mame," "Enter Laughing," "Riverside Drive" (OB), National Rep. Theatre productions of "The Madwoman of Chaillot," "The Rivals," and "The Trojan Women."

SIGGINS, JEFF. Born Sept. 22, 1943 in Warren, Pa. Appeared Off-Bdwy in "Anything Goes," "Ginger Man," and "All Women Are One" before making Broadway debut in 1965 in "The Impossible Years."

SILVER, JOE. Born in September 28, 1922 in Chicago. Attended U. of Wisc., American Theatre Wing. Made Broadway bow in 1942 in "Tobacco Road," followed by "The Doughgirls," "Heads or Tails," Off-Bdwy in "Blood Wedding," "Lamp At Midnight," "Joseph and His Brethren," "The Victors," "Nature's Way," "Gypsy," "The Heroine," "The Zulu and The Zayda."

SIMMONS, NAT. Born Nov. 17, 1936 in Richmond, Va. Reared in Red Bank, N. J. Attended Columbia. Appeared Off-Bdwy in "The Baptism," "Hatful of Rain," "Moon On A Rainbow Shawl," "Flowers For The Dead," and 1965 New York Shakespeare Festival before making Broadway bow Nov. 23, 1965 with APA in "You Can't Take It With You."

SINCLAIR, BETTY. Born Feb. 7, 1907 in Liverpool, Eng. Made Broadway debut in 1947 in "The Winslow Boy," followed by "The Deep Blue Sea," "The Doctor's Dilemma," "The Sleeping Prince," "The Apple Cart," "Lord Pengo," "Ivanov."

SKULNIK, MENASHA. Born in Poland, May 15, 1898. Began career at 10. Was Yiddish stage favorite for many years before making 1953 Broadway debut in "The Fifth Season," followed by "The Flowering Peach," "Uncle Willie," "The 49th Cousin," "The Zulu and The Zayda."

SMALL, NEVA. Born Nov. 17, 1952 in NYC. Made Broadway debut in 1964 in "Something More!," followed by "The Impossible Years."

SMITH, SAMMY. Born March 3, 1904 in Brooklyn. Graduate of Drake Business School. Has appeared in "Buckaroo," "Wish You Were Here," "Plain and Fancy," "Li'l Abner," "How To Succeed In Business Without Really Trying," "Oklahoma!" (CC).

SMITH, SANDRA. Born June 27, 1940 in Minneapolis. Made Broadway debut in "The Pleasure Of His Company," followed by "One By One," "Any Wednesday."

| mmy Steele | Frances Sternhagen | Dolph Sweet | Inga Swenson | Robert Symonds |

SMOLKO, JOHN. Born July 2, 1928 in Ambridge, Pa. Attended NYU. Has appeared in "Bless You All," "Paint Your Wagon," "Ankles Aweigh," "Kaleidoscope," "Mask and Gown," "It's A Bird . . . It's A Plane . . . It's Superman!"

SOBOLOFF, ARNOLD. Born Nov. 11, 1930 in NYC. Attended Cooper Union. Off-Bdwy credits: "Threepenny Opera," "Career," "Brothers Karamozov," and "Vincent." Made Broadway bow in 1960 in "Mandingo," followed by "The Egg," "The Beauty Part," "One Flew Over The Cuckoo's Nest," "Anyone Can Whistle," "Bravo Giovanni," "Sweet Charity."

SPINETTI, VICTOR. Born Sept. 2, 1932 in South Wales, British Isles. Attended Cardiff Drama College. Made New York debut in 1960 in "The Hostage," followed by "Oh, What A Lovely War!" for which he received a THEATRE WORLD Award, "La Grosse Valise."

STAPLETON, MAUREEN. Born June 21, 1925 in Troy, N. Y. Studied at Berghof Studio. Made Broadway debut in 1946 in "The Playboy Of The Western World," followed by "Antony and Cleopatra," "Detective Story," "The Bird Cage," "The Rose Tattoo" for which she received a THEATRE WORLD Award, "The Emperor's Clothes," "The Crucible," "Richard III," "The Seagull," "27 Wagons Full Of Cotton," "Orpheus Descending," "The Cold Wind and The Warm," "Toys In The Attic," "The Glass Menagerie" (1965).

STEELE, TOMMY. Born Dec. 17, 1936 in London. One of England's most popular performers before making Broadway debut April 25, 1965 in "Half A Sixpence" which he created in London.

STEHLI, EDGAR. Born July 12, 1884 in Lyons, France. Graduate of Cornell. Made Broadway bow in 1916 with Portmanteau Theatre repertory of one act plays. Among his many plays are "Jonathan Makes A Wish," "Liliom," "He Who Gets Slapped," "Hamlet," "Patience," "Love For Love," "The Greatest Show On Earth," "Arsenic and Old Lace," "The Happy Time," "Mid-Summer," "The Sin Of Pat Muldoon," "The Devils."

STERNHAGEN, FRANCES. Born Jan. 13, 1932 in Washington, D.C. Graduate of Vassar. Has appeared Off-Bdwy in "The Admirable Bashful," "Thieves' Carnival," "The Country Wife," "Ulysses In Nighttown," "The Saintliness Of Margery Kempe," "The Room" and "A Slight Ache." Made Broadway debut in 1962 in "Great Day In The Morning," followed by "The Right Honourable Gentleman."

STEVENS, PAUL. Born June 17, 1924. Graduate UCLA, Pasadena Playhouse. Off-Bdwy: "The Crucible," "Romeo and Juliet," "Two Gentlemen From Verona," "As You Like It," "Much Ado About Nothing," "Ivanov," and "The White Devil." Broadway bow in 1957 in "Compulsion," followed by "Girls Of Summer," "General Seegar," "Andorra," "The Advocate."

STEVENSON, MARGOT. Born Feb. 8, 1918 in NYC. Graduate of Brearley School. Made Broadway debut in 1932 in "Firebird," followed by "Evensong," "A Party," "The Barretts Of Wimpole Street," "Symphony," "Truly Valiant," "Call It A Day," "Stage Door," "You Can't Take It With You," "Golden Wings," "Little Women" (CC), "The Rugged Path," "The Leading Lady," "The Young and the Beautiful," "The Apple Cart," "Triple Play," toured with APA in 1961, "Lord Pengo," "Hostile Witness."

STEWART, DAVID J. Born in Omaha, Neb. Attended Omaha U., Neighborhood Playhouse, Actors Studio. Made New York debut in 1945 in "Antigone," followed by "Antony and Cleopatra," "That Lady," "The Rose Tattoo," "Barefoot In Athens," "Camino Real," "The Immoralist," "The Making Of Moo" (OB), "A Man For All Seasons," LC Rep. Co. Productions of "Marco Millions," "After The Fall," "Incident at Vichy," "Danton's Death."

STREISAND, BARBRA. Born April 24, 1942 in Brooklyn. Appeared Off-Bdwy in "Another evening With Harry Stoones" before making Broadway debut in 1962 in "I Can Get It For You Wholesale," followed by "Funny Girl."

STRICKLER, JERRY. Born Dec. 4, 1939 in Goose Creek, Tex. Attended Southwestern U. and American Theatre Wing. Made Broadway bow in 1962 in "Mr. President," followed by "Venus Is."

STRUDWICK, SHEPPERD. Born Sept. 22, 1907 in Hillsboro, N. C. Graduate of U.N.C. Made Broadway bow in 1929 in "The Yellow Jacket," followed by "Both Your Houses," "Let Freedom Ring," "End Of Summer," "As You Like It," "Christopher Blake," "Affairs Of State," "The Ladies Of The Corridor," "The Doctor's Dilemma," "The Seagull," "Night Curcus," "The Desert Incident," "Only In America," "J. B.," "Who's Afraid Of Virginia Woolf?," "The Devils."

SULLIVAN, JOSEPH. Born Nov. 29, 1918 in NYC. Attended Fordham, American Theatre Wing. Has appeared in "Sundown Beach," "Command Decision," "The Live Wire," "The Country Girl," "Oh, Men! Oh, Women!," "The Rainmaker," "The Best Man," "Fiddler On The Roof."

SUTTON, DUDLEY. Born June 4, 1933 in Surrey, Eng. Attended Royal Academy of Dramatic Arts. Made Broadway debut in 1960 in "The Hostage," followed by "Entertaining Mr. Sloane."

SWEET, DOLPH. Born July 18, 1920 in NYC. Graduate of Columbia. Made Broadway debut in 1961 in "Rhinoceros," followed by "Romulus," "The Advocate," "The Sign In Sidney Brustein's Window," Off-Bdwy in "The Dragon," "Too Much Johnson," and "Sergeant Musgrave's Dance," "The Great Indoors."

SWENSON, INGA. Born Dec. 29, 1932 in Omaha, Neb. Attended Northwestern, Actors Studio. Made Broadway debut in "New Faces of 1956," followed by "Twelfth Night," "The First Gentleman" for which she received a THEATRE WORLD Award, 1958 American Shakespeare Festival productions, "110 In The Shade," "Baker Street."

SYMONDS, ROBERT. Born Dec. 1, 1926 in Bristow, Okla. Attended Tex. U., Mo. U. A member of San Francisco Actors Workshop from 1954, and with group moved to Lincoln Center Rep. Theater where he acted in "Danton's Death" and "The Country Wife."

TANDY, JESSICA. Born June 7, 1909 in London. Attended Greet Acad. of Acting. Made Broadway debut in 1930 in "The Matriarch," followed by "The Last Enemy," "Time and the Conways," "The White Steed," "Geneva," "Jupiter Laughs," "Anne Of England," "Yesterday's Magic," "A Streetcar Named Desire," "Hilda Crane," "The Fourposter," "The Honeys," "A Day By The Sea," "The Man In The Dog Suit," "Triple Play," "Five Finger Exercise," "The Physicists," American Shakespeare, and Minneapolis Festival productions.

Richard Thomas   Angela Thornton   Mimi Turque   Philip Vandervort   Ted Van Griethuy

TANNER, TONY. Born July 27, 1932 in Hillingdon, Eng. Attended Webber-Douglas School of Dramatic Art. Appeared in London before making Broadway debut March 21, 1966 succeeding Tommy Steele in "Half A Sixpence."

THOMAS, RICHARD. Born June 13, 1951 in NYC. Attended Allen Stevenson School. Made Broadway bow in 1958 in "Sunrise At Campobello," followed by "Member Of The Wedding" (OB), "Strange Interlude" (1963), "The Playroom."

THORNTON, ANGELA. Born in Leeds, Yorkshire, Eng. Attended Webber-Douglas Dramatic School, London. Made Broadway debut in 1956 in "Little Glass Clock," followed by "Nude With Violin," "Present Laughter," "The Mousetrap" (OB), "Hostile Witness."

TOLAN, MICHAEL. Born in Detroit, Mich. Graduate of Wayne U. Studied with Stella Adler. Made New York bow Off-Broadway in "Coriolanus," followed by Broadway debut in 1955 in "Will Success Spoil Rock Hunter?," "A Hatful Of Rain," "The Genius and The Goddess," "Romanoff and Juliet," "A Majority Of One," "A Far Country," "The Journey Of The Fifth Horse" (OB).

TOWERS, CONSTANCE. Born May 20, 1933 in Whitefish, Mont. Attended Juilliard, and American Academy of Dramatic Arts. Toured in "Camelot" before making Broadway Debut Nov. 29, 1965 in "Anya," followed by Lincoln Center revival of "Show Boat."

TRACY, ANDREW. Born May 5, 1936 in Durban, S. A. Graduate of Oxford U. Made Broadway debut March 7, 1966 in "Wait A Minim!"

TRACEY, PAUL. Born June 5, 1939 in Durban, S. A. Attended Malvern College, Eng. Made Broadway debut March 7, 1966 in "Wait A Minim!"

TRACY, LEE. Born April 14, 1898. Attended Union College. Made Broadway bow in 1924 in "The Show-Off," followed by "Book Of Charm," "Glory Hallelujah," "Broadway," "The Front Page," "Oh Promise Me," "Louder Please," "Bright Star," "Every Man For Himself," "The Traitor," "Metropole," "Mr. Barry's Etchings," "The Show-Off" (1950), "Idiot's Delight" (CC), "The Best Man," "Minor Miracle."

TRUEX, ERNEST. Born in Red Hill, Mo., Sept. 19, 1890. Made Broadway bow in 1908 in "Wildfire," followed by "Rebecca Of Sunnybrook Farm," "Good Little Devil," "The Fall Guy," "Lysistrata," "Whistling In The Dark," "George Washington Slept Here," "Helen Goes To Troy," "Androcles and The Lion," "A Temporary Island," "Oh, Mr. Meadowbrook," "The Golden State," "4 Twelves Are 48," "Flahooley," "The Good Soup," "Venus At Large," "A Very Rich Woman."

TUCCI, MARIA. Born June 19, 1941 in Florence, Italy. Studied at Actors Studio. Has appeared Off-Bdwy in "Corruption In The Palace Of Justice," "Five Evenings," "The Trojan Women," and "The White Devil," in New York and American Shakespeare Festival productions, on Broadway in "The Milk Train Doesn't Stop Here Anymore," "The Deputy."

TURNER, DOUGLAS. Born May 5, 1930 in Burnside, La. Attended U. of Mich. Made Broadway bow in 1959 in "A Raisin In The Sun," followed by "One Flew Over The Cuckoo's Nest," Off-Bdwy in "The Iceman Cometh," "The Blacks," "Pullman Car Hiawatha," "Bloodknot," "Happy Ending," "Day Of Absence." Wrote last two.

TURNER, GEORGE. Born Feb. 19, 1902 in Findon Manor, Eng. Attended Royal Academy of Music. Made Broadway bow in 1924 in "The Way Things Happen," followed by "Oedipus Rex," "Hamlet," "Richard III," "Lady Windermere's Fan," "The Apple Cart," "Misalliance," "The Crucible," "The Complaisant Lover," "The Flowering Cherry," "Patate," "Epitaph For George Dillon," "Entertaining Mr. Sloane."

TURQUE (nee Strongin), **MIMI.** Born Sept. 30, 1939 in Brooklyn. Graduate of Brooklyn College. Made Broadway bow in 1945 in "Carousel," followed by "Seeds In The Wind," "The Enchanted," Off-Bdwy in "Johnny Summit," "The Dybbuk," "Romeo and Juliet," and "The Happy Journey," "Cry Of The Peacock," "Anniversary Waltz," "Carnival," "Man Of La Mancha."

VACCARO, BRENDA. Born Nov. 18, 1939 in Brooklyn. Attended Neighborhood Playhouse. Made Broadway debut in 1961 in "Everybody Loves Opal" for which she received a THEATRE WORLD Award, followed by "The Affair," "Children From Their Games," "Cactus Flower."

VALE, MICHAEL. Born June 28, 1922 in Brooklyn. Attended New School. Made Broadway debut in 1961 in "The Egg," followed by "Cafe Crown," "The Last Analysis," "The Impossible Years."

VANDERVORT, PHILIP. Born Sept. 29, 1945 in NYC. Attended NYU. Made Broadway debut in 1959 in "Sunrise At Campobello," followed by "The Zulu and The Zayda," Off-Bdwy credits: "More Sinned Against Than Usual," "It Pays To Advertise," "The Male Animal," and "Driftwood."

VANDIS, TITOS. Born Nov. 7, 1917 in Athens, Greece. Attended National Theatre of Greece Dramatic School. Made Broadway debut Oct. 17, 1965 in "On A Clear Day You Can See Forever."

VAN FLEET, JO. Born in Oakland, Calif. Graduate of College of Pacific. Attended Neighborhood Playhouse, Actors Studio. Made Broadway debut in 1946 in "The Winter's Tale," followed by "The World Over," "The Closing Door," "King Lear," "Flight Into Egypt," "Camino Real," "The Trip To Bountiful," "Look Homeward, Angel," "Oh, Dad, Poor Dad, Mamma's Hung You In The Closet and I'm Feelin' So Sad," "The Glass Menagerie" (1965).

VAN GRIETHUYSEN, TED. Born Nov. 7, 1934 in Ponca City, Okla. Graduate U. of Tex. Attended Yale, Royal Academy of Dramatic Arts. Made New York bow Off-Bdwy in "The Failures," followed by "Lute Song" (CC) American and New York Shakespeare Festival productions, "O Marry Me!" and "Red Roses For Me," Broadway debut in 1962 in "Romulus," followed by "The Moon Besieged," "Inadmissible Evidence."

VENORA, LEE. Born Feb. 16, 1932 in Bridgeport, Conn. Graduate of Julius Hartt College of Music. Made Broadway debut in 1959 in "Happy Town," followed by "Kean," Lincoln Center revivals of "The King and I" and "Kismet." Also appeared in opera.

VENUTA, BENAY. Born Jan. 27, 1911 in San Francisco. Attended Beaupre in Switz. Made Broadway debut in 1935 in "Anything Goes," followed by "Orchids Preferred," "Kiss The Boys Goodbye," "By Jupiter," "Nellie Bly," "Hazel Flagg," "Copper and Brass," "Dear Me, The Sky Is Falling," Lincoln Center revivals of "Carousel" and "Annie Get Your Gun."

vis Villiers   Sasha von Scherler   Sydney Walker   Marie Wallace   Susan Watson

VERDON, GWEN. Born Jan. 13, 1926 in Culver City, Calif. Made Broadway debut in 1950 in "Alive and Kicking," followed by "Can-Can," "Damn Yankees," "New Girl In Town," "Redhead," "Sweet Charity."

VESTOFF, VIRGINIA. Born Dec. 9, 1940 in NYC. Appeared Off-Bdwy in "The Boy Friend," "The Crystal Heart," and "Fallout" before making Broadway debut in 1960 in "From A To Z," followed by "Irma La Douce," "Baker Street," "New Cole Porter Revue" (OB).

VILLIERS, MAVIS. Born Dec. 10, in Sydney, Aust. Studied at Pasadena Playhouse. Appeared in London before making Broadway debut Feb. 16, 1966 in "Philadelphia, Here I Come!"

von SCHERLER, SASHA. Born Dec. 12, in NYC. Made Broadway debut in 1959 in "Look After Lulu," followed by "Rape Of The Belt," "The Good Soup," "The Great God Brown," "First Love," "Alfie." Off-Bdwy credits: "The Admirable Bashville," "The Comedian," "Conversation Piece," "Good King Charles Golden Days," "Under Milk Wood," "Plays For Bleecker Street," "Ludlow Fair."

VOSKOVEC, GEORGE. Born June 19, 1905 in Sazava, Czech. Graduate of Dijon U. Made New York bow in 1945 in "The Tempest," followed by "The Love Of Four Colonels," "His and Hers," "The Seagull," "Festival," "Uncle Vanya" (OB), "A Call On Kuprin," "The Tenth Man," "Big Fish, Little Fish," "Do You Know The Milky Way?," "Hamlet," "Brecht On Brecht" (OB), "The Physicists," "The World Of Ray Bradbury" (OB).

VYE, MURVYN. Born July 15, 1913 in Quincy, Mass. Attended Andover and Yale. Has appeared in "Hamlet," "As You Like It," "Oklahoma!," "One Touch Of Venus," "Carousel," "The Live Wire," "The Number," "Arturo Ui," "The Caucasian Chalk Circle" (LC).

WALBURN, RAYMOND. Born Sept. 9, 1887 in Plymouth, Ind. Made New York debut in 1912 in "The Greyhound," followed by "Manhattan," "The Awful Truth," "The Show-Off," "If I Were Rich," "Sinner," "The Great Necker," "Zeppelin," "Freddy," "Three Little Girls," "The House Beautiful," "Bridal Wise," "The Budget," "Man Bites Dog," "The Pursuit Of Happiness," "Park Avenue," "A Funny Thing Happened On The Way To The Forum," "A Very Rich Woman."

WALKEN, CHRISTOPHER (formerly Ronnie). Born March 31, 1943 in Astoria, New York. Attended Hofstra U. Made Broadway debut in 1958 in "J. B.," followed by "Best Foot Forward" (OB), "High Sprits," "Baker Street," "The Lion In Winter."

WALKER, SYDNEY. Born May 4, 1921 in Philadelphia. Attended Hedgerow Theatre School, Conservatoire Nationale de Musique, Paris. Has appeared Off-Bdwy in "Volpone," "Julius Caesar," "King Lear," "The Collection," and in repertory with the APA since 1963. Made Broadway bow in 1960 in "Becket," followed by APA's "You Can't Take It With You."

WALLACE, MARIE. Born May 19, 1939 in NYC. Attended NYU. Appeared Off-Bdwy in "Electra," "Harlequinade," and "Bell, Book and Candle," on Broadway in "Gypsy," "The Beauty Part," "Nobody Loves An Albatross," "The Right Honourable Gentleman."

WALLACH, ELI. Born Dec. 7, 1915 in Brooklyn. Graduate of U. of Tex., CCNY. Attended Neighborhood Playhouse, Actors Studio. Made Broadway bow in 1945 in "Skydrift," followed by "Henry VIII," "Androcles and The Lion," "Alice In Wonderland," "Yellow Jack," "What Every Woman Knows," "Antony and Cleopatra," "Mister Roberts," "The Lady From The Sea," "The Rose Tattoo" for which he received a THEATRE WORLD Award, "Mlle. Colombe," "The Teahouse Of The August Moon," "Major Barbara," "The Chairs" (OB), "The Cold Wind and The Warm," "Rhinoceros," "The Tiger" and "The Typists" (OB), "Luv."

WARD, JANET. Born Feb. 19 in NYC. Attended Actors Studio. Made Broadway debut in "Dream Girl," followed by "Anne Of The Thousand Days," "Detective Story," "The King Of Friday's Men," "Middle Of The Night," "Miss Lonelyhearts," "Chapparal" (OB), "J. B.," "Cheri," "The Egg," "The Typists" and "The Tiger" (OB), "The Impossible Years."

WARFIELD, WILLIAM. Born Jan. 22, 1920 in West Helena, Ark. Attended Eastman School of Music, Am. Theatre Wing. Made Broadway bow in 1948 in "Set My People Free," followed by "Regina," toured world in concert and as soloist, "Show Boat" (Lincoln Center).

WARREN, JOSEPH. Born June 5, 1916 in Boston. Graduate of Denver U. Attended Powers School of Theatre. Made Broadway bow in 1951 in "Barefoot In Athens," followed by "One Bright Day," "The Love Of Four Colonels," "The Hidden River," "The Advocate," "Brecht On Brecht" (OB), "Philadelphia, Here I Come!"

WARREN, LESLEY ANN. Born Aug. 16, 1946 in NYC. Studied with Stella Adler. Made Broadway debut in 1963 in "110 In The Shade," followed by "Drat! The Cat!"

WARRINER, FREDERIC. Born June 2, 1916 in Pasadena, Calif. Attended Pasadena City College, and Playhouse. Has appeared in "King Lear," "The Taming Of The Shrew," "Getting Married," "St. Joan," "The Clandestine Marriage," "The Doctor's Dilemma," "The Wayward Saint," "The Carefree Tree" (OB), "Major Barbara," "Time Remember'd," Am. Shakespeare Festival, "The White Devil" (OB).

WATERS, PAULETTE. Born Oct. 24, 1947 in NYC. Graduate of High School of Performing Arts. Made Broadway debut Nov. 23, 1965 with APA's revival of "You Can't Take It With You."

WATSON, SUSAN. Born Dec. 17, 1938 in Tulsa, Okla. Attended Juilliard School of Music. Appeared Off-Bdwy in "The Fantasticks," "Lend An Ear," and "Follies Of 1910." Made Broadway debut in 1960 in "Bye Bye Birdie," followed by "Carnival," "Ben Franklin In Paris," "Oklahoma!" (CC), "Carousel" (LC), "Where's Charley?" (CC).

WAYNE, DAVID. Born Jan. 31, 1916 in Traverse City, Mich. Attended Western Mich. U. Made Broadway bow in 1938 in "Escape This Night," followed by "Dance Night," "The American Way," "Scene Of The Crime," "The Merry Widow," "Peepshow," "Park Avenue," "Finian's Rainbow" for which he received a THEATRE WORLD Award, "Mister Roberts," "The Teahouse Of The August Moon," "The Ponder Heart," "The Loud Red Patrick," "Say, Darling," "Send Me No Flowers," "Venus At Large," "Too True To Be Good," with LC Rep. Co. in "Marco Millions," "But For Whom Charlie," and "Incident At Vichy," "The Yearling," "Show Boat" (LC).

251

Iris Whitney   Clyde Williams   Alan Yorke   Ron Young   Ed Zimmerm

WEAVER, FRITZ. Born Jan. 19, 1926 in Pittsburgh. Graduate of U. of Chicago. Appeared Off-Bdwy in "The Way of The World," "The White Devil" and "The Doctor's Dilemma" before making Broadway bow in 1955 in "The Chalk Garden" for which he received a THEATRE WORLD Award, "Protective Custody," "Miss Lonelyhearts," Phoenix production of "The Family Reunion," "The Power and The Glory," "Great God Brown," "Peer Gynt," and "Henry IV," "All American," "Lorenzo," "The White House," "Baker Street."

WEBB, ALAN. Born July 2, 1906 in York, Eng. Attended Royal Naval College. Made Broadway bow in 1938 in "Tonight At 8:30," followed by "George and Margaret," "The Winslow Boy," "Nina," "The Deep Blue Sea," "The Genius and The Goddess," "The Night Of The Iguana," "The Chinese Prime Minister," "UTBU."

WEDGEWORTH, ANN. Born Jan. 21 in Abilene, Tex. Attended U. of Tex. Has appeared in "Make A Million," "Blues For Mr. Charlie," "The Last Analysis," Off-Bdwy in "Chaparral," "The Crucible," "The Days and Nights of Beebee Fenstermaker," and "Ludlow Fair."

WETMORE, JOAN. Born in Sydney, Aust. Made Broadway debut in 1938 in "Two Bouquets," followed by "Two On An Island," "Kind Lady," "Counsellor-At-Law," "A New Life," "The Two Mrs. Carrolls," "For Keeps," "Hope For The Best," "The Small Hours," "A Girl Can Tell," "Advise and Consent," "A Very Rich Woman," "The Great Indoors."

WHITE, RUTH. Born in Perth Amboy, N. J. Graduate Douglass College. Made Broadway debut in 1956 in "The Ponder Heart," followed by "The Happiest Millionaire," "Rashomon," "The Warm Peninsula," "Whisper To Me" (OB), "Big Fish, Little Fish," "Happy Days" (OB), "Lord Pengo," "Absence Of A Cello," "Malcolm."

WHITNEY, IRIS. Born Feb. 20 in Pasadena, Calif. Attended UCLA. Made Broadway debut in 1937 in "Plumes In The Dust," followed by "Abe Lincoln In Illinois," "Juno and The Paycock," "The Flying Gerardoes," "The Strings, My Lord, Are False," "Dark Of The Moon," "The Remarkable Mr. Pennypacker," "A Touch Of The Poet," "Build With One Hand," "The Awakening Of Spring" (OB), "Three Bags Full."

WIDDOES, KATHLEEN. Born March 21, 1939 in Wilmington, Del. Studied at Theatre des Nations, Paris. Made Broadway debut in 1958 in "The Firstborn," followed by "The World Of Suzie Wong," "The Three Sisters" (OB), New York Shakespeare Festival productions, "The Maids" (OB), APA revival of "You Can't Take It With You."

WILLIAMS, CLARENCE III. Born Aug. 21, 1939 in NYC. Made Broadway bow in 1960 in "The Long Dream," followed by Off-Bdwy roles in "The Egg and I," "Walk In Darkness," "Double-talk," and "Sarah and The Sax," "Slow Dance On The Killing Ground" for which he received a THEATRE WORLD Award, "The Great Indoors."

WILLIAMS, CLYDE. Born in Cincinnati, O. Graduate of U. of Cinn. Made Broadway bow in 1963 in "Tambourines To Glory," followed by "Blues For Mr. Charlie," "Prodigal Son," "UTBU."

WINTER, EDWARD. Born June 3, 1937 in Roseburg, Ore. Attended U. of Ore. Member of San Francisco Actors Workshop, and has appeared with Lincoln Center Rep. Theater Co. in "The Country Wife," "The Condemned Of Altona," "The Caucasian Chalk Circle."

WINTERS, MARIAN. Born April 19, 1924. Attended Brooklyn College. Made Broadway debut in "Dream Girl" (CC), followed by "I Am A Camera," "The Dark Is Light Enough," "Auntie Mame," "Tall Story," "The 49th Cousin," "The Cherry Orchard" (OB), "Nobody Loves An Albatross," "Mating Dance."

WINWOOD, ESTELLE. Born Jan. 24, 1883 in Kent, Eng. Attended Lyric Stage Academy. Made Broadway debut in 1916 in "Hush," followed by "A Successful Calamity," "Too Many Husbands," "The Circle," "Trelawney Of The Wells," "Fallen Angels," "The Distaff Side," "The Importance Of Being Earnest," "Ladies In Retirement," "Ten Little Indians," "Lady Windermere's Fan," "The Madwoman of Chaillot," "The Cocktail Party," "Sabrina Fair," "Mr. Pickwick," "Mrs. Patterson," "Speaking Of Murder," "Crazy October," "Nathan Weinstein, Mystic, Conn."

WOOD, EUGENE R. Born Oct. 27, 1903 in Bowling Green, Mo. Graduate of Colo. State College and Cornell. Has appeared in "Porgy and Bess," "The Pajama Game," "Look Homeward, Angel," "Subways Are For Sleeping," "West Side Story," Off-Bdwy in "Borak," "The Crucible," "The Anvil," and "The Night Of The Auk," "Kiss Me, Kate" (CC), "The Devils."

WOODS, RICHARD. Born May 9, 1930 in Buffalo, N. Y. Graduate of Ithaca College. Has appeared in "Beg, Borrow and Steal," "Capt. Brassbound's Conversion," "Sail Away," Off-Bdwy in "The Crucible," "Summer and Smoke," "American Gothic," "Four-In-One," "My Heart's In The Highlands," "Eastward In Eden," "The Long Gallery," "The Little Hut," Am. Shakespeare Festival, with APA since 1962, and in its Broadway revival of "You Can't Take It With You."

WORLEY, JO ANNE. Born Sept. 6, 1937 in Lowell, Ind. Attended CCLA, Pasadena Playhouse. Made Broadway debut in 1961 in "The Billy Barnes People," followed by Off-Bdwy productions of "That Thing At The Cherry Lane," "Hotel Passionato," "The Mad Show."

YARNELL, BRUCE. Born Dec. 28, 1935 in Los Angeles. Attended CCLA. Has appeared in "Camelot," "The Happiest Girl In The World" for which he received a THEATRE WORLD Award, "Annie Get Your Gun" (LC revival).

YORKE, ALAN. Born Sept. 9, 1941 in NYC. Appeared in stock before making Broadway debut Jan. 11, 1966 in "Malcolm."

YOUNG, RON. Born June 11, 1941 in Tulsa, Okla. Graduate of Tulsa U. Appeared in stock and TV before making Broadway debut Jan. 16, 1964 in "Hello, Dolly!," "Mame."

ZIMMERMANN, ED. Born March 30, 1935 in NYC. Graduate of Columbia. Has appeared Off-Bdwy in "20 Poems of E. E. Cummings," and "Hamlet," on Broadway in "Luther," "The Right Honourable Gentleman," "Venus Is."

ZORICH, LOUIS. Born Feb. 12, 1924 in Chicago. Attended Roosevelt U., Goodman Theatre. Made Broadway bow in 1960 in "Becket," followed by "Moby Dick," "The Odd Couple," Lincoln Center Repertory Theater productions 1965-6. Off-Bdwy credits: "Six Characters In Search Of An Author," "Crimes and Crimes," "Henry V," "Thracian Horses," "All Women Are One," "Good Soldier Schweik," "Shadow Of Heroes."

Judy Holliday
1924-1965

OBITUARIES

Constance Bennett

Mary Boland

Nancy Carroll

BENNETT, CONSTANCE, 59, stage and screen actress, died July 24, 1965 in Walson Army Hospital, Fort Dix, N. J., of a cerebral hemorrhage. Born in NYC, daughter of actors Richard Bennett and Adrienne Morrison, she did not make her Broadway debut until 1939 in "Easy Virtue" after a successful movie career. Later appeared in "Without Love," "Skylark," "A Date With April," "Private Lives," "Sabrina Fair," and her last "Auntie Mame." Surviving are her fifth husband, Gen. John T. Coulter, two daughters by Gilbert Roland, an adopted son, and her sister Joan. Burial was in Arlington National Cemetery.

BOLAND, MARY, 83, veteran Broadway and film comedienne, died in her sleep at the Essex House in NYC. on June 23, 1965. During her career of more than 60 years she became famous for her fluttering dowagers. Born in Philadelphia, she made Broadway debut in 1905, and appeared in such plays as "Inconstant George," "Single Man," "Much Ado About Nothing," "Clarence," "The Torch Bearers," "Ada Beats The Drum," "The Vinegar Tree," "Jubilee," "The Rivals," "Open House," and her last in 1954 in "Lullaby." Never married, and left no survivors. Interment in Forest Lawn Memorial Park, California.

BROWNE, IRENE, 72, British stage and film actress, died of cancer in London, July 24, 1965. Made her Broadway debut at 14 in "The Red Mill," subsequently appearing in "The Blue Bird," "The Happy Husband," "Security," "Conversation Piece," "The Country Wife," "Call It A Day," "Jane," and last in 1963 in "The Girl Who Came To Supper."

BUNKER, RALPH, 77, stage and film actor, died in a nursing home of a stroke in NYC on April 28, 1966. Born in Boston, began his career as an assistant to Prof. Baker in his renowned 47 Workshop. His Broadway debut was in 1914 in "Omar, The Tentmaker." More recent credits include "Here Come The Clowns," "Early To Bed," "Goodbye, My Fancy," "Twentieth Century," "The Happy Time," "Paint Your Wagon," "Reclining Figure," and "Once More With Feeling."

CARROLL, NANCY, 60, stage and screen actress, was found dead of natural causes in her NYC apartment Aug. 6, 1965, when she failed to appear for a performance of "Never Too Late" in Nyack, N. Y. Born in NYC, made her Broadway debut in "The Passing Show of 1923," subsequently appearing in "Mayflowers," "Chicago," "Undesirable Lady," and "For Heaven's Sake, Mother." Appeared on TV as the mother in "The Aldrich Family." Three times married and divorced, an actress daughter, Patricia Kirkland Bevan, survives.

CLOGG, HALLYE (Mrs. Haritte Clogg Cannon), 86, a musical comedy chorus girl in the 1890's, and later a widely known wardrobe mistress, died July 6, 1965 in Bay Shore, L. I., N. Y. At retirement in 1963 she was reputedly the oldest woman in the New York Theatre. She was with the Theatre Guild for 30 years. Her last show was the musical "Tovarich" in 1963. She had no survivors.

COCHRANE, STEVE, 48, stage and screen actor, died June 15, 1965 of an acute lung infection, aboard his yacht in the Pacific off the coast of Guatemala where he was filming for his company. Born in Eureka, Calif., and attended U. of Wyo. before making Broadway bow in "Hickory Stick," followed by "Diamond Lil," which took him to Hollywood for films. Married and divorced three times. Survived by a daughter by his second wife, singer Fay McKenzie.

COLLINS, RAY, 75, stage, screen, and TV actor, died in Santa Monica's St. John's Hospital from a lung ailment on July 11, 1965. His career spanned 60 years. Born in Sacramento, son of a drama critic, he began his theatrical career at 14. On Broadway appeared with Mercury Theatre, and went with them to Hollywood in 1939 where he stayed to make more than 75 films. Best known in recent years as Det. Tragg on TV's "Perry Mason" series. His wife survives.

COLLINS, RUSSELL, 65, veteran character actor of Broadway and Hollywood, was found dead in his Hollywood apartment Nov. 14, 1965. Born in Indianapolis, made Broadway debut in 1932 in "Success Story," followed by more than 40 other plays, including "The Iceman Cometh," "Carousel," "The Moon Is Down," "Waiting For Lefty," "The Enchanted," "The Grass Harp," "Sabrina Fair," "A View From The Bridge," "Sunrise At Campobello," "Romulus," and his last in 1962 "The Calculated Risk." A sister survives.

CROUSE, RUSSEL, 73, writer-playwright-producer, died of pneumonia on April 3, 1966 in St. Luke's Hospital, NYC. Born in Findlay, O., came to NYC as a newspaper reporter, then became pressagent for the Theatre Guild. Met Howard Lindsay in 1934 and their collaboration made theatrical history. Their record-breaking (3,213 performances) "Life With Father" that opened in 1939 is probably their best known play, but other successes include "Red, Hot and Blue," "Hooray For What," "Strip For Action," "Life With Mother," "Call Me Madam," "Remains To Be Seen," "The Sound of Music," and their 1945 Pulitzer Prize "State Of The Union." As co-producers, they presented such plays as "Arsenic and Old Lace," "The Hasty Heart," "Detective Story," and "The Great Sebastians" which they also wrote. Their association lasted 32 years. Surviving are his second wife and two children.

DAVIS, IRVING KAYE, 65, playwright and former pressagent, died in NYC of a heart attack on Nov. 8, 1965. Wrote over 60 plays of which 12 were produced, one starring his wife Elsa Shelley. Included were "Diana," "Courtesan," "All Rights Reserved," "So Many Paths," and his last in 1944 "The Last Stop." Brought from Rumania to U.S. as a child. Became reporter, then pressagent for Lee Shubert, Earl Carroll and Rudolph Valentino. His wife survives.

DE MARCO, TONY, 67, top ballroom dancer, died Nov. 14, 1965 of a cerebral hemorrhage in Palm Beach, Fla. where he had retired. He was married to seven of his partners, but gained greatest fame with Renee, and Sally. Appeared with the latter in several Broadway musicals including "Boys and Girls Together," "Show Time," "The Gang's All Here," and "The Shining Hour." Retired in 1957 to Fla. where he bought a restaurant. His wife Sally survives.

DONEHUE, VINCENT J., 50, stage, film, and TV director, died Jan. 17, 1966 in NYC. Won a "Tony" Award for staging "Sunrise At Campobello" which he repeated in films. Other Broadway credits include "The Sound Of Music," "Peter Pan," and "Jennie."

FIELDS, JOSEPH, 71, co-author of many Broadway hits and movies, died in Beverly Hills, Calif., on March 3, 1966, of heart trouble. Born in NYC, son of comedian Lew Fields, much of his writing was done in collaboration with Jerome Chodorov, including "My Sister Eileen," "Junior Miss," "Anniversary Waltz," and "Wonderful Town." Other credits include co-authoring "Gentlemen Prefer Blondes," "Flower Drum Song," "Tunnel Of Love," and "The Doughgirls" which he wrote himself. His sister and younger brother, Dorothy and Herbert, also wrote for the theatre. His wife, two step-children, and sister Dorothy survive.

FLOWERTON, CONSUELO, 65, Ziegfeld Follies girl, night club entertainer, silent screen, and stage actress, died Dec. 21, 1965 in the New York Infirmary of cancer. During World War I, she was Christy's model for the Red Cross poster girl. Besides the Ziegfeld Follies, she was also seen in "Good Morning, Dearie," "Queen ot Hearth," "Minnie and Me," and "Let 'Em Eat Cake." Was a founder of AGVA. Surviving are her second husband, Robert Cushman, and a daughter, actress Nina Foch.

FRAWLEY, WILLIAM, 79, whose career spanned vaudeville, Broadway, Hollywood, and TV, died March 3, 1966 of a heart attack as he was walking down Hollywood Blvd. Born in Burlington, Iowa, he began as song and dance man in vaudeville, then appeared in several Broadway musicals including "The Gingham Girl" and "Sons O' Guns." Made over 100 films, but was probably best known for his regular appearances in the "I Love Lucy" TV show. Two brothers and a sister survive.

Steve Cochran

Russell Collins

Ruth Gates

William Harrigan

Hedda Hopper

Gareth Hughes

GATES, RUTH, 79, stage, radio, and TV actress who was protege of David Belasco, died May 23, 1966 of a heart attack while shopping near the Royalton Hotel in NYC where she had lived for many years. Made debut with David Warfield in "The Music Master," was leading lady for William Hodge and Wilton Lackaye; played in "Brass Ankle," "Post Road," "Kiki," "Ramshackle Inn," "That Old Devil," "I Remember Mama," "Not Herbert," "Up In Mabel's Room," "Substitute For Murder," "Pillar To Post," and her last role was Off-Bdwy in 1963 in "Opening Night" with Peggy Wood. Niece of Edwin Booth, she was born in Denton, Tex. and studied to be concert pianist. Her actor-husband, Ed Poulter, died in 1913. A sister survives.

GRACE, CHARITY, 86, who retired as a school-teacher at 60 and then fulfilled a lifelong ambition by becoming a successful actress, died of cancer in her St. Louis home Nov. 28, 1965. Appeared in several Broadway plays including "The Matchmaker" which took her to Hollywood where she made several films. A sister survives.

HARRIGAN, WILLIAM, 72, actor in more than 40 plays, died Feb. 1, 1966 in St. Luke's Hospital, NYC. Career began at 5 with his father writer-actor Edward Harrigan in "Reilly and The 400." Among his many appearances were "Bought and Paid For," "The Acquittal," "Polly Preferred," "The Dove," "The Great God Brown," "The Moon In The Yellow River," "The Animal Kingdom," "Criminal At Large," "Keeper Of The Keys," "Paths Of Glory," "Days To Come," "Mister Roberts," "Dear Ruth," "The Wayward Saint," and "A Shadow of My Enemy." He is survived by his third wife, two brothers, and a sister Nedda Harrigan Logan. He was buried in Arlington National Cemetery.

HARRINGTON, PAT, SR., 64, veteran comedian, died at an Islip, N. Y. nursing home after a long illness. He was born in Montreal and became famous for his Irish songs and parodies. Appeared in "Panama Hattie," "Star and Garter Revue," "Sailor Beware," "Call Me Madam," "The Live Wire," "Counsellor-at-Law," "Front Page," "Harbor Lights," "The Good Soup," and his last "Sunday in New York" in 1961. Surviving is his son, Pat Harrington, Jr., actor-humorist.

HOLLIDAY, JUDY, stage and film actress-singer, died of cancer June 7, 1965 in New York's Mt. Sinai Hospital. Born in The Bronx, she made her Broadway debut in 1945 in "Kiss Them For Me" for which she received a THEATRE WORLD Award, followed by unforgettable performances in "Born Yesterday" which she repeated in films and for which she was awarded an "Oscar," "Dream Girl" City Center revival, "Bells Are Ringing," for which she won a "Tony," and her last appearance was in "Hot Spot." She was divorced from musician David Oppenheim, and survived by her mother and one son.

HOPPER, HEDDA, 75, stage and film actress who became a syndicated Hollywood gossip columnist, died of pneumonia at Cedars of Lebanon Hospital in Hollywood on Feb. 1, 1966. Began career as a Broadway chorus girl, and after six Broadway productions embarked upon a screen career in 1916. She became a journalist in 1936, and wrote for papers and fan magazines. She was born Elda Furry in Hollidaysburg, Pa., and after cremation, her ashes were interred there. A son William by her husband, actor DeWolf Hopper, survives.

HOWARD, EUGENE, 84, vaudevillian, and straight man and manager to his late younger brother Willie, died Aug. 1, 1965 in Park West Hospital in NYC. Made Broadway bow in 1900 in "Million Dollars," followed by "The Belle of New York," and with Willie for many editions of "George White's Scandals" and "Ziegfeld Follies." Withdrew from act in 1940 to manage his brother. A brother, Sam Levkowitz, and a sister survive.

HUGHES, GARETH, 71, Welsh-born stage and screen actor, who renounced acting in 1944 to become a missionary among the Piute Indians, died Oct. 1, 1965 at Woodland Hills, California, Motion Picture Home where he had been hospitalized for over a year. For 15 years prior to going to Hollywood in 1919 he had played leads on Broadway, in such productions as "Eyes Of Youth," "Margaret Schiller," "Everyman," "Moloch," "The Guilty Man," "The Dunce Boy," and "Salome." Among the Indians he was known as Brother David.

INCE, ALEXANDER, 73, producer, director, and publisher, died Jan. 24, 1966 in NYC. In 1940 he fled Budapest for NYC, and began publishing a theatre magazine, Stage, which merged with Theatre Arts and he published until 1956. He produced many American plays in Budapest and Vienna, and in the U.S. "Miss Mabel" and "The Egg." A wife and daughter survive.

KEITH, MAXINE, 50, theatrical pressagent and drama critic for radio station WNYC, was found dead in her NYC apartment on March 12, 1966. She handled several legitimate shows during her career as well as publicity for other enterprises. She was chairman and hostess for The Drama Desk. Burial was at Valhalla, N. Y.

MARSHALL, HERBERT, 75, stage and film actor, died of a heart attack in his Beverly Hills home on Jan. 21, 1966. He left his native Eng. to appear on Broadway in 1921 in "The Voice From The Minaret," followed by "Fedora," "These Charming People," "The High Road," "Tomorrow and Tomorrow," "There's Always Juliet." Went to Hollywood for a successful career. There were five marriages. His fifth wife Dee Anne Kahmann survives, as do two sons and two daughters, one being actress Sarah Marshall.

MAUGHAM, WILLIAM SOMERSET, 91, prolific author of 30 plays, 21 novels, and 120 short stories, died Dec. 16, 1965 in his villa in Nice, France, after suffering a fall and stroke. Son of a solicitor in British Embassy in Paris, he became one of the most financially successful writers of all time. He retired with reservations in 1962. Many of his works were adapted for stage and films. Probably his best known works are "Of Human Bondage," "Miss Thompson" which became "Rain," and "The Razor's Edge," all of which were successful films. His plays include "Lady Frederick," "Penelope," "Mrs. Dot," "Smith," "The Land Of Promise," "Caroline," "Our Betters," "Too Many Husbands," "Caesar's Wife," "The Circle," "The Constant Wife," "The Letter," "The Sacred Flame," "For Services Rendered," "Sheppey," and "Theatre." A daughter, Lady John Hope, by his marriage to Lady Wellcome, survives. His ashes were interred in the grounds of Canterbury Cathedral.

MENKEN, HELEN, 64, Broadway and radio actress, and president of the American Theatre Wing, died of a heart attack March 28, 1966 while attending a social function at the Lambs Club in NYC. With her at the time was her third husband, broker George N. Richard. Born in NYC, she was a child actress who matured into a leading lady in such plays as "Seventh Heaven," "The Old Maid," "Mary of Scotland," "The Makropoulos Secret," "The Captive," "The Merchant Of Venice," "Hamlet," "Julius Caesar," "The Laughing Woman," and "The Skin of Our Teeth" in 1961 in a European tour for the State Dept. Dunging World War II she was producer for the Stage Door Canteen, and was organizer of annual Antoinette Perry Awards (Tonys) for Broadway achievement.

OWEN, CATHERINE DALE, 62, stage and film actress, died Sept. 7, 1965 in NYC. Born in Louisville, Ky., in 1925 was named one of 10 most beautiful women in the world. Made Broadway debut in 1921 in "Happy Go Lucky" while attending American Academy of Dramatic Arts, and subsequently appeared in "The Mountain Man," "Trelawney Of The Wells," "The Love City" and "The Play's The Thing." Her husband and son survive.

PATTERSON, ELIZABETH, 90, stage, screen, and TV actress, died Jan. 31, 1966 in Good Samaritan Hospital, Hollywood after a long illness. Made her Broadway debut in "A Midsummer Nights's Dream" in 1910, followed by "The Intimate Strangers," "The Lady Christilinda," "Peer Gynt," "Magnolia," "An Ideal Husband," "Lazy Bones," "Candida," "The Book Of Charm," "Paradise," "Rope," "The Marriage Bed," "Her Master's Voice," "But Not Goodbye," and her last in 1954 "His and Hers." She was active in TV until she was hospitalized. Interment was in her native Savannah, Tenn. A sister survives.

Herbert Marshall

Helen Menken

Catherine Dale Owen

Elizabeth Patterson

Alice Pearce

Carl Raymund

PEARCE, ALICE, 45, Broadway, Hollywood, and TV comedienne, died of cancer March 3, 1966 in her Hollywood home. She was also a popular night club entertainer. A native New Yorker, she made her Broadway debut in 1944 in "On The Town," followed by "Look, Ma, I'm Dancin'," "Small Wonder," "Gentlemen Prefer Blondes" (musical), "The Grass Harp," "John Murray Anderson's Almanac," "Dear Charles," "Fallen Angels," "Copper and Brass," "Bells Are Ringing," and "Sail Away." Her second husband, director Paul Davis, and parents survive.

PISCATOR, ERWIN, 72, German producer-director, died March 30, 1966 in Starnberg, Bavaria where he had undergone emergency gall bladder surgery. He came to U. S. in 1938 and until 1951 was active in theatre here, particularly as director of Dramatic Workshop of New School for Social Research. Returned to Germany in 1951 and became director-general of Freie Volksbrehne, Berlin. His wife, Maria Ley von Czada, a teacher-director, who lives in NYC, survives.

RAY, HELEN, 86, vaudeville, stage and film actress, died Oct. 2, 1965 in Wolfboro, N. H. after a brief illness. Made theatrical debut in 1900 and continued working until a few weeks before her death. Among her many Broadway plays are "Stage Door," "State Of The Union," "Arsenic and Old Lace," "The Connection," and "The Prescott Proposals." Appeared as mother in "Ethel and Albert" TV series. A daughter and brother survive.

RAYMOND, HELEN, 76, Broadway comedienne, died in NYC Nov. 26, 1965. Born in Philadelphia, made Broadway debut in 1915 in "Very Good Eddie," subsequently appearing in "Stepping Sisters," "The Peacock," "Broadway,". "The DuBarry," "Shady Lady," "Anything Goes," "A Private Affair," "One Touch Of Venus," and her last "The Music Man" which she played for three years.

RAYMUND, CARL, 50, associate assistant editor of THEATRE WORLD and SCREEN WORLD, died Feb. 25, 1966 in his NYC apartment of a heart attack. Prior to joining the staff of these annuals in 1959, he had worked for MGM. Burial was in his native Louisville, Ky. Several brothers and sisters survive.

RENNIE, JAMES, 76, for many years a Broadway leading man and film actor, died July 31, 1965 in NYC. Born in Canada, he made Broadway debut in 1916 in "His Bridal Night," followed by "Moonlight and Honeysuckle," "Spanish Love," "Shore Leave," "The Great Gatsby," "Young Love," "Alien Corn," "Abide With Me," "State Of The Union," "Mister Roberts," "Remains To Be Seen," "Four Winds," and his last "Annie Get Your Gun." His marriage to Dorothy Gish ended in divorce. His second wife survives.

RICHARDS, HOUSTON, 79, retired Broadway actor, died in Kingston, N. Y., Hospital after suffering a heart attack at a dinner party. Appeared in many musicals during the 1930's, including "Rosemarie," "Anything Goes," "Kiss The Boys Goodbye," "Jackpot," and "Lovely Me." After retirement, directed Coach House Players in Woodstock, N. Y. His wife survives.

RITZ, AL, 62, oldest of the zany Ritz Brothers comedy team, died Dec. 22, 1965 in New Orleans' Touro Infirmary. The brothers were playing an engagement in New Orleans. Born in Newark, the brothers were persuaded by Al to make their stage debut as a team in 1925. In 1929, made their Broadway debut in "Earl Carroll's Vanities," followed by "Florida Girl," and "Continental Varieties." Attained great popularity in films. They have not been too active professionally for several years. Surviving are his wife and two brothers.

ROGERS, EMMETT, 50, actor-producer, was found dead of undetermined causes in his New York apartment on Oct. 31, 1965. Began his acting career in 1933 in "Her Man Of Wax," followed by "Growing Pains," "The First Legion," "Strip Girl," "Richard II," "Hamlet," "Papa Is All," "The Linden Tree," "The Shop At Sly Corner," "Idiot's Delight" (City Center), and produced or co-produced "No Time For Sergeants," "Tall Story," "The Riot Act." No immediate survivors.

ROSE, BILLY, 66, producer, theatre owner, composer and lyricist, died Feb. 10, 1966 of lobar pneumonia in the Eldmire Nursing Home in Montego Bay, Jamaica, W. I., where he was recuperating from heart surgery. Began writing lyrics and sketches in 1926 for "Charlot's Revue," followed by "Padlocks of 1927," "Harry Delmar's Revels," "Fioretta," "Earl Carroll's Sketch Book," "Ziegfeld Follies." Produced "Sweet and Low," "Billy Rose's Crazy Quilt," "The Great Magoo," "Jumbo," "Clash By Night," "Carmen Jones," "Seven Lively Arts," "Concert Varieties," "The Immoralist," "The Wall." Owned the Ziegfeld Theatre and the Billy Rose Theatre (formerly National). Produced shows for several night club ventures such as his Billy Rose's Diamond Horseshoe Restaurant in NYC, and the World's Fair Aquacade. In addition to many popular songs, he contributed material to films. He also wrote a syndicated newspaper column. He was married to Fanny Brice, Eleanor Holm, Joyce Matthews, and Doris Warner Vidor, all of which were divorced. Two sisters survive.

ROSS, DAVID, 43, off-Bdwy producer-director, died April 13, 1966 in his native St. Paul, Minn. after a long illness. Prepared for acting career, but switched to producing and directing, specializing in Ibsen and Chekhov which he successfully presented at his Fourth St. Theatre, and later at Theatre Four. Received awards for his productions of "Uncle Vanya" and "Hedda Gabler." His second wife, and a son by his first marriage survive.

SCOTT, ZACHARY, 51, stage and screen actor, died Oct. 3, 1965 at his home in Austin, Tex. of a malignant brain tumor. After appearing in Eng., made Broadway debut in 1942 in "The Damask Cheek," followed by "This Rock," "Those Endearing Young Charms" which took him to Hollywood. Returned to theatre in 1956 for "King and I" at City Center, "Requiem For A Nun," and his last "A Rainy Day In Newark." Two daughters, and his second wife, actress Ruth Ford, survive.

SLOANE, EVERETT, 55, Broadway and Hollywood character actor, was found in his Brentwood, Calif. home dead from barbiturates by his wife on Aug. 6, 1965. Reportedly a suicide because of his failing eyesight. Born in NYC, he was a veteran of radio before making his Broadway bow in 1935 in "Boy Meets Girl," followed by "Native Son," and "A Bell For Adano." Surviving are his widow, actress Luba Herman, a son and a daughter.

STRASBERG, PAULA, 55, actress, director, and drama coach, died in her native NYC of a heart attack on April 29, 1966 in Beth Israel Hospital. As Paula Miller, first appeared with Civic Rep. Co. in 1928, followed by appearances with Group Theatre, and in "Till The Day I Die," "Waiting For Lefty," "Weep For The Virgins," "Case of Clyde Griffiths," "Johnny Johnson," "Many Mansions," "Cafe Crown," and "Me and Molly." Taught and directed at Actors' Studio with her husband Lee Strasberg who survives, as do two children, John and Susan, both actors.

STROOCK, JAMES E., 73, v.p. and general manager-director of Brooks-Van Horn Costume Co., died July 22, 1965 in New York. He had been the head of the largest costume company in the world for 30 years. Surviving are his wife Bianca, a sister, and two actress daughters, Geraldine and Gloria Brooks.

THORNE, ROBERT, 84, retired actor, died July 3, 1965 of a heart attack in his NYC home. Had appeared in "Daisies Won't Tell," "Taps," "Cyrano de Bergerac," "Mother Lode," "Thirsty Soil," "Othello," "Distant Drums." Two sisters survive.

THROCKMORTON, CLEON, 68, veteran stage designer, died Oct. 24, 1965 in his home in Atlantic City, N. J. Worked closely with and designed many of Eugene O'Neill's plays, in addition to more than 600 other productions, including "Porgy," "All God's Chillun Got Wings," "Bride Of The Lamb," "Burlesque," "Criminal At Large," "Alien Corn," "Another Language," "The Russian People," "Mr. Sycamore," "Across The Boards," and "Nathan The Wise." His wife survives.

James Rennie

Billy Rose

Zachary Scott

Everett Sloane

Sophie Tucker

June Walker

TUCKER, SOPHIE, 82, "The Last of The Red Hot Mamas," singer and actress whose career spanned 62 years, died of lung cancer and kidney failure Feb. 9, 1966 in her NYC home. She had been actively performing until four months before her death. She made her debut in 1905 in her father's cafe in Hartford, Conn. Besides vaudeville, films, and night clubs, she appeared on Broadway in "Ziegfeld Follies of 1909," "Earl Carroll's Vanities," "Gay Paree," "Follow A Star," "Leave It To Me," "High Kickers," and the "George Jessel Revue." She was married three times. A son by her first husband, and a brother survive. Burial was in Hartford.

VAN BUREN, A. H., 86, actor, and later director for more than 20 years, died in Los Angeles August 1, 1965, after being an invalid for many years as a result of a stroke. "The Trial Of Mary Dugan" was one of his best known directorial jobs. A daughter survives.

VANDAMM, FLORENCE, 83, who retired several years ago after being one of the foremost theatrical photographers, died of a stroke in NYC on March 15, 1966. With her late husband, George R. Thomas, photographed the majority of Broadway shows from 1925 to 1950. In 1961 the New York Public Library bought her collection. She was born in London, and is survived by a brother and two sisters.

WALKER, JUNE, 61, stage, film, and TV actress, died Feb. 3, 1966 in the home of her son actor John Kerr in Los Angeles. She had been in ill health for several years. A native of NYC, she was the first to play Lorelei Lee in "Gentlemen Prefer Blondes" in 1926. Her career began as a chorus girl at 16, and rose to play top roles in such plays as "Waterloo Bridge," "The Glass Slipper," "The Farmer Takes A Wife," "Green Grow The Lilacs," "Night of January 16," "They Knew What They Wanted," "Truckline Cafe," "The Hallams," "Ladies of The Corridor," "All Summer Long," "The Middle Of The Night," and "Blue Denim."

WALTON, VERA, 74, actress, died Sept. 1, 1965 as a result of an auto accident while she was appearing in "Baker Street." Among her numerous other Broadway roles were "Whoop-Up!," "Guys and Dolls," "Oklahoma!," and "The Sound Of Music." A son survives.

WARD, MARY, 78, pressagent and former actress, died of a heart attack in her home on May 2, 1966. Born in Maysville, Ky., became an actress and appeared in stock and touring companies before making Broadway debut in 1923 in "Pelleas and Melisande," followed by roles with Civic Rep. Co. for which she became company manager and pressagent. She was p.a. on many subsequent Broadway plays alone and as an associate with other pressagents. Was on Board of Directors of ATPAM. At the time of her death she was working with agents Sol Jacobson and Lewis Harmon. Was widow of actor J. Sayre Crawley. Three nephews and a niece survive. Her remains were cremated and the ashes scattered on the grounds of the Berkshire Playhouse, Stockbridge, Mass. where she had worked for many summers.

WATSON, MINOR, 75, veteran character actor of stage and screen, died July 28, 1965 in Alton, Ill. where he had been in retirement after a career of more than 45 years. Born in Marianna, Ark., made Broadway stage debut in 1922 in "Why Men Leave Home," followed by "The Magnolia Lady," "Trigger," "This Thing Called Love," "It's A Wise Child," "Reunion In Vienna," "End Of Summer," and "State Of The Union." Surviving are his wife and daughter.

WINTERS, LAWRENCE, 50, baritone who starred for last 4 years with Hamburg Opera, died of cancer Sept. 24, 1965 in Hamburg. Born Lawrence Wisonant in South Carolina, won prominence in 1946 Broadway production of "Call Me Mister." He was first Negro to sing "Rigoletto" at City Center and remained with the company for ten years. Appeared in several revivals of "Porgy and Bess," and "Show Boat," "My Darlin' Aida," and his last in 1960 "The Long Dream." His widow and two adopted sons survive.

INDEX

262

266

269